The New Corporate Bond Market:

A Complete and Insightful Analysis of the Latest Trends, Issues and Advances

Richard S. Wilson
Frank J. Fabozzi

PROBUS PUBLISHING COMPANY
Chicago, Illinois

Library of Congress Cataloging-in-Publication Data

Wilson, Richard S.
   The new corporate bond market : a complete and insightful analysis
of the latest trends, issues, and advances / Richard S. Wilson,
Frank J. Fabozzi.
      p. cm.
   ISBN 1-55738-128-3 : $55.00
   1. Bonds—United States.   I. Fabozzi, Frank J.   II. Title.
HG4963.W564 1990
332.63'23—dc20   90-8078
                                                           CIP

Printed in the United States of America

1   2   3   4   5   6   7   8   9   0

RSW to

Jean Wilson Thomas
William A. Wilson

FJF to

my parents,
Alfonso and Josephine Fabozzi

Available from Probus Publishing
Additional Titles by the Authors

Richard S. Wilson

Corporate Senior Securities, Richard S. Wilson

Frank J. Fabozzi

Active Total-Return Management of Fixed-Income Portfolios, Ravi E. Dattatreya and Frank J. Fabozzi

Advances and Innovations in the Bond and Mortgage Markets, Frank J. Fabozzi, Editor

Advances in Bond Analysis and Portfolio Strategies, Frank J. Fabozzi and Dessa Garlicki-Fabozzi, Editors

Asset Allocation, Robert Arnott and Frank J. Fabozzi, Editors

Fixed-Income Mathematics, Frank J. Fabozzi

Fixed-Income Portfolio Strategies, Frank J. Fabozzi, Editor

Floating Rate Instruments, Frank J. Fabozzi, Editor

Handbook of Fixed-Income Options, Frank J. Fabozzi, Editor

Handbook of Mortgage-Backed Securities, Revised Edition, Frank J. Fabozzi, Editor

Interest Rate Futures and Options, Mark Pitts and Frank J. Fabozzi

Mortgage-Backed Securities, Frank J. Fabozzi, Editor

The New Stock Market, Diana R. Harrington, Frank J. Fabozzi and H. Russell Fogler

Portfolio and Investment Management, Frank J. Fabozzi, Editor

Winning the Interest Rate Game, Frank J. Fabozzi, Editor

Forthcoming Titles

Asset Liability Management, Atsuo Konishi and Frank J. Fabozzi, Editors

The Japanese Bond Markets, Frank J. Fabozzi, Editor

Pension Fund Investment Management, Frank J. Fabozzi, Editor

Also Available from Probus Publishing
The Fabozzi Fixed-Income Calculator

Contents

Preface   ix

SECTION I

Chapter 1   **Overview of U.S. Corporate Bonds**   **3**
What Is a Corporate Bond?   3
Size of the Corporate Bond Market   7
Corporate Debt Ownership   9
Volume of New Corporate Bond Issues   13
Corporate Bond Trading   18
Corporate Bond Ratings   23
What Are Debt Ratings?   24
Limitations on the Uses of Ratings   28
Why Are Ratings Important to Market
    Participants?   31
Appendix A: Debt Rating Definitions   35

Chapter 2   **Bond Indentures**   **45**
Indentures   45
Secured Debt   63
Unsecured Debt   94

Chapter 3   **Maturity**   **107**
What Is Maturity?   107
Long-Term Debt   108
Bonds with Puts   116

Medium-Term Notes   120
Maturity Distribution in the Corporate Bond
    Market   123

Chapter 4   Interest Payments   135
General Characteristics   135
Interest Variations   141

Chapter 5   Debt Retirement   173
The Importance of Knowing a Bond Issue's
    Redemption Terms   173
Why the Concern About Premature
    Redemption?   176
Call and Refunding Provisions   177
Outright Redemptions   185
Sinking and Purchase Funds   188
Maintenance and Replacement Funds   197
Redemption Through the Sale of Assets and
    Eminent Domain   201
Net Worth, Merger, and Other Redemptions   205
Tenders   208
Defeasance   211
Conclusion   216

Chapter 6   Convertible Bonds   223
What Is a Convertible Bond?   223
Convertible Bond Provisions   227
Convertible Bond Concepts and Investment
    Characteristics   232
Liquid Yield Option Notes   239
Usable Securities   241
Traditional Convertible Strategies   244

Chapter 7   Speculative-Grade Bonds   255
What Are Speculative-Grade Bonds?   255
The Market   258
High-Yield Bond Performance and Default Rates   261
Who Owns the Junk?   272
Reducing Risk in a Speculative-Grade Portfolio   277

Defaulted and Bankrupt Issues   287
Summary   289

SECTION II

Chapter 8   **Bond Pricing and Traditional Yield Measures   299**
Pricing a Bond   300
Conventional Yield Measures   309
Traditional Analysis of Callable Bonds   314
Yield Measure for Floating Rate Securities   321

Chapter 9   **Analysis of Corporate Bonds Using the Horizon
      Return Framework   325**
Horizon Return   325
Applications of Horizon Analysis   327

Chapter 10   **Bond Price Volatility Fundamentals   339**
Bond Price Volatility Properties   339
Measures of Price Volatility   340
Relationship Among Price Volatility Measures   344
Use of Modified Duration and Convexity in Assessing
      Interest Rate Risk and Relative Value   351
Price Volatility of Callable Bonds   354
Appendix   356

Chapter 11   **Option-Adjusted Spread Approach to the Valuation
      of Corporate Bonds   361**
The Term Structure of Interest Rates   361
Estimating the Option-Adjusted Spread for a
      Corporate Bond   368
Effective Duration and Convexity   386
Price Performance   387
The Limitations of Option-Adjusted Spread
      Analysis   389

Chapter 12   **Basics of Options   391**
Options Defined   391
Profit/Loss Profile for Basic Option Positions   392
Option Price   396
Option Pricing Models   400
Price Sensitivity of the Option Price   402

Chapter 13 **An Options Approach to the Valuation of
Corporate Bonds   409**
Breaking a Callable Bond into its Component
Parts   409
Option-Adjusted Yield   416
Option-Adjusted Duration and Convexity   420
Using the Options Approach to Evaluate Corporate
Bonds with Other Embedded Interest Rate
Options   425
Horizon Return Analysis and Performance Profiles
of Callable Bonds   430
Using the Options Approach to Value Convertible
Bonds   436

Index   443

Preface

The corporate bond market has always been evolving with underwriters and issuers trying out new ideas and modifying older concepts. This was especially true in the decade of the eighties with the globalization of investment finance and the evolution of the junk bond market. There has been substantial participation in the new corporate bond market by issuers and investors who, ten years ago, hardly knew what bonds were. We have witnessed a proliferation of new debt instruments and experienced dramatic increases in price volatility. The quantitative aspects of fixed income securities have never been more important.

The New Corporate Bond Market is designed to help investors of all levels, professional as well as individual, to better understand the increasingly complex world of bonds. Reviewing the fundamentals of corporates from the qualitative and quantitative sides, it also discusses the dramatic changes that have occurred. Whether a market participant is a trader, investor, analyst or salesperson, increased knowledge of these markets will enhance performance over the longer term. This will become increasingly more apparent in the interesting years ahead.

ACKNOWLEDGMENTS

In an undertaking such as this, appreciation has to be extended to many who, in one way or another, helped make this book possible. Richard Wilson wishes to thank for their support, encouragement, suggestions and assistance over the years his many friends, colleagues and associates including (but not limited to) Eunice T. Reich of Citibank, NA; Loretta J. Neuhaus of Merrill Lynch Capital Markets; Gene Laber at the University of Vermont; Frank Reilly of Notre Dame University; James Grant of Grant's Interest Rate Observer; Leo McSherry of Fixed Income Resources, and the people at Fitch. Of course, his wife Barbara and daughters Jennifer and Kristina, should be commended for putting up with the foibles of a Wall Street author.

Frank J. Fabozzi wishes to thank the following individuals for their insights into the quantitative analysis of corporate bonds: Ravi Dattatreya of Sumitomo Bank Capital Markets; Chris Dialynas of PIMCO; Dessa Fabozzi of Merrill Lynch Capital Markets and CEO of Fabozzi Enterprises (honorary title); Laurie Goodman of Eastbridge Capital; Lakhbir Hayre of Prudential-Bache Capital Funding; Andrew Kalotay of Andrew Kalotay Associates; Bob Kopprasch of Hyperion Capital Management; Marty Leibowitz of Salomon Brothers; Sharmin Mossavar-Rahmani of Fidelity Management Trust Company; Mark Pitts of Shearson Lehman Hutton; Scott Richard of Goldman Sachs, and Yu Zhu of Merrill Lynch Capital Markets.

Richard S. Wilson and *Frank J. Fabozzi*

SECTION I

Chapter 1

OVERVIEW OF U.S.
CORPORATE BONDS

This chapter introduces nonconvertible, publicly issued, corporate bonds. It discusses the size of the market, ownership of the securities, new issue volume, secondary trading activity, and ratings. The general terms and features of bond indentures are discussed in Chapter 2. Maturity features, interest rate characteristics and retirement provisions are reviewed in Chapters 3, 4 and 5, respectively. Throughout this book we will use the term bond(s) in the general sense of corporate debt instruments; when required, we will use more specific terminology such as notes or debentures.

What Is a Corporate Bond?

A corporate bond used to be defined as a promise to pay a specified sum of money at a fixed date in the future along with periodic payments of interest. However, the bond instrument has undergone so many alterations over the past decade that the "plain vanilla" type of issue, so familiar to bond market investors and students only twenty years ago, may now be viewed by some as an anachronism. Bonds with gimmicks, often difficult for the investor to understand, for the salesman to sell, and for the trader to price, have become increasingly accepted in the 1980s.[1] In many cases, the interest rate changes weekly; the maturity date is not always fixed, as issuers can redeem the bonds prior to maturity and holders may demand prepayment; and the specified sum or principal payment due at maturity may fluctuate. Nonetheless, a bond is a debt instrument denoting the obligation of the issuer to satisfy the holder's claim; it is essentially an I.O.U., although more complex than the simple promissory note found in booklet form at legal supply stores.

These gimmicky bond issues can cause problems for corporations if the Internal Revenue Service (IRS) decides that they have more of the features or characteristics of equity instruments rather than debt. If a security is classified as debt, then the issuer is able to take a tax deduction for the interest payments in the determination of taxable income. If viewed as equity, the tax-deductability of interest is lost and the payments may be viewed as dividends. The distinction between debt and equity for income tax purposes has not been formally spelled out by the Treasury Department and no one characteristic is overriding in coming to a determination of debt versus equity. Rather, all of the characteristics are looked at and if it is determined that "it looks like a duck, quacks like a duck, and walks like a duck," then "it is a duck" (at least as far as the IRS is concerned).[2]

If the corporate security gives the holder a right to share in the profits of the enterprise while at the same time sharing in the risks, then the security may be viewed as equity. Debt, on the other hand, does not share in the profits of the business and holders do not have the risks attendant to equity. The payment of interest is mandatory; it ought to be paid regardless of profits or losses. Factors considered in the debt versus equity problem include, but are not limited to, the following:

- a promise to pay a fixed amount on demand or at a certain or ascertainable date, money in return for a consideration, at a specified interest rate;
- the source and adequacy of the interest payments and the ability of the issuer to defer interest payments;
- the debt leverage of the company (or "thin" capitalization);
- conversion into the company's equity;

- relationship or identity between the shareholders' equity interest and their debt holdings;
- the intent of the parties to the financing agreement and the indicia of the agreement;
- the participation, if any, in the management of the enterprise;
- the voting power accorded the investor;
- a maturity date or lack thereof, time to maturity, and provisions for redemption at the issuer's option or the holder's option;
- the place of the securities in the company's capitalization in comparison with other creditors, and
- enforcement upon default.

In 1986, Fox Television Stations, Inc. issued preferred stock in exchange for debentures and notes of Metromedia Broadcasting Corporation. As the Fox company counsel was unable to give an opinion as to whether the shares would be treated as equity or debt by the IRS, the Company decided to treat the stock as debt and deduct the dividend payments as interest. Corporate holders taking the opposite view that the payments are dividends would be eligible for the dividends received deduction. There are also other consequences to the issuer and the investor depending on how these securities are viewed by the taxing authorities.[3] A portion of the Fox shares were redeemed in 1987. Referring to the redemption, a company spokesman used the term "debt" instead of "stock" in describing the securities.

The issuer's (borrower's) rights and duties are spelled out in a loan agreement, also known as an indenture. The indenture may be fairly simple and straightforward, although, for most laymen it is complex and often runs to many pages—after all, it is a legal contract between two parties, debtor and trustee. The bond, or evidence of the debt obligation, is printed on a single sheet of paper which summarizes the more important sections of the loan agreement. Technically, this certificate is the agreement between the issuer and the lender.

The term *bond* actually refers to a debt instrument which is customarily secured by collateral, such as land and buildings or financial instruments. The indenture for secured debt contains a section describing the mortgaged or pledged collateral. A *debenture* is an unsecured loan also setting forth the rights and duties of the borrower in an indenture. In years past a note was characterized as a less formal obligation than a debenture or a bond. According to *Commentaries:*

> There is no basic or historically established distinction between "debentures" and "notes." There has emerged, however, a clear and useful distinction in modern usage. According to this usage, in the area of long-term debt securities, a security is properly termed a "note" when it is not issued pursuant to an indenture and there is no indenture trustee. However, it may be, and usually is, issued to one or a few purchasers pursuant to a purchase or loan agreement which, in addition to provisions dealing with the terms of purchase, includes many of the contractual rights found in an indenture. In today's nomenclature the security is properly termed a "debenture" when it is issued pursuant to an indenture and there is an indenture trustee.[4]

Thus, the popular "medium-term notes" are more properly called "medium-term debentures," as most have been issued under an indenture.[5] Today, however, "notes" has a slightly different meaning. To many, a note has more to do with the time remaining to a security's maturity than with the formality of the documentation; thus, notes are short- to intermediate-term maturity paper, while bonds and debentures are long-term issues. However, there can be short-term bonds and long-term notes. While we disagree with this usage to describe a corporate bond's remaining time to maturity, we can understand why many have adopted it; it is a fallout from the market for U.S. Treasury issues—government bonds are long-term, unsecured obligations, with original maturies of more than ten years while notes have maturities between one and ten years.

The physical bond used to be quite an attractive piece of paper, with some certificates of fairly large dimensions. Attached to or printed on the same page were interest coupons which holders would detach and send in for collection through normal banking channels. In this age of registered bonds, however, they are more uniform, generally the size of normal letter paper or a stock certificate. Coupons no longer are required as interest payments are made by check to the registered holder. The form of the bond is specified in the indenture. The front of the certificate has the company's name and other terms such as maturity date, interest rate, certificate number, and principal amount. It also bears the corporate seal and the signature(s) of the appropriate corporate officer(s) and of the trustee attesting to the authenticity of the certificate. Most important, it will have the name of the registered holder. The reverse of the certificate has a summary of the important indenture terms including call and redemption provisions, a printed bond power or a form of assignment and certain other forms, if needed. To reduce the risk of counterfeiting, the New York Stock Exchange has prescribed certain minimum standards for certificates of listed issues. These include requirements that certain portions of the face of the bond must be engraved and include a vignette.

Size of the Corporate Bond Market

According to the flow of funds accounts published by the Board of Governors of the Federal Reserve System, total corporate debt in the United States was an estimated $1.2 trillion dollars at the end of 1987, including $81 billion of foreign obligations (see Table 1–1a). This foreign debt, similar in form to that of U.S. business corporations, is issued by international treaty organizations such as the International Bank for Reconstruction and Development, foreign nations, their agencies and political subdivisions, and foreign corporations.

In the seventeen years since the end of 1970, total corporate-type debt has increased by $1 trillion dollars or 11.05% annually. Nonfinancial corporate debt (utility and industrial companies) accounted for nearly 83% of the total back in 1970; it has now fallen to less than 66% (see Table 1–1b). Commercial bank bonds increased at a 20.9% pace from only $3.2 billion in 1970 to nearly $81 billion in 1987. However, the catchall category of "CMO and other" rose from under $1 billion to $121 billion, an annual gain of 36.7%! Most of this increase occurred in 1984 to 1987 as new financing

Table 1–1a Corporate Bonds Outstanding by Issuer Type
($ billions)

	Total	Nonfinancial Corporate	Foreign	Commercial Banking	Finance Companies	CMO & Other
1987	$1,202.4	$789.6	$80.6	$80.8	$130.1	$121.3
1986	1,008.5	664.6	74.3	75.0	115.6	79.0
1985	815.7	542.9	71.8	69.4	93.1	38.5
1984	688.9	469.2	68.0	52.5	77.2	22.0
1983	602.7	423.0	64.2	39.6	67.7	8.2
1982	566.0	407.0	61.1	31.2	62.4	4.3
1981	527.9	388.3	54.5	25.2	56.0	3.9
1980	495.3	365.6	49.0	23.2	52.4	5.1
1979	464.9	337.9	47.8	21.9	52.3	5.0
1978	438.4	320.6	44.1	22.1	48.0	3.6
1977	405.4	299.5	40.1	21.1	41.6	3.1
1976	364.9	277.2	33.9	18.0	33.8	2.0
1975	327.0	254.3	25.3	14.5	30.7	2.2
1974	286.7	227.1	19.1	10.4	28.0	2.1
1973	261.9	207.5	17.0	9.2	26.2	1.9
1972	247.3	198.3	16.0	8.3	23.3	1.4
1971	227.0	186.1	15.0	5.2	19.7	1.0
1970	202.4	167.3	14.1	3.2	17.2	0.6

Note: Figures may not total due to rounding.
Source: Flow of Funds Accounts, Financial Assets and Liabilities, Year-End, 1963-87, Board of Governors of the Federal Reserve System.

techniques were developed. This was the start of the recycling, repackaging or securitization of financial assets, mostly mortgages but also automobile loans, credit card and other receivables, and leases, to name a few. Much of this did not involve the raising of corporate capital through the direct issuance of debt, but the sale of these financial assets to trusts and other third parties which would service the resulting obligations with the assets' cash flows.

Table 1–1b Corporate Bonds Outstanding by Issuer Type (percentage)

	Nonfinancial Corporate	Foreign	Commercial Banking	Finance Companies	CMO & Other
1987	65.67%	6.70%	6.72%	10.82	10.09%
1986	65.90	7.37	7.44	11.46	7.83
1985	66.56	8.80	8.51	11.41	4.72
1984	68.11	9.87	7.62	11.21	3.19
1983	70.18	10.65	6.57	11.23	1.36
1982	71.91	10.80	5.51	11.02	0.76
1981	73.56	10.32	4.77	10.61	0.74
1980	73.81	9.89	4.68	10.58	1.03
1979	72.68	10.28	4.71	11.25	1.08
1978	73.13	10.06	5.04	10.95	0.82
1977	73.88	9.89	5.20	10.26	0.76
1976	75.97	9.29	4.93	9.26	0.55
1975	77.77	7.74	4.43	9.39	0.67
1974	79.21	6.66	3.63	9.77	0.73
1973	79.23	6.49	3.51	10.00	0.77
1972	80.19	6.47	3.36	9.42	0.56
1971	81.98	6.61	2.29	8.68	0.44
1970	82.66	6.97	1.59	8.50	0.28

Source: Flow of Funds Accounts, Financial Assets and Liabilities, Year-End, 1963-87, Board of Governors of the Federal Reserve System.

Corporate Debt Ownership

Life insurance companies held more than 31% ($375 billion) of the corporate debt outstanding at the end of 1987 (Tables 1–2a and 1–2b), down slightly from 36.6% at the end of 1970. Trailing far behind in second position are foreign investors with $159 billion or 13.2%. Foreign ownership has grown at an annual rate of slightly more than 27% since the end of 1970 when holdings were a mere $2.7 billion. Private pension funds, with holdings in excess of $151 billion, accounted for 12.6% at the end of 1987 compared with $29.4

billion or 14.5% for 1970. Since 1983 households have increased their corporate bond investments by over $100 billion from $43.2 billion to $145.8 billion. This category accounts for 12.1% of the holdings compared with only 7.2% for 1983. However, as recently as 1976 household corporate bond investments were almost 21% of the total, ranking as the second largest investor category in corporates. Households also have exhibited more volatility in their year-to-year holdings, increasing the amount of bonds held for a few years, then becoming net sellers for several more, and again adding to their holdings. The other categories have mostly shown year-to-year additions to holdings.

The second time in this decade that public pension funds holdings declined was in 1987. Corporate bonds are relatively less important for public pension funds than in the recent past, accounting for 11.5% of the total corporate bonds outstanding versus 19.7% as recently as 1981. This may be due to the liberalization of the investment policies of many public pension funds over the years which now permit them to have more diversified portfolios. Investment managers have allocated a larger amount of assets to equities and real estate at the expense of corporate bonds. For example, in the 1981 through 1987 period, corporate debt holdings increased by 32.6% from $103.8 billion to $137.6 billion while the value of corporate equity investments rose 274.1% from $47.8 billion to $178.8 billion. A peak of $225.5 billion of equities at market value was reached at the end of 1987's third quarter, just prior to the stock market crash.

Banking and thrift institutions have increased their relative share of corporate bond investments over the years. In the case of some thrifts, corporate bonds have been a more liquid substitute for business loans, especially in the speculative grade issues, as deregulation and state laws broadened their investment horizons. In addition, collateralized mortgage obligations in the "CMO and other" category in Tables 1-1a and 1-1b have been used as a marketable substitute for direct holdings of mortgage loans.

Finally, the "Other" category, comprising mutual funds and securities brokers and dealers, has grown 12-fold since the end of 1970. While holding only 5.3% of total corporate bonds outstanding,

Table 1-2a Ownership of Outstanding Corporate Bonds
($ billions)

	Total	Household	Foreign	Banking & Thrift	Life Insurance	Private Pension	Public Pension	Other Insurance	Other*
1987	$1,202.4	$145.8	$159.1	$115.4	$375.0	$151.6	$137.6	$53.9	$63.8
1986	1,008.5	95.6	137.5	83.7	321.4	128.3	139.8	44.3	57.7
1985	815.7	60.9	97.1	60.0	280.6	121.0	129.0	33.9	33.1
1984	688.9	48.4	60.4	53.8	242.8	110.5	118.1	25.7	29.1
1983	602.7	43.2	45.5	43.6	219.1	100.3	106.6	21.6	22.8
1982	566.0	54.6	41.0	30.6	202.3	89.8	107.3	25.8	14.6
1981	527.9	54.0	30.4	28.7	186.1	83.3	103.8	26.3	15.4
1980	495.3	58.8	22.0	28.9	178.8	77.7	94.5	23.6	11.1
1979	464.9	72.0	13.8	27.6	170.1	63.7	85.0	23.6	9.1
1978	438.4	73.7	11.2	29.0	158.5	53.0	81.9	21.6	9.7
1977	405.4	77.9	9.3	29.2	141.2	44.6	72.9	19.8	10.7
1976	364.9	76.4	5.5	28.1	122.4	40.1	66.9	16.1	9.4
1975	327.0	65.9	4.6	25.9	105.5	42.4	61.8	12.2	8.6
1974	286.7	59.1	4.0	20.6	96.4	35.0	54.9	10.0	6.7
1973	261.9	51.5	3.1	18.7	92.5	32.9	48.4	8.0	6.7
1972	247.3	51.2	3.1	19.4	86.6	29.4	43.2	8.1	6.2
1971	227.0	46.5	3.0	15.9	79.6	28.6	39.0	8.9	5.5
1970	202.4	36.2	2.7	11.1	74.1	29.4	35.1	8.6	5.2

* Other is comprised of mutual funds and brokers and dealers in securities.
Note: Figures may not total due to rounding.
Source: Flow of Funds Accounts, Financial Assets and Liabilities, Year-End 1963-87. Board of Governors of the Federal Reserve System.

Table 1-2b Ownership of Outstanding Corporate Bonds (Percentage)

	Household	Foreign	Banking & Thrift	Life Insurance	Private Pension	Public Pension	Other Insurance	Other*
1987	12.13%	13.23%	9.60%	31.19%	12.61%	11.45%	4.48%	5.31%
1986	9.48	13.63	8.30	31.87	12.72	13.86	4.39	5.75
1985	7.47	11.91	7.36	34.40	14.84	15.82	4.16	4.06
1984	7.03	8.77	7.81	35.25	16.04	17.15	3.73	4.22
1983	7.17	7.55	7.23	36.35	16.64	17.69	3.58	3.78
1982	9.65	7.24	5.41	35.74	15.87	18.96	4.56	2.58
1981	10.23	5.76	5.44	35.25	15.78	19.66	4.98	2.92
1980	11.87	4.44	5.83	36.09	15.68	19.08	4.76	2.24
1979	15.49	2.97	5.94	36.59	13.70	18.28	5.08	1.96
1978	16.80	2.55	6.61	36.14	12.08	18.67	4.92	2.21
1977	19.21	2.29	7.20	34.81	11.00	17.97	4.88	2.64
1976	20.94	1.51	7.70	33.54	10.99	18.33	4.41	2.58
1975	20.15	1.41	7.92	32.26	12.97	18.90	3.73	2.66
1974	20.61	1.40	7.19	33.62	12.21	19.15	3.49	2.33
1973	19.66	1.18	7.14	35.32	12.56	18.48	3.05	2.61
1972	20.70	1.25	7.84	35.02	11.89	17.47	3.28	2.55
1971	20.48	1.32	7.00	35.07	12.60	17.18	3.92	2.43
1970	17.89	1.33	5.48	36.61	14.53	17.34	4.25	2.57

* Other is comprised of mutual funds and brokers and dealers in securities.
Source: Flow of Funds Accounts, Financial Assets and Liabilities, Year-End 1963-87. Board of Governors of the Federal Reserve System.

it still comes to nearly $64 billion. The last couple of years have witnessed an increased interest in bonds—corporate, municipal and government—by investment companies. Many individual investors have begun to realize some of the advantages offered by diversified investment portfolios under professional management. It has dawned on them that bonds are not simply "buy-and-hold" investments; bond portfolios need to be managed just as much as equity investments.

Volume of New Corporate Bond Issues

While the total amount of corporate debt is quite large, much of it is not of direct concern to many bond investors as it has been privately placed with, or issued directly to, banks, insurance companies and other financial intermediaries. We are mostly concerned with publicly issued debt which can be traded either on the established securities exchanges or in the unlisted over-the-counter markets. At the end of 1988, the outstanding amount of publicly issued domestic corporate bonds (including convertibles) taken at par value was estimated at $570 billion; excluded from these figures are zero coupon issues and floating and adjustable rate debt.[6]

As interest rates declined in 1984 to 1986, corporations issued an increasing amount of nonconvertible debt in the public markets through underwritten offerings. In 1986, a record-setting $142.6 billion of fresh corporate new issues came to market, four times the volume of only three years earlier. New issue activity slowed in 1987 and 1988 as interest rates drifted upwards, but the amounts issued were the second and third largest. Tables 1–3a to 1–3c show the amount of public offerings for 1973 through 1988. Excluded are non-underwritten offerings such as those sold on a best-efforts basis, medium-term notes, debt issued in exchange for stock or other debt, and structured transactions such as asset-based financings which represent a sale of assets and are based on the nature of the asset and the offering's structure rather than the issuer's credit.

The composition of the new issue market by issuer type has changed since 1980 when utilities accounted for 36.5% of the total volume followed by industrials with 33.4% and financial institutions for 29%. In 1988, utility debt was only $10.8 billion or only

Table 1-3a Public Financing in the Taxable Bond Markets by Issuer Classification, 1973-1988 (Nonconvertible Bond Offerings—Par Value ($ millions))

	Total	Communi-cations	Electrics	Gas and Water	Industrials	Finance	Banks and Thrifts	Transpor-tation	Inter-national
1988	$ 98,867	$ 638	$ 7,653	$2,512	$45,104	$22,949	$13,616	$2,480	$3,915
1987	104,634	2,495	12,283	2,848	42,056	24,329	13,945	1,593	5,085
1986	142,562	10,231	21,893	2,825	60,364	22,837	15,644	3,750	5,018
1985	80,118	3,210	6,354	1,566	32,161	19,817	9,638	1,427	5,945
1984	48,890	830	5,000	825	19,510	10,223	8,255	1,247	3,000
1983	35,697	1,965	5,400	1,470	9,391	5,927	6,758	896	3,890
1982	44,168	720	7,170	1,665	14,281	8,373	5,217	1,062	5,680
1981	40,655	3,820	6,425	1,640	12,729	7,175	1,975	1,316	5,575
1980	36,695	5,975	6,418	1,000	12,257	5,310	2,025	1,445	2,265
1979	24,941	3,700	4,760	555	6,114	3,236	2,200	991	3,385
1978	20,799	2,880	4,708	170	3,287	4,140	630	734	4,250
1977	25,929	2,625	5,306	302	4,472	5,723	1,520	873	5,108
1976	30,165	2,200	5,012	1,058	7,635	5,510	1,185	1,270	6,295
1975	34,918	3,035	6,932	1,319	14,100	2,538	920	967	5,107
1974	26,663	3,396	7,642	752	7,853	2,125	2,325	920	1,650
1973	13,315	3,149	4,757	449	1,235	1,923	555	522	725
Total	$809,016	$50,869	$117,713	$20,956	$292,549	$152,135	$86,408	$21,493	$66,893

Source: Derived from *Moody's Bond Survey*, various issues.

Table 1-3b Public Financing in the Taxable Bond Markets by Issuer Classification, 1973-1988 (Nonconvertible Bond Offerings—Percentage Distribution)

	Communi-cations	Electrics	Gas and Water	Industrials	Finance	Banks and Thrifts	Transpor-tation	International
1988	0.65%	7.74%	2.54%	45.62%	23.21%	13.77%	2.51%	3.96%
1987	2.38	11.74	2.72	40.19	23.25	13.33	1.52	4.86
1986	7.18	15.36	1.98	42.34	16.02	10.97	2.63	3.52
1985	4.01	7.93	1.95	40.14	24.73	12.03	1.78	7.42
1984	1.70	10.23	1.69	39.91	20.91	16.88	2.55	6.14
1983	5.50	15.13	4.12	26.31	16.60	18.93	2.51	10.90
1982	1.63	16.23	3.77	32.33	18.96	11.81	2.40	12.86
1981	9.40	15.80	4.03	31.31	17.65	4.86	3.24	13.71
1980	16.28	17.49	2.73	33.40	14.47	5.52	3.94	6.17
1979	14.83	19.08	2.23	24.51	12.97	8.82	3.97	13.57
1978	13.85	22.63	0.82	15.80	19.90	3.03	3.53	20.43
1977	10.12	20.46	1.16	17.25	22.07	5.86	3.37	19.70
1976	7.29	16.61	3.51	25.31	18.27	3.93	4.21	20.87
1975	8.69	19.85	3.78	40.38	7.27	2.63	2.77	14.63
1974	12.74	28.66	2.82	29.45	7.97	8.72	3.45	6.19
1973	23.65	35.72	3.37	9.27	14.44	4.17	3.92	5.44
Average 1973-88	6.29%	14.55%	2.59%	36.16%	18.80%	10.68%	2.66%	8.27%

Source: Derived from Moody's Bond Survey, various issues.

10.9% of the year's volume. Industrial financing rose to $45.1 billion or 45.6%. Financial institutions raised $36.6 billion or 37% of the year's volume. In the sixteen-year period from 1973 through 1988, industrial companies raised the largest amount of public debt, $292.5 billion, or 36.2% of the total. Financial institutions are in second place with $238.5 billion (29.5%) trailed by utilities at $189.5 billion (23.4%).

Another way of looking at new issue volume is by quality or rating category (see Table 1–3c). Using the Moody's Investors Service rating designations, we note that there has been a considerable decline in new issues of prime rated (Aaa) credits, falling from a high of 41.7% of 1977's volume to only 4.8% in 1984, before a modest recovery to nearly 12% in 1988. For that matter, the two highest rating classifications (Aaa and Aa) accounted for more than 50% of the primary volume each year prior to 1982. The rating sector at the other extreme end of the scale (Ba and lower including nonrated issues we assigned to this category due to speculative characteristics) posted tremendous growth for much of this period. From a low of only $145 million in 1975, volume rose to more than $30 billion in 1986. New speculative grade issues of $26.5 billion for 1988 accounted for just under 27% of the year's primary market activity. An increasing share of the new issue volume has also been captured by lower medium grade credits (Baa). In the last few years an increasing number of professional investors have viewed this category as "semi-speculative," the last stop before degradation.

Table 1–4 shows that since the early seventies the average corporate bond issue has nearly tripled in size from slightly under $56 million in 1973 to more than $162 million in 1988. Generally, the larger issues are easier to buy and sell in the secondary market as they often have more market makers and greater investor interest. Increased market competition often means smaller spreads between the price which the dealer is willing to pay for the bond (bid) and the price at which he is willing to sell the bond (offer or asked). This liquidity factor is very important to actively managed investment portfolios. Illiquid and poorly marketable corporate bonds may involve higher transaction costs if one can find a counterparty to the transaction.

Table 1-3c Public Financing in the Taxable Bond Markets by Issuer Classification, 1973-1988
(Nonconvertible Bond Offerings—Par Value ($ millions))

	Total	Aaa	% of Total	Aa	% of Total	A	% of Total	Baa	% of Total	Ba and Lower	% of Total
1988	$ 98,868	$11,758	11.89%	$13,501	13.66%	$32,494	32.87%	$14,639	14.81%	$26,476	26.78%
1987	104,634	10,587	10.12	21,860	20.89	30,521	29.17	16,475	15.75	25,191	24.07
1986	142,562	12,253	8.59	37,943	26.62	40,159	28.17	21,866	15.34	30,341	21.28
1985	80,118	9,016	11.25	16,539	20.64	27,953	34.99	9,772	12.20	16,838	21.02
1984	48,890	2,350	4.81	13,730	28.08	15,117	30.92	4,145	8.48	13,548	27.71
1983	35,697	3,920	10.98	11,110	31.12	9,030	25.30	5,125	14.36	6,512	18.24
1982	44,168	6,072	13.75	14,659	33.19	15,340	34.73	4,274	9.68	3,823	8.65
1981	40,655	11,835	29.11	9,980	24.55	12,662	31.15	4,085	10.05	2,093	5.14
1980	36,695	10,109	27.55	10,721	29.22	11,900	32.43	2,540	6.92	1,425	3.88
1979	24,941	10,400	41.70	5,712	22.90	5,780	23.17	1,744	6.99	1,305	5.24
1978	20,799	7,967	38.30	5,646	27.15	4,415	21.23	1,618	7.78	1,153	5.54
1977	25,929	11,046	42.60	5,239	20.21	5,033	19.41	2,093	8.07	2,518	9.71
1976	30,165	9,907	32.84	8,786	29.13	8,039	26.65	3,023	10.02	410	1.36
1975	34,918	11,348	32.50	8,932	25.58	12,011	34.40	2,482	7.11	145	0.41
1974	26,663	7,420	27.83	8,510	31.92	7,500	28.13	1,933	7.25	1,300	4.87
1973	13,315	4,046	30.39	3,225	24.22	4,052	30.43	519	3.90	1,473	11.06
Total	$809,016	$140,033	17.31%	$196,093	24.24%	$242,006	29.91%	$96,333	11.91%	$134,552	16.63%

Ba and lower category includes non-rated issues.
Source: Derived from *Moody's Bond Survey*, various issues.

Table 1-4 Average Size of Issue, 1973–1988 Public Financing in the Taxable Bond Markets (Nonconvertible Bond Offerings—Par Value ($ millions))

	Total Financing	Number of Issues	Average Size of Issue
1988	$ 98,868	609	$162.34
1987	104,634	706	148.21
1986	142,562	987	144.44
1985	80,118	655	122.32
1984	48,890	403	121.32
1983	35,697	379	94.19
1982	44,168	467	94.58
1981	40,655	333	122.09
1980	36,695	378	97.08
1979	24,941	250	99.76
1978	20,799	244	85.24
1977	25,929	328	79.05
1976	30,165	395	76.37
1975	34,918	471	74.14
1974	26,663	350	76.18
1973	13,315	238	55.95

Source: Derived from data in *Moody's Bond Survey,* various issues.

Corporate Bond Trading

Many believe individuals should confine their corporate bond investments to those issues listed on the New York Stock Exchange (or on the smaller American Stock Exchange) and avoid unlisted issues trading in the over-the-counter (OTC) market. Professional investors find that the over-the-counter market is the only one for their needs for a very simple reason: listed trading activity is primarily small orders for "retail" or individual investors in lots of as small as $1,000 par value. An institutional investor wanting to sell a block of $5 million par value of an issue would find that the listed auction market would not be able to handle it; the trade has to be done in the negotiated unlisted market. In most cases, the investment firm will act as a dealer and purchase the bonds for its own account and risk as it may not be able to find an institutional purchaser right away. It will hold the bonds hoping that it will quickly find a purchaser for them at a profit. The business of the dealers or market makers is not investment in the traditional sense of a bond portfolio but the trading and turnover of their inventory.

Most individual investors like to see their bonds quoted in the newspaper; unlisted corporate bonds are not normally quoted unless, perhaps, they are recent new issues with institutional interest. Many retail stock brokers can easily obtain the last sale, current quotation, and size of the bid and offering from their quotation machines. Unlisted quotations and bids and offers are less readily obtained by the salesmen handling small investors. Of course, brokers can more easily get investors lists of offerings from the firm's own inventory, but these may not always be issues of the investor's choosing.

This does not mean that the listed market will always provide investors with higher bid and lower offering prices than the unlisted market. The two markets can behave independently of one another. The listed market and its quotes can easily be impacted by small trades. It is not uncommon to see the price of a bond fall several points on a sale of a few thousand dollars principal amount only to have it regain that loss on a succeeding purchase. This may occur because the broker has not carefully placed the order. More than likely, the order was to sell (buy) "at the market" without regard to the size of the current bid or offering. It is often better to place limits on orders, especially for those less actively traded issues. Also, inactive issues are just that—they do not trade every day. In some cases the several point rise or fall may be due to changes in the interest rate levels since the last listed trade weeks or months ago. The current transaction represents today's interest levels, not those of the past.

Many investors place limit orders when trading in stocks which have very active and liquid markets but ignore limit orders for thinly traded bonds. As Ben Weberman said in *Forbes Magazine*, "The listed market is so small and thin, it is easy to manipulate."[7] This may sound a little extreme, but there is more than a grain of truth to it. However, despite some of the drawbacks, the listed bond market provides many investors with the needed peace of mind as the transaction prices are published for all to see.

Bond trading on The New York Stock Exchange is subject to what is known as "the nine bond rule." This is Rule 396 which requires that all orders for nine bonds or less be sent to the floor of the Exchange for execution. If the order can be executed at a better price after the floor market has been diligently sought and ascertained, it may then be executed "upstairs" in the over-the-counter market. Some of the larger stock brokerage firms may extend this rule to 25 or 50 bonds. That is, they will normally send all orders up to that size to the floor.

There are no minimum requirements for the listing of bonds on the New York Stock Exchange. However, the public distribution and aggregate size must be wide and large enough to warrant a listing. Appropriate distribution might mean a minimum of 250 to 300 bondholders, or an issue size of about $20 million. If the aggregate market or principal value fall to less than $1 million, the Exchange may delist the bonds. Also, if the company defaults and files for bankruptcy, the bonds may be delisted, but not in all cases. In recent years such companies as Manville, Global Marine, Storage Technology, to name but a few, kept their bonds listed on the New York Stock Exchange. In our opinion, this is the time when many holders need the listed market, and the Exchange is to be commended for retaining the listings. There are fewer and different market participants in bankrupt issues than in conventional bonds which makes for a less liquid market, especially over-the-counter. The spread or difference between the bid and asked prices may be wider, trading activity tends to diminish, and price volatility may increase. The information flow coming from the corporation is often less than prior to the bankruptcy and fewer Wall Street analysts follow the companies making for increased speculative activity on the part of more uninformed participants. Thus, the individual investor needs the additional market support or liquidity provided by the listed market.

The New York Stock Exchange charges a one-time fee for listing bonds but there were annual fees from 1981 through 1984. Several companies including New York Telephone, Southern Bell Telephone and Southwestern Bell Telephone refused to make these payments. In 1985 the Exchange delisted 58 issues of the three telephone companies after negotiations failed to move the squabblers from their respective positions. Subsequently, Southwestern Bell Telephone Co. listed 12 of its debenture issues on the American Stock Exchange. *The Wall Street Journal* reported: "Since the vast majority of the holders . . . affected by the dispute are institutions, the companies said they don't believe trading in the bonds will be affected."[8]

In 1986, bond volume set a record for the New York Stock Exchange with nearly $10.5 billion (including convertibles and a small amount of foreign issues) traded; this is a daily average of $41.4 million. Listed secondary trading activity followed the new issue trend in 1987 and 1988 with the average daily volume falling to $30.4 million. The lowest average daily volume of $1.8 million was posted in 1913. The lowest daily volume on record in the twentieth century was only $500,000 on August 13, 1900, while the highest single day's activity was on September 6, 1939, when $83.1 million traded. Investors may have thought that the U.S. exchanges would close for a period as much of Europe was declaring war on one another. They remembered August 1914 when the lamps were "going out all over Europe" and the U.S. exchanges closed for several months.

The Securities Industry Association began keeping figures for unlisted corporate bond trading in May 1985. For the year from May through December the average daily corporate bond volume was $10.070 billion. In 1986 daily volume averaged $14.593 billion, in 1987 $14.890 billion, and for 1988 it declined to $13.182 billion. Thus, the New York Stock Exchange trading volume is less than one-half of one percent of the over-the-counter market. These data amply demonstrate that listed trading is very insignificant compared with total corporate bond trading volume. It is safe to guess that a decade ago the average OTC trading volume was consider-

Table 1–5 Selected Details New York Stock Exchange Bond Trading, 1980–1988 (Par value—$ millions)

	Annual Volume	Daily Average	Number of Trades	Number of Bonds per Trade	Number of Issuers	Number of Issues	Par Value	Market Value
1988	$7,702.1	$30.4	522,173	14.00	846	3,106	$1,610,310	$1,561,031
1987	9,727.1	38.4	659,231	14.76	885	3,346	1,650,263	1,621,263
1986	10,464.1	41.4	774,890	13.50	951	3,611	1,379,545	1,457,603
1985	9,046.5	35.9	726,279	12.46	1,010	3,856	1,327,375	1,339,238
1984	6,982.3	27.6	620,547	11.25	1,024	3,751	1,083,674	1,021,791
1983	7,572.3	29.9	712,877	10.62	1,034	3,600	965,252	898,064
1982	7,155.4	28.3	686,186	10.43	1,031	3,233	792,529	766,105
1981	5,733.1	22.7	636,572	9.01	1,049	3,110	681,237	573,893
1980	5,190.3	20.5	594,449	8.73	1,045	3,057	601,527	507,770

Source: New York Stock Exchange Fact Book, 1988, 1989.

ably less. The increase has been due to a number of factors including more participants in a much larger market and the shorter-term view taken by portfolio managers which encourages turnover. Bonds are no longer bought and held to maturity (if they ever were) for they can readily be traded as they get under and overvalued relative to one another. Bond investment constantly requires assessing the relative value of one issue with another in a market that is not always "efficient." The increasing internationalization of the debt markets and new trading techniques including the use of options and futures in portfolio hedging strategies are two other factors contributing to the greater trading volume nowadays.

Listing a company's debt on a stock exchange is not without cost. It involves the payment of fees to the exchange and the opportunity cost of the time spent by management on listing documentation, among other things. In recent years, the New York Stock Exchange has lost more than 150 issuers. The number of listed bonds is down by more than 500 from the peak although the par value is at record levels. Of what value is a listing? The over-the-counter market is much bigger and works rather well. We have not come across any studies that show that listing reduces an issuer's interest costs or flotation expenses. With the exception of some small odd-lot trading activity, it is questionable that marketability is even improved. Thus, while individuals with small investments in corporate bonds may find the exchange market more suitable for their needs due to increased confidence in the New York Stock Exchange, it offers the issuer little except possibly some added prestige. After all, the market for municipal and U.S. Treasury bonds is also the unlisted market.

Corporate Bond Ratings

A bond rating is an indicator or assessment of the issuer's ability to meet its principal and interest payments in a timely manner in accordance with the terms of the issue. In the United States, debt ratings are issued by five recognized agencies, i.e., organizations whose ratings are generally accepted by the vast majority of investment professionals and by regulatory authorities. They are capable of rating the full range of debt securities from commercial paper to term bonds, corporate and governmental, domestic and international. For years Moody's Investors Service, Inc. (Moody's) and Standard & Poor's Corporation (S&P) have been the two most widely accepted of the services because of the breadth and depth of their coverage and their wide publication activities. Fitch Investors Service, Inc. (Fitch), the smallest of the three old-line bond raters, was revitalized in 1988 by a new investor group and is gaining stature and credibility among professional investors. The last two agencies, while smaller, younger and less well-known, nevertheless perform important functions for their subscriber/investors. They are Duff & Phelps Inc. (D&P) and McCarthy, Crisanti & Maffei, Inc. (MCM).

What Are Debt Ratings?

Ratings are normally assigned to the particular issue, not the issuer; this is the reason why a company may have a couple of different ratings on its debt. For example, S&P assigns a "AA" rating to the senior debt of Ford Motor Credit Corporation while the subordinated debt has a rating of "AA-." Moody's gives three different ratings to the various debt securities of the Public Service Company of New Hampshire. The first mortgage bonds and the general and refunding mortgage bonds are rated "Caa," the deferred interest third mortgage bonds are rated "Ca," and the debentures "C." Prior to the 1988 bankruptcy, Moody's rated the issues "B1," "B2," "B3" and "Caa," respectively. Even though the first mortgage bonds and the general and refunding mortgage bonds are paying their interest, Standard & Poor's rates all of the debt "D" as the company is in bankruptcy. Fitch rates them "D" and Duff & Phelps "CCC." MCM does not rate the debt although it is covered by their speculative grade high yield research service. Table 1–6 summarizes the rating categories; the definitions may be found in the Appendix.

In brief, a thorough analysis is done of the issuer's (and guarantor's, if applicable) operations and need for funds. An assessment is made of the industry and the issuer's position within the industry. Finally, the caliber of the issuer's management is reviewed even though it is largely reflected in the financial statements of the company. The financials are, to some extent, a report card on management. In conducting a credit review the analyst considers the three C's of credit—Character, Collateral, and Capacity. The character of the management, the collateral, if any, behind the repayment of the debt, and the capacity of the issuer to service its debt. While bond analysts rely on numbers and calculate many ratios to get a picture of the company's debt servicing capacity, a rating is an opinion or judgment of an issuer's ability to meet all of its obligations when due, whether during prosperity or during times of stress. The purpose of bond ratings is to rank issues in terms of the probability of default.

Ratings are not based on where we are in an economic or business cycle but on the fundamentals of the company and the issue. A corporation may have a poor year but this does not necessarily mean that a downgrading is imminent. If the raters feel, based on their experience and analysis, that the downturn is only temporary, the rating may remain unscathed. However, if the rating review reveals that the deterioration may be of a more permanent nature, the rating can be lowered. In many cases, the reason for a lower rating is that the issuer has increased its debt burden to such an extent that a return to the former levels is not anticipated. Also, business conditions may be such that profit margins may weaken causing deterioration in various debt related measurements. This all adds up to less protection for the debt holder. But ratings also increase. Higher ratings may be due to better operations and profit margins after reorganization, and improved management, increased financial management conservatism reflecting less leverage or "trading on the equity," improved industry position and strengthened finances, among other factors.

Indentures have some bearing on debt ratings. An important factor is where the issue stands in the capitalization of the company. Is it subordinated or senior, secured or unsecured? Generally, the more senior the issue, the higher the rating. In late 1988, Moody's and Standard & Poor's expressed concern about rating downgrades due to "event risk," the increased leverage of a company's capital structure caused by decapitalizations, restructurings, recapitalizations, mergers, acquisitions and leveraged buyouts, among other things.[9] Both agencies established committees to look into the matter of investor protection in the case of downgradings triggered by designated events. Moody's said that it "will recognize meaningful

Table 1-6 Summary of Rating Symbols and Definitions

Moody's	S&P	Fitch	D&P	MCM	Meaning
Investment Grade—High Creditworthiness					
Aaa	AAA	AAA	AAA	AAA	Gilt edge, prime, maximum safety
Aa1	AA+	AA+	AA+	AA+	
Aa2	AA	AA	AA	AA	Very high grade, high quality
Aa3	AA–	AA–	AA–	AA–	
A1	A+	A+	A+	A+	
A2	A	A	A	A	Upper medium grade
A3	A–	A–	A–	A–	
Baa1	BBB+	BBB+	BBB+	BBB+	
Baa2	BBB	BBB	BBB	BBB	Lower medium grade
Baa3	BBB–	BBB–	BBB–	BBB–	
Distinctly Speculative—Low Creditworthiness					
Ba1	BB+	BB+	BB+	BB+	
Ba2	BB	BB	BB	BB	Low grade, speculative
Ba3	BB–	BB–	BB–	BB–	
B1	B+	B+	B+		
B2	B	B	B	B	Highly speculative
B3	B–	B–	B–		

Moody's	S&P	Fitch	D&P	MCM	Meaning
Predominantly Speculative—Substantial Risk or in Default					
	CCC+				
Caa	CCC	CCC	CCC		Substantial risk, in poor standing
	CCC–				
Ca	CC	CC			May be in default, extremely speculative
C	C	C			Very extremely speculative
	CI				CI=Income bonds—no interest is being paid
		DDD			Default
		DD		DD	
	D	D			

indenture protection against event risk in its ratings of individual issues where significant event risk is present.. . . . Insofar as we determine that meaningful protection is afforded against this heightened source of risk, we will change ratings of individual issues appropriately." [10] Thus there can be two different ratings for senior debt if one issue has satisfactory event risk protection and the other does not. Other terms and provisions affecting the issuer's ability to service the debt, if decidedly weak, may be taken into consideration. But redemption provisions and similar features are generally not factors in a rating decision. Rating agencies do not rate or grade bond indentures per se, they rate only ability of the issuer to repay the debt and the protection afforded bondholders.

It used to be said that ratings were assigned for the life of the issue. While still applicable today, things seem to change more rapidly than previously with rating changes occurring more often than was the case two decades ago. True, there are now more rated issues but continual economic change and the resulting impact on the individual company and industry is the major influence on rating revisions nowadays.

Table 1–7 is a summary of Moody's rating changes for corporate issuers in recent years. In 1985, 277 corporations had their debt ratings changed by Moody's. Upgrades were given on about $129 billion of debt of 124 companies. Downgrades covered 153 issuers with $108 billion of rated debt. Of the downgrades 102 or 67% ($67 billion) were caused by negative changes in the company's fundamentals. However, the remaining downgrades—51, or 33% ($41 billion)—were caused by what Moody's calls "decapitalizations" or "special events," up from 24% in 1984. In 1989, rating changes affected $294 billion of debt of 477 issuers. Of these, 138 issuers with $86 billion of debt were upgraded and 339 with $208 billion of debt were downgraded. Special event risk caused the downgrades of 77 issuers impacting $50 billion of debt.

Limitations on the Uses of Ratings

Ratings are only a guide to the "credit quality" of an issue. They are not "buy," "hold" or "sell" indicators. They will not, in and of themselves, state if a bond issue is rich, cheap or fairly priced. Ratings will not tell one if the bond's price is going to go up or down. The "1" "3" and "+" "−" modifiers are not directional signals pointing the way to an upgrade or a downgrade. Some issues at the upper end of a rating category may be vulnerable to a downgrading while others at the lower end might be in an uptrend. They can not help investors to determine the issue's vulnerability to early redemption. The rating agencies have devoted much copy to the use of ratings. The following is from *Moody's Bond Guide*, May 1989:

Table 1-7 Summary of Moody's Rating Changes, 1984–1989

	1989		1988		1987		1986		1985		1984	
	Up	*Down*	*Up*	*Down*	*Up*	*Down*	*Up*	*Down*	*Up*	*Down*	*Up*	*Down*
Number of Issuers												
Financials	49	113	40	61	16	37	33	39	16	14	10	16
Industrials	81	181	76	147	70	119	61	183	62	124	70	90
Utilities	8	45	26	29	14	20	49	24	46	15	81	42
Total	138	339	142	237	100	176	143	246	124	153	161	148
% of Total	29%	71%	37%	63%	36%	64%	37%	63%	45%	55%	52%	48%
Dollar Volume (billions)												
Financials	$28	$44	$18	$76	$5	$46	$23	$50	$8	$11	$7	$11
Industrials	55	124	61	108	73	64	22	117	67	72	36	30
Utilities	3	40	32	36	13	35	45	31	54	25	56	40
Total	$86	$208	$110	$220	$90	$145	$90	$197	$129	$108	$100	$81
% of Total	29%	71%	33%	66%	38%	62%	31%	69%	54%	46%	55%	45%

Table continues

Table 1-7 Summary of Moody's Rating Changes, 1984–1989   (Continued)

	1989 SE	1989 Fund	1988 SE	1988 Fund	1987 SE	1987 Fund	1986 SE	1986 Fund	1985 SE	1985 Fund	1984 SE	1984 Fund
Number of Issuers												
Financials	5	108	4	57	6	31	3	36	0	14	2	14
Industrials	69	112	70	77	40	78	64	119	49	75	31	59
Utilities	3	42	1	28	0	20	3	21	2	13	2	40
Total	77	262	75	162	46	129	70	176	51	102	35	113
% of Total	23%	77%	32%	68%	26%	74%	28%	72%	33%	67%	24%	76%
Dollar Volume (billions)												
Financials	$1	$43	$5	$71	$8	$38	*	$50	$0	$11	*	$10
Industrials	49	75	42	66	26	38	$37	79	38	34	$15	16
Utilities	*	39	1	35	0	35	*	2	3	23	1	39
Total	$50	$157	$48	$172	$34	$111	$38	$160	$41	$67	$16	$65
% of Total	24%	76%	22%	78%	23%	77%	19%	81%	38%	62%	20%	80%

* less than $500 million.

Note: Columns may not total due to rounding.   SE = special events; Fund = fundamentals.
Source: *Global Outlook 1990 Overview*, Moody's Investors Service, January 1990, pp. 10-11.

Bonds carrying the same rating are not claimed to be of absolutely equal quality. In a broad sense they are alike in posi-tion, but since there are a limited number of rating classes used in grading thousands of bonds, the symbols cannot reflect the fine shadings of risks which actually exist. Therefore, it should be evident to the user of ratings that two bonds identically rated are unlikely to be precisely the same in investment quality.

As ratings are designed exclusively for the purpose of grading bonds according to their investment qualities, they should not be used alone as a basis for investment operations. For example, they have no value in forecasting the direction of future trends of market price. Market price movements in bonds are influenced not only by the quality of individual issues but also by changes in money rates and general economic trends, as well as by the length of maturity, etc. During its life even the best quality bond may have wide price movements, while its high investment status remains unchanged.

The matter of market price has no bearing whatsoever on the determination of ratings which are not to be construed as recommendations with respect to "attractiveness." The attractiveness of a given bond may depend on its yield, its maturity date or other factors for which the investor may search, as well as on its investment quality, the only characteristic to which the rating refers.

Since ratings involve judgments about the future, on the one hand, and since they are used by investors as a means of protection, on the other, the effort is made when assigning ratings to look at "worst" potentialities in the "visible" future, rather than solely at the past record and the status of the present. Therefore, investors using the rating should not expect to find in them a reflection of statistical factors alone, since they are an appraisal of long term risks, including the recognition of non-statistical factors.

Why Are Ratings Important to Market Participants?

Prudent investment management requires that definite standards be applied in the selection of securities. This is true for equities as well as bonds, and institutions as well as for individuals. As Charles D. Ellis wrote:

> In investment management, the real opportunity to achieve superior results is not in scrambling to outperform the market, but in establishing and adhering to appropriate investment policies over the long-term—policies that position the portfolio to benefit from riding with the main long-term forces in the market. Investment policy, wisely formulated by realistic and well-informed clients with a long-term perspective and clearly defined objectives, is the foundation upon which portfolios should be constructed and managed over time and through market cycles.[11]

Despite their limitations, ratings are, nonetheless, important to market participants for several reasons. Many institutions and governmental bodies have established investment parameters that allow them to invest in corporate bonds of only certain quality levels, namely, in the investment grade range (the four highest rankings). Of course, there may be additional criteria as part of the overall portfolio or investment policies. Some institutions look upon Baa/BBB issues as semi-investment grade and thus are restricted to the top three grades. In a number of cases, the investment guidelines may allow a small portion of the investment portfolio to be in noninvestment grade issues, but most of the bonds must be of respectable quality. This allowance for noninvestment grade issues is often called "a basket clause."

S&P has determined that qualified investments for "AAA" rated structured financings can include, among many others, obligations rated "AAA."[12] The commercial paper rates in the Board of Governors of the Federal Reserve System's *Statistical Release H.15 (519)— Selected Interest Rates* are those of companies whose bond rating is "AA" or the equivalent. These rates are used in the determination of dividends for auction market and remarketed preferred stock. Many mutual funds and investment companies have limitations on their investments based on debt ratings of the major agencies, both for short-term defensive purposes and for longer-term investment. In the 1930s, the Comptroller of the Currency, working with Fitch, issued regulations governing the bond investments of banks under its control. Bonds thus eligible for investment were those in the top four investment grades.

A lower bond rating means that it will cost the issuer more to raise funds than if the security were higher rated due to the increased risk of default as one moves down the quality ladder, all other things being equal. It only makes sense that investors want to get paid more for taking on additional risk, and ratings are an indication of that risk. Some floating rate or variable rate bonds have the interest rate based on the prevailing rating at the time the new coupon is determined. Ratings are also important to issuers as a lower rating may mean that the security may not even come to market. In May 1970, Standard & Poor's Corporation gave a "BB" rating to the proposed $100 million debt offering of Pennsylvania Co., a real estate company in the Penn Central System. The deal never made it to the market and was another event leading up to the subsequent bankruptcy filing of Penn Central.

Ratings are also important in the determination of the value for an investment-grade fixed income instrument. The value of a bond is determined by a number of factors. One factor is the yield curve, i.e., the maturity of the issue, its coupon and the level of interest rates, with U.S. Treasury issues as the benchmark. Another is the indenture features including protective covenants and redemption terms. Finally, the actual or perceived quality of the bond issue must be reflected in the bond's valuation. As mentioned above, increased default risk means that investors will want a greater return. If analysis suggests that the issue may be upgraded, investors may be willing to pay a higher price. If it appears vulnerable to downgrading, investors will want the bonds at a cheaper price (higher yield). Other factors of lesser importance affecting bond evaluation include the amount outstanding, how much of a sinking fund issue is controlled by a few investors, whether it is a public or privately placed issue, and whether it is a foreign or domestic issue. These factors affect liquidity and marketability of the bond and thus impact what investors and traders are willing to pay for an issue.

After the issue's quality and expected rating trend, its vulnerability to premature redemption, and its place on the yield curve have been determined, a value will be given to the bond. Depending on the issue, it might be given a valuation of 110 basis points above the level of the Treasury yield curve at a similar maturity date. Another issue of similar but slightly different terms might be valued at 100 basis points above the yield curve. Thus, at that time, they should trade at a spread of ten basis points from one another. If the actual spread is different, then a trade might be accomplished by selling the richer bond and buying the cheaper one. Investors constantly compare one bond with another since bond investment is, to a great extent, based on relative valuation.

Finally, what about split ratings—ratings that differ between the major rating agencies. Moody and S&P ratings are often the same, but not always. Ratings, after all, are subjective; differences of opinion do occur.

> We find that in general split ratings represent random differences of opinion on issues whose creditworthiness is close to the borderline between ratings. The respective positions of the two agencies could easily have been reversed; i.e., on another day or with a slightly different set of analysts, either agency might assign a different rating. In only a decided minority of cases do splits appear to represent a more fundamental difference of opinion, and in those cases the differences appear to be with respect to aspects of the issue other than public accounting information.
>
> . . . therefore, split ratings evidence the complexity and subjectivity of bond creditworthiness evaluations and it is this subjectivity that leads most users to demand a second rating.[13]

And split ratings do affect what investors are willing to pay for bonds. A study on split ratings and reoffering yields on new debt issues appeared in *Financial Management* in the summer of 1985. It concluded:

> The paper's empirical analysis reveals that the reoffering yields on split-rated bonds are not significantly different from the yields on the lower rating involved in the split while they are significantly different from the yields on the higher rating involved in that same split. It thus appears that investors' perceptions of the true default risk of a split-rated issue are more accurately represented by the lower of the two ratings . . . [14]

Therefore, in doing the bond value analysis, split ratings must be considered.

Appendix A: Debt Rating Definitions

The *Fitch Rating Register* says:

> A Fitch Bond Rating provides a guide to investors in determin-
> ing the investment risk attached to a security. The rating repre-
> sents our assessment of the issuer's ability to meet the obliga-
> tions of a specific debt issue . . . . [It goes on to say that] the
> rating takes into consideration special features of the issue, its
> relationship to other obligations of the issuer, the record of the
> issuer and of any guarantor, as well as the political and
> economic environment that might affect the future financial
> strength of the issuer. Bonds which have the same rating are of
> similar but not necessarily identical investment quality since the
> limited number of rating categories cannot fully reflect small dif-
> ferences in the degree of risk. Moreover, the character of the risk
> factor varies from industry to industry and between corporate,
> health care and municipal obligations.

Moody's Bond Record states:

> Limitations to Uses of Ratings: Bonds carrying the same rating
> are not claimed to be of absolutely equal quality. In a broad
> sense they are alike in position, but since there are a limited
> number of rating classes used in grading thousands of bonds,
> the symbols cannot reflect the fine shadings of risks which ac-
> tually exist. Therefore, it should be evident to the user of ratings
> that two bonds identically rated are unlikely to be precisely the
> same in investment quality.

Standard & Poor's Bond Guide bases its bond ratings primarily on
the following factors:

I.   Likelihood of default-capacity and willingness of the obligor
as to the timely payment of interest and repayment of principal in
accordance with the terms of the obligation;

II.   Nature and provisions of the obligation;

III.   Protection afforded by, and relative position of, the obligation
in the event of bankruptcy, reorganization or other arrangement
under the laws of bankruptcy and other laws affecting creditors'
rights.

In order to use ratings properly, it is important to know the precise definitions of the rating categories—what they are and what they are not.

Fitch Investors Service, Inc.

AAA: rated bonds are considered to be investment grade and of the highest quality. The obligor has an extraordinary ability to pay interest and repay principal, which is unlikely to be affected by reasonably foreseeable events.

AA: rated bonds are considered to be investment grade and of high quality. The obligor's ability to pay interest and repay principal, while very strong, is somewhat less than for AAA rated securities or more subject to possible change over the term of the issue.

A: rated bonds are considered to be investment grade and of good quality. The obligor's ability to pay interest and repay principal is considered to be strong, but it may be more vulnerable to adverse changes in economic conditions and circumstances than bonds with higher ratings.

BBB: rated bonds are considered to be investment grade and of satisfactory quality. The obligor's ability to pay interest and repay principal is considered to be adequate. Adverse changes in economic conditions and circumstances, however, are more likely to weaken this ability than bonds with higher ratings.

BB: rated bonds are below investment grade and considered speculative. The obligor's ability to pay interest and repay principal is not strong and is considered likely to be affected over time by adverse economic changes.

B: rated bonds are considered highly speculative. Bonds in this class are lightly protected as to the obligor's ability to pay interest over the life of the issue and repay principal when due.

CCC: rated bonds may have certain characteristics which, with the passing of time, could lead to the possibility of default on either principal or interest payments.

CC: rated bonds are minimally protected. Default in payment of interest and/or principal seems probable.

C: rated bonds are in actual or imminent default in payment of interest or principal.

DDD, DD, D: rated bonds are in actual default and in arrears in interest and/or principal payments. Such bonds are extremely speculative and should be valued only on the basis of their value in liquidation or reorganization of the obligor.

Plus (+) Minus (-) Signs

These signs are used after a rating symbol to designate the relative position of a credit within the rating grade. The + and - signs are carried in ratings from "AA" to "B."

Moody's Investors Service, Inc.

Aaa: Bonds which are rated **Aaa** are judged to be of the best quality. They carry the smallest degree of investment risk and are generally referred to as "gilt edge." Interest payments are protected by a large or by an exceptionally stable margin and principal is secure. While the various protective elements are likely to change, such changes as can be visualized are most unlikely to impair the fundamentally strong position of such issues.

Aa: Bonds which are rated **Aa** are judged to be of high quality by all standards. Together with the **Aaa** group they comprise what are generally known as high grade bonds. They are rated lower than the best bonds because margins of protection may not be as large as in **Aaa** securities or fluctuation of protective elements may be of greater amplitude or there may be other elements present which make the long term risks appear somewhat larger than in **Aaa** securities.

A: Bonds which are rated **A** possess many favorable investment attributes and are to be considered as upper medium grade obligations. Factors giving security to principal and interest are considered adequate but elements may be present which suggest a susceptibility to impairment sometime in the future.

Baa: Bonds which are rated **Baa** are considered as medium grade obligations, i.e., they are neither highly protected nor poorly secured. Interest payments and principal security appear adequate for the present but certain protective elements may be lacking or may be characteristically unreliable over any great length of time. Such bonds lack outstanding investment characteristics and in fact have speculative characteristics as well.

Ba: Bonds which are rated **Ba** are judged to have speculative elements; their future cannot be considered as well assured. Often the protection of interest and principal payments may be very moderate and thereby not well safeguarded during both good and bad times over the future. Uncertainty of position characterizes bonds in this class.

B: Bonds which are rated **B** generally lack characteristics of the desirable investment. Assurance of interest and principal payments or of maintenance of other terms of the contract over any long period of time may be small.

Caa: Bonds which are rated **Caa** are of poor standing. Such issues may be in default or there may be present elements of danger with respect to principal or interest.

Ca: Bonds which are rated **Ca** represent obligations which are speculative in a high degree. Such issues are often in default or have other marked shortcomings.

C: Bonds which are rated **C** are the lowest rated class of bonds and issues so rated can be regarded as having extremely poor prospects of ever attaining any real investment standing.

In April 1982, Moody's added numerical modifiers, "1," " 2," and "3," to each rating category from **Aa** through **B**. The modifier "1" indicates that the security ranks in the higher end of its generic rating category; the modifier "2" indicates a mid-range ranking; and the modifier "3" indicates that the issue ranks in the lower end of its generic rating category.

Standard & Poor's Corporation

AAA: Debt rated **AAA** has the highest rating assigned by Standard & Poor's. Capacity to pay interest and repay principal is extremely strong.

AA: Debt rated **AA** has a very strong capacity to pay interest and repay principal and differs from the higher rated issues only in small degree.

A: Debt rated **A** has a strong capacity to pay interest and repay principal although it is somewhat more susceptible to the adverse effects of changes in circumstances and economic conditions than debt in higher rated categories.

BBB: Debt rated **BBB** is regarded as having an adequate capacity to pay interest and repay principal. Whereas it normally exhibits adequate protection parameters, adverse economic conditions or changing circumstances are more likely to lead to a weakened capacity to pay interest and repay principal for debt in this category than in higher rated categories.

BB: Debt rated **BB** has less near-term vulnerability to default than other speculative issues. However, it faces major ongoing uncertainties or exposure to adverse business, financial or economic conditions which could lead to inadequate capacity to meet timely interest and principal payments.

The **BB** rating category is also used for debt subordinated to senior debt that is assigned an actual or implied **BBB-** rating.

B: Debt rated **B** has a greater vulnerability to default but currently has the capacity to meet interest payments and principal repayments. Adverse business, financial or economic conditions will likely impair capacity or willingness to pay interest or repay principal.

The **B** rating category is also used for debt subordinated to senior debt that is assigned an actual or implied **BB** or **BB-** rating.

CCC: Debt rated **CCC** has a currently identifiable vulnerability to default, and is dependent upon favorable business, financial and economic conditions to meet timely payment of interest and repayment of principal. In the event of adverse business, financial and economic conditions, it is not likely to have the capacity to pay interest and repay principal.

The **CCC** rating category is also used for debt subordinated to senior debt that is assigned an actual or implied **B** or **B-** rating.

CC: The rating **CC** is typically applied to debt subordinated to senior debt that is assigned an actual or implied **CCC** rating.

C: The rating **C** is typically applied to debt subordinated to senior debt that is assigned an actual or implied **CCC-** rating.

CI: The rating **CI** is reserved for income bonds on which no interest is being paid.

D: Debt rated **D** is in default.

The **D** rating category is also used when interest payments or principal repayments are expected to be in default at the payment date, and payment of interest and/or repayment of principal is in arrears.

The concept of an implied senior debt rating is critical to the interpretation of S&P's rating. This is particularly so in the junk bond sector, which is largely a subordinated debt universe. S&P rates specific debt securities rather than overall creditworthiness, and generally assigns different ratings to debt securities of a single issuer based on their relative ranking in liquidation or bankruptcy. The likelihood of default, however, is virtually the same for all debt securities of a single issuer, and is indicated by the senior debt rating. Likewise, senior debt of one issuer may be rated the same as subordinated debt of another, although the risk of default for the first is higher. For instance, senior debt rated "B+" has a higher risk of default than subordinated debt rated "B+."

If senior debt is not rated, an implied senior rating is determined. If the actual or implied senior debt rating is speculative, namely "BB+" or lower, subordinated debt, with few exceptions, will be rated two designations below the senior rating.

Plus (+) or Minus (–): The ratings from "AA" to "CCC" may be modified by the addition of a plus or minus sign to show relative standing within the major rating categories.

Notes

[1] "'Hybrids' that Buoy Eurobonds." *Business Week*, August 3, 1982, p. 78. This interesting article, while about bonds sold in Europe, is relevant for debt sold in the U.S. market. Referring to these gimmicky debts, one investment banker said, "It's a sign of desperation. All these bastardizations are trying to get investors to take a long-term view when they really don't want to. It's an inflation induced madness." Another said: "We're scrambling to create gimmicks to get cash because most corporations don't want to pay today's [high] interest rates. Gimmicks do help; they're a function of trying to gain the investor's attention." Finally another claimed, "If plain vanilla can't be sold, you need to make tutti-frutti." There will be more about gimmicks in the other chapters.

[2] William T. Plumb, Jr., "The Federal Income Tax Significance of Corporate Debt: A Critical Analysis and a Proposal." *Tax Law Review*, Vol. 26: 1971. This lengthy article thoroughly discusses the distinction between equity and debt.

[3] Prospectus of Fox Television Stations, Inc., Increasing Rate Exchangeable Guaranteed Preferred Stock, February 27, 1986. The prospectus states:

An instrument labeled "preferred stock" by an issuer will not necessarily be characterized as preferred stock for Federal income tax purposes. Many cases and authorities have considered the issue of characterizations, and no single test or factor has been deemed controlling. Rather, the characterization of an instrument as debt or equity depends upon an examination of all of the terms and conditions of the instrument and all of the facts and circumstances surrounding its issuance. Some of the terms that are characteristic of debt instruments include a definite maturity date, an obligation to pay fixed amounts of interest on definite dates regardless of earnings, and a right to share with creditors and in priority to equity holders in the case of the issuer's bankruptcy. Some of the terms tending to indicate that an instrument is equity include the holding of the instrument by stockholders in proportion to their stock holdings, the absence of a fixed maturity date, inadequate or "thin" capitalization of the issuer (i.e., a high debt-to-equity ratio), a right to receive distributions only out of corporate earnings, which makes such distributions dependent upon the success of the venture for payment.

In the case of Fox Television Preferred Stock, the guaranty by News America and News Corporation of the payment of dividends, interest on accrued and unpaid dividends, redemption price, liquidation preference, and repurchase obligations upon exercise of the Rights, the ability of Fox Television to redeem the Fox Television Preferred Stock immediately after issuance, the acceleration provision entitling the holder to cause the Fox Television Preferred Stock to be redeemed if certain dividends are not timely paid and the fixed maturity date support characterization of the Fox Television Preferred Stock as debt. The facts that the Fox Television Preferred Stock is denominated "preferred stock," and that dividends are payable only when and if declared by the Board of Directors out of funds legally available for payment of dividends, support characterization of such stock as preferred stock. Accordingly, although the treatment of the Fox Television Preferred Stock is uncertain, based on an analysis of all the facts and circumstances Fox Television intends to treat Fox Television Preferred Stock as debt for Federal income tax purposes. Holders of Debt Securities debt for Federal income tax purposes. Holders of Debt Securities should be aware, however, that the Service [IRS] is likely to challenge this position, and may do so successfully. Although, as noted above, judicial authority in the debt-equity area is unclear and inconsistent, substantial authority exists that would support the characterization of an instrument having the terms of the Fox Television Preferred Stock as equity. Furthermore, to the extent that holders of Debt Securities elect not to exchange such [Metromedia] securities for cash and/or Fox Television Preferred Stock, the argument that the Fox Television Preferred Stock is equity may be strengthened. The fact that such outstanding Debt Securities are likely to constitute debt of Fox Television for Federal income tax purposes may allow the Service to assert that Fox Television is thinly capitalized, thereby increasing the likelihood that the Fox Television Preferred Stock will be treated as equity.

[4] American Bar Foundation Corporate Debt Financing Project. *Commentaries on Model Debenture Indenture Provisions 1965 Model Debenture Indenture Provisions All Registered Issues 1967 and Certain Negotiable Provisions Which may be Included in a Particular Incorporating Indenture* (Chicago, IL: American Bar Foundation, 1971). This work henceforth will be called *Commentaries or Commentaries on Indentures*.

[5] Medium-term notes will be more fully discussed in Chapter 3. Normally issued in maturities ranging from nine months to 15 years, they are usually offered continually on a best efforts basis by some of the major investment banking firms acting as agents for the issuers.

[6] These estimates have been derived from data from the Merrill Lynch Taxable Bond Indices.

[7] For additional insight into listed bond trading, see David Henry, "Patience Rewarded." *Forbes*, May 19, 1986, p. 82. See also Ben Weberman, "Comparison Shopping." *Forbes*, October 6, 1986, p. 203.

[8] Ann Monroe, "Big Board Suspends Trading in Bonds of 3 Phone Firms." *The Wall Street Journal*, July 10, 1985.

italization" is defined as those "management actions which result in a leveraging of company financials following treasury stock purchases, leveraged buyouts, or acquisitions financed through borrowings. It is not intended to include events such as asset write-offs or operating losses." See also *Moody's Bond Survey*, February 16, 1987, and January 18, 1988.

[10] "Indenture Protection and Event Risk." *Moody's Special Comment*, November 18, 1988. This comment says that "since its inception, Moody's philosophy has been to rate fixed-income obligations on the basis of the specific risk characteristics of individual issues. In addition to priority and collateral, our ratings have at times reflected differential indenture protection with respect to various obligations of a single issuer."

[11] Charles D. Ellis, *Investment Policy: How to Win the Loser's Game* (Homewood, IL: Dow-Jones Irwin, 1985).

[12] *Standard & Poor's CreditWeek.* July 14, 1986, p. 7.

[13] Louis H. Ederington, "Why Split Ratings Occur." *Financial Management*, Vol. 15, no. 1, Spring 1986, p. 46.

[14] Randall S. Billingsley, Robert E. Lamy, M. Wayne Marr, and G. Rodney Thompson, "Split Ratings and Bond Reoffering Yields." *Financial Management*, Vol. 14, no. 2, Spring 1985, p. 65.

Chapter 2

BOND INDENTURES

This chapter reviews the indenture, the legal document issued in connection with debt issues.[1] Webster's *New Universal Unabridged Dictionary* defines indenture thusly: "in law, a deed or written agreement between two or more parties: indentures were originally in duplicate, laid together and indented or cut in a waving line, so that the two papers or parchments corresponded to each other."

Indentures

The buyer of a bond in a secondary market transaction becomes a party to the contract even though he wasn't, so to speak, present at the creation. Yet many investors are not too familiar with the terms and features of the obligations they purchase. They know the coupon rate and maturity but they often are unaware of many of the issue's other terms, especially those that can affect the value of their investment. In most cases—and as long as the company stays out of trouble—much of this additional information may be unnecessary and thus considered superfluous by some. But this knowledge can become valuable during times of financial stress when the company is involved in merger or takeover activity. It is especially important when interest rates drop as the issue may be vulnerable to premature or unexpected redemption. Knowledge is power, and the informed bond investor has a better chance of avoiding costly mistakes.

45

Let us briefly look at what indentures contain (some indenture provisions and articles will be discussed more fully in succeeding chapters). For corporate debt securities to be publicly sold they must (with some permitted exceptions) be issued in conformity with the Trust Indenture Act of 1939 (TIA). The TIA requires that debt issues subject to regulation by the Securities and Exchange Commission have a trustee. Also, the trustee's duties and powers must be spelled out in the indenture. Some corporate debt issues are issued under a blanket or open-ended indenture; for others a new indenture must be written each time a new series of debt is sold. A blanket indenture is often used by electric utility companies and other issuers of general mortgage bonds, but it is also found in unsecured debt, especially since the shelf registration procedure became widely accepted in the early eighties. The initial or basic indenture may have been entered into 30 or more years ago but as each new series of debt is created, a supplemental indenture is written. For instance, the original indenture for Baltimore Gas and Electric Company is dated February 1, 1919, but it has been supplemented and amended many times since then due to new financings.[2]

A more recent example of an open-ended industrial debenture issue is found in the Eastman Kodak Company debt prospectus dated March 23, 1988 and supplemented October 21, 1988, which says that "the Indenture does not limit the aggregate principal amount of debentures, notes or other evidences of indebtedness ("Debt Securities") which may be issued thereunder and provides that Debt Securities may be issued from time to time in one or more series." The indenture of Fruehauf Finance Company, according to its prospectus dated December 11, 1985, gives the Company the ability to "reopen" a previous issue of securities and to issue additional securities having terms and provisions identical to any such previous issues of debt. An example of an indenture limiting the amount of debt is Harris Corporation's dated December 1, 1988, which authorizes debt in the amount of $150 million of 10 ⅜% Debentures due December 1, 2018.

The model indenture described in *Commentaries* has 15 articles and a preamble, or preliminary statement, called parties and recitals. The model mortgage bond indenture form has 16 articles and a preliminary statement.[3] Of course, the number of articles depends on the terms of the debt being issued. The consolidated mortgage bonds of Illinois Central Gulf Railroad Company, as supplemented, has 23 articles. The preliminary statements note that the bonds or debentures have been authorized by the corporation's board of directors and that it has the authority to execute the indenture. The introductory statements contain granting clauses describing the mortgage property, which is necessary for secured debt.

Definitions, Form of Securities and Denominations

The first article of an indenture usually includes the definitions of special words and phrases used in the indenture and certain provisions of a general nature or application covering acts of bondholders, notices to the trustee, the company and debtholder, and governing law, among other things. The second article covers the form of the bond or debenture. It spells out what is to appear on the actual security certificate. The third article is called "The Bonds" or "The Debentures," as the case may be. Here the securities' title or series is stated as well as the form (coupon, registered) and denominations. Today, practically all domestically issued corporate bonds are in registered form—i.e., the ownership is registered with the transfer agent (normally the trustee) and a check for the interest payment is sent to the registered holder. In late 1986, a form of registered corporate bond called book-entry appeared. The book-entry form had been used by the Federal government and its agencies for some time, but Ford Motor Credit Company was the first nongovernmental entity to do so when it issued $200 million of 7⅛% Notes due October 15, 1989, under a prospectus dated October 7, 1986. With this type of registration, only one global registered note is issued; it is deposited with, and held by, the Depository Trust Company (DTC) in New York City and registered in the DTC's nominee name. The global note may only be transferred in whole to another nominee of DTC or to a successor of DTC. Buyers of the notes really acquire ownership of beneficial interest in them, records of which are kept by the participating firms (banks, brokers, dealers, clearing corporations) and the depository.

The Depository Trust Company is a limited-purpose trust company established to hold securities and to facilitate the clearance and settlement of its participants' securities transactions through the electronic book-entry changes in the accounts of the participants. Because of restrictions on the transfer of the global note, some investors may not hold book-entry form securities. These would be those who, by state law or other regulations, must have physical delivery in definitive form of the underlying securities that they own. As the book-entry method becomes more acceptable, these rules and regulations will probably be modified. It should be noted that as the Depository's nominee is the sole owner of the global note, owners of beneficial interests will not be considered owners or holders thereof under the indenture. The prospectus states that "neither Ford Credit, the Trustee [The Chase Manhattan Bank] . . . has any direct responsibility or liability for the payment of principal or interest on the Notes to owners of beneficial interests in the Global Note." But it goes on to say: "Payments by Participants and indirect participants to owners of beneficial interests in the Global Note will be governed by standing instructions and customary practices, as is now the case with securities held for the accounts of customers in bearer form or registered in "street name," and will be the responsibility of the participants and indirect participants." Since Ford Credit's first book-entry issue, other issuers have followed suit. Book-entry is used by all issuers of auction market and remarketed preferred stock.

The usual denomination of registered corporate debt is $1,000 (par value) and multiples thereof, although, in some cases, a minimum of $5,000 or $10,000 (and even $100,000 or more) may be required. In cases where the interest is payable in the same security (payment-in-kind or "PIKs"), rights offerings, debt issued in exchanges or on emergence from bankruptcy, the indenture may provide for denominations of less than $1,000, such as $100 or $500 pieces. These smaller denominated issues are called "baby bonds." There have even been a few issues where the minimum denomination or par value was as low as $20 each. As the normal unit of trading is in multiples of $1,000, prices may vary for trades in units other than the conventional $1,000.

The third article also discusses the authentication, delivery, dating and the registration, transfer and exchange of the bonds as well as mutilated, destroyed, lost and stolen bonds. Finally, it sets forth the record dates for interest and the interest payment dates.

Remedies

There are several other articles common to both types of debt although one may be, for example, article 12 in one indenture and article 8 in the other. Article 9 in the model mortgage indenture (article 5 in the model debenture indenture) concerns remedies—the steps that are available in case the company defaults. The trustee is responsible for enforcing the available remedies; while it is only the debtholders' representative, it is ultimately responsible to the majority of the bondholders. In this article events of default are defined and may include the following: (i) failure to pay interest on the date due or within the grace period (usually 30 days); (ii) failure to make a principal payment on the due date; (iii) failure to make a sinking fund payment when due; (iv) failure to perform any other covenants and the continuation of that failure for a certain period after notice has been given by the trustee to the debtor company, and (v) certain other events of bankruptcy, insolvency or reorganization which may include defaults of other debt obligations of the company.

If an event of default is continuing, either the trustee or the holders of 25% of the principal amount of the outstanding issue may declare all of the bonds of the particular series immediately due and payable along with unpaid and interest due up to the date of acceleration. This may pressure the obligor to cure the defaults (if it is able to do so) and thus rescind the acceleration or to seek waivers of the defaults while it is trying to find a solution. But such acceleration might force the debtor to seek protection of the bankruptcy courts; it might have been better to work with the debtor and help him on the path to recovery. The article also provides limits to lawsuits which individual bondholders may bring against the company with a default under the indenture provisions. However, no provision may impair the bondholders' absolute and unconditional right to the timely payment of principal, premium (if any) and interest on the bond, and the right to bring legal action to enforce such payment.

The Trustee

While the rights and duties of the trustee are mentioned in various articles throughout the indenture, articles 6 and 10 in the model indentures give certain specifics regarding the trustee and its activities including resignation or removal. Investors should clearly understand that the trustee is paid by the debt-issuing company and can only do what the indenture provides. The article may begin with wording such as: "... the Trustee undertakes to perform such duties and only such duties as are specifically set forth in this Indenture, and no implied covenants or obligations shall be read into this Indenture against the Trustee. . . ." Further, ". . . the Trustee shall exercise such of the rights and powers vested in it by this Indenture, and shall use the same degree of care and skill in their exercise, as a prudent man would exercise or use under the circumstances in the conduct of his own affairs," or, "No provision of this Indenture shall be construed to relieve the Trustee from liability for its own negligent action, its own negligent failure to act, or its own wilful misconduct. . . ." Of course, certain exceptions are listed.

One of the duties of the indenture trustee as enumerated in this article is the notification to bondholders of a default under the indenture (except in certain cases such as a cured default or provided that the board of directors or "responsible officers" of the trustee, etc., in good faith determine that withholding of the notice is in "their best interests"). Also, the trustee is under no obligation to exercise the rights or powers under the indenture at the request of bondholders unless it has been offered reasonable security or indemnity. This seems reasonable in this age of frivolous lawsuits, but it could possibly be used by the trustee as a reason not to proceed with an action which it ought to do. The trustee is not bound to make investigations into the facts surrounding documents delivered to it, but it may do so if it sees fit.

Another section of the article requires the issuer to pay the trustee reasonable fees for its services, provide reimbursement for reasonable expenses, and to indemnify it for certain losses which might arise from administering the trust. A subsection states that in case of a conflict of interest, the trustee will either eliminate the conflict or resign within 90 days of the date of determining that a conflict of interests exists. Not an uncommon occurrence, one often

will see in the financial press legal advertisements of the resignation of a trustee and the appointment of a successor trustee. As
there must always be a trustee, no resignation is effective until a
new trustee has been secured. Such potential conflicts often occur
where the trustee bank is also a creditor of the issuing company.
The prospectus for the $600 million May Department Stores offer-
ing on June 8, 1988 says that "the Company maintains deposit accounts with and engages in banking transactions in the ordinary
course of business with each [of the trustees]." One bank is a trustee
of various employee benefit plans and both trustees have credit
agreements with May. In 1984 Citibank, N.A., resigned as trustee
for the first mortgage bonds of Long Island Lighting Company citing a potential conflict of interest between its obligations to bondholders as trustee and as a creditor to LILCO. It can't very well
serve the bondholders' interests and its own creditor interests at the
same time.[4] There is also provision for the removal of a trustee,
with or without cause, upon the action of a majority of the
debtholders.

The prospectus (dated September 14, 1988) for K N Energy's
10 ¾% Sinking Fund Debentures due September 1, 2008 says that
the indenture contains "certain limitations on the right of the
Trustee, should it become a creditor of the Company, to obtain payment of claims in certain cases, or to realize for its own account on
certain property received in respect of any such claim as security or
otherwise. The Trustee will be permitted to engage in certain other
transactions; however, if it acquires any conflicting interest . . . it
must eliminate such conflict or resign."

Reports

The next article (7 and 11 in the model debenture and mortgage
indentures, respectively), dealing with debtholders' lists and reports
by the trustee and company, is rather short but has caused many
investors concern. Under this article, the company is required to
furnish the trustee with semi-annual lists of bondholders and their
addresses and preserve this information until a new list is available.
This is to enable the requisite number of bondholders to communi-
cate with other bondholders about their rights under the indenture.
The trustee must submit to the bondholders certain brief reports or

statements concerning its continued eligibility as a trustee, any advances made by the trustee to the corporation, any other indebtedness owed by the company to the trustee, and any property or funds of the company held by the trustee. An interesting question is how many bondholders have actually received these reports or have even seen them? More than likely, very few; perhaps the many nominees such as stockbrokers and banks have failed to send them to the beneficial owners because of the added (and possibly unreimbursed) costs.

The bone of contention between bondholders and issuers concerns corporate financial reporting. Indentures of public debt issues sold in the United States require an issuing company to file with the trustee copies of annual reports and other reports which it must normally file with the Securities and Exchange Commission (SEC). But there is no requirement (unless specifically mentioned) that a company send these reports to debtholders. These reports can be inspected at the SEC or the offices of the trustee, not always convenient for a creditor. Investors desiring such information are often up against the wall, especially when the issuer of public debt securities is privately owned. Private companies with fewer than 300 security holders do not have to file regular reports with the SEC. Holders of some debt issues of special purpose financing corporations sold by American issuers in the Eurodollar market have discovered this when trying to evaluate their holdings several years after the prospectuses were issued. Many years ago bondholders may have been content with little or no information; that is not so today. Bondholders have a right, although it is not spelled out, to be treated fairly. All holders and other interested parties should be able to obtain from any public debt issuer or its trustee audited annual reports and quarterly statements, at the very least. If a corporation does not want to divulge this information, then it should not come to the public markets. One of the costs of entry to the public markets should be that of full and proper financial disclosure.

A rating agency cannot rate an issuer's debt if it is not provided with adequate information and a corporation cannot be forced to provide information if it is not legally bound to do so. At the beginning of 1989, McCarthy, Crisanti and Maffei withdrew their coverage of the bonds of SCI Television, Inc. This certainly doesn't benefit the holder but what good is an opinion based on faulty or no knowledge of the latest operations of the debtor? At that time Moody's gave SCI Television debt ratings of B2 and B3 while S&P gave B– and CCC+ ratings. MCM stated that "Although the company issued bonds publicly in October 1987, it has not filed financial statements with the SEC since December 1987. SCI TV will not make financial reports available to us unlike some other companies which are also not subject to filing requirements, such as Heritage Communications and Continental Cablevision. These companies have indicated that they are providing us with information in order to enhance liquidity for bondholders."

Page 81 of SCI's prospectus dated October 21, 1987 says: "The Company intends to distribute to the holders of the Securities annual reports containing audited consolidated financial statements and an opinion thereon by the Company's independent certified public accountants and quarterly reports containing unaudited consolidated information for the first three quarters of each fiscal year." One would think that SCI's investment bankers would want a client to provide such information in order to have a better market for the bonds.

In contrast to SCI, Adelphia Communications in its December 19, 1988, bond offering said, "The Company has agreed to provide the Trustee and the Holders, and to file with the Commission, copies of quarterly and annual reports and other information, documents and reports substantially equivalent to those specified in Sections 13 and 15(d) of the Exchange Act as long as the Notes are outstanding (whether or not the Company would otherwise be subject to such reporting requirements.)"

However, annual and quarterly reports are normally written for shareholders and may not fully disclose all of the information a prudent bondholder needs. For example, just a simple look at the debt part of the capital structure may often reveal the inadequacy of the financial disclosure. Often the outstanding amount of a particular bond issue may not be clear from the financial statements. A common description such as "4 5/8%-10 3/8% sinking fund debentures due 1993-2010 . . . $387.5" does not clearly state the outstanding amount of the 4 5/8s and each of the other issues.

In the early 1980s one of the authors wrote to the Ford Motor Credit Company and Dart & Kraft, Inc. requesting information about the amounts outstanding for individual issues as the annual reports and Forms 10K were unsatisfactory. Dart & Kraft's Director of Corporate Finance responded on April 25, 1984: "Regarding your request . . . for principal amounts of Dart & Kraft's publicly issued debt, we presently do not disclose that information other than the amounts disclosed in our 1983 Annual Report." The Treasurer's Office of Ford Motor Credit replied on April 30, 1984: "I regret to inform you that it is now our policy to not disclose detailed information on principal amounts outstanding on specific debt issues."

Shades of the robber barons of the 1890s! An article in *The New York Times* said: "It is ironic that most public companies today, despite the importance of debt financing and the increasingly dynamic nature of the bond market, still regard holders of their debt as second-class citizens when it comes to giving them information."[5] This was written in 1975 but it still pertinent today.

Consolidation, Merger, Conveyance and Lease

Common to indentures of secured and unsecured debt are model articles 12 and 8 dealing with consolidation and merger, or the conveyance, transfer or lease of assets. There might be some indentures which expressly forbid the debtor company to merge or consolidate with another corporation, but most indentures for public debt issues allow corporate mergers, consolidations and the sale of substantially all of the corporation's assets if certain conditions are satisfied. Transfer or sale of less than substantially all of the corporation's property are usually not subject to control by this article. One such condition is that the company be the surviving party to the merger/consolidation or, if not, that the other party be organized and existing under federal or state law. The new or surviving corporation must assume the terms of the indenture including the timely payment of principal, interest and premium (if any) on the subject debt securities, and the successor company is substituted for the predecessor company in the indenture. Of course, if secured, the terms of the transaction (unless waived by bondholders) must provide for the preservation of the security lien and the trustee's rights and powers. The merger, consolidation, or asset sale cannot take place if it would cause an event of default under the indenture's various covenants. Some indentures might place other restrictions on these transactions, including tangible net worth tests of the surviving corporation.

Supplemental Indentures and Covenants

As times change so may corporate law and practices. An indenture that was satisfactory when entered into many years ago may not be so today. Thus, article 13 in the mortgage indenture and article 9 in the debenture indenture provide for supplemental indentures and the amendments to the original indenture. The most common supplemental indenture is one issued under a blanket indenture for new and additional series or issues of debt securities. The supplemental indenture sets forth the terms and conditions for the issuance of the new securities, including authorized amounts of the new issue, interest rate, maturity, and redemption provisions. It may also include restrictive provisions not found in the basic or blanket indenture but, more often than not, at least nowadays, may contain much less restrictive provisions. Of course, the more restrictive provisions of preceding and still outstanding debt issues remain in force until the debt is extinguished or until the original indenture is changed or amended.

Certain provisions may be made without bondholders' consent. These include the addition of provisions for the debtholders' benefit or the surrender of company rights to correct inconsistencies and errors in the original indenture and to bring the original indenture into conformity with new and applicable laws concerning corporate trust indentures. Other provisions may require the assent of a two-thirds (or greater) majority of the debt outstanding; changes of a substantive or essential nature require a 100% vote. The latter category includes changes in the maturity, interest rate, redemption premium, place of payment, currency in which the debt is payable, or any provision which would impair the right to start legal suit for the enforcement of any defaulted payment. Some of the changes sought may include the extension of the maturity, reduction of the interest rate, or the payment of interest in common stock at the company's option. In some cases, the company may seek amendments to the indenture and offer to exchange new securities for old.

If the old indenture received the required number of votes, the indenture would be changed and would govern any old securities that were not exchanged for new ones. The new securities issued in the exchange would have a new indenture.

In order for Peoples Express, Inc. (PEI) to merge into Texas Air Corporation in late 1986, the debtholders of People Express Airlines, Inc., a subsidiary of PEI, were required to exchange their old securities for new ones with longer maturities and lower interest rates and to consent to amendments to the old indenture (66⅔% vote of the outstanding principal amount of each issue was required). The amendments included the elimination of provisions restricting the payment of dividends by the Company and the acquisition of shares of common stock. Bondholders who did not tender and who did not vote for the indenture amendments nevertheless would be bound by the new supplemental indenture concerning dividends and stock repurchases even though they kept their original securities.

The debtor seeking indenture amendments often will give consideration to the debtholders in the form of increased interest payments or a one time fee. Companies' solicitations will, of course, often carry the boiler plate statements such as "Management of the Company believes that the proposed changes are in the best interests of the Company and the holders of each issue are being asked to consent to the proposed indenture changes." Many of these proposed changes weaken some of the existing covenants. For example, in 1985 Houston Natural Gas (HNG) asked some of its debenture holders to eliminate the interest coverage test which required available earnings to be at least 2.5 times annual interest charges on consolidated senior funded debt before it could issue new senior funded debt. The proxy statement said, "HNG wishes to change its debt incurrence tests to reflect current practice as it applies to corporate obligors of HNG's caliber and to improve HNG's financing flexibility in order to permit HNG to be able to respond to rapid changes in the business and financial environment in which it operates." With no change HNG would have been permitted to issue about $240 million of additional debt on October 31, 1984, assuming a 12% interest rate. With the restrictions eliminated, it would have been able to issue $1,773 million of additional debt under a less restrictive capitalization test. As the proxy statement said, "to the extent that as a result of the proposed amendment HNG increases its leverage through the issuance of additional Senior Funded Debt beyond its ability to reasonably service such debt, the holders of the Debentures would be adversely affected thereby."

In 1977 and 1978 a number of electric utility companies sought changes in their indentures issued between 1928 and 1945. The reasons given were basically about the same, namely, their desire to modernize the indentures by eliminating obsolete and unnecessary restrictions and to increase their financial flexibility. The changes allowed the companies to issue additional debt in greater amounts or at an earlier date than previously. Many dramatic changes occurred in the economy since the indentures were written, and the high capital costs and rising fuel expenses caused by the runaway inflation of the seventies wrought havoc in the utility industry. Of course, weakening of debt restrictions may cause little problem in the short run; indeed, most of the time these changes will not of themselves cause a downgrade in the company's debt rating. But it is at the time of crisis that investors probably wish that less restrictive covenants were not granted so freely. Investors should carefully review any proposed indenture changes. The less restraint on corporate managements in their financing activities might mean more problems for the debtholders.

Covenants

Articles 14 of the mortgage indenture and article 10 of the debenture indenture are concerned with certain limitations and restrictions on the borrower's activities. Some covenants are common to all indentures, such as (1) to pay interest, principal and premium, if any, on a timely basis; (2) to maintain an office or agency where the securities may be transferred or exchanged and where notices may be served upon the company with respect to the securities and the indenture; (3) to pay all taxes and other claims when due unless contested in good faith; (4) to maintain all properties used and useful in the borrower's business in good condition and working order; (5) to maintain adequate insurance on its properties (some indentures may not have insurance provisions since proper insurance is routine business practice); (6) to submit periodic certificates to the trustee stating whether the debtor is in compliance with the loan agreement; and (7) to maintain its corporate existence. These are often called *affirmative* covenants since they call upon the debtor to make promises to do certain things.

Negative covenants are those which require the borrower not to take certain actions. These are usually negotiated between the borrower and the lender or their agents. Setting the right balance between the two parties can be a rather difficult undertaking at times. In public debt transactions the investing institutions normally leave the negotiating to the investment bankers, although they will often be asked their opinion on certain terms and features. Unfortunately most public bond buyers are unaware of these articles at the time of purchase and may never learn of them throughout the life of the debt. Borrowers want the least restrictive loan agreement available, while lenders should want the most restrictive, consistent with sound business practices. But lenders should not try to restrain borrowers from accepted business activities and conduct. A company might be willing to include additional restrictions (up to a point) if it can get a lower interest rate on the loan. As we have seen, when companies seek to weaken restrictions in their favor, they are often willing to pay more interest.

What do some of these negative covenants cover? Obviously, there is an infinite variety of restrictions that can be placed on borrowers, depending on the type of debt issue, the economics of the industry and the nature of the business, and the lenders' desires. Some of the more common restrictive covenants include various limitations on the company's ability to incur debt, since unrestricted borrowing can lead a company and its debtholders to ruin. Thus, debt restrictions may include limits on the absolute dollar amount of debt that may be outstanding or may require ratio tests—for example, debt may be limited to no more than 60% of total capitalization or that it cannot exceed a certain percentage of net tangible assets. An example is Jim Walter Corporation's indenture for its 9 ½% Debentures due April 1, 2016. This indenture restricts senior indebtedness to no more than the sum of 80% of net instalment notes receivable and 50% of the adjusted consolidated net tangible assets. The indenture for The May Department Stores Company 7.95% Debentures due 2002 prohibits the company from issuing senior funded debt unless consolidated net tangible assets are at least 200% of such debt. More recent May Company indentures have dropped this provision.

There may be interest coverage tests, requiring that the company maintain earnings available for interest charges at a given minimum level in order to do additional borrowing. There could also be cash flow tests or requirements and working capital maintenance provisions. The prospectus for Federated Department Stores, Inc.'s debentures dated November 4, 1988, has a large section devoted to debt limitations. One of the provisions allows net new debt issuance if the consolidated coverage ratio of earnings before interest, taxes and depreciation to interest expense (all as defined) is at least 1.35 to 1 through November 1, 1989, 1.45 to 1 through November 1, 1990, 1.50 to 1 through November 1, 1991, and at least 1.60 to 1 thereafter.

Some indentures may prohibit subsidiaries from borrowing from all other companies except the parent. Indentures often classify subsidiaries as restricted or unrestricted. Restricted subsidiaries are those considered to be consolidated for financial test purposes; unrestricted subsidiaries (often foreign and certain special-purpose companies) are those excluded from the covenants governing the parent. Often, subsidiaries are classified as unrestricted in order to allow them to finance themselves through outside sources of funds.

Limitations on dividend payments and stock repurchases may be included in indentures. Often, cash dividend payments will be limited to a certain percentage of net income earned after a specific date (often the issuance date of the debt and called the "peg date") plus a fixed amount. Sometimes the dividend formula might allow the inclusion of the net proceeds from the sale of common stock sold after the peg date. In other cases, the dividend restriction might be so worded as to prohibit the declaration and payment of cash dividends if tangible net worth (or other measures, such as consolidated quick assets) declines below a certain amount. There are usually no restrictions on the payment of stock dividends. In addition to dividend restrictions, there are often restrictions on a company's repurchase of its common stock if such purchase might cause a violation or deficiency in the dividend determination formulae. Some holding company indentures might limit the right of the company to pay dividends in the common stock of its subsidiaries. For example, Citicorp, the holding company parent of Citibank, N.A., is restricted, under certain circumstances, from paying dividends in shares of Citibank. The prospectus dated August 20, 1986, states:

> Citibank covenants . . . as long as any of the notes which mature more than ten years after their issuance are outstanding, it will not declare or pay any dividends, or make any distribution to its stockholders ratably, payable in shares of stock of Citibank, if after giving effect thereto, the Adjusted Stockholders' Equity of Citicorp would be less than 200% of Senior Long-Term Indebtedness; provided, however, that Citicorp may declare and pay such dividends and make any other distributions without regard to the foregoing provisions so long as the aggregate amount . . . of the value . . . of the shares of Stock . . . does not exceed 20% of the Adjusted Stockholders' Equity of Citicorp . . .

Another part of the covenant article may place restrictions on the disposition and the sale and leaseback of certain property. In some cases, the proceeds of asset sales totaling more than a certain amount must be used to repay debt. This is seldom found in indentures for unsecured debt but at times some investors may have wished they had such a protective clause. At other times, a provision of this type might allow a company to retire high coupon debt in a lower interest rate environment, thus causing bondholders a loss of value. It might be better to have such a provision where the company would have the right to reinvest the proceeds of asset sales in new plant and equipment rather than retiring debt, or to at least give the debtholder the option of tendering his bonds. The April 15, 1986, indenture of CSX Corporation does not prohibit the sale by the Company or any subsidiary of any stock or indebtedness of any restricted subsidiary. The main restricted subsidiaries of this transportation and energy company are The Chesapeake and Ohio Railway Company, The Baltimore and Ohio Railroad Company, CSX Transportation, Inc., Texas Gas Resources Corporation, American Commercial Lines, Inc. and Texas Gas Transmission Company. One hopes that management has the bondholders' welfare in mind in case they decided to dispose of a substantial operation that may provide some degree of security for the eventual repayment of the debt. A sale/leaseback transaction involves the sale of the property and the simultaneous leasing back of the same property for a fixed number of years. Restrictions on these transactions might be limited to certain property owned, or to an amount of property which can be included in such a transaction, or to the use of the proceeds therefrom.

Some indentures restrict the investments that a corporation may make in other companies, through either the purchase of stock or loans and advances. As *Commentaries* states:

> By restricting the amount of cash or property which the borrower may invest in other enterprises, it is expected that the available assets of the borrower will be applied and devoted primarily to the basic business and purposes of the enterprise. If the borrower does not need the money in that enterprise, it may then be encouraged to use it for accelerated debt repayment. Such a covenant is not commonly used but when used it is more often found in directly placed issues than in public issues.[6]

The May Department Stores Credit Company has a provision in the indenture for its 9% Debentures due 1989 stating that,

> The Company will not . . . invest a substantial part of its assets in securities other than Deferred Payment Accounts, certain governmental securities maturing not more than eighteen months after the date of purchase, prime commercial paper and securities of a Subsidiary of the Company or May engaged in a business similar to that of the Company. The Company may also acquire debt securities of May in certain circumstances.

Finally, there may be an absence of restrictive covenants. The shelf registration prospectus of Transamerica Financial Corporation dated November 25, 1987, forthrightly says:

> The Indentures do not contain any provision which will restrict the Company in any way from paying dividends or making other distribution on its capital stock or purchasing or redeeming any of its capital stock, or from incurring, assuming or becoming liable upon Senior Indebtedness, Subordinated Indebt-

edness or Junior Subordinated Indebtedness or any other type of debt or other obligations. The Indentures do not contain any financial ratios or specified levels of net worth or liquidity to which the Company must adhere. In addition, the Subordinated and Junior Subordinated Indentures do not restrict the Company from creating liens on its property for any purpose.

Let the Buyer Beware! If corporate managements and boards of directors viewed themselves as fiduciaries for all of the investors in the company, from stockholders to bondholders, indentures with many restrictive covenants might be unnecessary. But in most instances, that is not the case; they strive to increase shareholder wealth (or their own), not the wealth of the total firm, and often at the expense of the senior security investor. In this age of corporate raiders and managements' apparent lack of concern or fiduciary duty towards debt investors, perhaps some consideration ought to be given to the resurrection of good, old-fashioned restrictive provisions. That is, at least until the courts and state legislatures have acted to protect bondholders.

One observer of bondholders' rights summarizes,

> Contrary to popular belief, indentures do not have numerous detailed covenants that regulate the bondholder-stockholder conflict. Indeed, an indenture may have no restrictive covenants at all. Such covenants are costly. Other constraints on stockholder gain at bondholder expense are ineffective. Since fiduciary duties are a substitute for costly contracts, directors should have fiduciary duties to bondholders as well as to stockholders. The exclusive focus of corporate law on stockholders is too narrow for modern corporate finance. Bondholders and stockholders are all security holders in the enterprise and equally deserving of board protection.[7]

Covenants Change Over Time

Debt covenants can change over the years as companies issue new debt under new and more modern indentures. For example, Kansas-Nebraska Natural Gas Company, Inc., now K N Energy, Inc., has issued debt during the past twenty years under three indentures with the same indenture trustee. In each of the indentures there were differences between the various provisions. Table 2–1 summarizes some of the more important covenants as disclosed in the prospectuses for the particular issues.

The 1976 and 1982 issues have provisions limiting dividend payments and share repurchases; the 1988 issue does not. The two earlier issues have a debt issuance test whereby debt cannot exceed 60% of pro forma capitalization; the 1988 issue does not have such a test. The 1976 issue has an interest coverage test for debt issuance which is not in the 1982 and the 1988 indentures.

Secured Debt

Since we have been introduced to corporate bonds in general, let us get to some specifics. The starting point will be bonds that are secured by some form of collateral, the first of the three Cs of credit: the *collateral*, which is pledged to ensure repayment of the debt; the *character* of the borrower, which ensures that the obligation will be paid on a timely basis, and the *capacity* of the borrower, which ensures that it will have the means of repaying the debt.

Utility Mortgage Bonds

The largest issuers of debt secured by property, i.e. mortgage debt, are the electric utility companies. Of the major electric companies which periodically issue debt, there is but one—The United Illuminating Company in Connecticut—which issues only unsecured debt; all the others have mortgage debt as the primary debt vehicle in their capital structures. Other utilities, such as telephone companies and gas pipeline and distribution firms, have also used mortgage debt as sources of capital but generally to a lesser extent than electrics.

Most electric utility bond indentures do not limit the total amount of bonds that may be issued. This is called an *open-ended mortgage*, a contribution to American corporate finance attributed to Samuel Insull, the pioneer of the electric utility business who once served as the secretary to Thomas Alva Edison.[8] The mortgage generally is a first lien on the company's real estate, fixed property, and franchises, subject to certain exceptions or permitted encumbrances owned at the time of the execution of the indenture or its supplement. The after-acquired property clause also subjects to the

Table 2–1 Comparison of Three Debentures as Outlined in the Prospectuses of Kansas-Nebraska Natural Gas Company, Inc. and K N Energy, Inc.
Indenture Trustee: Continental Illinois National Bank and Trust Company of Chicago

	$20,000,000 *9% Debentures* *January 1, 1996*	*$25,000,000* *13% Debentures* *October 1, 2002*	*$35,000,000* *10 3/4% Debentures* *September 1, 2008*
Indenture date:	February 1, 1948	October 1, 1982	September 1, 1988
Supplement date:	January 1, 1976		
Prospectus date:	January 27, 1976	October 20, 1982	September 14, 1988
Restrictions:			
Payment of dividends and acquisitions of stock:	Company may not declare or pay any dividend or make any distribution on its common stock or purchase or redeem any shares of its capital stock of any class (exceptions include sinking fund on $5.65 Class A Preferred) except out of (x) surplus and income earned and accrued after 12/31/74 and (y) $10,000,000. No subsidiary is permitted to purchase any shares of capital stock of K-N.	Company may not pay or declare nor make any distribution on any capital stock, nor may K-N or any subsidiary make any payment to acquire shares (exceptions for fixed dividends and purchase fund payments) if such payments subsequent to 12/31/81, including the above exceptions, would exceed the sum of (a) consolidated net earnings subsequent to 12/31/81, (b) $25,000,000, (c) proceeds from the sale of stock after 12/31/81, and (d) debt converted into capital stock after 12/31/81.	No Provision.

	$20,000,000 9% Debentures January 1, 1996	$25,000,000 13% Debentures October 1, 2002	$35,000,000 10 3/4% Debentures September 1, 2008
Payment of dividends and acquisitions of stock:	Neither K-N nor any subsidiary may purchase, redeem or acquire any capital stock or take any action by way of dividends or distribution resulting in the decrease in the par or stated value of its capital stock or surplus if the consolidated funded indebtedness of K-N shall exceed 60% of total consolidated capitalization.		
Debt issuance Capitalization test	Neither K-N nor any subsidiary may create, incur, assume or guarantee, any additional funded debt, unless the consolidated funded debt including the additional debt shall not exceed 60% of the total consolidated capitalization.	Neither K-N nor any subsidiary may incur, directly or indirectly, any funded debt if consolidated funded debt, giving effect to the proposed additional debt and the receipt and application of proceeds thereof, would be more than 60% of pro forma consolidated capitalization	No Provision.

Table continues

Table 2-1 Comparison of Three Debentures (Continued)

	$20,000,000 9% Debentures January 1, 1996	$25,000,000 13% Debentures October 1, 2002	$35,000,000 10 3/4% Debentures September 1, 2008
Interest coverage test	In addition, in order to issue such debt, consolidated net income for 12 consecutive months out of the 15 immediately preceding months must be at least 2 ½ times total interest charges on pro forma funded debt (3 times coverage required as long as any debentures issued prior to 1975 remain outstanding.	No Provision.	No Provision.
Consolidation, merger and sale of assets	No Provision.	Company may consolidate with, or merge into or transfer all or substanitially all of its assets to, one corporation if (i) the corporation assumes K-N's obligations under the indenture, (ii) after the transaction the consolidated debt is not greater than 60% of the consolidated capitalization of the resulting corporation, (iii) no default will occur as a result of the transaction, (iv) the surviving company is organized under the law of the United States or one of the states.	Company may, without the consent of any holders of debt securities, consolidate with, or merge into or transfer all or substantially all of its assets to one or more other entities, provided (i) the surviving company is organized under the laws of the United States or one of the states and assumes all of the Company's obligations on the debt securities under the indenture, and (ii) no default will occur as a result of the transaction.

Table continues

	$20,000,000 9% Debentures January 1, 1996	$25,000,000 13% Debentures October 1, 2002	$35,000,000 10 3/4% Debentures September 1, 2008
Prohibition of Advances	Kansas-Nebraska may not make or have outstanding any advances or extensions of credit, except to a Subsidiary, otherwise than in the ordinary course of its business.	No Provision.	No Provision.
Events of Default	Failure to pay interest or any sinking fund installment for 30 days;	Default for 30 days in payment of interest;	Failure to pay interest when due, which failure continues for 30 days;
	Failure to pay principal (and premium, if any) when due;	Default in payment when due of principal of, or premium, if any;	Failure to pay principal of or premium, if any, when due;
			Failure to deposit any sinking fund payment, when due;
	Failure to perform any other covenant for 60 days after notice;	Failure by K-N for 90 days after notice to it to comply with any of its other agreements in the;	Failure to observe and perform any other covenant in the Indenture which continues for 90 days after written notice;

Table continues

Table 2-1 Comparison of Three Debentures (Continued)

$20,000,000 9% Debentures January 1, 1996	$25,000,000 13% Debentures October 1, 2002	$35,000,000 10 3/4% Debentures September 1, 2008
	Default under an agreement or instrument under which there is issued funded debt in excess of $1,000,000 with the result that such debt shall have been declared due and payable prior to the date on which it would otherwise become due and payable, or failure by the Company to pay or refund any debt in excess of $1,000,000 within 30 days after maturity or extended maturity;	Default under any mortgage, indenture or instrument under which funded debt is issued in a principal amount exceeding $2,000,000 with the result that such debt shall have been declared due and payable prior to the date on which it would otherwise become due and payable, or failure by the Company to pay or refund any debt in excess of $2,000,000 within 60 days after the maturity or extended maturity has not been cured or waived;
Certain events in bankruptcy, insolvency or reorganization	Certain events of bankruptcy or insolvency.	Certain events in bankruptcy, insolvency or reorganization

Source: Company prospectuses.

mortgage property acquired by the company after the filing of the original or supplemental indenture. For example, the prospectus for Sierra Pacific Power Company's 10 ⅛% First Mortgage Bonds due 2018 says that the "New Bonds will be secured . . . by a first lien on substantially all properties and franchises owned by the Company at October 31, 1940 [the indenture is dated December 1, 1940] and on property and franchises subsequently acquired which in each case are used or useful in the business of furnishing electricity, water or gas, or in any business incidental thereto or operated in connection therewith, except properties released pursuant to the Mortgage. . . ." Property which is excepted from the lien of the mortgage may include nuclear fuel (it is often financed separately through other secured loans); cash, securities and other cash items and current assets; automobiles, trucks, tractors and other vehicles; inventories and fuel supplies; office furniture and leaseholds; property and merchandise held for resale in the normal course of business; receivables, contracts, leases and operating agreements, and timber, minerals, mineral rights and royalties. In Sierra Pacific Power's case, "there are specifically excepted from the lien of the Mortgage certain current assets, securities and other personal property; timber; oil and other minerals; certain other property owned at October 31, 1940; and all property subsequently acquired, not used or useful to the Company in its utility business."

Permitted encumbrances might include liens for taxes and governmental assessments, judgments, easements and leases, certain prior liens, minor defects, irregularities and deficiencies in titles of properties and rights-of-way which do not materially impair the use of the property. For example, the mortgage for Indiana & Michigan Electric Company as supplemented in 1987 for the issuance of 9 ⅛% First Mortgage Bonds due 1997, is "(a) a first lien on substantially all of the fixed physical property and franchises of the Company . . . and (b) a lien, subject to the lien of IMPCo's mortgage, on the fixed physical property acquired in connection with the merger of IMPCo into the Company. . . ." These and other bonds issued after July 1, 1986, were subject to some $24 million of judgment liens, the enforcement of which had been stayed. These judgment liens, according to the prospectus dated June 23, 1987, may have a priority senior to the first mortgage lien of the bonds. Citizens Utilities Company 7 ⅞% First Mortgage and Collateral Trust Bonds due 1996 are secured by a direct first lien on substantially all of the public utility properties located in Arizona, Colorado, Idaho and Vermont, and a direct second lien on property located in Hawaii (there was a small prior mortgage on the Hawaiian properties).

Historically bonded debt—at least for the electric utility industry—was viewed as permanent capital and, as such, was not expected to be repaid, only rolled over or refunded. This is the current view taken of the federal government's debt. Prior to the mid-1970s, most of the new issues were long-term with maturities of thirty years or so. Sinking funds were either nonexistent or, if insignificant, could usually be satisfied with additions to property and not with actual debt retirement. It made little sense to repay permanent debt if one only had to borrow the amount that was just repaid. Therefore, other protective measures were incorporated in the indenture to satisfy the lender that the mortgaged property was being cared for.

To provide for proper maintenance of the property and replacement of worn-out plant, maintenance fund, maintenance and replacement fund, or renewal and replacement fund provisions were placed in indentures. These clauses stipulate that the issuer spend a certain amount of money for these purposes. Depending on the company, the required sums may be around 15% of operating revenues, as defined; in other cases, the figure is based on a percentage of the depreciable property or amount of bonds outstanding. These requirements usually can be satisfied by certifying that the specified amount of expenditures has been made either for maintenance and repairs to the property or by gross property additions. They can also be satisfied by depositing cash or outstanding mortgage bonds with the trustee; the deposited cash can be used for property additions, repairs and maintenance or in some cases—to the concern of holders of high-coupon debt—the redemption of bonds. More will be said on this topic in Chapter 5.

Another provision for bondholder security is the release and substitution of property clause. If the company releases property from the mortgage lien (such as through a sale of a plant or other property that may have become obsolete or no longer necessary for use in the business, or through the state's power of eminent domain), it must substitute other property or cash and securities to be held by the trustee, usually in an amount equal to the released property's fair value. It may use the proceeds or cash held by the trustee to retire outstanding bonded debt. Certainly, a bondholder would not let go of the mortgaged property without substitution of satisfactory new collateral or adjustment in the amount of the debt, as he should want to maintain the value of the security behind the bond. In some cases the company may waive the right to issue additional bonds. System Energy Resources, Inc.'s prospectus for its 14% First Mortgage Bonds due November 15, 1994, says: "Property may be released upon the bases of (i) the deposit of cash or, to a limited extent, purchase money mortgages, (ii) property additions, after adjustments in certain cases to offset retirements and after making adjustments for qualified prior lien bonds outstanding against property additions, and (iii) waiver of the right to issue First Mortgage Bonds, without applying any earnings tests."

Although the typical electric utility mortgage does not limit the total amount of bonds that may be issued, there are certain issuance tests or bases that usually have to be satisfied before the company can sell more bonds. New bonds are often restricted to no more than 60 to 66 ⅔% of the value of net bondable property. This generally is the lower of the fair value or cost of property additions, after adjustments and deductions for property that had previously been used for the authentication and issuance of previous bond issues, retirements of bondable property or the release of property, and any outstanding prior liens. Bonds may also be issued in exchange or substitution for outstanding bonds, previously retired bonds, and bonds otherwise acquired. Bonds may also be issued in an amount equal to the of cash deposited with the trustee. Sierra Pacific Power Company's $70 million of 10 ⅛% First Mortgage Bonds due 2018 were issued against the early retirement of $60 million 15 ⅜% First Mortgage Bonds due 1991. The remaining $10 million 10 ⅛s were issued on the basis of unfunded additional property additions at 60%.

A further earnings test found often in utility indentures requires interest charges be covered by pretax income available for interest charges of at least two times. The Connecticut Light and Power Company prospectus for its 9 ¾% First and Refunding Mortgage

Bonds, Series QQ due November 1, 2018, states:

> . . . the Company may not issue additional bonds under the B
> Provisions unless its net earnings, as defined and as computed
> without deducting income taxes, for 12 consecutive calendar
> months during the period of 15 consecutive calendar months
> immediately preceding the first day of the month in which the
> application to the Trustee for authentication of additional bonds
> is made were at least twice the annual interest charges on all the
> Company's outstanding bonds, including the proposed addi-
> tional bonds, and any outstanding prior lien obligations.

The coverage figures for the twelve months ended December 31,
1987 and February 29, 1988, were, based on the bonds and prior
lien obligations outstanding, 3.41 times and 3.57 times, respectively.

Mortgage bonds go by many different names. The most common
of the senior lien issues are *First Mortgage Bonds* as used by The
Cincinnati Gas & Electric Company, Long Island Lighting Company, Public Service Company of New Hampshire and Sierra Pacific Power Company, among others. Baltimore Gas & Electric
Company has the title of *First Refunding Mortgage Bonds* (*First and
Refunding Mortgage Bonds* for Connecticut Light and Power Company) while Canal Electric Company, a wholesale electric generator,
uses First and General Mortgage Bonds. The Baltimore issue, subject to a first mortgage lien (with certain exceptions), is also secured
by a pledge of 100,000 shares each of Class A stock and Class B
stock of Safe Harbor Water Power Corporation, an operator of a
hydroelectric plant in Pennsylvania. The Baltimore bonds are also
secured by the common stock of other directly owned subsidiaries
but not stock of second level subsidiaries, i.e., subsidiaries of subsidiaries. The Canal Electric lien is broad-based, covering all of its
property adjacent to the Cape Cod Canal, after-acquired property
and pledged contracts relating to a couple of its generating units.
Texas Utilities Electric Company issues *First Mortgage and Collateral
Trust Bonds*. These are secured by Class "A" Bonds held by the
trustee, which are first mortgage bonds issued by former subsidiaries (now divisions), and a first mortgage lien on certain other property of the Company. Texas Utilities has also issued Secured Medium-Term Notes as a series of the First Mortgage and Collateral

Trust Bonds under the December 1, 1983, Mortgage and Deed of Trust.

There are instances (excluding prior lien bonds as mentioned above) when a company might have two or more layers of mortgage debt outstanding with different priorities. This situation usually occurs because the companies cannot issue additional first mortgage debt (or the equivalent) under the existing indentures. Often this secondary debt level is called *General and Refunding Mortgage Bonds* (G&R). In reality, this is mostly second mortgage debt. Long Island Lighting Company first issued G&R bonds in June 1975.

Let us take a look at the mortgage debt issues of Public Service Company of New Hampshire (PNH). Besides having first mortgage bonds and general and refunding mortgage bonds with varying degrees of security, it also has third mortgage bonds as well as publicly issued unsecured debt. All in all, there are four levels of claims against the company and its properties. PNH, the largest electric utility in the state, supplies power to about 75% of the population of New Hampshire. Along with a number of other neighboring utilities, it embarked on the construction of an ambitious nuclear project located at Seabrook, New Hampshire. As did many other nuclear facilities under construction during the late 1970s and early 1980s, it encountered rapidly increasing construction costs, skyrocketing financial costs, and regulatory delays due to consumer and other opposition to nuclear facilities. (In 1976, a prospectus estimated that Seabrook Unit #1 would be in service in 1981; by the end of 1988 it still had not yet been placed on stream.) The end result was a strain on the finances of the Company, especially internally generated cash flow, which resulted in a lack of financial flexibility. The Company finally omitted common and preferred stock dividends in May 1984 and, on January 28, 1988, filed a petition for reorganization under Chapter 11 the Bankruptcy Reform Act of 1978.

Due to provisions contained in the Company's First Mortgage Bond indenture which restricted the issuance of additional senior mortgage debt, PNH entered into a General and Refunding Mortgage Bond Indenture in August 1978. The terms of this indenture are somewhat similar to the First Mortgage with the exception of

the removal of the restrictions on the issuance of additional debt
and a modification relating to the use of the allowance for funds
used during construction in the earnings test. The G&R bonds have
a lien on substantially all of the property and franchises owned by
the company (as do the first mortgage bonds), " . . . *subject*, however, to the payment of the Trustee's charges, to the lien of the First
Mortgage, to the lien on after-acquired property existing at the time
of acquisition or created in connection with the purchase thereof . . .
and to Permitted Liens."[9]

The G&R indentures (as supplemented) also provide that the
bonds are additionally secured by a pledge of the maximum
amount of first mortgage bonds which may be issuable at the time
of the issuance of the G&R debt. Thus, the G&R constitutes a second mortgage on the property of the Company and, in some cases,
backed up by a first mortgage. At the end of 1987 PNH had six
G&R issues outstanding of which four had the additional security
of first mortgage bonds as shown in Table 2–2. The prospectus
states that the principal benefit to the holders of G&R bonds that
have first mortgage bonds pledged as additional security would be
in reorganization or insolvency when the allocation to the holders
of these G&R bonds might be increased by the reason of their participation in the First Mortgage through the pledged bonds. Upon
the retirement of all non-pledged First Bonds (2006 or earlier) the
G&R bonds would become the equivalent of first mortgage debt as
the original First Mortgage would have been discharged or satisfied.

The next level of debt in PNH's capitalization represents a third
mortgage through the issuance in early 1986 of $225 million of
13 ¾% Deferred Interest Third Mortgage Bonds Series A due 1996.
The Company resorted to this level due to the G&R earnings test,
which permitted the issuance of only about $26 million of G&R
debt at December 31, 1985. The prospectus states: "The . . . Bonds,
. . . are secured by a mortgage on substantially all of the Company's
New Hampshire properties. The Third Mortgage is junior and subordinate to the liens of the First Mortgage and the G&R Indenture
. . ." While the Third Mortgage does not have an earnings test, additional bonds under the indenture may only be issued if the total

Table 2–2 Selected Data on General & Refunding Mortgage Bonds, Public Service Company of New Hampshire at December 31, 1987 ($ thousands)

	General & Refunding Bond Issue		G & R Amount Outstanding	Pledged First Mortgage Bonds	Percent of G & R Collateralized by FMB
"A"	10.125%	1993	$ 32,700	$ 9,658	29.54%
"B"	12.00%	1999	60,000	9,126	15.21
"C"	14.50%	2000	30,000	None	0
"D"	17.00%	1990	23,000	None	0
"E"	18.00%	1989	50,000	24,135	48.27
"H"	Variable	1991	112,500	10,080	8.96

Source: Form 10-K for fiscal year ended December 31, 1987.

of the outstanding First, G&R and Third Mortgage Bonds does not exceed 90% of the book value of the Company's New Hampshire properties subject to the Third Mortgage. The final stratum of debt is unsecured, consisting of promissory notes and debentures. PNH is a rare bird among electric utility companies (or even among non-railroad companies) due to its capital structure. Most companies might not have more than two—or at the most three—different types of debt on the books.

After the bankruptcy filing, holders of the mortgage bonds brought suit in court to have the Company resume interest payments on the secured debt. The Court granted the motions of the First Mortgage and General and Refunding bond holders and interest was resumed, and defaulted interest paid, in June 1988. The Court found that the value of the bond collateral exceeded the amount of the debt and thus post-petition interest on this debt is an allowed claim. Further, current and projected cash flow were adequate to allow payment of interest, and the payment of such interest would avoid future litigation expense which might arise from continued nonpayment of the interest. As the property was in use and decreasing in value due to depreciation and wear and tear, the holders were entitled to receive adequate compensation; in this case interest payments.

In allowing the interest payments, the Court order said: "Accrual of unpaid interest on senior secured debt erodes the position of junior secured debt and, therefore, current payment of interest on the Debt will provide a measure of protection of interests in the Bond collateral which are junior in priority to the liens securing the Debt because such payment will reduce the amount of the secured claim of the holders of the Debt for interest regarding any period during which such interest is currently paid." Resumption of interest payments or adequate protection was denied the Third Mortgage Bonds. Apparently, they were found to be not fully secured as the Seabrook nuclear generating unit's status was not clear at that time. Seabrook only has value if permitted to generate electricity. Whether the Third Mortgage Bonds' claim for accrued and unpaid interest is satisfied in the ultimate reorganization will depend greatly on Seabrook operating.

As stated earlier, electric companies utilize mortgage debt more than other utilities. However, other utilities, such as telephone and gas companies, also have mortgage debt. Among the telephone companies with mortgage bonds are some of the subsidiaries and affiliates of the GTE Corporation system. Illinois Bell Telephone Company and New York Telephone Company issued first mortgage debt until the early 1970s, when the mortgage was closed and they started to issue unsecured debenture debt. Prior to the Bell System's breakup, the mortgage bonds and debentures of the Bell subsidiaries carried the same rating. For example, the bonds and debentures of New York Telephone and Illinois Bell were rated triple-A by Moody's and Standard & Poor's. After the divestiture, however, Moody's applied different ratings to the secured and unsecured debt, while S&P had the same rating whether the debt was first mortgage or debenture. In late 1988, Illinois Bell's mortgage debt was rated Aaa/AAA and the debentures Aa1/AAA. Similarly, New York Telephone's secured debt was rated Aa2 and AA+, while the unsecured carrried Aa3 and AA+ designations.

Gas companies also used mortgage debt to some extent. Here, again, the issuance tests are similar to those for the electric issues, as are the mortgage liens. However, the pipeline companies may have an additional clause subjecting certain gas purchase and sale contracts to the mortgage lien.

Other Mortgage Debt

Non-utility companies do not offer much mortgage debt nowadays; the preferred form of debt financing is unsecured. In the past, railroad operating companies were frequent issuers of mortgage debt. In many cases, a wide variety of secured debt might be found in a company's capitalization. One issue may have a first lien on a certain portion of the right of way and a second mortgage on another portion of the trackage, as well as a lien on the railroad's equipment, subject to the prior lien of existing equipment obligations. For example, Burlington Northern Railroad Company's 10% Consolidated Mortgage Bonds, Series J, due November 1, 1997, has direct and indirect liens on various parts of the railway's property as follows:

> (1) a second lien on the railroad properties subject to the first lien of the Great Northern General Gold Bond Mortgage (including approximately 4,086 miles of main line and 2,814 miles of branch line); (2) an indirect first lien on such Great Northern Railroad properties through the pledge under the Consolidated Mortgage of $350,135,000 principal amount of Great Northern General Mortgage Bonds; (3) a third lien on railroad properties subject to prior liens on the Northern Pacific Prior Lien Mortgage and Northern Pacific General Lien Mortgage (including approximately 2,398 miles of main line and 1,360 miles of branch line); (4) a third lien on the railroad properties subject to a first lien of the former Chicago, Burlington and Quincy Railroad Company (CB&Q) First and Refunding Mortgage and to the second lien of the Great Northern General Mortgage (including approximately 4,963 miles of main line and 1,543 miles of branch line); (5) an indirect first lien on such CB&Q properties through the pledge under the Consolidated Mortgage of $70,000,000 principal amount of CB&Q First and Refunding Mortgage Bonds; and (6) a first lien on approximately 8 miles of Great Northern branch line, approximately 169 miles of Northern Pacific main line and approximately 718 miles of Northern Pacific branch line, and approximately 19 miles of branch line of Colorado and Southern Railway Company.

There are certain railroad properties which are not subject to the lien of the above Consolidated Mortgage. Other exclusions include (1) lands not used or acquired for use in the railroad transportation service, (2) any lands adjacent to the lines of the railroad, used or acquired by the Company for industrial purposes and not for use in the railroad transportation service, (3) all timber and all oil, gas, coal and other minerals, (4) all air rights which may be used without unreasonable interference or adverse effect on the use for railroad purposes of surface land, and (5) all certificates of convenience and necessity for motor and water carrier operations and equipment used in connection therewith. The mortgage lien does not attach to property or improvements which are not appurtenant to any property subject to the lien thereof.

Another example is Chesapeake and Ohio Railway Company's Refunding and Improvement Mortgage Bonds, 3½% Series due May 1, 1996, which has a direct lien on 2,406.59 miles of track (819.32 miles as a first lien, 1,354.88 miles as a second lien, and 232.39 miles as a third lien), on the company's interest in 9 miles operated under leasehold agreements, and 411 miles operated under trackage rights, on C&O's owned equipment, and on its leasehold interest in equipment, subject to prior mortgage liens and outstanding equipment trust obligations. Railroad mortgages are often much more complex and confusing to bond investors than other types of mortgage debt.

In the broad classification of industrial companies, only a few have first mortgage bonds outstanding. The steel industry's Inland Steel Company, National Steel Corporation, Youngstown Sheet and Tube Company and Jones & Laughlin Steel Corporation have mortgage debt. The latter two are now part of the bankrupt LTV Steel complex. While electric utility mortgage bonds generally have a lien on practically all of the company's property, steel company mortgage debt has more limited liens. The prospectuses for Inland and National Steel describe the particular steel properties subject to the mortgage lien and make special mention that "various other properties of the Company . . . are not now subject to the lien of the Mortgage."[10] The mortgages of Youngstown and Jones & Laughlin retained the respective liens on their respective properties after their own merger and the subsequent merger with Republic Steel.

Mortgages may also contain maintenance and repair provisions, earnings tests for the issuance of additional debt, release and substitution of property clauses, and limited after-acquired property provisions. In some cases, shares of subsidiaries might also be pledged as part of the lien.

Some mortgage bonds are secured by a lien on a specific property rather than on most of a company's property as in the case of an electric utility. For example, Humana Inc. has sold a number of small issues of first mortgage bonds secured by liens on specific hospital properties. The 16 ½s of 1997 are secured by a first lien on a 267-bed hospital in Orlando, Florida, while the 16 ¼s of 1996 have lien on a 219-bed hospital in St. Petersburg, Florida. Although technically mortgage bonds, the basic security is centered on Humana's continued profitable operations. Because the security is specific rather than general, investors are apt to view these bonds as less worthy or of a somewhat lower ranking than fully secured or general lien issues. As the prospectuses say, the bonds are general obligations of Humana Inc. and also secured by the first mortgage. Standard & Poor's has mentioned that "It is difficult to assure that debtholders secured by specific collateral such as a hotel or hospital will, following a bankruptcy and liquidation of assets, realize values which make them whole."[11] The ultimate realization under these adverse circumstances greatly depends on the value of the property obtained in liquidation or assigned as part of the reorganization process. In many cases, by the time a company must resort to bankruptcy action, the properties are not worth what they once were. Any deficiency between what is owed and the value of the property then becomes a general unsecured claim against the debtor.

Other Secured Debt

Debt can be secured by many different assets. Forstmann & Company, Inc. issued $60 million 11 ¾% Secured Senior Extendible Notes due April 1, 1998, secured by a first priority lien on substantially all of its real property, machinery and equipment, and by a second priority lien on its inventory, accounts receivables and intangibles; the first priority lien on these latter assets is held by General Electric Credit Corporation (GECC) for its revolving credit loan. The revolving credit at August 3, 1986, amounted to nearly $44 million and may go to as much as $72 million in the future. The prospectus points out:

> There can be no assurance that the fixed assets of the Company are currently, or in the future will be adequate collateral for the Notes. While the Fair Market Value of the Company's fixed assets (assuming a continuation of current operations) has been appraised by American Appraisal Associates, Inc., an independent appraising firm, at $89,616,000 and the Company believes the replacement value of those assets to be more than $150,000,000, the Orderly Liquidation Value of those assets (assuming a piecemeal disposition over a reasonable period of time) has been appraised at $38,481,000. In addition, there can be no assurance that the Company's current assets will, after satisfaction of the claims of GECC, provide any collateral for the Notes.[12]

In the view of Forstmann's management, "it is highly unlikely that the assets of the Company would be sold in a liquidation situation because of the greater marketability of the Company if sold as a going concern."

Collateral trust debentures, bonds and notes are secured by financial assets such as cash, receivables, other notes, debentures or bonds, and not by real property. Louisville and Nashville Railroad Company's 11% Collateral Trust Bonds due July 15, 1985, were secured by a pledge of L&N's 11% First and Refunding Mortgage Bonds, Series P, due April 1, 2003, in an amount equal to 120% of the collateralized bonds. The mortgage bonds were a direct first lien on 3,949 miles of road, a direct second lien on 1,373 miles, and a third lien on 512 miles. In 1969 the Canadian company, Hudson's Bay Oil and Gas Company Limited, sold an issue of 7.85% Collateral Trust Bonds due 1994 in the United States. These bonds were secured by an equivalent amount of U.S. dollar payable First Mortgage Sinking Fund Bonds (covering the Company's Canadian properties) with the same maturity, interest rate and payment dates and redemption and sinking fund provisions as the collateral bonds. The pledged securities, being nearly similar in every way to the collateralized bonds are called "shadow bonds" by some, and "mirror bonds" by others. Thus, the collateral bond indenture constitutes a first lien on the pledged bonds and an indirect lien ranking pari passu (equally) with the holders of the Company's other First Mortgage Bonds on the Company's property as described in the Deed of Trust and Mortgage dated May 1, 1955, and supplemented.

Collateral trust notes and debentures have been issued by companies engaged in vehicle leasing, such as RLC Corporation, Leaseway Transportation Corporation, and Ryder System, Inc. The proceeds from these offerings were advanced to various subsidiaries in exchange for their unsecured promissory notes which, in turn, were pledged with the trustees as security for the parent company debt. These pledged notes may later become secured by liens or other claims on vehicles. Protective covenants for these collateralized issues may include limitations on the equipment debt of subsidiaries, on the consolidated debt of the issuer and its subsidiaries, on dividend payments by the issuer and the subsidiaries, and on the creation of liens and purchase money mortgages, among other things.

Debt can be secured by the pledge of assets such as a partnership notes (DCS Capital Corporation 12.20% Series A Notes due 1994 or Pembroke Capital Company Inc. 14% Notes due 1991). DCS Capital Corporation is owned by DCS Capital Partnership, whose general partners are The Dow Chemical Company, Union Carbide Corporation and Shell Canada Limited. The partnership note is secured by a cash deficiency agreement and performance guarantees with the three partners on a several basis, initially in the following proportions: Dow 52%; Union Carbide 27%; and Shell, 21%. These agreements and guarantees are not assigned directly to the holders of the Series A Notes, but the trustee has the right to enforce them if the notes are not paid when due. The Pembroke issue is secured by a partnership note of Pembroke Cracking Company, a partnership of Texaco Limited and Gulf Oil (Great Britain) Limited, wholly owned subsidiaries of American corporations. If the Pembroke Capital Note is not paid on a timely basis, the general partners are severally obligated to make, or caused to be made, payments sufficient to pay the principal and interest on the notes if their respective subsidiaries fail to do so.

Since 1985, **LOBs** (for Lease Obligation Bonds), **SLOBs** (for Secured Lease Obligation Bonds) and **SFBs** (for Secured Facility

Bonds) have been issued as a result of sale and leaseback transactions of electric utility companies. Some utilities have sold interests in generating plants and transmission facilities to third parties, which, in turn, leased the assets back to the utilities. A utility enters into these transactions essentially for tax purposes as it may have limited near-term use for depreciation allowances. It essentially substitutes lease rental payments for depreciation and capital recovery requirements associated with ownership. The third party lessor in these leveraged lease transactions obtains the funds to purchase the assets from the sale of these SLOBs, LOBs, and SFBs. The source of repayment for these bonds is from the rentals paid by the utility to the lessor in amounts sufficient to provide for the payment of principal and interest on the bonds. Additional security may be pledged lessor notes which, in the case of SLOBs, are secured by a lien on and a security interest in the ownership interest in the leased property. LOBs do not have any security interest in the leased property although, under certain circumstances, the lease indenture trustee may acquire a lien and security interest on the property. SFBs are secured by a lien and security interest in the leased assets and the lessor's rights under the lease.

Private Export Funding Corporation (PEFCO) issues secured notes with the pledged security being an equivalent principal amount of obligations backed by the full faith and credit of the United States of America, such as guaranteed importer notes, or cash. The interest on PEFCO's secured notes is unconditionally guaranteed by the Export-Import Bank of the United States, a U.S. government agency. Thus PEFCO's paper carries the highest ratings, Aaa/AAA.

Thrift institutions, either directly or indirectly through special purpose financing corporations, secure some of their debt obligations in order to enhance the credit standing of the paper. The securities are backed by eligible collateral such as federally insured or guaranteed mortgages and deeds of trust on real property, Government National Mortgage Association Certificates, Federal National Mortgage Association Certificates, Federal Home Loan Mortgage Corporation Certificates, and conventional mortgages. These secured issues are obligations of the thrift or the special purpose subsidiary, not of any special trust, and do not constitute deposits or savings accounts. The security is still owned by the thrift, although pledged for repayment of the debt created. Proceeds from the sale of the secured bonds and notes (not from the sale of mortgages) are used by the thrift for general purposes. If, following a default, the proceeds from the liquidation of the pledged property are insufficient to pay the entire amount of the bonds, the bondholders would then become general unsecured creditors of the issuer to the extent of the deficiency ranking on a parity with other general unsecured creditors.

The eligible collateral is held by a trustee and periodically marked to market to ensure that the market value has a liquidation value in excess of the amount needed to repay the entire outstanding bonds and accrued interest. If the collateral is insufficient, the issuer must, within several days, bring the value of the collateral up to the required amount. If the issuer is unable to do so, the trustee would then sell collateral and redeem bonds. Another collateralized structure allows for the defeasance or "mandatory collateral substitution" which provides the investor assurance that it will continue to receive the same interest payments until maturity. Instead of redeeming the bonds with the proceeds of the collateral sale, the proceeds are used to purchase a portfolio of U.S. government securities in such an amount that the cash flow is sufficient to meet the principal and interest payments on the mortgage-backed bond. Because of the structure of these issues, the rating agencies have assigned triple-A ratings to them. The rating is based on the strength of the collateral and the issues' structure, not on the issuers' credit standing.

Equipment Trust Financing—Railroads

Railroads and airlines have financed much of their rolling stock and aircraft with secured debt. The securities go by various names such as equipment trust certificates (ETCs) in the case of railroads, and secured equipment certificates, guaranteed loan certificates and loan certificates in the case of airlines. We will look at railroad equipment trust financing first for two reasons: (1) The financing of railway equipment under the format in general public use today goes back to the late 1800s, and (2) it has had a superb record of safety of principal and timely payment of interest, more traditionally known as dividends. Railroads probably comprise the largest and oldest group of issuers of secured equipment financing.[13]

Probably the earliest instance in U.S. financial history in which a company bought equipment under a conditional sales agreement (CSA) was in 1845 when the Schuylkill Navigation Company purchased some barges.[14] Over the years secured equipment financing proved to be an attractive way for railroads—both good and bad credits—to raise the capital necessary to finance rolling stock. Various types of instruments were devised—equipment bonds (known as the New York Plan), conditional sales agreements (also known as the New York CSA), lease arrangements, and the Philadelphia Plan equipment trust certificate. The New York Plan equipment bond went the way of the dodo bird in the 1930s. The Philadelphia Plan ETC is the form used for most, if not all, public financings in today's market.

The ratings for equipment trust certificates are higher than on the same company's mortgage debt or other public debt securities. This is due primarily to the collateral value of the equipment, its superior standing in bankruptcy compared with other claims, and the instrument's generally self-liquidating nature. The railroad's actual creditworthiness may mean less for some equipment trust investors than for investors in other rail securities or, for that matter, other corporate paper. However, that is not to say that financial analysis of the issuer should be ignored. Table 2–3 compares the ratings on equipment trust certificates of a number of railroad companies with the ratings on some of their other public debt. In some cases, the differences between the two securities are slight; in others they comprise a complete rating grade.

Equipment trust certificates are issued under agreements that provide a trust for the benefit of the investors. Each certificate represents an interest in the trust equal to its principal amount and bears the railroad's unconditional guarantee of prompt payment, when due, of the principal and dividends (the term *dividends* is used as the payments represent income from a trust and not interest on a loan). The trustee holds the title to the equipment, which when the certificates are retired, passes to, or vests in, the railroad. But the railroad has all other ownership rights. It can take the depreciation and can utilize any tax benefits on the subject equipment.

The railroad agrees to pay the trustee sufficient rental for the principal payments and the dividends due on the certificates, together with expenses of the trust and certain other charges. The railroad uses the equipment in its normal operations and is required to maintain it in good operating order and repair (at its own expense). If the equipment is destroyed, lost or becomes worn out or unsuitable for use (that is, suffers a "casualty occurrence") the company must substitute the fair market value of that equipment in the form of either cash or additional equipment. Cash may be used to acquire additional equipment unless the agreement states otherwise.

The trust equipment is usually clearly marked that it is not the railroad's property. One equipment trust agreement states:

> Section 4.6. The Railroad agrees that at or before the delivery to the Railroad of each unit of the Trust Equipment, there shall be plainly, distinctly, permanently and conspicuously placed and fastened upon each side of such unit a metal plate bearing the words [Missouri Pacific Equipment Trust, Series No. 22, Chemical Bank, Trustee, Owner and Lessor] . . ., or such words shall be otherwise plainly, distinctly, permanently and conspicuously marked on each side of such unit, in either case in letters not less than one-half inch in height. Such plates or marks shall be such as to be readily visible and as to indicate plainly the Trustee's ownership of each unit of the Trust Equipment. In case . . . such plates or marks shall at any time be removed, defaced or destroyed, the Railroad shall immediately cause the same to be restored or replaced. The Trust Equipment may be lettered "Missouri Pacific Railroad," "Missouri Pacific Lines", "M.P." or with the name, insignia, emblem or initials of any Affiliate which . . . is authorized to use the equipment . . . for convenience of identification of the leasehold interest of the Railroad therein. During the continuance of the lease . . . the Railroad shall not allow the name of any person, association or corporation to be placed on any of the Trust Equipment as a designation which might be interpreted as a claim of ownership thereof by the Railroad or by any person, association or corporation other than the Trustee.[15]

Immediately after the issuance of an ETC the railroad has an equity interest in the equipment that provides a margin of safety for

Table 2–3 Ratings of Debt Securities of Selected Railroad Companies (January 1, 1990)

Company	ETC Ratings			Senior Public Debt	
	Moody's	S&P		Moody's	S&P
Atchison, Topeka & Santa Fe	A3	A+	General Mortgage	Baa3	BBB+
Baltimore & Ohio Railroad	Aa2	AA-	First Consolidated	A2	A-
Burlington Northern Inc. (RR)	Aa3	A+	(RR) Consolidated	A3	BBB+
Chesapeake & Ohio Railway	Aa2	AA-	General Mortgage	A2	A-
Illinois Central Gulf R.R.	A2	A	First Mortgage	Ba2	B+
Louisville & Nashville	Aa2	AA-	1st & Refunding Mortgage	A2	A-
Missouri Pacific Railroad	Aa1	AA+	First Mortgage	A1	A+
Norfolk & Western Railway	Aaa	AAA	1st Consolidated	Aa1	AA
Southern Pacific Transport.	A3	A	1st & Refunding	Baa3	BB+
Southern Railway	Aaa	AAA	1st Consolidated	Aa2	AA
Texas & Pacific Railway	Aa2	AA+	First Mortgage	A1	A+
Union Pacific Railroad	Aa1	AA+	General Consolidated	Aa3	A+

Source: Moody's Bond Record and Standard & Poor's Bond Guide, January 1990.

the investor. Normally, the ETC investor finances no more than 80% of the cost of the equipment and the railroad the remaining 20%. The Union Pacific Railroad Company's 8 ¾% Equipment Trust No. 1 of 1987 issued January 28, 1988, was for $101,200,000, equal to 80% of the original cost of the equipment financed. This equipment consisted of 75 Dash diesel-electric road freight locomotives with a cost of $83,668,950 (cost per locomotive, $1,115,586), 25 diesel-electric road freight locomotives with a cost of $29,357,500 (cost per locomotive, $ 1,174,300), and 345 center partition bulkhead flat cars costing $13,467,906 ($39,037 each) for a total of $126,494,356. Although modern equipment is longer-lived than that of many years ago, the ETC's length of maturity is still generally the standard 15 years (there are some exceptions noted below). Assuming a 20-year equipment life with straight line depreciation, there will be a positive margin of equity in the trust at normal maturity date. Actually, however, much of the equipment can remain in service for thirty to forty years without a major overhaul.

The structure of the financing usually provides for periodic redemption of the outstanding certificates. The most common form of ETC is the serial variety; The ETC is issued in 15 equal serial maturities, each coming due annually from the end of the first year to the end of the fifteenth. The Norfolk and Western Railway Company 8 ⅞% Equipment Trust Series 19 dated May 15, 1988, consisted of 15 serial maturities of $1,200,000 due each May 15 from 1989 through 2003. The reoffering yields ranged from 7.50% for the first serial due May 15, 1989, to 9.40% for the tranches maturing on May 15, 2000 to 2003. Consolidated Rail Corporation issued its 1988 Equipment Trust Certificates, Series A, with serial maturities of unequal principal amounts due annually October 15, 1991 to October 15, 2004. There are single-maturity (or "bullet maturity") ETCs such as the previously mentioned Union Pacific 8 ¾% Equipment Trust No. 1 of 1987. This 7-year issue does not have a sinking fund and the entire issue matures on January 15, 1995. There are also sinking fund equipment trust certificates where the ETCs are retired through the operation of a normal sinking fund, one fifteenth of the original amount issued per year. Thus the Louisville and Nashville Railroad Company's 12.30% Equipment Trust Certificates, Series 10, due February 1, 1995 (original issue $53,600,000), has an annual sinking fund of $3,575,000, designed to retire 93.4% of the issue prior to maturity.

The standing of railroad or common carrier equipment trust certificates in bankruptcy is of vital importance to the investor. As the equipment is needed for operations, the bankrupt railroad's management will more than likely reaffirm the lease of the equipment because, without rolling stock, it is out of business. One of the first things the trustees of the Penn Central Transportation Company did after the firm filed for bankruptcy on June 21, 1970, was to reaffirm its equipment debt. On August 19, the court issued the required equipment debt assumption orders.[16] There were outstanding about $90.7 million of equipment trust certificates, $442.9 million of conditional sales agreements, and unexpired lease rental payments on other contracts of $594 million. It was not until the end of 1978 that investors and speculators started to recover something from the other Penn Central obligations. Cases of disaffirmation of equipment obligations are very rare indeed. But if equipment debt were to be disaffirmed, the trustee could repossess and then try to release or sell it to others. Any deficiency due the equipment debtholders would still be an unsecured claim against the bankrupt railway company. Standard gauge, non-specialized equipment should not be difficult to release to another railroad.

The Bankruptcy Reform Act of 1978 provides specifically that railroads be reorganized, not liquidated, and subchapter IV of Chapter 11 grants them special treatment and protection. One very important feature found in Section 77(j) of the preceding Bankruptcy Act was carried over to the new law. Section 1168 states that Section 362 (the automatic stay provision) and Section 363 (the use, sale, or lease of property section) are not applicable in railroad bankruptcies. It protects the rights of the equipment lenders while giving the trustee the chance to cure any defaults.[17] Railroad bankruptcies usually do not occur overnight but creep up gradually as the result of steady deterioration over the years. New equipment financing capability becomes restrained. The outstanding equipment debt at the time of bankruptcy often is not substantial and usually has a good equity cushion built in.

Equipment debt of noncommon carriers such as private car leasing lines (Trailer Train, Union Tank Car, General American Transportation etc.) does not enjoy this special protection under the Bankruptcy Act. Standard & Poor's says that it accordingly rates this debt only as the senior security of the lessor. Signal Capital Corporation through its Pullman Leasing Company division (a non-common carrier) leases rail freight cars to shippers and railroads and finances the equipment through the issuance of equipment trust certificates. In 1988, Signal Capital issued $100 million of 9.95% Certificates due February 1, 2006, to reduce short-term borrowings incurred to finance the railcar leasing division. The ETC agreement provided for the sale, assignment and transfer to the trustee of 5,156 freight cars with a depreciated final cost of at least $125 million. None of the equipment would have been in use prior to January 1, 1975! The prospectus states:

> In the event of bankruptcy or reorganization of the Company or any sublessee, the rights of the trustee to repossess or dispose of equipment covered by the Trust would be subject to the effect of the federal bankruptcy laws upon enforcement of lessor's rights. These laws, among other things, impose automatic stays upon rights of repossession as against the Company and non-railroad sublessees; may invalidate lease termination clauses which become effective by reason of bankruptcy and certain other insolvency-related events; and allow a trustee in bankruptcy (or the Company or sublessee if it should be a debtor-in-possession) to assign or terminate an unexpired lease not-withstanding a provision in the Agreement or the sublease which prohibits, restricts, or conditions such assignment or termination.

Equipment trust certificates have even been issued in reorganization. An interesting example due to the dividend yields is the issue of Chicago & North Western Railway Company Trustees' Equipment Trust Certificate, 2 ½% of 1939. The $1,800,000 offering made on November 24, 1939, was sold at yields ranging from 0.45% for the December 15, 1940, maturity to 2.85% for the December 15, 1949, paper. The funds raised paid approximately 76.2% of the equipment's cost.

During the twentieth century losses have been rare and delayed payments of dividends and principal only slightly less so. Detroit, Toledo and Ironton Railway Company defaulted in December 1907 or June 1908 on $40,000 of 4 ½% Equipment Notes. The face value less a small amount of expenses was eventually realized.[18] The Seaboard Airline Railroad and the Wabash Railway Company required holders of maturing equipment obligations to extend their maturities for a short period or to exchange them for Trustees' or Receivers' Certificates of lower coupon. There were a couple of other delays of principal and/or dividend payments but they were often limited to the grace period. Due to the strong position of the lien on equipment and loans by the Reconstruction Finance Corporation (RFC) to some railroads, losses were minimal during the Great Depression. This is especially noteworthy in view of the sharp drop in commodity prices and traffic which resulted in a decline in the value of much of the equipment.

One railroad that defaulted and caused investors a loss was Florida East Coast Railway Company. In most Wall Street literature on equipment financing, this case appears only as a historical footnote; however, it is interesting even though it is history and laws have changed. The railroad overextended during the boom times of the 1920s but reality caught up with it and so FEC entered bankruptcy on September 1, 1931. In 1932 the road experienced difficulty in meeting its equipment obligations. In 1936 the receivers disaffirmed the lease and the equipment was sold in a public sale. After a subsequent sale of the equipment in 1937 and further court battles, a judgment was finally paid in 1944. The final payment came in 1950, nearly twenty years after the initial bankruptcy filing. In sum, after all expenses and fees were paid, the net recovery by the equipment certificate holder was between 68 and 70% of the claim.[19]

Airline Equipment Debt

Airline equipment debt has some of the special status that is held by railroad equipment trust certificates. Of course, it is much more recent, having developed since the end of World War II. Many airlines have had to resort to secured equipment financing, especially since the early 1970s. Like railroad equipment obligations, certain equipment debt of certified airlines, under Section 1110 of the Bankruptcy Reform Act of 1978, is not subject to sections 362 and 363 of the Act, namely the automatic stay and the power of the court to prohibit the repossession of the equipment. The creditor must be a lessor, a conditional vendor, or hold a purchase money security interest with respect to the aircraft and related equipment. The secured equipment must be new, not used.[20] Of course, it gives the airline 60 days in which to decide to cancel the lease or debt and to return the equipment to the trustee. If the reorganization trustee decides to reaffirm the lease in order to continue using the equipment, it must perform or assume the debtor's obligations which become due or payable after that date, and cure all existing defaults other than those resulting solely from the financial condition, bankruptcy, insolvency or reorganization of the airline. Payments resume including those that were due during the delayed period. Thus, the creditor will get either the payments due according to the terms of the contract or the equipment.

The equipment is an important factor. If the airplanes are of recent vintage, well maintained, fuel efficient and relatively economical to operate, it is more likely that a company in distress and seeking to reorganize would assume the equipment lease. On the other hand, if the outlook for reorganization appears dim from the outset and the airplanes are older and less economical, the airline could very well disaffirm the lease. In this case, releasing the aircraft or selling it at rents and prices sufficient to continue the original payments and terms to the security holders might be difficult. Of course, the resale market for aircraft is on a plane-by-plane basis and highly subject to supply and demand factors. Multimillion-dollar airplanes have a somewhat more limited market than do boxcars and hopper cars worth only $30,000.

Most of the publicly offered equipment loans in the 1970s financed approximately 70 to 75% of the cost of new aircraft and related parts. The 25 to 30% equity was invested mostly by outside financial institutions which could take advantage of the depreciation deduction and the investment tax credit. These issues generally had maturities of 15 to 16 years. Some of the equipment deals done in the 1980s had maturities out to 23 or so years. But in many cases the debt portion of the financing amounted to 50 to 60% of the equipment's cost, providing a greater equity cushion. The lease agreement required the airline pay a rental sufficient to cover the interest, amortization of principal, and a return to the equity participant. The airline was responsible for maintaining and operating the aircraft, as well as providing for adequate insurance. It must also keep the equipment registered and record the equipment trust certificate and lease under the Federal Aviation Act of 1958.

In the event of a loss or destruction of the equipment, the company may substitute similar equipment of equal value and in as good operating condition and repair and as airworthy as that which was lost or destroyed. It also has the option to redeem the outstanding certificates with the insurance proceeds. In 1975, a portion of the Trans World Airlines 10s of 1985 was redeemed due to the destruction of one of the Boeing 727-231 aircraft securing the loan. A problem could arise under Section 1110 in the case of a bankrupt airline with outstanding ETCs secured with substituted equipment. Recent ETC financings have stated that the owner trustee as lessor should be entitled to the benefits of Section 1110 with regard to the initially delivered aircraft and equipment. But the prospectuses go on to say that "it is doubtful whether, after an Event of Loss to an Aircraft or Engine or a voluntary substitution of an engine by Piedmont, any replacement aircraft or engine subjected to the lien of the applicable Equipment Trust Agreement would have the benefits of Section 1110."[21]

An important point to consider is the equity owner. If the airline runs into financial difficulty and fails to make the required payments, the owner may step in and make the rental payment in order to protect its investment. The carrier's failure to make a basic rental payment within the stipulated grace period is an act of default but is cured if the owner makes payment. The Piedmont Aviation prospectus says:

> In the event Piedmont fails to make any semi-annual basic rental payment when due under a lease, and as long as no unrelated event of acceleration under the related Equipment Trust Agreement shall have occurred and be continuing, within 15 days of the expiration of the grace period for rental payments the Owner Participant or the applicable Owner Trustee may furnish to the Equipment Trust Trustee . . . the amount of such rental payment, together with any interest thereon on account of the delayed payment thereof, in such event such Equipment Trust Trustee and the holders of outstanding Certificates of the Series to which such failure relates may not exercise any remedies otherwise available under such Equipment Trust Agreement or

such Lease as the result of such failure to make such rental payment, unless such failure is the fourth consecutive or seventh cumulative failure to make such rental payments. The Owner Participant of the Owner Trustees may also cure any other default by Piedmont in the performance of its obligations under the leases that can be cured by the payment of money.[22]

Thus, a strong owner lends support to the financing, and a weak one little.

Airline equipment debt should be considered by many investors but it pays to investigate before investing. Do not be misled by the title of the issue just because the words secured or equipment trust appear. Investors should look at the collateral and its estimated value based on the studies of recognized appraisers compared with the amount of equipment debt outstanding. Is the equipment new or used? Do the creditors benefit from Section 1110 of the Bankruptcy Reform Act? As the equipment is a depreciable item and subject to wear, tear and obsolescence, a sinking fund starting within several years of the initial offering date should be provided if the debt is not issued in serial form. Of course, the ownership of the aircraft is important as mentioned above. Obviously, one must review the obligor's financials as the investor's first line of defense depends on the airline's ability to service the lease rental payments. Failure to do adequate research and digest what has been studied could lead to a costly and possibly unwise investment.

Many investors have probably wished that they had more closely read the prospectus of People Express Airlines, Inc., 14 ⅜% Secured Equipment Certificates due April 15, 1996, and dated April 17, 1986. Full of certain risk factors, it shows the company's heavy leverage and recent lack of fixed charge coverage. It points out that the aircraft to be secured are used, ranging in age from 4.5 to 18.0 years, and with estimated useful lives from 12.0 to 20.5 years, as well as the possible impairment to the trustee's right to repossess the aircraft in the event of default. All in all, investors were buying a weak security. The truth was revealed all too quickly. Less than six months later—before the first interest payment was made—the company informed its creditors that they had to make concessions in order for Texas Air Corporation to proceed with its acquisition of Peoples. Probably the most hurtful concession was that requesting that the equipment certificate holders exchange their old paper for new with interest rates 2 ¼ percentage points less. Thus, the 14 ⅜% owners would get new certificates with a 12 ⅛% interest rate. While buyers paid $1,000 per certificate on delivery on April 24, 1986, the worth was only about $700 each on September 12 and a somewhat better $800 each on October 3. But, that 14 ⅜% coupon was certainly attractive in April!

A borrower can pledge any type of asset for a loan in order to obtain lower cost monies, if the security is satisfactory to the lender. In some cases, the lender's claim or access to the property is somewhat moot insofar as the debtor, even in bankruptcy, will continue to use the collateral under court supervision. A mortgage could be closed off and unsecured financing utilized, as with New York Telephone Company, Illinois Bell Telephone and some others. Expenses associated with issuing unsecured debt are usually less than those of secured obligations, and the mortgage may be considered an anachronism to many observers of the financial scene. But in other cases, a borrower may be unable to get any financing unless the security is adequate. Thus, it may be necessary for one to "hock the family ranch" in order to get the financing.

Unsecured Debt

We have discussed many of the features common to secured and unsecured debt. Take away the collateral and we have unsecured debt. In this connection, the remaining two Cs of credit—character and capacity—become increasingly important.

Unsecured debt, like secured debt, comes in several different layers or levels of claim against the corporation's capitalization. But in the case of unsecured debt, the nomenclature attached to the debt issues sounds less substantial. For example, "General and Refunding Mortgage Bonds" may sound more important than "Subordinated Debentures," even though both are basically second claims on the corporate body. In addition to the normal debentures and notes, there are junior issues; for example, General Motors Acceptance Corporation, in addition to senior unsecured debt, had public issues designated as senior subordinated and junior subordinated notes, representing the secondary and tertiary levels of the capital structure. The difference in a high-grade issuer may be considered insignificant as long as the issuer maintains its quality. But in cases of financial distress, the junior issues usually fare worse than the senior issues. Only in cases of very well-protected junior issues will they come out whole—in which case, so would the senior indebtedness. Thus, many investors are more than willing to take junior debt of high-grade companies; the minor additional risk, compared to that of the senior debt of lower-rated issuers, may well be worth the incremental income.

Looking at General Motors Acceptance Corporation's Senior Subordinated Notes, 14 3/8% due April 1, 1991, we see that they "are subordinate in right of payment . . . to all indebtedness for borrowed money . . . now outstanding or hereafter incurred, which is not by its terms subordinate to other indebtedness of the Company." The Junior Subordinated Notes, 8 1/8% of April 15, 1986, say that they are subordinate and junior, with the remaining wording similar to that of the senior subordinate debt. The junior debt subordination wording further implies that in the event of bankruptcy or insolvency proceedings, liquidation, reorganization or receivership, all principal, premium (if any) and interest on superior or senior and senior subordinated indebtedness will be paid in full before any payment is made on junior subordinated indebtedness. Many of these legal proceedings actually involve negotiation and compromise between the various classes of creditors. Even junior creditors can receive some consideration, although, under strict application of priority, they normally may be entitled to little or nothing.

Subordination of the debt instrument might not be apparent from the issue's name. This is often the case with bank and bank related securities. Chase Manhattan Bank (National Association) had some 8 3/4% Capital Notes due 1986. The term "Capital Notes" would not sound like a subordinated debt instrument to most inexperienced investors unfamiliar with the jargon of the debt world. Yet capital notes are junior securities. The subordination section of the issue's prospectus says, "The indebtedness . . . evidenced by the Notes . . . is to be subordinate and junior in right of payment to its obligations to depositors, its obligations under banker's acceptances and letters of credit and its obligations to any Federal Reserve Bank and (except as to any Long Term debt as defined ranking on a parity with or junior to the Notes) its obligations to its other creditors. . . ." This issue was debt of the bank and thus had prior claim on the assets of the bank in case of receivership, conservatorship or the like, over and above the claim of the Bank's sole shareholder (and the creditors of that shareholder), the Chase Manhattan Corporation.

Credit Enhancements

Some debt issuers have other companies guarantee their loans. This is normally done when a subsidiary issues debt and the investors want the added protection of a third-party guarantee. The use of guarantees makes it easier and more convenient to finance special projects and affiliates although guarantees are extended to operating company debt. Examples of third party (but related) guarantees include U S West Capital Funding, Inc. 8% Guaranteed Notes due October 15, 1996 (guaranteed by U S West, Inc.). The principal purpose of Capital Funding is to provide financing to U S West and its affiliates through the issuance of debt guaranteed by U S West. This guarantee reads: "U S West will unconditionally guarantee the due and punctual payment of the principal, premium, if any, and interest on the Debt Securities when and as the same shall become due and payable, whether at maturity, upon redemption or otherwise. The guarantees will rank equally with all other unsecured and unsubordinated obligations of U S West." Citicorp has guaranteed the payment of principal of interest on a subordinated basis for some of the debt issues of Citicorp Person-to-Person, Inc., a holding company providing management services to affiliates offering financial and similar services. PepsiCo, Inc. has guaranteed the debt of its financing affiliate, PepsiCo Capital Resources, Inc., and The Standard Oil Company (an Ohio Corporation) has unconditionally guaranteed the debt of Sohio Pipe Line Company. The Seagram Company Ltd., a Canadian corporation, has "unconditionally guarantee[d] the due and punctual payment of principal and interest on the [9.65% Debentures of Joseph E. Seagram & Sons, Inc., an Indiana corporation], when and as the same shall become due and payable, whether at the maturity date, by declaration of acceleration or otherwise."

There are also other types of third party credit enhancements. Some captive finance subsidiaries of industrial companies enter into agreements requiring them to maintain fixed charge coverage at such a level so that the securities meet the eligibility standards for investment by insurance companies under New York State law. The required coverage levels are maintained by adjusting the prices at which the finance company buys its receivables or other financial from the parent company or through special payments from the parent company. These supplemental income maintenance agreements, while usually not part of indentures, are very important considerations for bond buyers.

Another type of support agreement is found in the BellSouth Capital Funding Corporation's 9 ¼% Notes due January 15, 1998. This support agreement between the company and its parent, BellSouth Corporation, stipulates that the parent (1) agrees to cause Bell-South Capital to maintain a positive tangible net worth in accordance with generally accepted accounting principles; (2) will provide the necessary funds to pay debt service if the subsidiary is unable to meet the obligations when due; and (3) shall own, directly or indirectly, all of the outstanding voting capital stock of the subsidiary throughout the life of the support agreement. In addition, in case of a default by the parent in meeting its obligations under the default agreement, or in the case of default by the subsidiary in the payment of principal and/or interest, the holders of the securities or the trustee may proceed directly against the parent. However, they do not have any recourse to or against the stock or assets of the parent's telephone subsidiaries.

Another credit enhancing feature is the letter of credit (LOC) issued by a bank. A LOC requires the bank to make payments to the trustee when requested so that monies will be available for the bond issuer to meet its interest and principal payments when due. Thus the credit of the bank under the LOC is substituted for that of the debt issuer. For example, in February 1988, Holiday Inns, Inc., a subsidiary of Holiday Corporation, issued $200 million each of 8 ⅝% Notes due 1993 and 9% Notes due 1995. The principal and interest on the notes are payable by drawings under an irrevocable, direct-pay letter of credit issued by The Sumitomo Bank, Limited, acting through its New York City branch. The notes also carry the guarantee of Holiday Corporation. These credit enhanced securities were rated Aaa by Moody's Investors Service while Holiday Inns unsecured senior debt is rated B1, hardly investment grade. The adjusted capitalization of Holiday Corporation at the time of the offering showed $250 million of short-term debt, $2,385 million of long-term debt, and a stockholders' deficit of $766 million. The LOC is not given out gratis. In addition to an initial fee for granting the LOC, Holiday Inns must pay an annual fee and a drawing fee for each payment made thereunder. Both Inns and the parent must reimburse the bank for all payments made under the LOC. These reimbursement obligations are secured by first mortgages/deeds of trust on certain hotel/casino properties and first priority interests in certain related properties in Nevada. Sumitomo was also named the trustee of the notes. Interest savings for the company were estimated at a substantial 200 basis points. In other words, the interest rates on the debt would have been around 10 ⅝% and 11%, respectively, and the total cost increased by $8 million annually or some $48 million over the life of the notes.

Insurance companies also lend their credit standing to corporate debt, both new issues and outstanding secondary market issues. One leader is Financial Security Assurance (FSA) which has unconditionally and irrevocably guaranteed the scheduled payments on new issues such as Columbus Southern Power Company's 8 ⅝% First Mortgage Bonds due 1996 and County Savings Bank 10.15% Bonds due 1998. In the secondary market FSA has applied its TAGSS program (Triple-A Guaranteed Secondary Securities) to numerous blocks of bonds issued by Texas Utilities Electric, Commonwealth Edison and Georgia Power, among others. The ratings on these enhanced securities is Aaa/AAA, not the rating that would be on the securities if they were "stand alones." FSA usually requires that the issue to be insured must be investment grade on its own merits and also be collateralized so as to reduce the insurer's risk of loss. The investor in these issues gets a greater degree of safety through the higher rating and protection against the underlying issuer's credit deterioration. In addition, the issue's liquidity could be enhanced as more investment firms may be willing to make a market in the insured bonds. From the new issuers' perspective, the interest savings more than offset the cost of the insurance premium leading to a lower net interest cost. Certainly, utility rate regulators like to see companies under their supervision take steps to reduce their overall costs.

While a guarantee or other type of credit enhancement may add some measure of protection to a debtholder, caution should not be thrown to the wind. In effect, one's job may even become more complex as an analysis of both the issuer and the guarantor should be performed. In many cases, only the latter is needed if the issuer is merely a financing conduit without any operations of its own. However, if both concerns are operating companies, it may very well be necessary to analyze both, as the timely payment of principal and interest ultimately will depend on the stronger party. A downgrade of the enhancer's claims paying ability reduces the value of the bonds.

Negative Pledge Clause

One of the important protective provisions for unsecured debt holders is the negative pledge clause. This provision, found in most senior unsecured debt issues and a few subordinated issues, prohibits a company from creating or assuming any lien to secure a debt issue without equally securing the subject debt issue(s) (with certain exceptions). Designed to prevent other creditors from obtaining a senior position at the expense of existing creditors, "it is not intended to prevent other creditors from sharing in the position of debenture holders."[23] Again, it is not necessary to have such a clause unless the issuer runs into trouble. But like insurance, it is not needed until the time that no one wants arrives.

A book on international lending says that "the chief value of such a clause is that no future loan can be secured without at the same time securing equally or ratably all other loans which contain the negative pledge clause. It is obvious that such a clause does not prevent the borrower from contracting other obligations in the future." It also points out a stronger version of the clause specifying that if the issuer should pledge revenues as security for a new loan, the older loan would have priority as to the pledged security.[24]

One negative pledge clause section reads as follows:

> The Company and its Restricted Subsidiaries will not create, incur, assume or suffer to exist any mortgage, pledge or other

> lien or encumbrance upon any Principal Property or any shares
> of capital stock or indebtedness of any Restricted Subsidiary,
> whether now owned or hereafter acquired, if after giving effect
> thereto the aggregate principal amount of indebtedness secured
> by any mortgage, pledge or other lien or encumbrance would be
> in excess of 5% of Consolidated Net Worth unless the Deben-
> tures will be secured equally and ratably with (or prior to) such
> other obligations, indebtedness or claims; . . . Exceptions include
> purchase money mortgages securing debt not exceeding the fair
> cost of the property, liens securing certain construction and im-
> provement loans, liens in connection with government contracts,
> liens on the property of a restricted subsidiary at the time it be-
> came a restricted subsidiary, and certain liens in favor of an in-
> strumentality of the United States, or any state or subdivision
> thereof to secure debt to finance the acquisition, construction or
> improvement of property.[25]

Another restrictive covenant has the following limitation on liens:

> FFC will not, and will not permit any Designated Subsidiary to,
> issue, assume, incur or guarantee any indebtedness for bor-
> rowed money . . . secured by a mortgage, pledge, lien security
> interest or other encumbrance upon any share of capital stock of
> any Designated Subsidiary unless the Securities . . . shall be se-
> cured equally and ratably with such Debt.[26]

Negative pledge clauses are not just boiler plate material added
to indentures and loan agreements to give lawyers extra work.
They have provided additional security for debtholders when prog-
noses for corporate survival was bleak. International Harvester
Company and International Harvester Credit Company had negative pledge clauses that became operative when they secured sorely
needed bank financing.

As we have seen, corporate debt securities come with an infinite
variety of features; yet we have just scratched the surface. We will
look at many more in subsequent chapters. For now, the reader
should realize that participation in the corporate bond ring involves
careful analysis and study. Failure to do one's homework—whether
one is a trader, an investor, an investment banker, or a salesman—
may lead to disaster. While prospectuses may provide most of the

needed information, the indenture is the more important document. Read it and don't be afraid of its length and complexity.

Notes

[1] See Robert I. Landau, *Corporate Trust Administration and Management*, 3d ed. (New York, NY: Columbia University Press, 1985). This book is a good reference on corporate trust indenture trends and practices.

[2] See Thomson King, *Consolidated of Baltimore 1816-1950* (Baltimore, MD: privately published by Consolidated Gas Electric Light and Power Company of Baltimore, now Baltimore Gas and Electric Company, 1950). It says,

> On April 30, 1919, the Board of Directors approved a new bond indenture, so designed that it would in time become the first mortgage upon all the company's properties. Provision was made so that considerable future growth could be financed under the new indenture, for it provided that as much as $100,0000,000 of the bonds could be outstanding at any one time. Little did the directors realize how much the Company was to grow; in less than 30 years it became necessary to remove the $100,000,000 limitation.

[3] American Bar Foundation, *Mortgage Bond Indenture Form 1981* (Chicago, IL: American Bar Foundation, 1981).

[4] On September 28, 1984, a notice appeared in *The Wall Street Journal* addressed to the holders of BankAmerica Corporation's Money Multiplier Notes due in 1987, 1990, 1991 and 1992. The indenture trustee, The Bank of California, had issued this notice citing a conflict of interest under the indenture due to its merger with Mitsubishi Bank. Apparently, two years earlier a subsidiary of Mitsubishi Bank had acted as underwriter for an overseas offering of BankAmerica notes that were now causing the conflict under the indenture and the Trust Indenture Act. The last paragraph of the notice is interesting:

> The Bank does not intend to resign from its position as Trustee, as we feel that this development in no way impairs

our ability to perform the duties and obligations required by the Indenture. We at the bank will continue our efforts to provide the best possible service to you and will be happy to answer your questions. . . .

[5] Harold Wolfson, "Tell It to the Bondholder, Too." The *New York Times*, May 18, 1975.

[6] *Commentaries*, p. 458.

[7] Morey W. McDaniel, "Bondholders and Corporate Governance" *The Business Lawyer*, vol. 42, no. 2, (February 1986), pp. 413-460. See also Morey W. McDaniel, "Bondholders and Stockholders." *The Journal of Corporation Law*, vol. 13, no. 2, (Winter 1988), pp. 205-315. These articles review the position of bondholders in today's world of leveraged buyouts, corporate reorganizations and decapitalizations. Another interesting article is "Fiduciary Duties of Directors: How Far Do They Go?" *Wake Forest Law Review*, vol. 23 (1988), pp. 163-180. Two Delaware court decisions in 1988 reaffirmed that corporate managements and directors do not owe bondholders any fiduciary duty. In *Shenandoah Life Insurance Company* v. *Valero Energy Corporation*, the Chancery Court said that "no breach of fiduciary duty occurred because neither an issuing corporation, nor its directors, owed fiduciary duties to holders of corporate debt."—(as reported in *Delaware Corporation Law Update*, vol. 4, no. 6, (October 1988), pp. 1, 8-11. The Delaware Supreme Court found in *Simons* v. *Cogan* (No. 429, 1987, DelSupCt, 10/19/88, Lexis 328) that "the issuer of certain convertible debentures owed no fiduciary duty to a debenture holder. . . ." Further, "a debenture is a credit instrument which does not devolve upon its holder an equity interest in the issuing corporation. It is apparent that unless there are special circumstances which affect the rights of the debenture holders as creditors of the corporation, e.g., fraud, insolvency, or a violation of a statute, the rights of the debenture holders are confined to the terms of the indenture agreement pursuant to which the debentures were issued."

[8] Forrest McDonald, *Insull* (Chicago, IL: University of Chicago Press, 1962). See also Peter Furhman, "Do It Big, Sammy," *Forbes*, (July 13, 1987), p. 278.

[9] Prospectus for $30,000,000 Public Service Company of New Hampshire General and Refunding Mortgage Bonds, Series C 14½% due 2000, dated January 22, 1980.

[10] Prospectus for $125,000,000 Inland Steel Company First Mortgage 7.90% Bonds, Series R due January 15, 2007, dated January 12, 1977.

[11] "Rating 'Secured' Industrial Debt." Standard & Poor's *Credit Week*, August 16, 1982, p. 944.

[12] Prospectus for 60,000 Units Forstmann & Company, Inc., dated September 26, 1986.

[13] See Michael Downey Rice, *Railroad Equipment Obligations* (New York, NY: Salomon Brothers, 1978). This book, privately published and sponsored by the investment banking firm of Salomon Brothers, gives a good historical and legal background on the instrument. It does not, however, incorporate the effects of the Bankruptcy Reform Act of 1978, which became effective October 1, 1979.

[14] Arthur Stone Dewing, *The Financial Policy of Corporations* (New York, NY: The Ronald Press Company, 1926), p. 178.

[15] Missouri Pacific Railroad Equipment Trust Series No. 22, Equipment Trust Agreement Dated as of October 15, 1982, between Chemcial Bank Trustee and Missouri Pacific Railroad Company.

[16] Rice, *Railroad Equipment Obligations*, p. 125.

[17] *Bankruptcy Reform Act of 1978*, P.L. 95-598 (Chicago, IL: Commerce Clearing House). Section 1168 states in part,

> The right of a secured party with a purchase-money equipment security interest in, or of a lessor or conditional vendor of, whether as trustee or otherwise, rolling stock equipment or accessories used on such equipment, including superstructures and racks, that are subject to a purchase-money equipment security interest granted by, leased to, or conditionally sold to, the debtor to take possession of such equipment in compliance with the provisions of a purchase-money security agreement, lease or conditional sale contract, as the case may

be, is not affected by Section 362 or 363 of this title or by any
power of the court to enjoin such taking of possession, . . .

[18] Dewing, *The Financial Policy of Corporations*, p. 216.

[19] Richard S. Wilson, *Corporate Senior Securities* (Chicago, IL: Probus
Publishing Company, 1987), pp. 48-52.

[20] Some secured issues are not affected by Section 1110 of Federal
Bankruptcy Code and thus would be treated as any regular secured creditor. This includes issues secured by used aircraft,
engines and parts. If the airline could use the aircraft, it could
continue as a debtor-in-possession and the trustee would be
prohibited from exercising its right of repossession. The secured creditor must be given "adequate protection," but the
term has not been explicitly defined. It is generally meant to
protect the interest of the secured debtor in the collateral. This
may be accomplished by cash payments or the granting of additional security. Peoples Express Airlines, Inc., in its offering
circular and consent solicitation of October 8, 1986, explained
why its secured equipment certificates likely would not qualify
for treatment under Section 1110:

> In view of the fact that all of the aircraft were originally ac-
> quired by the Company with the proceeds of other financings,
> the Company believes that in the event of . . . seeking relief
> under the Federal Bankruptcy Code, . . . the . . . limitations on
> remedies available to the Trustee would not be affected by
> Section 1110 . . . which allows for repossession of Aircraft in
> certain instances. Accordingly, the Company does not believe
> that the Trustees will have the legal ability to realize upon the
> Aircraft collateral promptly after the institution of a bank-
> ruptcy case. Any delay in the exercise of the Trustees' legal
> remedies may adversely affect the collateral value of the Air-
> craft.

[21] Prospectus for $89,600,000 Piedmont Aviation, Inc. 1988 Equip-
ment Trust Certificates, Series D, E, F and G, dated September
23, 1988, p. 23.

[22] Ibid., p. 29.

[23] *Commentaries*, p. 350.

[24] John T. Madden and Marcus Nadler, *Foreign Securities* (New York, NY: Ronald Press Company, 1929), pp. 162, 163.

[25] Prospectus for $150,000,000 Harris Corporation 10 3/8% Debentures due 2018, dated November 29, 1988. The 5% allowance for secured debt used to be a standard indenture provision. However, with the weakening of indenture protection afforded bondholders over the last decade, this limitation has also been expanded in a number of cases. For example, Eastman Kodak Company's 9 7/8% Notes due 2004, issued in October 1988, allows secured debt up to 10% of consolidated net tangible assets. Recent issues of The May Department Stores Company permits liens to amount to up to 15% of consolidated net tangible assets; it formerly had been a 5% limitation.

[26] Prospectus for $150,000,000 *Fireman's Fund Corporation* 9 5/8% Debentures due 2016, dated October 16, 1986.

Chapter 3

MATURITY

The date stated in a bond's title may not always mean that the security will mature as specified. This chapter looks at the maturity characteristics of corporate debt, from retractable and extendible issues to bonds with puts; these features allow the holder to alter the stated maturity date. We will also look at the trend of maturities of new issues over the recent past.

What Is Maturity?

Webster's defines maturity as as being full-grown, ripe, or fully developed; or a being perfect, complete or ready.[1] While these definitions might apply to some bond market participants, we are interested in the financial definition: the coming due of a security, i.e., the termination or the end of a period of a note, debenture, bond or other obligation. A debt issue's maturity is fully set forth in the indenture and is usually part of the issue's title. For example, we might refer to "May 10 7⁄8s of '18" for The May Department Stores Company 10 7⁄8% Debentures due September 1, 2018, or the "long bond" to mean the most recently issued and longest-maturing bond of the United States Treasury. Most people assume that the issue's principal will be paid on the maturity date and interest will cease to accrue after that date. But this is not really so; the maturity is the latest date at which the principal amount will be paid. In a majority of cases (at least those of investment-grade or higher-quality issues), the maturity date probably should be taken with a grain of salt. Often the issuer can retire or redeem an issue prior to maturity (i.e., prematurely). In other cases, the bondholder can get the principal back upon request before the stated maturity date due to special features in the bond contract.

Obviously, when working with time spans we can use all sorts of measurements. The bond world usually is concerned with short-term, intermediate-term, and long-term bonds. Some use these descriptions without fully understanding what they mean; various bond market practitioners and theoreticians might give different estimates of maturity. As a starting point, let us regard any debt obligation due within one year as the equivalent of cash items. Commercial paper is in this category, since its maturity cannot be more than 270 days from the date of issuance. Also included is any debt, regardless of its original time to maturity, that is scheduled to be retired within 12 months from the date of inquiry.

One of the authors informally surveyed analysts, traders, salesmen, and bond portfolio managers in order to get their viewpoints on the time span for the maturity of bonds due beyond one year. To this select group, short-term debt meant issues with maturities of from one to five years, though several said that two years was their outside limit and one tolerated issues due up to seven years. A majority said that intermediate-term corporate debt matures within five to ten years of issuance. Some held out for 12-year issues and one even included issues with maturities as long as 15 years. Long-term bonds, then, would be those with maturities longer than those of intermediate-term issues. Some would include a category between intermediate-and long-term, but the market generally thinks in terms of only three maturity categories.

For our purposes, we will consider short-term corporate debt as that having maturities from one to five years. Intermediate-term debt is debt that matures in more than 5 years and goes out no more than 12 years. Finally, long-term debt matures in more than 12 years.

Long-Term Debt

What is considered long-term today may have been relatively short-term in another generation. Over the years investors' perceptions of bond maturity have undergone substantial changes. If one asked if any long-term bonds have been issued recently, the reply would be yes; however, using the definitions of a half century ago, the answer may have been "no," with a possible exception or two. Dewing's classic work says this about bond maturity:

> The length of their life varies greatly according to the credit market at the time of issue, the prejudices of investors, the type of security behind the bonds, and the character of the business in which the issuing corporation is engaged. A classification of periods is little more than approximate; yet such phrases as "short-term" and "long-term" have crept into the vocabulary of finance. Without holding too rigidly to the limits given, one may say that obligations which mature in less than five years are the nature of notes, meaning by note merely a short-term bond in which the safeguards described in the indenture under which they are issued refer much more to the temporary credit of the corporation than to the ostensibly permanent character of its property. Bonds which run from five to fifteen years may be conveniently designated as short-term, while those that run from fifteen to forty years may be called medium-term bonds. Those which will not mature for more than forty years should be called long-term bonds and belong to a special class because of the difficulty of projecting conceptions of property value into the distant future.[2]

Probably no corporate bond market participant today would agree with Dewing's maturity classification. There is no doubt that a bond with a maturity greater than forty years is in the long-term category, but most would take exception to Dewing's short-term and intermediate-term views.

Today's bond investors are little aware of a truly long-term bond. Yet such bonds do exist. In 1988, Swedish Export Credit Corporation issued $150 million 9 7/8% debentures maturing in 2038, the first 50-year public issue sold in the U.S. market in an untold number of years. Many investment banking firms were reluctant to participate in the offering, feeling that the market would not be receptive to such a long maturity. But the managing underwriter, along with two others, went ahead with the offering which was reported

85% sold at the end of the first day of marketing. This should be viewed as a commendable performance considering the maturity.

U.S. investors can buy a perpetual issue of Canadian Pacific Limited, listed on the New York Stock Exchange. ("Perpetual" means that the debt can be outstanding indefinitely and thus has no maturity). The issue is called 4% Perpetual Consolidated Debenture Stock. Despite the word "stock" in the title, it is debt. According to *Moody's Transportation Manual*, the debenture stock is a perpetual obligation of the Company constituting ". . . a first charge on the whole of the undertaking, railways, works, rolling stock, plant, property and effects of the company." This issue is truly perpetual as it is cannot be called or redeemed by Canadian Pacific. As it has no maturity, there can be no yield-to-maturity; current yield (the 4% interest rate divided by the market price) is the common yield measurement for this security.

In November 1986, Citicorp, the large bank holding and financial services company, sold a $500 million perpetual issue overseas. This was supposedly a first for a U.S. banking concern, although other foreign banks have sold similar undated debt securities. Citicorp can utilize the perpetuals as equity for regulatory capital purposes but as debt for Internal Revenue Service purposes. The tax authorities have viewed debt without maturity as equity and thus have not allowed interest expense to be deducted for income tax purposes. But this particular issue can be redeemed at Citicorp's option starting in 1991, at the option of the holder in 2016, and annually thereafter. On redemption in 2016 or later, however, the holder will get in exchange not cash but securities, such as common stock, perpetual preferred stock or other marketable permanent capital. This optional redemption on the holder's part apparently caused the Internal Revenue Service to view the issue as debt. In contrast to the Canadian Pacific perpetuals, the Citicorps are not thought of as truly infinite securities, since they can be redeemed by either party.

Is a perpetual security too long? Then what about the Green Bay & Western Railroad's Income Debentures? The Class "A" and Class "B" debentures are due only when the railroad is sold or reorganized! At the end of 1986 only $2,000 par amount of Series "A" debentures were outstanding out of an originally authorized $600,000. Class "B" debentures outstanding were $6,298,000 out of an authorized $7,000,000. While not perpetual issues, they come pretty close. They are interesting items in several respects. First, they are not callable. Second, the disposition of the income is quite unique. After all operating expenses have been paid, then 2 ½% of the par value will be paid on the Class "A" debentures and then 2 ½% on the common stock (based on $100 par value). The two securities will then share, on a pro rata basis, up to an additional 2 ½% (5% in total). Any excess earnings may be declared and distributed to the holders of the Series "B" debentures with no limitation upon the directors' approval. This is a case of a debenture that ranks behind common stock in the disposition of earnings and yet can receive a payment limited only by earnings and management's discretion. But of course, management is elected by the common shareholders, and they have the final say.

Between 1904 and 1934, payments on the "A" debentures and stock were between 2 ½% and 5%; in 1935 they were 2 ½% on the debentures and 1% on the stock; in 1936 and 1937, both issues received a payment of 7 ½%; nothing was paid in 1938; and 5% was paid on both securities from 1939 to 1978, the latest years for which payment information is available. As the Class "B" income debenture payments come from what is left over and also must be declared by management, they have been relatively meager, ranging from zero in 1921, 1932 to 1936, 1938 and 1939, 1946 to 1948, 1950, 1953, 1955, and 1961 to 3% in 1965. *Moody's Transportation Manual* for 1988 says that payments in the 1970s were 2% for 1970 to 1972, ¼% for 1973, 1% for 1974, ¾% for 1975, and ½% for 1976, the latest recorded payment.

The Class "A" debentures and the common stock share equally in liquidation on a pro rata basis up to their par value. Also, upon the sale of the railroad, 75% of the stockholders must agree to accept the par value ($100 per share) for their stock. Any remaining balance of liquidation proceeds go to the Class "B" debenture holders.[3] The capital structure has been described as the "English recapitalization" and "a railroad which cannot be placed in receivership or undergo financial difficulty as long as it can earn enough to pay its operating expenses."[4] Finally, the following poem (attributed to S. C. Barnett, a reporter from the Green Bay Press-Gazette) has been written about the Series "B" debentures:

THE SONG OF THE B'S

By Homer

I've classed among my foolish ventures
My purchase of Class B: debentures;
Those bonds which say in language deft,
"With all else paid, you get what's left,
(Unless the Board makes declaration
It's needed for depreciation!)"

But once in many years, I find
The gloomy cloud is silver-lined;
The long-dead-ghost perambulates,
The eagle sh——er defecates,
And there I see, upon my desk
A Winthrop letter, labeled "Esq."

I feel a kinship, quite complete,
With mighty figures of "The Street:"
The railroads' thundering symphony
Is earning dough for them—and me!
And midst its tones, like some great organ,
I'm one with Vanderbilt and Morgan!

I've got my bonds, I'm glad I've held'em,
But payments STILL are goddam seldom![5]

For investors who feel more confident with a definite maturity, financial history provides a few examples. Still outstanding and paying are the 4% First Mortgage Gold Bonds of the Toronto, Grey & Bruce Railway Company dated January 1, 1884, and maturing June 14, 2883. The bonds come only in coupon form in denominations of £100 sterling. The coupons (40 to a sheet and enough for 20 years) are payable in Montreal (in Canadian dollars, as payments in gold are restricted) or London (in sterling). According to *Moody's Transportation Manual*, the company's properties were leased to the Ontario & Quebec Railway Company for 999 years at an annual rental equal to interest on 4% first mortgage bonds. On January 1, 1884, the lease was transferred to the Canadian Pacific Railway Company, now Canadian Pacific Limited. The bonds are truly long-term as they are not callable for life. Canadian Pacific said that of the £719,000 outstanding, it owns £307,900.[6]

Of a somewhat shorter maturity (but at least of a U.S. company) are the Elmira and Williamsport Railroad Company's 5% Income Bonds due October 1, 2862. The bonds were guaranteed as to interest by the Northern Central Railway but were assumed by the Pennsylvania Railroad Company in 1914 for 999 years from 1863, and eventually became an obligation of the Penn Central Transportation Company. While not subject to call, the bonds were paid in full ($1,468 representing principal and accrued and unpaid interest) in late 1978 upon the reorganization of Penn Central.

Another relatively long bond also involved in the Penn Central reorganization is the West Shore Railroad Company's 4% First Mortgage Bonds due January 1, 2361. The noncallable bonds were issued in 1886, guaranteed by the New York Central and Harlem River Rail Road Company, and eventually assumed by Penn Central on February 1, 1968. The lien was on 306 miles of track from Weehawken, New Jersey to Buffalo, New York, a historic line dating back to early American railroading. Penn Central's reorganization plan provided that each $1,000 principal amount of West Shore 4s receive $140 in cash, $131 principal amount of Penn Central Corporation's 7% Series "A" General Mortgage Bonds due 1987, $265 principal amount of Series "B" Bonds due 1987, 19.8 shares of Series "B" Convertible Preference Stock, and 8.92 shares of common stock.

The Decline of the Long-Term Bond Market

Today one will find few real long-term bonds such as the above. Certainly, an occasional issuer such as the Swedish Export Credit Corporation may attempt an offering but American corporations probably will not be among them. Even the aforementioned Citicorp perpetual can be called. In 1985 one major business publication said, "The long-term corporate bond is beginning to look like an endangered species. . . . The mainstay of the credit markets only ten years ago, fixed-rate issues with maturities of twenty years or more shrank . . . and shriveled. . . . The long-term fixed rate sector is now speculative and not a financing market. . . ."[7] The decline is attributed to many factors, including the high inflation and soaring interest costs of the seventies which wrought havoc on the values of long-term debt instruments. Investors wanted instruments of shorter maturity. For example, insurance companies changed emphasis from the traditional whole-life policy with its focus on the long-term investment of reserves and the buildup of cash values to the more short-term-oriented term life and other policies designed more for pure insurance purposes than for savings and investment.

Companies used to finance their long-term assets with long-term debt and short-term assets, such as receivables and inventories, with commercial paper and bank loans. If they borrowed long, they invested long; if they borrowed short, they invested short. In effect, corporate financial officers would try to match the maturity their assets with their liabilities. If they borrowed short and invested long, they could face a crisis at maturity. They might not have the liquid assets available to pay the loan when due, and refinancing might be very difficult due to adverse market conditions. A well-run and structured corporation with sound practices and financial policies will seldom face a crisis at maturity, as it will have managed its cash flow carefully and in accordance with solid principles.

One way to look at asset life is in terms of a company's depreciation policies. The lower the depreciation as a percentage of gross plant, the longer the assets' book lives. Most new-issue debt of the Bell Telephone system, both before and after the divestiture, typically has had 40-year maturities. Of course, depreciation measurements may not tell the whole story. If the plant has been under-depreciated due to obsolescence, the debt's maturity may not match the asset's life. In the telephone industry, copper wire may last for 40 or more years—but with fiber optic cable available, will it continue to be used? Is the copper wire today worth what it is carried at in the company's financials? Perhaps telephone debt should have shorter maturities more closely matching asset life in this age of technological change.

If a company's long-term growth prospects are good, lenders may be more willing to lend to it on a longer-term basis. However, the decadent decade of the seventies with stagflation and low-to-no-growth attitudes of many public officials and big business leaders contributed to the shortening of investors' maturity preferences. Even if borrowers would be better served by longer-term loans, it is investor demand that must be satisfied if financing is to be obtained at relatively reasonable cost.

With our society's great emphasis on the short-term—ranging from debt financing to managing corporate income statements for quarterly results to youngsters with newly minted degrees but without a good foundation in the basics of business and ethics wanting to become overnight millionaires—it is no wonder that government leaders and major businesses have failed to provide the inspiration needed for America's premier place in the world. The deficit is always going to be cured in the next few years. New laws will shortly lead to a better life (but will botch things up in the long run). The general attitude is "What are you doing for me right now? Let's get ours while we can." While people want action, what is needed is thought. Companies cannot adequately plan for the future if they must constantly be concerned with rolling over maturing debt. This short-term viewpoint does little to improve the soundness of one's bond investment.

Recent Changes

The 1970s witnessed many changes in the maturity characteristics of corporate bonds. In many cases, the stated maturity was shortened to suit the investors' needs. In others, the effective maturity of the bond could be shortened or retracted by the investor or the issuer. Still others permitted the parties to lengthen or extend the maturity.

There are few truly extendible bonds in the marketplace, i.e., issues whose maturities may be extended at the issuer's option. Most investors would not buy bonds which give the issuer the sole right to lengthen the maturity unless they got something in return. The few bonds have been mostly issued by speculative grade companies such as Turner Broadcasting and Texas Air Corporation. For example, Texas Air's Senior Increasing Rate Extendible Notes provide for their maturity on each interest payment date commencing August 15, 1986, unless the company extends the maturity to the next interest payment date. Issued in February 1986 with an initial interest rate of 12.50%, the rate is increased by 50 basis points per quarter during the first year (payments due on the 15th of May, August, November, 1986, and February 1987), and by 25 basis points per quarter starting May 15, 1987. However, the final maturity can be no later than February 15, 1991.

The increase in the coupon rate is the extra consideration Texas Air pays for the right to extend maturity; the investor is getting something in return. However, since this can be pretty expensive money, Texas Air has the right to pay off the whole issue on any maturity date, extend the whole issue's maturity to the next interest payment date, or extend only part of the issue and redeem the balance of the bonds at the early maturity date. The minimum amount of bonds whose maturity may be extended is $25 million. The scheduled interest rate would be 14 ½% for the quarter starting February 15, 1987, rising to 15 ½% on February 15, 1988 and finally to 18 ¼% for the quarter starting November 15, 1990, and payable February 15, 1991. Turner Broadcasting has only extended the maturity on part of its increasing rate extendible notes, redeeming a large portion at the maturity dates in late 1986.

Bonds with Puts

Most bonds with "extendible" (or "extendable") in their titles are considered mislabeled by some; they should be called retractable bonds, since the issuer has the right to shorten the maturity from that stated. This is, in effect, an exercise of the company's right to call the bonds. Many variable-rate issues give the company the right to call the bonds at a number of dates prior to the final maturity. For example, The CIT Group Holdings, Inc. has an extendible note issue with a final maturity of March 28, 1996. The coupon is 7 ⅝% to March 28, 1990, at which date CIT may redeem the bonds (retraction of maturity) or determine a new interest rate, interest period and redemption terms. This latter action is generally referred to as extending the maturity. But the terminology is not really all that important as what is retractable to one is extendible to the other.

This bond has another interesting feature, one that was not often used until the mid-seventies—a put. This provision gives the investor the option to either ask for repayment on a certain date(s) prior to the stated maturity or to hold the bond to either the next put date (if any) or maturity. In the case of the above CIT issue, the holder has the right to put the notes back to the issuer on March 28, 1990 (the date at which the new interest rate and terms would commence), or to hold them until the next put date when the opportunity for redemption occurs once again. This option is not a separate instrument but embedded in the bond contract itself. The valuation of embedded options is discussed in Section II.

In most cases, bond investors are at the issuer's mercy. They have loaned money for what they expect to be a certain number of years, but this period could very well be shortened if the issuer decides to call the bonds. A call or premature redemption often occurs when the situation is advantageous for the borrower and less attractive for the lender, namely in periods of lower interest rates when the lender would have to reinvest the proceeds at yields that more than likely would reduce the overall rate of return (or at least the promised rate of return at the time of the initial investment). Chapter 8 will discuss price compression of higher coupon bonds in a lower interest rate environment. In periods of high interest rates when bond prices are depressed, few issuers have any interest in retiring their debt. However, holders of optional maturity bonds or bonds with puts can turn the tables in their favor. If the coupon rate is below the going market rate, investors need not hold the debt until maturity or even sell it in the market place; they can turn it back to the issuer for repayment at the principal amount and reinvest the proceeds in a security having a current market interest rate. The issuer will usually cancel the repurchased bonds but some issues provide for a remarketing of the put bonds through an investment banker to other investors.

The right to put the bonds back to the issuer is an important option which the bondholder should not forget. Bondholders should be aware of the period during which the issuer or trustee must be notified. If the notification is not properly given, the holders will continue to own the bonds, which could be to their detriment. Besides a loss in value, they could be left owning a much less marketable security. Generally, the put option, once exercised, cannot be revoked. But there are some cases of floating rate notes which provide that if the interest coupon is increased after bonds have been put but prior to the effective put date, the holder may revoke the put request and have the bonds returned. The lead time for notifi-

cation varies from as few as four to fifteen days before the put date
to as long as six to eight months.

The importance of heeding the put date cannot be overstressed.
For example, in 1979 Beneficial Corporation sold $250 million of
debentures with a coupon of 11 ½% to January 15, 1984, and 9%
thereafter to maturity on January 15, 2005. The put notification period was from September 15 through October 14, 1983. The bonds
were worth close to par at that time as they could be redeemed on
January 15, 1984. However, for those who did not exercise the put
the market price plunged; a few investors were left holding a now
9% note due in 21 years. The 9% notes traded at about 71 in late
1984—quite a penalty for negligence. Less than $6.5 million are out-
standing.

Put Bonds with a Morbid Touch

Some put provisions have certain restrictions on the holder's right
of redemption. For example, a few issues provide that not more
than a certain amount of bonds will be repurchased from any
holder at any one put date. In addition, there may be an aggregate
limitation on the total amount of bonds which may be redeemed at
any one time. CP National Corporation's 15 ¼% Debentures due
1997 provide for an annual put subject to not more than $25,000
principal amount from any debentureholder and not more than
$500,000 principal amount in aggregate.

Some issues have a death redemption benefit; to enjoy this put
you have to be deceased! The legal representative of a deceased
holder or the surviving joint tenant may tender their bonds to the
issuer for redemption. In some cases these puts have priority over
the requests of living debtholders. In the case of The Cato Corporation 10 ½% Subordinated Debentures due 1996, the death benefit is
only applicable to the initial beneficial owner of the debentures. The
death benefit provisions are mostly found in smaller issues which
have generally been underwritten by regional and local investment
banking firms. It can provide an estate with a market for the bonds
which might otherwise be difficult to sell.

Poison Puts

About 1986, in reaction to the increased activity of corporate raiders and mergers and acquisitions, some companies incorporated "poison puts" in their indentures. These were designed to thwart unfriendly takeovers by making the company proposed to be acquired unpalatable to the acquirer. All too often in recent years companies have been taken over or substantially restructured and debt substantially increased with the result that the bond ratings get lowered and bond prices decline. The common shareholder might come out all right but the bondholders do not. Bondholders consider this an unfair transfer of wealth from one class of investors to another.

Basically, poison put provisions may not deter a proposed acquisition but could make it more expensive. In addition, uncertainty is increased as the put payment is not made, in most cases, until 100 days after the change in control occurs. Thus, the management has no way of knowing exactly how many bonds will be tendered for redemption. Of course, if the board of directors approves the change in control, i.e., it is a "friendly" transaction (and all takeovers are friendly if the price is right), the poison put provisions would not become effective. The designated event of change in control generally means either that continuing directors no longer constitute a majority of the board of directors or that a person, including affiliates, becomes the beneficial owner, directly or indirectly, of stock with at least 20% of the voting rights. In a couple of cases (such as in ITT Corporation's 7 7/8% Notes due 1993 and Kerr-McGee Corporation's 9 3/4% Debentures due 2016) a rating change is also part of the requirement to set the put in motion.

The prospectus for ICN Pharmaceuticals, Inc. Debenture offering commented on the Change-in-Control Put as follows:

> The Change-in-Control Put may deter certain mergers, tender offers or other present or future takeover attempts and may thereby adversely affect the market price of the Common Stock. Since a Change-in-Control Put may deter takeovers where the person attempting the takeover views itself as unable to finance

the repurchase of the principal amount of Debentures which may be delivered to the Company for repurchase upon occurrence of such Change-in-Control. To the extent that the Debentures are repurchased pursuant to the Change-in-Control Put, the Company will be unable to utilize the financing provided by the sale of the Debentures. In addition, the ability of the Company to obtain additional Senior Debt based on the existence of the Debentures may be similarly adversely affected.[8]

These poison puts lacked teeth and in 1988 investors got particularly upset at the continuing activity in corporate restructurings. It was the leveraged buyout of RJR Nabisco Inc. that was "the straw which broke the camel's back." The whole industrial bond market was affected as bond buyers withdrew from the market and new issues postponed. Trading of industrials in the secondary market nearly came to a standstill as prospectuses and indentures were checked and rechecked for protective covenants. Bond analysts sharpened their pencils and did event risk studies to try to identify companies which appeared vulnerable for some type of restructuring. Investors demanded better covenants in public issues and, in some cases, got them. New poison put language was developed and incorporated in the new indentures. Essentially, if both a designated event and a rating downgrade to below investment grade occur within a certain period, the company is obligated to repurchase the bonds at par. It does not matter if the takeover is friendly or hostile. One issue provided that if the market value of the debentures was less than par due to the event and rating downgrade, it could elect to redeem all of the issue at par. If it failed to redeem the bonds, it would have to reset the interest rate to such a level which would have resulted in the bonds being worth par on the day after the downgrading date.[9]

Medium-Term Notes

Medium-term notes (MTNs) are new-issue debt instruments offered continuously over an extended period of time. An extension of commercial paper issuance, maturities normally range from nine months to 15 years, although some may be as short as six months. In recent years an increasing number of programs have set the maximum maturity at 30 years. From 1972 to 1982, the major captive automobile finance companies accounted for most of the issuance and offered their medium-term notes directly to the public. But with the advent of shelf registrations by the Securities and Exchange Commission and Rule 415 which provides the issuer of public securities considerably more flexibility than before, medium-term note programs took on a new life. Issuers made arrangements with the major Wall Street investment banking firms to market their medium-term notes as agents of the issuer on a best efforts or a reasonable efforts basis.[10] In addition, in order to broaden the market for the securities, investment bankers make a secondary market in the MTNs of the issuers for which they act as agent. Providing increased liquidity and needed marketability, this gives investors another outlet for their MTN investments in case circumstances change since they would no longer be locked-in until maturity.

Accurate figures on the outstanding volume of MTNs is not available but at the end of 1988 it probably was in excess of $100 billion. Growth was particularly strong in 1987 and 1988 with the trade publication *Investment Dealers' Digest* (IDD) reporting that new domestic programs more than doubled from $40.2 billion to $81.3 billion in 1988. According to one observer, the growth of MTNs came at the expense of commercial banks and their term loans. The cost to the issuer is often less than term loans at many banks. "Many large corporate borrowers have as good or better credit ratings than all but a very few of the banks lending in this market. Moreover, for large borrowers the banks no longer have any special expertise in assessing the creditworthiness of potential borrowers. Much of the relevant information is public and readily available to any potential investor."[11] The cost to the issuer of MTNs is generally less than with a conventional note issue. Agents' commissions typically range from .125% to .75% of the principal amount, depending on the maturity of the note. Costs of conventionally underwritten debt issues can run higher.

An issuer with an active MTN program will post the rates for the maturity ranges that it wishes to sell. Generally, the maturity ranges might be from nine months to one year, from one year to 18 months, from 18 months to two years, and then annually out to the final maturity date. Depending on the issuer, the note may have a fixed rate or a variable rate. Fixed rate interest payments are typically on a semiannual basis with the same interest payment dates applicable to all of the notes of a particular series of an issuer. Of course, the final interest payment is made at maturity. Interest on floating rate and variable rate MTNs may have more frequent interest payments. If the interest rate market is volatile, posted rates may change, sometimes more than once a day. The notes are priced at par which appeals to many investors; they don't have to be concerned about amortizing premiums and the accretion of discounts. Any change in new rates will not affect the rates on previously issued notes.

The purchaser may usually set the maturity as any business day within the offered maturity range, subject to the borrower's approval. This is a very important benefit of MTNs as it enables a lender to match maturities with its own specific requirements. As they are continuously offered, an investor can enter the market when his needs require and will usually find suitable investment opportunities. With underwritten issues, the available supply, both in the new issue and secondary markets, might not be entirely satisfactory for the portfolio's needs. A particular series of medium-term notes may have many different maturities but all will be issued under the same indenture. The bulk of the notes sold have maturities of less than five years with the two to three year range the most preferred. The notes generally are noncallable for life, although some issuers have leeway to add redemption features to unsold notes.

The initial issuers were the automobile finance companies needing vast sums of medium-term funds in order to finance car sales. Soon other consumer and commercial finance companies entered the market as they found it a good area in which they could immediately get funds in a specific amount and maturity. Banks and bank holding companies and thrift institutions have also borrowed through medium-term notes. According to IDD, financial institutions in 1988 accounted for approximately 70% of the new programs, industrial companies 17%, sovereigns, their agencies and international lending organizations some 10%, and utility and others the remaining 3%.

The medium-term note market is primarily institutional with individual investors being of little import for a couple of reasons. For one, the majority of issues require a minimum purchase of $100,000. Also, commissions on MTNs are less than on many other competing investments and individual salesmen would more than likely steer their clients to investments which are more rewarding to their pocketbooks. Banks and bank trust departments are the biggest holders of MTNs, followed by thrift institutions, insurance companies and nonfinancial corporations. Commercial banks and thrifts have used medium-term notes as part of their arbitrage activities. They might borrow in Europe or get funds through term certificates of deposit and reinvest the monies in higher yielding MTNs with similar maturities, taking the spread between the two instruments. Of course, if they needed funds to meet increased loan demand, the MTN secondary market provides an outlet.

Not all medium-term notes are sold on an agency basis; some have been underwritten. C.I.T. Financial Corporation issued $200,000,000 of 8% Medium-Term Notes due March 1, 1989, at a discount price of 99.875% on February 27, 1986. A few weeks later through a different set of underwriters, it issued $100,000,000 of 7.75% notes due April 15, 1993. These notes are redeemable at the issuer's option on and after April 15, 1991. Equitable Life Leasing Corporation sold 12.62% Medium-Term Notes with a final maturity of November 1, 1988. This issue is interesting in that the Company makes level monthly payments representing interest and principal repayment. Equitable has also issued serial medium-term notes with each series maturing every six months. Finally, United States Steel Corporation sold 9% Intermediate-Term Notes due in 1992.

Maturity Distribution in the Corporate Bond Market

Over the years there have been a number of studies on the maturity distribution of the bond market. Of major importance is the work of Hickman covering most of the first half of this century.[12] Table 3–1 is condensed from his study. Note that well over 50% of the outstanding corporate debt at the turn of the century had maturities longer than 30 years. About $3.5 billion out of the total of $5.9 billion matured after 1930 with nearly 23% due in more than 50 years. There were 96 issues amounting to $1,214.7 million due in 1975 and beyond but the bulk of these consisted of railroad debt. By 1916, debt maturing in more than 30 years amounted to 43% of the total outstandings. In 1928, it was 25%, in 1936 about 26%, and in 1944 around 17%. (Hickman's study does not go beyond 1944.) Much of this decline in the extreme long-term outstandings has been more than likely due to the extinguishment of debt through bankruptcy and reorganization.

Over the 1900 to 1943 period, the number of issues and par amount of super long-term offerings (30 years and longer) declined. In the 1900 to 1907 period, Hickman tabulated 1,692 new super long-term issues with a par value of $4,090.1 million. The length of maturity of new offerings generally declined in importance over each succeeding period (the exception being 1924 to 1931). In 1940 to 1943, only 6.35% of the issues offered were 30 years or longer in maturity. This amounted to $674.7 million or a touch more than 11% of the total par amount offered. The five years in the 1900 to 1943 period with the greatest volume of these super long-term issues are shown in Table 3–2. Table 3–3 presents the par amount of offerings classified by term to maturity.

Maturity Composition of Today's Corporate Bond Market

The average maturity of the outstanding investment grade corporate bond has declined over the past decade (see Table 3–4). The Merrill Lynch Taxable Bond Index, Corporate Master, which includes all investment grade corporate issues with $10 million or more outstanding, had an average maturity of 20.08 years at the end of 1974. This has steadily declined to under 19 years at the end of 1978, under 18 years at the end of 1981, less than 16 years at the end of 1983 and 14 ¼ years at year end 1987. The average maturity approximated 13 years and seven months at December 31, 1988. The average maturity of new issue investment grade corporate issues declined as interest rates rose into the double-digit area starting in 1979. The low point was reached in 1984 when maturity averaged only 9.87 years.

Table 3–5 shows the breakdown of investment-grade new issue volume by maturity classification. Through 1980 long-term issues

Table 3–1 Outstanding Issues Classified by Term to Maturity: 1900 to 1944
($ million/% of total)

Year	Total Outstanding	Over 1, to 5 Years	Over 5, to 15 Years	Over 15, to 30 Years	Over 30, to 50 Years	Over 50 Years
1900	$5,882.7	$252.3	$775.0	$1,388.6	$2,149.5	$1,337.3
		4.29%	12.83%	23.62%	36.54%	22.73%
1916	$15,957.1	$1,116.8	$3,030.4	$4,949.8	$4,909.9	$1,950.2
		7.00%	18.99%	31.02%	30.77%	12.22%
1928	$25,352.0	$2,209.2	$6,110.9	$10,643.0	$3,853.6	$2,535.3
		8.71%	24.10%	41.98%	15.20%	10.01%
1936	$22,081.9	$1,376.3	$6,059.8	$8,941.1	$3,198.4	$2,506.3
		6.23%	27.44%	40.49%	14.48%	11.36%
1944	$19,687.0	$1,140.0	$5,092.3	$10,028.8	$1,538.5	$1,895.4
		5.79%	25.87%	50.90%	7.82%	9.63%

Note: Excludes issues due within one year and those for which information is lacking. Data are for January 1.
Source: W. Braddock Hickman, *Statistical Measures of Corporate Bond Financing Since 1900* (Princeton, NJ: Princeton University Press, 1960), Table 40.

(maturities of 12 or more years) constituted over half of the volume. Short-term debt was insignificant with less than 10% of the volume for any year prior to 1982. In that year short-term offerings increased substantially, rising to 21.48% of the investment grade offerings. In 1984 long-term new issues were only a mere 14.39% of all investment grade corporates. It should be noted that in our calculations, if an issue has a put exercisable at the option of the holder, the maturity is considered to be the first put date, not the nominal stated maturity. Also, medium term note offerings under a best efforts basis are not included in our figures.

Table 3–6 indicates the average maturity for new-issue investment-grade offerings by industry classification. The industry with the longest maturity debt on average is telecommunications, although, as far as new issues are concerned, it lost that status in 1988. Bell System issuers have traditionally used relatively long-term bonds in their financing activities with maturities up to forty years. Electric utilities have also been among the issuers of long maturity debt in the 30 to 35 year range. But investor demand for shorter maturities even affected the utility industries. In 1981 the average new telephone and electric issue was of considerably shorter maturity than several years prior. Industrial companies, another traditional user of long-term funds, had to shorten the maturities of their new-issue offerings. The average maturity has come down from slightly under 20 years in 1974 to 11.79 years in 1988. The average maturity of bank and thrift issues has fallen by more than half from 17.87 years in 1974 to 6.58 years in 1988. Finance company issues have also experienced a sharp reduction in average maturity, especially since 1978. Is this new-issue trend because investors want shorter maturity issues due to the difficulties these financial institutions have faced in the eighties? Are investors concerned about the quality of the loans held by these lenders? After all, consumer loans to residents of troubled areas, loans to over-extended farmers, borrowings by third world nations which will never have the capacity nor the character to repay, and loans for corporate decapitalizations may give investors good reason to avoid the long end of the market. Are these investors thinking that a shorter maturity may provide them greater protection and peace of mind than a longer issue in the case of a troubled thrift or bank?

**Table 3–2 Top Volume Years for Super Long-Term Offerings:
1900 to 1943 (Par Amount, $ millions)**

Over 30, to 50 Years		Over 50, to 75 Years		Over 75 Years	
1927	$1,111.5	1903	$173.9	1922	$219.8
1928	902.8	1939	158.1	1930	125.3
1901	854.4	1936	106.6	1900	107.8
1931	770.3	1924	105.1	1915	101.5
1930	767.2	1930	88.3	1902	100.3

Source: W. Braddock Hickman, *Statistical Measures of Corporate Bond Financing
Since 1900* (Princeton, NJ: Princeton University Press, 1960), Table 94.

Part of the answer is yes, but new-issue maturity in other industry classifications has also decreased. The rest of the answer is that portfolio managers want reduced bond price volatility which can be obtained in shorter-dated issues. The effect of maturity on price volatility is explained in Section II.

Investors seeking refuge in a shorter maturity of a troubled issuer should not receive much comfort. The shorter maturity structure of corporate debt over the past decade increases pressures on corporate financial managers. The more frequent refinancings needed to replace a heavier volume of maturing debt also adds to management's burden and to the pressures and distortions in the bond market. More of a corporation's cash flow may have to be directed away from potentially profitable investments, research and development activities to the repayment of obligations as they become due. We have often heard corporations and other borrowers say that while their assets exceed their liabilities, they are in a temporary cash bind because of maturing debt obligations.

Table 3-3 Par Amount of Offerings Classified by Term to Maturity: 1900 to 1943 ($ millions / % of total)

Period of Offerings	Total	Over 1, to 5 Years	Over 5, to 15 Years	Over 15, to 30 Years	Over 30, to 50 Years	Over 50 Years
1900-1907	$8,592.5	$659.1 7.67%	$726.9 8.46%	$3,116.4 36.27%	$3,270.2 38.06%	$819.9 9.54%
1908-1915	$9,249.1	$1,510.4 16.33%	$918.0 9.93%	$3,651.8 39.48%	$2,536.7 27.43%	$632.2 6.83%
1916-1923	$12,138.0	$2,076.0 17.10%	$3,594.6 29.61%	$4,676.7 38.53%	$1,263.1 10.41%	$527.6 4.53%
1924-1931	$20,764.7	$1,565.0 7.53%	$4,059.0 19.55%	$9,415.7 45.35%	$4,873.6 23.47%	$850.5 4.10%
1932-1939	$13,533.0	$610.1 4.51%	$3,793.3 28.03%	$7,888.1 58.29%	$840.9 6.21%	$400.6 2.96%
1940-1943	$6,115.5	$55.3 0.91%	$1,600.4 26.17%	$3,785.1 61.89%	$494.9 8.09%	$179.8 2.94%
1900-1943	$70,392.8	$6,475.9 9.20%	$14,693.1% 20.87%	$32,533.8 46.22%	$13,279.4 18.87%	$3,410.6 4.48%

Source: W. Braddock Hickman, *Statistical Measures of Corporate Bond Financing Since 1900* (Princeton, NJ: Princeton University Press, 1960), Table 94.

Table 3-4 Average Maturity of Investment-Grade Corporate Bonds (Years)

Year	Merrill Lynch Corporate Master Index	New Issues	Moody's Composite Corporate Bond Average
1988	13.57	11.05	10.18%
1987	14.27	12.54	9.91
1986	15.00	15.79	9.71
1985	15.08	12.86	12.05
1984	15.50	9.87	13.49
1983	15.83	15.37	12.78
1982	17.42	12.90	14.94
1981	17.55	15.70	15.06
1980	18.16	18.42	12.75
1979	18.23	22.01	10.12
1978	18.52	23.10	9.07
1977	18.72	22.83	8.43
1976	18.80	20.39	9.01
1975	19.07	17.99	9.57
1974	20.08	19.93	9.03

1988 average maturity for speculative grade debt, 10.34 years
1987 average maturity for speculative grade debt, 10.42 years.
1986 average maturity for speculative grade debt, 11.33 years.

Table 3–5 Percentage Distribution of Volume—New Issue Investment-Grade Corporate Offerings by Maturity Classification

Year	Short-Term 1-5 Years	Intermediate-Term > 5 and < 12 Years	Long-Term > 12 Years
1988	39.67%	37.34%	22.99%
1987	32.35	40.00	27.65
1986	22.65	34.51	42.84
1985	30.26	38.34	31.40
1984	42.74	42.87	14.39
1983	28.00	31.55	40.45
1982	21.48	45.80	32.72
1981	7.02	51.01	41.97
1980	8.98	38.90	52.12
1979	2.78	25.27	71.95
1978	8.75	23.71	67.54
1977	6.39	14.70	78.91
1976	7.34	26.36	66.40
1975	1.73	41.80	56.47
1974	5.64	28.18	66.18

Table 3–6 Average Maturity of Corporate New Issues by Industry Classification All Rating Categories (Selected Years)

Industry	1988	1987	1986	1985	1981	1978	1974
Telephone	16.00	23.60	27.54	29.35	26.50	37.24	31.87
Electric	18.55	19.14	21.91	23.60	16.87	25.49	20.39
Gas and Water	15.68	14.82	19.77	12.44	12.81	17.77	16.00
Industrials	11.70	14.26	15.56	14.25	17.79	19.79	19.87
Finance	7.52	7.32	8.26	6.41	11.55	16.82	10.48
Banks & Thrifts	6.58	8.34	7.57	8.21	6.38	15.87	17.87
Transportation	11.21	16.43	16.18	15.29	17.28	18.00	19.85
International	15.12	13.87	19.38	12.72	11.35	17.83	22.69

Notes

[1] *Webster's New Universal Unabridged Dictionary*, 2d ed. (New York, NY: Dorset & Baber, 1983).

[2] Arthur Stone Dewing, *The Financial Policy of Corporations* (New York, NY: The Ronald Press Company, 1941), p. 180.

[3] In addition to the description of the issues in *Moody's Transportation Manual*, see Ray Specht and Ellen Specht, *The Story of the Green Bay and Western*, Bulletin 115, October 1966, The Railway and Locomotive Historical Society.

[4] Ibid, 28.

[5] Ibid, 29.

[6] Letter to one of the authors, March 24, 1981. These bonds are listed on the London Stock Exchange and are also quoted in Glasgow.

[7] Elizabeth Kaplan, "The Waning of the Long-Term Bond." *Dun's Business Month* (June 1985), pp. 40-42.

[8] Prospectus for $100,000,000 ICN Pharmaceuticals, Inc. 12 7/8% Sinking Fund Debentures due July 15, 1998, dated July 17, 1986.

[9] Moody's Investors Service issued two interesting special comments on the topic of event risk. These are "Indenture Protection and Event Risk," November 18, 1988, and "Event Risk: Moody's Amplified Its Views on Indenture Protection Issues," January 5, 1989.

[10] Some prospectuses of issues contain wording such as "The Notes are being offered on a continuing basis by the Company through [the agents] who have agreed to use their best efforts to solicit purchasers of the Notes." Others may have slightly different phraseology such as "Offers to purchase the Notes are being solicited, on a reasonable efforts basis (or on a reasonable best efforts basis), from time to time by the Agents on behalf of the Company. Is a best-efforts basis better than a reasonable (best) efforts basis?

[11] Ben Weberman. "Watching $40 Billion Walk Out the Door." *Forbes* (October 20, 1986), pp. 33-34.

[12] W. Braddock Hickman, *Statistical Measures of Corporate Bond Financing Since 1900* (Princeton, NJ: Princeton University Press, 1960).

Chapter 4

INTEREST PAYMENTS

A main factor affecting a bond's value is the nature of the coupon or interest payments. This chapter reviews the many variations of interest payments ranging from zero and nominal interest rates to those which fluctuate periodically based on an index or other measurement. The effect of interest payments on the price, yield and price volatility of a bond is covered in greater detail in Section II.

General Characteristics

Investors lend money and in return they expect to receive some form of consideration, usually periodic payments in the form of interest, for the use of that money. The most common form of interest rate is one which is set for the life of the issue, the so-called straight or fixed coupon. Since the early seventies the floating rate or variable coupon bond has attracted increased investor demand. These bonds, where the interest rate fluctuates over the life of the issue, are more fully described below. Sometimes the debt instrument provides for no periodic payment of interest at all but a lump sum payment at maturity; thus the zero coupon issue. Bond market convention calls these payments coupons even though all bonds now sold in the United States are in registered form. Interest payment or interest rate would be the more accurate terminology. Coupon, of course, comes from years ago when bonds were old with coupons attached representing the interest payments to be made over their lives. So when you hear a trader ask "What's the coupon on that bond?" take it to mean "What is the interest rate?"

Timing of Interest Payments

Most debt issues sold in the United States provide for the payment of interest twice a year at six month intervals. If the interest rate on a bond is 10%, then each $1,000 bond will have two payments of $50 each every year. In the case of medium-term notes, interest is paid semi-annually and at maturity if the maturity date does not coincide with the interest payment date; this is called a "short coupon." Another type of short coupon is found on some new issues where the interest might accrue from the date the trade settles, that is, the date payment is made by the purchaser to the underwriter. For example, if a new issue is sold with a settlement date of September 15 but with interest payment dates of March 1 and September 1, the price of the bond may not include interest from September 1. In this case, the first interest payment on March 1 will represent interest on the use of the money for 5 ½ months. If the offering terms call for the purchaser to pay the offering price plus accrued interest from September 1 until the settlement date of the transaction, then the first interest payment due on March 1 will be a full coupon payment.

If this bond were sold in August and settled on August 27, then the first interest payment would be called a "long coupon" as it would be for slightly more than six months' interest. An example of a long coupon is found in Younkers, Inc. 9.35% Bonds due September 1, 1994. The bonds were sold in August 1987 with delivery to purchasers on August 27th. Interest is payable monthly starting with the October 1, 1987, payment. While each subsequent payment represents one month's interest, the first payment was for 35 days from August 27, the date from which interest began to accrue (also known as the "dated date").

Thus, semi-annual payments may be each January and July 1, or March and September 15. In many bond publications these would be abbreviated as J&J1 and M&S15. The first or the fifteenth of the month are the more common interest payment dates although there are a number of issues which pay at the end of the month or some other odd date. For example, John Deere Crèdit Company has several fixed-rate issues with interest payments due on April 30 and October 31, and a subordinated note paying on May and November 1. Illinois Bell Telephone has several debenture issues with interest payments dates such as J&D10, F&A18, and A&O22.

Bonds with only one interest payment a year (annual coupons) are the norm for issues in the overseas markets but they are seldom issued in the United States. However, this does not mean that they don't exist. Ford Motor Credit Company sold several issues in the public market which pay interest only once each year. For example, its annual adjustable rate notes due March 31, 1997, pay interest only on March 31; the normal semi-annual payments would likely be March 31 and September 30. Upon emerging from reorganization in 1984, Wickes Companies, Inc. issued 12% Debentures due January 31, 1994. The interesting feature about this issue is that interest was paid annually on January 31, 1986, (accruing from February 1, 1985) and 1987 and then it changed to semi-annual payments commencing July 31, 1987. Bond issues with more than two interest payments a year are also fairly scarce. There are a number of domestically issued floating rate notes with quarterly interest payments such as John Deere Credit due September 25, 1991, with payments due on March, June, September and December 25. Few straight or fixed coupon bonds pay other than semi-annually. However, CP National Corporation 10.375% Debentures of 1991 and its 16.50% Debentures due 1996 pay interest on the last day of May, June, September and December.

Bonds with monthly interest dates are infrequently encountered. However, in August 1982 General Motors Acceptance Corporation sold $60 million of Notes due September 1, 1997. The issue was divided into two tranches or parts with the only difference the interest rate and the frequency of the interest payment. The 12.90% Notes totalled $54,350,000 and paid interest March 1 and September 1. The balance of $5,650,000 was 12.50% notes with interest payable on the first of each month starting October 1. The prospectus said that, "The lower stated interest rate on the Notes with interest payable monthly . . . reflects in part the earlier and more frequent payment of interest on the Monthly Notes than on the Notes with interest payable semiannually. . . ."

Are these two rates equivalent? The buyers of the 12.50% monthly notes receive $10.41667 per $1,000 each payment or a total of $125.00 a year. The 12.90% semi-annual issue pays $64.50 every six months or $129.00 annually. Are the buyers of the monthly payment notes getting $4.00 less per note per year? The answer is yes, they are getting paid less. But also, the two yields are not equivalent. Compounding, a very important element to investment returns, will be illustrated in Chapter 8. But briefly, the concept of yield to maturity involves some basic assumptions such as the interest earned from an investment will be reinvested at a rate equal to the purchase yield of that investment. As a matter of fact, interest on interest for long-term bonds can account for a substantial portion of the total return from the investment. Of course, no one knows the exact reinvestment rates which will be obtained in the future. If the reinvestment rate averages more than the purchase yield, then the actual total return will be greater. If the actual reinvestment rate averages less than the purchase yield, the actual total return will be less than that initially expected. Thus, promised rates of return as expressed through yields to maturity may not be the realized rates of return.

Normally, interest payments (as well as principal payments) due on a Sunday or holidays are paid on the next business day without additional interest for the extra period. Indentures might have a clause covering this in the covenant section or in the miscellaneous provisions article. Beneficial Corporation has the following pro-vision:

> Section 14.03. *Payments Due on Sundays and Holidays.* In any case where the date of maturity of principal of or interest on any Securities or the date fixed for redemption of any Securities shall be a Sunday or legal holiday or a day on which banking institutions in the State of New York are authorized by law to close, then payment of interest or principal and premium, if any, may be made on the next succeeding business day with the same force and effect as if made on the date of maturity or the date fixed for redemption and no interest shall accrue for the period after such date.[1]

Payment and Record Date

Since most corporate bonds are now in registered form, interest is paid to the holder by check on the interest payment date. The interest check is normally mailed on the business day preceding the interest payment date to the holder of record. The record date, usually fifteen days prior to the payment date, is the date the trustee prepares the list of bondholders entitled to the approaching interest payment. The interest for the General Motors Acceptance Corporation issues described above is payable to holders of record on the 15th of the month preceding the interest payment date. The record dates for the semi-annual payments are February 15 and August 15. Interest payments for bonds in coupon or bearer form are collected in a fashion similar to the clearance of checks. The investor deposits the coupons with his bank for collection through the banking system from the issuer's bank or paying agent. The agent checks the coupons to see that they are in order and then will credit the depositor's bank or correspondent for eventual credit to his account.

There may be instances when corporations of shaky credit standing will not be able to make the interest payment on time. In such situations the regular interest record date is void and any purchaser of the bonds after that date may receive the interest when paid and if the new owner is a holder of record on the required date. When the company obtains the necessary funds, a new record date will be established for that interest payment. Let us assume that August 31 is the original record date and the interest payment date is September 15. Funds are not on hand and thus the interest payment is not made on September 15. Several weeks later monies become available allowing payment to be made. A new, special record date will be set for the late interest payment, generally no more than 15 nor less than 10 days prior to the new payment date. Holders of record on that new date, not the old date, will be entitled to the interest payment. Section 307 of the registered version of the Model Debenture Indenture makes provision for the payment of defaulted interest.

Accrued Interest

The purchase of a coupon bond usually requires the payment of an amount equal to the agreed-upon sales price (including commission, if any) plus the interest which has accrued from the last interest payment date to the settlement date of the transaction. If the bond is an income bond or in default—that is, not currently paying interest—then there is no accrued interest and none will be paid. The bond is said to "trade flat" when it does not trade with accrued interest. The seller is entitled to accrued interest only if the bond is in good standing. If one sells a bond that settles after the interest record date and before the interest payment date (i.e., the seller is still a holder of record) the purchaser will have paid the seller accrued interest up to the date of settlement. As the purchaser is entitled to the full interest payment on the payment date, the seller (or his broker/dealer) will attach a due bill to the bonds which assigns the rights for the upcoming interest payment to the purchaser. For sake of argument, let us assume that the accrued interest for the trade settling after the record date is $55 and that a full six months interest is $60. The purchaser has paid the record holder the proper amount accrued, namely $55. The seller's broker gives a due bill for the $60 interest payment to the purchaser so that he will be paid when the interest payment is received by the seller. Thus, the seller has received his $55 of interest and the buyer has the $5 he is owed for the rest of the interest ($60 due bill less the $55 accrued interest paid at purchase). If the corporation fails to make payment after the record date, the due bill becomes void and the new holder is entitled to received nothing from the seller. He now has the right to receive payment from the company.

Some speculative grade bond investors have found out a hard fact of life: They bought bonds and paid the accrued interest only to have the issuer fail to meet the next interest payment when due. The seller received payment including accrued interest at the time the transaction settled but if the new holder were to sell, the price would probably be lower and no accrued interest would be received. In addition, the investor now has no assurance that it will ever be paid in full because bankruptcy is more likely. This adds substantially to the monetary and psychic cost of a junk bond. It is difficult to admit that one has been duped, to acknowledge that one's timing was wrong. The issuer defaulted shortly after the investment was made and the new holder hasn't yet seen any return when one was expected. This was dramatically noted in mid-June 1989 when Integrated Resources announced that it would halt interest payments and seek an accomodation with its various lenders; it could no longer roll-over its maturing commercial paper. Trading in the debt securities went from "with accrued interest" to "flat." One publicly traded senior subordinated note, the 13 1/8s of 1995 with interest due each January and July 15, had just about five months of accrued interest when trading went to the flat status; this is equal to nearly $55 per $1,000 note.

A calendar year has 365 days (or 366 days in the case of a leap year) but for purposes of computing corporate bond interest a year consists of only 360 days. Each month in a corporate bond calendar is 30 days whether or not it is February, April, or August. A 12% corporate bond will pay $120 per year, equal to $10 per month. Interest will accrued in the amount of $0.33333 per day. The accrued interest on a 12% bond for 3 months is $30; for 3 months and 25 days, $38.33, and so forth. The corporate calendar is referred to as 30/360. Day count conventions will be explained in Chapter 8.

Interest Variations

Most corporate bonds are the "plain vanilla" type, just a semiannually paying issue with the same interest rate throughout its life. But starting in the seventies, new tools became available allowing financial engineers, the Doctors Frankenstein of finance, to devise increasingly complex new structures and features for investors and issuers.[2] Some of these variations or unconventional features are beneficial in that they allow firms to offset increased finance risks of one type or another; these received a warm response from various market participants and have lasted since they served the needs of both sides of the transaction. These include floating rate and variable rate securities and zero coupon bonds. Others that had little value were discarded. In some cases only one or two issues could be sold as they apparently did not fulfill the current needs of investors. In this category are such issues as money market notes, dual coupon debentures, and maximum reset notes and debentures.

As long as there is interest rate, exchange rate and other financial volatility, as long as the world is a risky place, there will be continual development in financial instruments, whether we like it or not. We will look at a number of these creations by the modern day offspring of Mary Shelley.

Currencies

Most bonds sold in the United States are denominated in legal tender dollars, and the interest is paid in dollars. (We were inclined to say "good, old-fashioned" dollars until we remembered that dollars now represent little except good faith. They are not backed by specie and they do not constitute a promise to pay anything. Look at a dollar bill and just wonder what it really means!) This makes sense as the funds raised are mostly used to finance activities within this country. Monies required for financing of foreign subsidiaries and other nondomestic purposes can be raised overseas in international and local markets, and through banks and other lending institutions. Even dollars can be raised outside the borders of the United States in the Eurodollar market. Starting in the early 1980s some American companies sold issues in the United States denominated in foreign currencies and "faux-currencies," as both fixed coupon and floating rate issues. For example, in March 1985, Hercules Incorporated sold 10⅛% Bonds due March 15, 1992, for 50 million European Currency Units (ECU).[3] The purchasers could pay for the bonds in ECU or in U.S. dollars; if paid for in dollars, such payments would have to be converted into ECU through the agent of the underwriters.

The ECU bonds were issued in registered form to U.S. buyers; foreign buyers could get bonds in coupon form. Only bearer (coupon) bonds can be exchanged for registered bonds; registered bonds cannot be exchanged for the coupon form. One interesting point is that the registered bonds are not callable for life. But the coupon bonds can be called at the option of the company at any time in the event of certain changes in the United States tax laws which would cause the company to pay additional amounts in respect of bearer bonds. If called, the holder can avoid having his bonds redeemed by exchanging coupon for registered bonds. Principal and semi-annual interest payments are in ECU but may be paid in dollars for registered bonds at the holder's option. The actual dollar amount to be received will depend on the exchange rate prevailing two business days preceding payment. If the ECU ceases to exist, the indenture provides that payment will be in the dollar equivalent of the ECU as determined by a major bank to be selected by the trustee. It would be based on the composition of the ECU on the last day that the ECU was used.

Bonds have also been issued in the United States in real foreign currencies such as the New Zealand dollar (NZ$), the Australian dollar (A$) and the Canadian dollar (C$), by such companies as Chrysler Financial Corporation, Citicorp, and Security Pacific Corporation. Generally, interest and principal payments will be converted into U.S. dollars unless the holders want to receive the foreign currency. The holders bear any costs in connection with the currency conversion, which are deducted from such payments. Semiannual interest payment dates are not the usual first or 15th of the month but odd days such as the third, nineteenth, or twenty-second. Holders of large amounts may receive their payments by wire transfer from the trustee instead of by check. The governing law for the issues is New York statutes. In the event of a legal action any judgment would likely be made in U.S. dollars but the prospectuses state that it is unclear as to whether or not the exchange rate between the foreign currency and the U.S. dollar would be taken into account.

Foreign currency issues can provide investors with another avenue for portfolio diversification, but they aren't without risk. As a matter of fact, another risk element is assumed in these bonds—currency or exchange risk—in addition to the usual credit or business risk and interest rate risk. With foreign exchange risk we do not know what the value of our interest payments will be after the payment is exchanged for U.S. dollars, nor, for that matter, do we know the U.S. dollar value of the principal of our investment at maturity, the sale date, or any date in between. True, this could apply to many investments, but the added element of currency risk just makes the problem increasingly more complicated. For this reason many individual investors might be better served by investing in these bonds through mutual funds and other intermediaries, rather than buying them directly. Large, knowledgeable professional investment managers have the staffs, resources and contacts necessary to follow and analyze international economic and political activity and the resulting effects on the currency markets. They can also engage in hedging transactions to reduce the exchange risk if they deem it necessary. But even the most sophisticated investment manager can misread, misinterpret, and make errors in judgement.

The high nominal interest rates on some of these issues should not disguise the currency risk. If the foreign currency depreciates, it will be converted into fewer U.S. dollars. Currencies do fluctuate against one another. For example, at the end of December in the years listed the Australian dollar was equal to U.S. $0.90 in 1983, U.S. $0.83 in 1984, U.S. $0.68 in 1985, U.S. $0.65 in 1986, $0.72 in 1987 and $0.86 in 1988. To put it another way, at the end of 1983, one United States Greenback would buy $1.11 of Australian dollars. In 1984 it would be worth A$1.20; in 1985, A$1.47; in 1986, A$1.54; in 1987, A$1.39; and in 1988, A$1.16. In early 1989 *Barron's* noted that even skilled professionals can find the currency markets hazardous.

> Yields are up Down Under, but the Australian dollar is down. That combination adds up to hefty losses for American investors who have flocked to Aussie fixed-income investments in their global quest for the highest yields.

> The Australian dollar plunged to 82.35 U.S. cents, from its 1989 high, touched Monday, of just over 89 cents. Most of the decline followed Thursday's report that the nation's current account deficit widened dramatically in January, to A$1.54 billion from $924 million in December. (Estimates called for an unchanged deficit in the current account which counts trade and service flows.)

> For U.S. investors in Australian bonds, the double-whammy of a plunging currency and surging interest rates [Australian government bond yields rose 150 basis points since the beginning of the year] was devastating. For instance, *First Australian Prime Income Fund*, a closed-end fund that invests in Down Under debt, plummeted in heavy trading. It was the most active issue trading on the American Stock Exchange Friday, closing at 8 13/16

from 9 ⅜ last week, a 6% loss. That was more than double its 3% total return for January, which placed First Australia Prime Income seventh among closed-end bond funds last month, according to data from Lipper Analytical Services. Last week's losses also took a hefty chunk out of the robust returns of 28.50% in the 12 months ended January 31, when the A-dollar was rising while rates were falling.[4]

Dual Coupon Issues

With the exception of floating rate debt whose interest payment might vary as often as weekly due to changes in the underlying financial benchmark, most bonds have one interest rate for life. However, there have been some issued with an interest payment which automatically changes after it has been outstanding for awhile. Beneficial Corporation's Debentures due 2005 had an 11 ½% interest rate to January 15, 1984, and 9% rate thereafter. This is called a *stepped-down* interest rate. Others have been issued with increasing interest rates; these are known as *dual coupon* or *stepped-up* coupon issues. In September 1982, The Charter Company proposed to issue $100 million of Dual Coupon Subordinated Debentures due 2002. Preliminary pricing talk indicated that the interest rate for the first five years would be 7%, increasing to 9 ½% for the final 15 years. The bonds were to be priced at 50% of face value, raising $50 million before underwriting fees. Instead of this offering, Charter sold $60 million face amount of 14 ¾% Subordinated Debentures due 2002. It defaulted on its interest payments two years later. Another dual coupon issue resulted from the reorganization of Wickes Companies. It issued 20-year debentures due January 31, 2005, with interest accruing at a 7 ½% rate from February 1, 1985, until January 31, 1994, and at a 10% rate thereafter to maturity.

In February 1986, the herd instinct resurfaced once again in Wall Street as American Express Credit, Gannett Company, Hertz Corporation and Household Finance Corporation each sold a $100 million issue with stepped-up coupons, all within three weeks of each other. These noncallable issues had interest rates of 8.40% to 8.50% for the first five or six years, stepping-up in 1990 or 1991 to 9.30% to 9.55% to the maturity date.

A number of lower-rated companies have issued increasing rate or progressive rate notes in which the interest rate is raised by a fixed number of basis points periodically, usually 25 or 50 basis points each quarter. These issues have no ceiling or cap on the maximum interest rate which can ultimately be set (except, possibly, state usury laws) and so they can become pretty costly. This should encourage the debtor to redeem the notes at the earliest possible time, if at all possible.

Participating Bonds

A bond which can participate in the fortunes of an enterprise over and above the coupon rate is called a *participating bond*. We are not referring to convertible issues which may rise in price because the underlying common share price increases, but to those issues which share in the company's profits or participate in the appreciation of certain assets. Not too many have been issued. Of interest to students of American financial history is the Union Pacific Railroad Company/Oregon Short Line Railroad Company 4% Participating Gold Bonds due August 1, 1927, because of its involvement with the historic antitrust case of the Northern Securities Company, a railroad holding company. The bonds, dated August 1, 1902, were secured by common stock of the Northern Securities Company. Besides requiring an annual 4% interest payment beginning in 1903, the holders were to receive an additional amount equal to any dividends and interest in excess of 4% paid on the collateral, namely the common stock of Northern Securities. On March 14, 1904, the U. S. Supreme Court rendered a decision in the Northern Securities case under the Sherman Antitrust Act which prohibited the company from receiving dividends from railroad stock it owned. The decision also put "an end to the holding company as a legal instrumentality for the attainment of monopoly [powers]."[5] Therefore, Northern Securities could not pay dividends on its shares and the participating feature of the bonds was rendered meaningless. They were redeemed at 102.50 on February 1, 1905.

Another type of bond may participate in any appreciation of certain real estate. In 1982, The Koger Company, a real estate operating concern, sold $30 million of Real Estate Appreciation Notes due June 1, 2000. The notes had a fixed 9% rate to June 1, 1988, at which time the coupon was reset to 8%. The next reset will be on June 1, 1994, when the rate will be the greater of 8% or the capitalization rate used by the independent appraisal company in appraising the company's properties. In addition, on these dates the principal amount of the notes may be increased by the amount of additional interest accrued to the preceding December 31 based on an increase in the appraisal of the company's properties. Fixed interest is payable on this increase in the principal amount.

In 1982, Hovnanian Enterprises, Inc. issued 16⅞% Participating Senior Subordinated Debentures due May 15, 1994. The fixed rate is paid quarterly but on each May 15 an additional sum may be paid based on a percentage of the company's pretax net income, as defined. As long as Hovnanian Enterprises has earnings and the bonds are outstanding, an additional amount will be paid. In the case of Northern Pacific's 15% Subordinated Participating Debentures due February 15, 1998, additional interest is payable if the adjusted earnings of the company exceed certain levels, but only up to an additional $60 per debenture. The additional amount may be paid in cash or additional debentures.

Income Bonds

Much maligned, held in low esteem, and seldom encountered nowadays are income bonds, a hybrid security superior in the capitalization ranking to preferred equity but generally of a subordinated status as debt. Today, one would think that with all of the varieties of debt instruments being created, and the burgeoning market for speculative grade bonds, the positive features of income bonds would appeal to at least some issuers and investors. But as time marches on, the income bond recedes into the depths of financial memory. Most of the outstanding income bonds issued have been created as a result of financial reorganizations. Some observers feel that the stigma of financial failure attached to these obligations is the reason why they have been shunned by issuers and investors alike.

Income bonds came out of the railroad reorganizations of the 19th century. Interest payments were contingent, not fixed, and would only be paid if earned. But earnings can be juggled and "interest disbursements often depended on the judgement of the board of directors who were likely to reflect the interests of the stockholders who elected them rather than the income bondholders who were creditors of the corporation. As a result, the board might favor directing earnings towards enlarged expenditures for maintenance of property and equipment rather than toward income bond payments."[6] Because of this, a carefully worded definition of earnings, and a requirement that interest be paid if earned, are necessary protective features. Also, interest payments, if not earned and paid, should be cumulative without limitation.

Failure to pay interest (if unearned) on an income bond is not an act of default and would not, in and of itself, be a cause for bankruptcy. Failure to pay interest on other obligations or failure to meet other terms of the income debt agreement may be grounds for legal proceedings. It is this factor that is important to both parties to the contract; it lessens the financial burdens on a company in times of financial stress. By not being required to pay interest when it does not have earnings, the management of the company under temporary difficulty may be able to gain enough time to straighten things out for the benefit of the creditors and equity owners. It is this feature that makes income bonds similar to preferred stocks; failure to pay preferred stock dividends, whether or not earned, is not an act of default although it is an indication of financial problems. Dividends can be suspended at management's whim. While they are payable from after-tax net income, income bond interest, while contingent, is payable from pretax income and so the net cost to the issuer is reduced. But income bonds occupy a creditor position in case of bankruptcy while preferred shares are in an equity position.

There are only a score or so of income bonds in the public markets today. Most are railroad issues, a number of which are in arrears on their payments. About half have annual interest payments and the rest provide for semiannual or even quarterly payments. The bonds trade flat and have a record date for registered holders. Like preferred stocks, they will trade "ex-interest" a week prior to the record date. Some companies publish interest payment notices in the financial press prior to the interest payment date but one can often fail to notice these. A reliable source for income bond payments is a special section in the *Standard & Poor's Called Bond Record.*

Besides being issued as part of bankruptcy reorganizations, income bonds and debentures have been issued to replace preferred stock, for the refunding of higher interest rate income bonds and to raise capital for general corporate purposes. They have been issued with warrants with the income debenture usable in lieu of cash of the exercise price of the warrant. One major issuer of the 1960s and 1970s was Gamble-Skogmo, Incorporated, which first sold them through its own securities sales organization and then through an outside regional securities firm. The bonds were offered mostly on a best-efforts basis to thousands of investors in middle America.

Income bonds can be used in mergers and acquisitions instead of preferred stock and junior debt. They can have any type of feature as more conventional issues, such as being convertible or participating. They can be designed with features such as sinking funds and call provisions, and be of any priority and security. They can be designed with debt-like features so as to satisfy the Internal Revenue Service that they are debt instruments, not equity (or "debtquity" as some refer to junk bonds). Certainly, an income obligation of a creditworthy issuer should find a receptive market and be generally evaluated as any other senior security. The income obligation of a speculative grade issuer should be viewed as no worse than much of the other similar debt outstanding. While the certainty of interest payment is less than with conventional debt, at least the investor may received some cash flow from the investment; that is more than can be said for low grade zero coupon issues. But as with all securities, it is important for the investor to know the terms of the issue so that a proper bond analysis can be made.

Missouri Pacific Railroad Company (MoPac) has several issues of income bonds outstanding. Two issues are general income mortgage bonds and one is an income debenture. The income mortgage bonds are rated Baa1 by Moody's and the income debentures Baa2. All three issues are rated AA− by Standard & Poor's. These securities were issued in the 1956 reorganization of the company. The bonds are secured by a general mortgage on all properties and assets of the railroad, subject to the rights of the first mortgage. Interest has been paid on a timely basis to date. Interest is payable to the extent earned from available net income (as defined) up to the stated amount, and cumulative up to 13 ½% (three years of unpaid interest).[7] The Board of Directors, in its own discretion and subject to the limitation that the funds are not required for needed and desirable betterments, may, out of lawfully available monies, make payment of the accumulated and accrued interest on the bonds. But past due interest on the Series B bonds cannot be paid unless the unpaid interest on the Series A bonds has been paid or set aside for payment. The interest on the debentures is not cumulative but, again, may be paid at the discretion of the Board, whether or not earned, provided the senior issues have been taken care of.

Hudson & Manhattan Railroad Company issued an interesting income bond in 1913 called the "Five Per Cent. Adjustment Income Bonds due February 1, 1957," with interest payable April and October 1 and at maturity. Issued under a plan of readjustment of the company's debt, each $1,000 principal amount could also be paid in pounds sterling in London at the rate of £205/11s per $1,000 bond (a dual currency bond). Interest was noncumulative prior to January 1, 1920, but cumulative after that date. The company entered bankruptcy proceedings in December 1954, and emerged from reorganization January 1, 1962. The income bond holders received only 3 ½ shares of class "B" stock. In September 1962, the company was taken over by the Port of New York Authority in condemnation proceedings resulting in the eventual payment of $531.60 per class "B" share.

In October 1981, the trustee of The Curtis Publishing Company's 6% Income Debentures due 1986 notified the Company that it was in default since it had not made the interest payments due April 1 and October 1, 1981 (plus some earlier payments), even though it had net income for 1979, 1980 and 1981. In fact, the unpaid principal amount for the debentures at the end of 1981 amounted to $943,000 and the accrued interest to $870,000. The company claimed that because it had an accumulated deficit it could not pay interest on the debentures even if earned unless ordered to do so by the court. The company's counsel opined that it would violate Pennsylvania law to pay the interest as debt issued in exchange for stock (as in this case) was considered stock for purposes of the law and any interest payments would be considered as dividend payments. Also, dividends were prohibited as long as there was an accumulated deficit.

In 1983, Curtis reached an agreement with the trustee under which a standby letter of credit of a national bank was issued covering interest obligations on the debentures for 1980 through 1983. It agreed to build up cash reserves to pay the principal at maturity on October 1, 1986. The payments due during the disputed time, from the beginning of 1980 through April 1, 1983, were paid with interest on the past due amounts. It is interesting to note that while payments due from October 1, 1983 (coupon number 54), to the April 1, 1986, coupon were earned and available for payment, most holders, according to a company spokeswoman, did not send in their coupons for collection.

Original Issue Discount Bonds with Coupons

Original issue discount bonds (OIDs) are those that have been deliberately priced at less than par value because their interest rates at issuance are below current market levels. For tax purposes, the OID may be ignored if it is less than 0.25% of the par value times the number of years to maturity. If a five-year bond is originally offered at 98.75 or higher, no OID is deemed to exist. The cutoff point for a ten-year bond is 2 ½ points or 97 ½ and higher, 95 for a 20-year issue, and so on. In the case of many speculative grade issues, the interest coupons may appear to be fairly current, but if the issuer were to sell a bond priced at par, the interest rate would have to be even higher. In some cases, management's reluctance to have a high coupon on the books may be the reason for the issuance of a bond at an original issue discount. Also, the actual out-of-pocket cash interest expense outlay is less for a deep discount OID than for a bond with only a moderate discount or a full coupon.

While OIDs are not a phenomenon of the eighties, the deep discount issues took the market by storm in 1981 and 1982, especially in the investment grade area. Prior to this time most original issue discount bonds were issued by speculative grade companies. While some investment grade OIDs were issued on a private placement basis in 1980, the first public issue of this era was offered on March 10, 1981; $175 million par value of Martin Marietta Corporation's

7% Debentures due March 15, 2011, sold at 53.835 to yield 13.25% to maturity. This was quickly followed a number of other issues of General Motors Acceptance Corporation, J.C. Penney Company and Transamerica Financial, among others. By the end of the year nearly $7 billion par value ($3.3 billion of proceeds) was being traded. In the first five months of 1982 another $1.6 billion of par value ($745 million of proceeds) was issued. Most of these had interest rates in the 5 ½% to 7% range.[8] However, certain changes in the tax laws made issuance after May less attractive to many companies, and volume fell drastically. Since then, the majority (but not all) of original issue deep discount bonds have been issued by companies with debt quality ratings below investment-grade.

Original issue deep discount debt offered corporations a number of advantages. The interest cost was less than full coupon debt for several reasons; some have placed the savings over conventional fixed coupon debt at 50 to 100 basis points. Investors were willing to make this yield sacrifice because it enabled them to lock in the return on the discount portion of the investment, and reduce the reinvestment risk on the coupon portion in case interest rates declined. Most coupon OIDs were currently callable, but this provision was not too meaningful. Thus, these issues afforded considerable protection from premature redemption compared with current coupon issues for few companies would want to call a six or seven percent coupon bond at 100, especially when rates are higher than the coupon rate. In addition, the issuer could amortize the original issue discount for tax purposes on a ratable or pro rata basis over the life of the issue and utilize the compound interest or economic interest method for financial reporting purposes.

In the early years of the issue, the amount deducted or amortized for tax purposes exceeds that of the interest method. The company reduces its nearby tax burden and increases cash flow; the amortization of the discount, although called interest expense, is not a cash outlay. Cash flow is important to the issuer and it has the use of this additional money until the debt is repaid. The 1982 tax law change made the tax reporting and financial reporting methods the same for subsequent new issues of original issue discount debt, namely the economic or true interest basis. Under this method the amortization of the original issue discount steadily increases over the years by the rate at which the bond was issued. It reduces the cash flow benefit in the early years from original issue deep discount bonds but it does not eliminate it. The accretion of the discount is still a non-cash charge to the income statement.

Some have said that because the interest imputed by the discount is taxable, it would discourage many potential buyers. This is true for investors who, unless in a low marginal tax bracket, must pay taxes on the accreted discount even though it is not cash interest. Individuals generally would be better off in tax-advantaged investments such as municipal bonds.[9] However, one must not overlook the fact that the main buyers of taxable corporate bonds are not taxable individuals for their own accounts but institutions with little or no tax liabilities such as pension funds, including individual retirement accounts, and other self-directed plans. These original discount issues provided those investors with a debt instrument well-suited their needs.

While the 1982 tax changes dampened the incentive of investment-grade companies to issue new deep discount bonds, there were several other reasons. In times of high interest rates, investors look for ways and instruments with which to lock in yields and their promised returns. Interest rates peaked in mid-1982 making subsequent OID investments somewhat less appealing to many investors. In a lower interest rate environment, compounding or interest on interest is less important than when yields are high. Investors may hesitate to invest in what seems like a relatively low-guaranteed rate of return if they think that rates will rise again and thus enable them to reinvest at higher yields. Also, the lower interest rates reduce cash flows for corporate issuers and the resulting tax advantages, making OIDs less attractive from their viewpoint. Finally, we can expect even less future interest in OIDs due to lower marginal tax rates as the after-tax cash flow advantages are further reduced. However, some will undoubtedly continue to be issued.

Zero Coupon Bonds

The ultimate in original issue deep discount bonds is the bond with no coupon or periodic interest payment, called the *zero coupon bond* or *zero* for short. This is really just the principal portion of an issue, similar to stripping away the coupons from a coupon bond. Remove the coupons and what is left? Only the principal portion due at some future maturity date. There is nothing special about a zero coupon bond. It has the advantages of the original issue discount bond but even more so, offering complete lack of reinvestment risk as there is nothing to reinvest. Call protection is even greater than with coupon OIDs, in most cases. Some are noncallable for life but most are currently callable at par. A few are similar to municipal zero coupon bonds as they are callable at a premium to the accreted value. While most are bullet issues, that is bonds with one maturity and no provision for periodic retirement as with a sinking fund, a few issuers have opted for serial maturities. For example, PepsiCo Capital Resources, Inc. sold $850 million of zeros due annually from April 1, 1988, to April 1, 2012.

It was only a matter of weeks after the first OID was issued for the zero coupon corporate OID to hit Wall Street. On April 22, 1981, J.C. Penney Company, Inc. offered $200 million principal amount of zero coupon notes due May 1, 1989, at 33.247 ($332.47 per $1,000 bond) for a yield to maturity of 14.25%. (Six days earlier it had issued $200 million of 6% Debentures due in 2006 for a 14.85% yield.) The next issuer came to market two months later on June 24 when General Motors Acceptance Corporation issued $750 million principal amount of discount notes due July 1, 1991. The price was 25.245 for a 14.25% yield to maturity. In 1981 $2.475 billion par value ($778 million of proceeds) of zeros were issued. In 1982 another $6.89 billion ($1,652 million of proceeds) came to market. Since then, new issue activity greatly diminished as it did for deep discount coupon OIDs.

While these issues were new to the corporate bond market, the concept of a zero coupon debt instrument is well-established with American investors. They have bought noninterest bearing Series "E" and Series "EE" United States savings and war bonds for years. Interest is paid in a lump sum along with the original purchase price at maturity. Many term savings certificates and accounts can be viewed as just another form of a zero coupon bond. An investor buys the certificate or makes a deposit at a stated interest rate for a certain period of time. The interest is not paid out but allowed to be reinvested and compounded until maturity. Overseas they might call these "capitalization certificates" or bonds or deposits with capitalized interest. Late in the War of the Rebellion (also know as the War of Secession to our southern friends), the Federal government issued circulating legal tender compound interest Treasury notes in denominations of $10, $20, $50, $100, $500 and $1,000. The notes accrued interest at a rate of 6% compounded each six months (3% per period) and were repayable at the end of three years. The obverse of the note stated: "Three years after date the United States will pay the bearer . . . dollars with interest at the rate of six per cent compounded semi-annually." The reverse side had the following: "By Act of Congress this note is a legal tender for . . . dollars but bears interest at six per cent compounded every six months though payable only at maturity as follows [here is found the accrued interest and the worth of the note at the end of six semi-annual periods] . . . This sum $ . . . will be paid the holder for principal and interest at maturity of note three years from date." In April 1879, the Treasury issued refunding certificates in $10 denominations that accrued interest at a 4% annual rate for an indefinite period. But in 1907, Congress stopped the accrual of interest when it reach $11.30 for each $10 certificate.

In bankruptcy, the claim of an original issue discount bond, whether it has a coupon or no coupon, is not the principal amount of $1,000 but the accreted value up to the date of bankruptcy; this is the original offering amount plus accrued and unpaid interest. These bonds, especially zero coupon issues, have been sold at deep discounts and the liability of the issuer at maturity may be substantial. Thus, there is the accretion of the discount but this is not put away in a special fund for retirement purposes. There are no sinking funds on most of these issues. One hopes that corporate managements properly invest the proceeds and run the corporation for the benefit of all investors so that there will not be a cash crisis at maturity. The potentially large balloon repayment creates a cause for concern among investors. It is most important to invest in higher quality issues so as to reduce the risk of a potential problem. If one wants to speculate in lower rated bonds, then that investment should throw off some cash return.

Many investors have been confused by yields and returns of zero coupon bonds. There is no current return, as zero divided by the price is zero. Yet one of the authors has heard from many bond market participants that they bought a zero with a current return of 20% or 25%. That is impossible under conventional fixed income mathematics. Where these investors went wrong is to assume that the accretion of the original issue discount is a dollar return or yield and have divided that amount by the price of the security. This is a bookkeeping matter only, not cash in the pocket. A $500 investment that will grow to $1,000 in five years produces a gain of $500 or 100% of the original amount invested. Some might say that the return is 20% annually. This method of calculation is specious and out of step with accepted bond world conventions. Other investors have confused simple interest with compound interest, the generally accepted investment measurement. While the results may look good, they are incorrect and could lead to false conclusions.

An important question for the bond investor is whether the total cash flow or return from a zero will be greater or less than that from a coupon bond over the same time span? To make this determination one must estimate what could be earned on coupon reinvestment over the investment horizon. If the estimated return on the coupon bond is greater than that of the zero, then the coupon issue may be the preferred investment. In high interest rate markets, the zero with its automatic compounding, is probably the more attractive investment. In low interest rate environments, where the compounding effect is less and the probability of higher interest rates greater, the coupon bond might be the better. While forecasting is one of the more difficult tasks to do with any degree of accuracy, it is necessary for making intelligent investment decisions. As with all senior security investments, these forecasting decisions must be continually made and monitored as circumstances change. Generally, bond portfolios should not be static but changed as time and outlook dictates. Individual issues and sectors get overvalued and undervalued from time to time, and zero coupon securities are no exception.

Zero/Coupon Deferred Interest and Payment-in-Kind Bonds (DIBs and PIKs)

A hybrid zero coupon bond is the deferred interest bond (DIB), also known as the zero/coupon bond (zero *slash* coupon). Issued through exchange offers, leveraged buyouts, recapitalizations or mergers, as well as being conventionally underwritten, these are generally (but not always) subordinated issues of lower rated industrial firms. They have been issued by companies such as Colt Holdings Inc., Container Corporation of America and Owens-Corning Fiberglas Corporation, and there is even the Deferred Interest Third Mortgage Bond of Public Service Company of New Hampshire. Most of the issues are structured so that they do not pay cash interest for the first five years. At the end of the deferred interest period cash interest accrues, generally between 13 and 18%, and paid semi-annually to maturity, unless the bonds are redeemed earlier. The deferred interest feature allows newly restructured, highly leveraged and other companies with less than satisfactory current cash flows to defer the payment of cash interest over the early life of the bond. Hopefully, when cash interest payments start, the company will be able to service the debt. If it has made excellent progress in restoring its financial health, it may be able to redeem or refinance the debt rather than have high interest outlays.

A variation of the deferred interest debenture is the pay-in-kind (PIK) debenture. With PIKs, cash interest payments are deferred at the issuer's option until some future date. Instead of just accreting the OID as with DIBs or zeros, the interest rate is paid out in smaller pieces of the same security, namely other pieces of the same paper. The option to pay cash or in-kind interest payments rests with the issuer, but in many cases the issuer has little choice as provisions of other debt instruments often prohibit cash interest payments until certain tests are satisfied. The holder just gets more pieces of paper, but these at least can be sold in the market without giving up one's original investment; DIBs and zeros do not have provisions for the resale of the interest portion of the instrument. Again, an investment in this type of bond, as it is issued by speculative grade companies, requires careful analysis of the issuer's cash flow prospects and ability to survive.

Harcourt Brace Jovanovich, Inc., issued $250 million of 14¾% Subordinated Pay-In-Kind Debentures due September 15, 2002, on September 18, 1987. The PIKs were issued in registered form only in minimum denominations of $1,000 and multiples thereof, with cash interest accruing from September 15, 1992, payable March 15,

1993, and each six months thereafter. HBJ has the option of paying any interest payment not exceeding $100 to any holder in cash. Additional PIKs issued in lieu of cash payments, may be issued in any denomination. Thus, the holder would receive a 14 ¾% debenture (or the in-lieu cash payment) in the denomination of $73.75 every six months for each $1,000 face amount of PIK debenture. Each PIK payment would increase on every interest date as in compound interest, with the holder getting an increasing amount of paper (unless previously sold), since the base or principal amount is increasing every six months.

The holders of these deferred interest securities, if they were deemed to have been issued with original issue discounts for tax purposes, would have to pay income taxes on the accretion of any OID. The tax treatment of PIKs appears to be rather complex. Obviously, tax laws, regulations, and their interpretation change over time; investors should therefore consult with their tax consultants who are familiar with each individual's particular tax situation and type of instrument for appropriate advice.

Debt with Variable Coupons

Late in 1973 an innovation appeared in the U.S. bond market with the introduction of the floating rate note (FRN). Instead of a fixed coupon rate, the interest rate fluctuated at 1 ½% (150 basis points) over the prime lending rate, subject to the minimum rate of 8% and a maximum rate of 12%. Only two issues totalling $35 million were issued that year, but in 1974 activity picked up with 11 issues amounting to some $1.3 billion being sold. Ten of these had the coupon based on the secondary market yields for 3-month U.S. Treasury bills. For the next three years not one variable coupon issue came to the public market. In 1978 only one offering for $200 million was made, followed by a jump to 18 issues for $2.7 billion in 1979. A few other benchmarks for rate determination purposes were tried. Underwriting volume slipped again until 1982, when it resurged, hitting a peak of more than $17 billion in 1985.

Investor demand was stimulated by increasingly volatile bond markets. Market participants wanted an instrument with an income stream that would rise when other interest rates increased, one that offered some protection against interest rate volatility. Issuers with floating rate assets could now have a counterbalance on the liability side of the balance sheet. Both parties could better match their assets and liabilities from an interest rate standpoint. Many of the issues also offered some principal protection against any sustained downturn in market prices through the use of puts. Cash managers have increasingly used floating rate notes as a high-quality substitute for other short-dated instruments in the core portion of their portfolios. One reason is the better yields on these securities. Another reason for their popularity is that transaction costs are reduced because of the less frequent rollover of maturing short-term paper.

The term "floating rate note" or "floaters" covers several different types of securities with one common feature: Interest will vary over the life of the instrument. The rate may be based on a financial benchmark such as the London Interbank Offered Rate (LIBOR) or the U. S. Treasury bill auction rate, or it can be determined at the issuer's discretion. Some have been based on nonfinancial benchmarks such as the price of gas, oil and copper, or the volume of stock trading on the New York Stock Exchange.[10] Floating rate debt usually has coupons based on a short-term money market rate or index that reset (change) more than once a year, such as weekly, monthly, quarterly or semi-annually. One of the earliest and largest issues based on the interest yield equivalent of the 3-month U.S. Treasury bill was Citicorp's Floating Rate Notes due June 1, 1989, issued in July 1974. Interest was reset and payable each June 1 and December 1; in addition, investors had the right to require the company to redeem the notes at par on those dates. Another is Wells Fargo & Company's Floating Rate Subordinated Capital Notes due August 1, 1996, resetting weekly at 1/16th of 1% over the 3-month LIBOR rate and payable quarterly. This is an example of a "mismatched" floater, that is, the interest resets a number of times during the period based on the benchmark rate applicable to the whole period. The interest rate is based on 3-month LIBOR, not one-week LIBOR.

"Adjustable-" or "variable-rate debt" include those issues with coupons based mostly on a longer-term index and reset not more than annually. This category includes those issues based on the one-year and longer Treasury constant maturity rate as published by the Board of Governors of the Federal Reserve System.[11] Some issues may have such terms as the interest rate, the interest period and the redemption features determined by the issuer periodically during the note's life. In effect, the corporation has issued a series of short to intermediate-term securities, of which only the first has known provisions. All have puts available to the holder, for without them, the investor would be at the issuer's mercy.

Volume Comment

Table 4-1 shows that more than 440 variable rate debt issues have been underwritten since 1973 with a total par value of more than $72 billion. This excludes floating rate medium-term notes (about $9 billion) and certificates of deposit (estimated at $75 billion). At the end of 1988, it was estimated that some $60 billion of the underwritten issues were still outstanding. Some issues have matured, a few have been converted or exchanged for other types of securities, others have been called, and several have entered the realm of the bankruptcy courts. Banks, bank holding companies and thrift institutions have issued the greatest amount of floaters, some $26.5 billion or 36% of the total. This shouldn't be surprising considering that these floating rate liabilities are a partial match for some of their floating rate assets. In second place with $21.7 billion (30%) are finance companies such as the captive automobile finance subsidiaries and stock brokerage firms. Industrial and transportation companies with $20 billion issued account for about 28% of the amount issued. Other issuers include sovereign nations, international financial institutions such as the International Bank for Reconstruction and Development, branches of foreign banks and utilities.

The most popular benchmark or rate determination classification is the Treasury constant maturity and the somewhat similar category where the rate is determined at the discretion of the issuer (see Table 4-2). Close to $22 billion of this type has been issued through the end of 1988. Close behind are those issues where the interest rate is based on the U.S. Treasury bill, either the auction of new issues or the secondary market. In third place are the issues with the rate determined by LIBOR.

Table 4-1 Floating Rate Debt by Industry Type

Year	Banks & Thrifts	No. of Issues	Finance & Related	No. of Issues	Inter-national	No. of Issues	Industrial Transportation & Others	No. of Issues	Utilities	No. of Issues	Total $ Mil.	Total No. of Issues	% of Total Amount Issued	% of Total Number of Issues
1988	$3,695.0	19	$6,889.7	31	–	–	2,691.0	19	–	–	$13,275.7	69	18.32%	15.54%
1987	1,825,0	15	1,031.6	5	–	–	1,516.0	9	125.0	1	4,497.6	30	6.21	6.76
1986	3,768.6	19	2,514.2	16	–	–	1,436.3	8	–	–	7,719.1	43	10.65	9.68
1985	3,934.8	38	4,425.0	31	553.5	4	7,630.6	22	575.0	5	17,188.9	100	23.62	22.52
1984	5,295.0	42	3,315.0	26	2,500.0	5	5,052.0	30	275.0	3	16,437.0	106	22.68	23.87
1983	3,710.0	20	1,025.0	9	100.0	1	300.0	4	100.0	1	5,235.0	35	7.22	7.88
1982	350.0	3	1,890.0	13	–	–	775.0	7	–	–	3,015.0	23	4.16	5.18
1981	250.0	1	25.0	1	–	–	85.0	1	–	–	360.0	3	0.50	0.68
1980	250.0	1	250.0	1	–	–	52.0	1	–	–	552.0	3	0.76	0.68
1979	2,041.5	14	250.0	2	–	–	400.0	2	–	–	2,691.5	18	3.71	4.05
1978	200.0	1	–	–	–	–	–	–	–	–	200.0	1	0.28	0.23
1974	$1,160.0	8	10.0	1	–	–	157.5	2	–	–	1,327.5	11	1.83	2.48
1973	–	–	35.0	2	–	–	–	–	–	–	35.0	2	0.05	0.45
Total	$26,479.9	181	$21,660.5	138	$3,153.5	10	$20,095.4	105	$1,075.0	10	$72,464.3	444		
% of Total	36.54	40.77	29.89	31.08	4.35	2.25	27.73	23.65	1.48	2.25				

Review of the Terms and Features

Because financial engineers have created debt instruments with a variety of terms, investors and other market participants should carefully review the prospectus and offering documents of issues in which they are interested, especially floaters.

Only a few of the issues have sinking funds requiring the periodic retirement of a portion of the bonds. Unlike conventional debt, many have call features permitting the company to redeem the bonds only on specific dates, often the date on which the holder may put the bond. Others have fairly standard call features and a fair number are not callable at all. The put feature varies, with some permitting the holder to require the company to redeem the bonds on any interest payment date. Others allow the put to be only exercised when the coupon is adjusted. In cases of extendible notes where the new terms, including the coupon and the interest period are reset only every few years, the put may be used only on those dates. Of course, the time required for prior notification to the issuer or its agent varies from as little as four days to as much as a couple of months. For example, Transamerica Commercial Finance Company's 8 5/8% Extendible Notes due June 15, 1997, have interest reset dates of June 15, in 1991 and 1994. The notes are redeemable by the company at par, and may be put by the holder, only on those interest reset dates. Fifteen days prior notice is required for the put to be exercised.

Most of the issues sold in the United States are payable in U. S. dollars. But there are also issues denominated in ECU, Australian dollars and New Zealand dollars (also called ANZAC or Kiwi issues). In most cases, the coupon is set at a certain premium to the base or benchmark rate. For those based on the Treasury constant maturity, it might be at a minimum percentage of the base rate (and may be set higher at the issuer's discretion). For example, Primerica Corporation's Extendible Notes August 1, 1996, were scheduled for an interest rate change on August 1, 1987. The coupon was 13.25%, but as interest rates were considerably lower, the corporation set the rate from August 1, 1987, through July 31, 1992, at 8.40%, about 105% of the five-year Treasury constant maturity of 8.00%. The minimum percentage under the indenture was 102.5%. Apparently this rate was not satisfactory to the holders and many notes were

Table 4-2 Floating Rate by Benchmark Type

Year	Prime, Commercial Paper and Other	No. of Issues	Libor	No. of Issues	Treasury Bills	No. of Issues	TCM or Rate Determined by Issuer	No. of Issues	Kiwi or ANZAC	No. of Issues	Stepped-up Coupons	No. of Issues	Miscellaneous	No. of Issues	Total
1988	$4,579.0	22	$1,200.0	6	$1,700.0	7	$2,585.0	10	$ 65.7	1	–	–	$3,146.0	23	$13,275.7
1987	1,025.0	11	825.0	5	–	–	1,395.0	6	187.6	3	$140.0	1	925.0	4	4,497.6
1986	300.0	1	1,400.0	10	2,185.0	8	2,160.0	11	497.8	6	400.0	4	776.3	3	7,719.1
1985	290.0	4	8,237.4	42	2,803.5	19	5,476.0	30	–	–	–	–	312.0	5	17,118.9
1984	2,000.0	3	2,950.0	26	5,012.0	34	6,050.0	41	–	–	–	–	425.0	2	16,437.0
1983	100.0	1	400.0	2	3,585.0	23	1,150.0	9	–	–	–	–	–	–	5,235.0
1982	–	–	–	–	1,000.0	7	2,015.0	16	–	–	–	–	–	–	3,015.0
1981	–	–	–	–	–	–	335.0	2	–	–	–	–	25.0	1	360.0
1980	–	–	–	–	250.0	1	250.0	1	–	–	–	–	52.0	1	552.0
1979	–	–	–	–	2,441.5	17	250.0	1	–	–	–	–	–	–	2,691.5
1978	–	–	–	–	200.0	1	–	–	–	–	–	–	–	–	200.0
1974	7.5	1	–	–	1,320.0	10	–	–	–	–	–	–	–	–	1,327.5
1973	35.0	2	–	–	–	–	–	–	–	–	–	–	–	–	35.0
Total	$8,336.5	45	$15,012.4	91	$20,497.0	127	$21,666.0	127	$751.0	10	$540.0	5	$5,661.3	39	$72,464.2
% of Total	11.50	10.14	20.72	20.50	28.29	28.60	29.90	28.60	1.04	2.25	0.75	1.13	7.81	8.78	

Note: Kiwi or ANZAC issues are denominated the Australian or New Zealand dollars. TCM = Treasury Constant Maturity.

either put back to the company during the first two weeks of July or the holders threatened to do so. In any event, several days prior to the commencement of the new rate and interest period a notice appeared in the newspaper of record announcing that the company "... is exercising its option under the terms of the Extendible Notes due 1996 to establish an interest rate higher than the rate previously announced. . ." The rate was increased to 8.875%, equal to 110.9% of the Treasury constant maturity. The notice further stated, "Holders of the Notes who have previously elected repayment of their Notes may revoke such election (and thereby become entitled to receive the increased interest rate). . . ." by notice ". . . to the Company or the Trustee no later than 5:00 P.M., New York City time on the first business day following publication of this Notice."

In other cases the rate might be set at a certain number of basis points above or below the base rate, as the case may be. Many 3-month LIBOR-based issues have the rate set at LIBOR plus ⅛ or ¼ of 1% (12.5 or 25 basis points), while some 3-month Treasury bill-based issues are spread from 100 basis points to as much as 450 basis points over the base rate. The spread over the base rate tends to be high for relatively low yielding indices and lower for higher yielding ones, all other things being equal. In certain cases the spread may be a discount from the base rate. In general, the progression of the benchmark rates from the lowest spread to the highest starts with the prime rate, followed by LIBOR, federal funds, commercial paper, certificates of deposit to the 11th District cost of funds, and finally Treasury bills often having the widest spreads. The 11th District index is a weighted average of interest costs for thrift liabilities in the 11th district of the Federal Home Loan Bank System.

Some issues provide for a change in the spread from the base rate at certain intervals over the life of the floater. For instance, the coupon for Citicorp's floater due September 1, 1998, was based on the interest yield equivalent of the market discount rate for 6-month Treasury bills plus 120 basis points from March 1, 1979 through August 31, 1983, and then 100 basis points over the base rate to August 31, 1988. It is currently 75 basis points over until maturity. *Step-down floaters* have the same characteristic of a lower spread as maturity approaches. Chemical Banking Corporation's two-year

Step-Down Floating Rate Notes due July 18, 1990, have a 25 basis point premium to the 1-month commercial paper index for the first year, declining to a 20 basis point premium in the second year. Some issues are on an either or basis. One such example is Barclays-American Corporation Floating Rate Subordinated Notes due November 1, 1990. Interest is payable quarterly and calculated monthly at the higher of (i) the prime rate minus 125 basis points or (ii) the 30-day commercial paper rate plus 25 basis points. Other issues have their coupon rates determined through a Dutch auction procedure or remarketing process, with the applicable interest rate the one at which all sell orders and all buy orders are satisfied.

One usually expects that as interest rates rise, the coupon on the floater will increase, and as rates fall, the coupon will decrease. This makes sense to most people but there are some issues that might even confuse many bond professionals. With yield curve notes the interest rate is reset and payable twice a year based on a certain percentage rate (depending on the issue) *minus* the 6-month LIBOR rate. For example, the General Motors Acceptance Corporation's Yield Curve Notes due April 15, 1993, are based on 15.25% minus 6-month LIBOR. If LIBOR is at 8%, the rate on the notes would be 7.25%. If LIBOR increases to 10%, the yield curve note drops to 5.25%, and if LIBOR falls to 6%, the yield curve note would have a rate of 9.25%. It appears that only those investors who are bullish on the direction of interest rates would care for these issues. Another type of issue for interest rate bulls are the maximum reset notes and debentures. The two issues (one of each) which came to market in late 1985 were not warmly received by investors according to some traders. The initial coupon rates were 10.625%. Interest is adjusted and payable semiannually, and if, at the interest determination date, 6-month LIBOR exceeds 10.50%, then the interest rate for the period will be reduced from 10.625% by the amount of the excess, with the minimum rate being zero percent. With LIBOR at 12%, the rate on these notes would decline to 9.125%. *At least if LIBOR exceeds 21 ⅛% the holder will not have to pay the issuer anything.*

Some of the issues have floors below which the interest rate can not go. A number of the LIBOR-based issues have minimum rates of 5.25%. Others have declining minimums such as the Citicorps due September 1, 1998. The minimum rate is 7.50% through August 31, 1983, then 7.00% through August 31, 1988, and then 6.50% to maturity. Certain issues have ceilings or maximum rates, often because of state usury laws. Many issues state that the maximum rate is 25% due to New York State's usury law but holders of $2.5 million or more of an issue are exempt from this. Some issues of Texas bank holding companies had a 17% maximum rate. In 1974, Crocker National Corporation sold $40 million of floating rate notes due 1994 with a 10% maximum rate due to uncertainties with California law. For several years the coupon rate was below the ceiling but in 1979 interest rates shot up, restricting the interest to 10%. As the notes had a put feature, many investors put the bonds back to the company and reinvested the proceeds in more attractive instruments. Had there been no put option, those investors would have been out of pocket for a number of years. One should certainly relate the ceiling rate with the spread over the base rate: Is the spread satisfactory enough to compensate for the limit to the income stream in case rates rise, or is the ceiling too close to the base rate?

Several floating rate issues have both a floor and a ceiling, which together are called *collars*. Baltimore Gas & Electric Company issued a couple of floaters in 1985 with collars. Based on the 91-day Treasury bill auction rate (bond equivalent basis) the spreads are 110 basis points for one and 112.5 basis points for the other. The collars are 8% and 12%, and 7.90% and 11.90%, respectively. These appear to be relatively narrow bands within which the interest rate may vary but the lower ceiling is offset to some extent by the higher floor. Other issuers of collared floaters include California Federal Savings and Loan Association, Citicorp, and Student Loan Marketing Association.

The Market for Floaters

Individual investors found the first series of floating rate notes quite appealing. The two-year delay in the put feature was a small negative, but it was used to mollify the thrift interests which did not view these retail debt instruments kindly. They feared an outflow of deposits to these new securities. From the investor's viewpoint, they were, at worst, two-year instruments and then six-month instruments once the puts became effective. Price fluctuations were relatively narrow because of the put. When the second batch of floaters hit the market in 1979 they were also warmly received by investors. Many investors did not care that the new generation of floating rate paper did not have any puts. They thought that as long as the coupon rate was adjusted every six months the bonds would naturally stay around par. How mistaken they were! There was nothing to keep them at par when all around was changing. The spread was fixed at market levels which existed at the time the issues were priced. They did not have puts and, as interest rate movements became increasingly more volatile later in the year, their prices sank. These new issues were just intermediate to longer-term securities with a coupon that happened to fluctuate. If the credit quality of the issuer deteriorated, prices would be reduced. Because of rapid movements in interest rates, the interest rates, when reset, were often below the market rates. Prices had to adjust for this gap between the floater rate and the market rate. The semi-annual coupon change did not provide the needed support. In the January 1980 to June 1981 period, based on end-of-week prices on the New York Stock Exchange, Citicorp's June 1, 1989, floater with a put had a price range of only 96 to 103 ¼. In comparison, floaters without puts had wider price fluctuation. Manufacturers Hanover floating rate notes of May 1987 moved between 86 ¼ and 101 ½, while Chase Manhattan's due in 2009 had a low of 82 and a high of 100 ½.

In early 1980, as interest rates fell sharply, the floaters that were hurt the most in the preceding few months, moved rapidly from the low 80s and 90s to the par area. For example, the Chase Manhattan 2009s went from 86 to about 100 in 15 weeks. But retarding some prices were the investors who wanted to get even; they wanted to get rid of an investment that had not measured up to their initial unreal performance expectations. After the rally, prices took another tumble as rates once again rose. This history shows how important the put feature can be. Of course, it also helps if you know the risks and rewards of the specific instruments one happens to be investing in.

Many investors in the floating rate note market are financial institutions with floating rate liabilities of one sort or another. Other investors use floaters as substitutes for money market instruments, although those without put features are not perfect substitutes for short-dated instruments. Money market funds are large buyers of floaters with puts within one year. They have been used as hedges against rising interest rate markets. If interest rates are thought to be on the increase, floaters with frequent resets should provide increasing income. Their defensive characteristics should lend them price stability. A mismatched floater might be suitable. Resetting weekly to increasingly higher levels with interest payable quarterly or semi-annually, the holder is not locked into one rate for three or six months. LIBOR has historically been at higher levels than Treasury bill rates and the relationship between the two should be analyzed prior to investing. If the spread between the two is relatively narrow, and one's interest rate outlook is cautious, then LIBOR-based floaters might be considered so as to take advantage of a possible widening of the spread relationship.

Investors looking for a decline in interest rates may prefer floaters with less frequent resets (such as extendible notes) and deferred resets (so as to maintain the higher coupon for as long as possible). Of course, large investors don't have to limit themselves to just what is available in the domestic market; the supply of floating rate paper in the foreign markets is considerable. The major investment firms with their worldwide trading capabilities, participate in these markets 24 hours a day.

Notes

[1] *Indenture dated as of June 15, 1983, between Beneficial Corporation and Bankers Trust Company, Trustee, Providing for the Issuance of Debt Securities.*

[2] In its December 8, 1986 issue, *Barron's National Business and Financial Weekly* carried an interview with James Rogers, a private investor and professor of finance at the Columbia University Graduate School of Business. Rogers said, in part:

> But since no economy in the world is near as strong as the financial markets, all this money has been flowing into financial assets all over the world. Investment bankers are staying up late, trying to come up with and invent new financial instruments to soak up all this money that's sloshing around. I

keep up a little bit with these things, even in my retirement, but there are financial instruments now that I have never heard of. Some of the things they have created in the Eurodollar market—I just don't know what's going on anymore. And I've got former students who are out there trading interest-rate swaps and mortgage-backed securities and foreign currency swaps, and they don't have a clue as to what they're doing. They don't have a clue on what the ultimate ramifications, or who the ultimate creditor is, or anything else about these things. All they know is it's trading and they're making a lot of money.

In sum, many market participants have an insufficient understanding of the risks associated with their activities.

[3] The European Currency Unit (ECU) is a "faux-currency" as it is not money in circulation such as the pound sterling or the United States dollar. There is no central bank issuing ECU notes although financial institutions issue travelers' cheques and other financial instruments denominated in ECU, and it is increasingly recognized in international transactions. The ECU is a synthetic, composite, or basket currency, consisting of specific amounts of currencies from each of the member nations of the European Economic Community. One ECU was worth approximately U.S. $1.11 in November, 1989.

[4] Randall W. Forsyth, "Current Yield." *Barron's National Business and Financial Weekly* (February 20, 1989), pp. 39-40.

[5] William Z. Ripley, *Trusts, Pools and Corporations* (Boston, MA: Ginn and Company, 1916), p. 491.

[6] Sidney M. Robbins, *An Objective Look at Income Bonds* (Boston, MA: Envision Press, 1974), pp. 6-7. Another interesting article endorsing the use of income bonds in corporate capital structures is Leo Barnes' "A Do-It-Yourself Way to Cut Taxes," *Business Week* (May 5, 1975), pp. 21-25.

[7] For a fairly complete definition of available net income and the disposition of income, see *Moody's Transportation Manual* (New York, NY: Moody's Investors Service, Inc.).

8   Ford Motor Credit Company issued $100 million of 1% Original
    Issue Discount Notes due August 15, 1990, at 63.52 to yield
    10.571% to maturity. The current yield was 1.574%, not too
    substantial. General Motors Acceptance Corporation also is-
    sued 1% Notes due October 22, 1990, on April 27, 1987. The
    yield to maturity was 7.45% and the current yield 1.243%. Spe-
    cially designed for large institutional investors, the minimum
    denomination was $5 million for the Ford Credits and $1 mil-
    lion for GMAC.

9   There are only three zero coupon bonds called deferred interest
    debentures on which taxable holders pay no taxes on the ac-
    creted interest, although they could incur some capital gain tax
    liability. Issued in 1982 through recapitalizations under the tax
    code, the issues are Exxon Shipping Company's Guaranteed
    Deferred Interest Debenture due September 1, 2012, General
    Motors Acceptance Corporation Deferred Interest Debentures
    due December 1, 2012, and another issue due June 15, 2015.
    The debentures are callable at any time, in whole or in part, at
    the principal amount plus accrued interest computed on a
    straight-line basis.

10 Two examples of interest-indexed issues are Magma Copper
    Company's Copper Interest-Indexed Senior Subordinated
    Notes due 1998, and Presidio Oil Company's Senior Subordi-
    nated Gas Indexed Notes due 1999. Magma Copper's notes pay
    interest quarterly each February, May, August and November
    15. The initial rate was 18% paid on May 15, 1989. Thereafter,
    the quarterly rate will pay interest based on the average price
    of copper during the preceding quarter, subject to a minimum
    of 12% (copper price $0.80 a pound) to a maximum of 21%
    (copper at $2.00 a pound). If copper averages less than 80 cents
    a pound, Magma has the right to pay half of the interest in
    additional notes. Presidio's notes also pay interest quarterly
    with the base rate 13 ¼% and the maximum rate 18%. Addi-
    tional interest is paid each quarter that the 12-month moving
    average of the gas index price exceeds $1.75 per million British
    thermal units. The additional interest is 2.5 basis points for
    each $0.01 by which the gas index exceeds $1.75. In effect, these

securities are somewhat like participating bonds in that the holder participates in the price rise of the company's main commodity.

[11] The Federal Reserve Statistical Release H.15 (519), *Selected Interest Rates*, describes the Treasury constant maturity series as follows:

> Yields on Treasury securities at "constant maturity" are estimated from the Treasury's daily yield curve. This curve, which relates the yield on a security to its time to maturity, is based on the closing market bid yields on actively traded Treasury securities in the over-the-counter market. These market yields are calculated from composites of quotations reported by five leading U.S. Government securities dealers to the Federal Reserve Bank of New York. The constant yield values are read from the yield curve at fixed maturities, currently 1, 2, 3, 5, 7, 10 and 30 years. This method permits estimation of the yield for a 10-year maturity, for example, even if no outstanding security has exactly 10 years remaining to maturity.

Chapter 5

DEBT RETIREMENT

The main reason corporations retire their debt prior to maturity is because declining interest rates make it economical. The issuer may substitute new and lower cost debt for older issues with higher interest rates, or may redeem the debt through cash on hand built up through the retention of earnings or the sale of assets. The lower debt expense may lead to improved earnings and cash flow. Other reasons include the desire by the issuer to eliminate restrictive or onerous covenants from its indenture and to improve or change the corporation's capital structure, so as to increase its financial and managerial flexibility. Describing the various call features found in corporate bond indentures, this chapter is important for anyone who wants to value the embedded options found in callable bonds. The techniques for doing so are explained in Section II.

The Importance of Knowing a Bond Issue's Redemption Terms

Without knowledge of financial history, many bond market participants are thus unprepared when events occur in the market that are similar to past events. This is especially true when interest rates decline, particularly from lofty levels. Being unfamiliar with the financial past, traders and investors do not understand what may happen under present or future conditions. Portfolios and trading positions have been structured based on considerations that may have been appropriate at one time, but may now be inadequate under changed conditions and outlook. In many cases, investors' eagerness for increased yield makes their bond holdings vulnerable to premature retirement. This, coupled with an unfamiliarity with the issue's terms, makes bond investment riskier than it ought to be. Investors should read the prospectuses and indentures of the issues they own, especially for the higher-coupon bonds. Redemption provisions vary from issue to issue, even among those of the same company and under the same general indenture. How often do you hear someone say, "I don't have time to read a prospectus"? This is not an adequate response and market participants must take the time to diligently study their holdings' provisions in order to be able to take proper action at the appropriate time.

The importance of knowing the terms of bond issues, especially those relating to redemption, cannot be overstressed. Yet there have appeared numerous instances of investors, professional and others, who acknowledge that they don't read the documentation. For example, the following statements were attributed to some stockbrokers: "But brokers in the field say they often don't spend much time reading these [official] statements," "I can be honest and say I never look at the prospectus. . . . Generally, you don't have time to do that", and "There are some clients who really don't know what they buy. . . . They just say, 'That's a good interest rate.'"[1] The following are from legal decisions involving debt redemptions:

> Although she received prospectuses for her investment, plaintiff . . . never read any FPL [Florida Power & Light Company] prospectus or other description of the 10 ⅛ bonds before she purchased the 10 ⅛ bond . . .

> . . . did not possess or read any FPL prospectus describing the 10 ⅛ bonds before he purchased the . . . bonds . . . in the after market.

> . . . did not read or rely on prospectuses when buying bonds in the after market. . . .

As the Fifth Circuit Court also pointed out in *Alabama Power*:

> . . . it is reasonable (for the issuer) to assume that investors who (purchase) their bonds would familiarize themselves with the

conditions under which they were issued, and particularly the terms of redemption, by reading the few short paragraphs on the face of the bonds.

The plaintiffs offered little, if any, evidence of their own due diligence in making their investment decisions, which respectively involved a reckless disregard for, or deliberate inattention to, the contents of the FPL prospectus, which none of them read or consulted, as well as an apparent and knowledgeable willingness to "gamble" on the part of the more sophisticated investor, . . .[2]

We note initially that bondholders are charged with knowledge of the contents of the trust indenture where the bond certificate refers to the terms of the indenture.[3]

A professional analysts' journal stated:

To infer that all money managers and other analysts do not read prospectuses is a quantum and incorrect leap, yet uneasy feelings exist about the number that do. Why read a prospectus, 10K or any other fully disclosed information? Is someone out there saying something and analysts not listening? One would surmise that, if prospectuses contained value, they would be read. Is there a delusionary safe harbor in believing too strongly that all known information is reflected in market prices and well diversified portfolios insure against all but market risks? [4]

Retirement of debt before the stated maturity is not a new phenomenon. James Grant said, "At the turn of the century the risk to bondholders was default . . . or the early redemption of sound securities. . . ."[5] It occurs periodically whenever interest rates decline. Hickman stated:

During periods of rising interest rates few issues are called, many are paid off at maturity, and though realized yields may rise with money rates, call premiums may be insufficient to offset default losses, and substantial capital losses may result. In periods of falling money rates the reverse appears to be true: few issues are paid off at maturity, many are called, and even though default losses may be substantial, call premiums may be more than sufficient to offset them, and capital gains may occur.[6]

Recent periods of major debt redemption activity include 1963, 1975 through 1978, and 1983 to 1989. Times of generally declining interest rates, they provided ample opportunity for corporations to rid themselves of high-coupon debt. Bond calls are common, and yet they have caused the unwary investor much consternation over the years. Investors have suffered unwarranted losses of principal that might been have avoided had they heeded one warning: Know the terms of the bond contract. Remember that investors are parties to the bond contract even though they may have purchased the issue in the secondary market long after the bonds were first publicly offered. The subsequent buyer is as much a party to the bond contract as is the initial purchaser; he succeeds to the contract.

It is common knowledge that bond market participants are unaware of indenture provisions, especially those relating to redemption and the options given to the issuer. Bondholders often have mistaken ideas as to what a corporation may do when it comes to debt retirement. It should always be kept in mind that corporate managements generally do not have bondholders' interests at heart; they are elected by, and beholden to, the owners of the business, namely the common shareholders. Their duty is to increase shareholder wealth, not that of bondholders. They do not owe any fiduciary duty to bondholders, their only responsibility is contractual.

Why the Concern About Premature Redemption?

Some might ask, "Why is there all the concern about premature bond redemption?" After all, we get our money back and can reinvest it. But *that* is the concern: In most cases, a company will call its high-coupon bonds when interest rates are lower; therefore, investors lose their high income and must reinvest the bond proceeds in a lower interest rate environment. The promised yield expected at purchase may be reduced. While lower interest rates may reduce the interest-on-interest component of the expected total return from a bond, at least many investors still expect to get the relatively high interest payment coming in. But corporations are run by managements who do what individuals often try to do. If they see an opportunity to reduce their expenses by calling high-coupon debt, they will usually do so. If homeowners rush to refinance their home mortgages when rates drop, why can't companies refinance their outstanding high-cost debt?

Besides suffering a decline in interest income and the resulting interest-on-interest, the bonds are called at prices which are often lower than recent market prices. The call price may be at a premium to par but the redemption price may be only par. Examples of calls at levels well below the prevailing market price of the bonds are presented later in this chapter.

Yield-oriented investors are among those often hurt by premature bond redemptions. They are attracted by the relatively high yield to maturity without realizing that this is most likely due to one of two reasons: increased risk of default or increased risk of call. Seldom is the high yield due to inefficiencies in the market. Whenever a bond offers above-average yield, the investor should ask why. One does not usually get something for nothing in the financial markets.

Call and Refunding Provisions

A company wanting to retire a debt issue prior to maturity usually must pay a premium over the par value for the privilege. The initial call premium on long-term debt traditionally has been the interest coupon plus par or the initial reoffering price (in some cases it is the higher of the two). Thus, a 30-year bond initially priced at 100 with a 10% coupon may have a call price of 110% for the first year, scaled down in relatively equal amounts to par starting in year 21 to maturity. Anheuser-Busch Companies, Inc. offered $200 million of 10% debentures in mid-1988 at 100% of par; the maturity is July 1, 2018. Table 5–1 shows the redemption schedule for the bonds. Note that the initial call price is equal to the coupon plus the reoffering price. Subsequent redemption prices are in decrements of 50 basis points (0.5 of 1%) to par starting July 1, 2008. Some issues only show the call premium such as 8.583%, 8.154%, 7.725%, instead of the whole price.

The prices shown in Table 5–1 are called the *regular* or *general redemption prices*. There are also special redemption prices for debt redeemed through the sinking fund and through other provisions such as the maintenance and replacement fund, the proceeds from the confiscation of property through the right of eminent domain, and the release and substitution of property clauses. The special redemption price is usually par, but in the case of some utility issues it initially may be the public offering price, which is amortized down to par (if a premium) over the life of the bonds. Carolina Power & Light Company's 9 ¾% bonds due May 1, 2004, have a special redemption price that is a discount. The bonds, issued in 1974 at 99.75, have a special redemption price starting at 99.75 and accruing to par for the final year starting May 1, 2003. This price can be used for redemptions for the improvement fund, the maintenance and replacement fund, or with the proceeds of released property. In other instances, the special redemption price is the same as the regular redemption price. This makes the debt redemption somewhat more costly for the issuer and provides the bondholder an additional premium. Rules of thumb for corporate bond characteristics applicable a generation ago cannot be safely used today; there are too many exceptions for one to be able to ignore the documentation. In the case of shorter-maturity debt, the initial call premium will usually not be the full coupon but some fraction thereof, scaled down to par; it may even be par for the issue's life.

The Anheuser-Busch debentures are currently callable—that is, the company may redeem the bonds at any time at the above general redemption prices subject only to the ten-year prohibition against lower cost refunding. Other issues may not be called for any reason for a certain number of years. For example, there is usually a five-year noncallable period for long-term debt of the former members of the American Telephone and Telegraph Company family. Therefore, the call price at the time the bond may first be called is not par plus the coupon, but the amortized price in five years after issuance obtained by the par plus the coupon calculation. If the telephone bond had the same coupon and reoffering price as the Anheuser issue, the initial call price would be 107.5 for the 12-months beginning July 1, 1993.

In 1979 some of the Bell System companies attempted to change the call price formula. Instead of basing the premium on the initial

Table 5–1 Redemption Schedule for Anheuser-Busch Companies, Inc.
10% Sinking Fund Debentures due July 1, 2018

Redemption

The Debentures will be redeemable at the option of the Company at any time in whole or in part, upon not fewer than 30 nor more than 60 days' notice, at the following redemption prices (which are expressed in percentages of principal amount) in each case together with accrued interest to the date fixed for redemption:

If redeemed during the 12 months beginning July 1,

1988	110.0%	1999	104.5%
1989	109.5%	2000	104.0%
1990	109.0%	2001	103.5%
1991	108.5%	2002	103.0%
1992	108.0%	2003	102.5%
1993	107.5%	2004	102.0%
1994	107.0%	2005	101.5%
1995	106.5%	2006	101.0%
1996	106.0%	2007	100.5%
1997	105.5%	2008 and	
1998	105.0%	thereafter	100.0%

provided, however, that prior to July 1, 1998, the Company may not redeem any of the Debentures pursuant to such option, directly or indirectly, from or in anticipation of the proceeds of the issuance of any indebtedness for money borrowed having an interest cost of less than 10% per annum.

Source: Prospectus dated June 23, 1988.

coupon, it was arbitrarily set at half of the coupon rate. On August 21, 1979, Northwestern Bell Telephone offered $300 million of 9 ½% bonds due in 37 years at 99.7 with the initial call price after five years at 104.75. Other affiliates tried the same call price formula over the next several months, but investors did not care for it. The lower call price meant that interest rates did not have to decline as much in order for the company to profitably redeem the debt, and thus vulnerability to call was increased. In addition, if the bonds were called, investors would be receiving substantially less than under the older formula. The experiment was unsuccessful and the more traditional call pricing resumed.

If a debt does not have any protection against early call, then it is said to be a *currently callable issue*, as is the Anheuser issue. But most new bond issues, even if currently callable, usually have some restrictions against certain types of early redemption. The most common restriction is that prohibiting the refunding of the bonds for a certain number of years. Aware of the dangers of generalizations, industrial company long-term debt issues often have ten years of refunding protection while electric and gas utilities normally provide five years.[7] Many telephone, bank and finance issues provide deferred call provisions. Both call prohibitions and refunding prohibitions may be for a certain number of years or for the issue's life. Bonds that are noncallable for the issue's life are more common than bonds which are nonrefundable for life but otherwise callable.

Many investors are confused by the terms *noncallable* and *nonrefundable*. Hess and Winn said: "The terms 'noncallable' and 'nonrefundable' are often used rather loosely as interchangeable entities, although from a technical standpoint they have different meanings."[8] Call protection is much more absolute than refunding protection. While there may be certain exceptions to absolute or complete call protection in some cases (such as sinking funds and the redemption of debt under certain mandatory provisions), it still provides greater assurance against premature and unwanted redemption than does refunding protection. Refunding prohibition merely prevents redemption only from certain sources, namely the proceeds of other debt issues sold at a lower cost of money. The holder is only protected if interest rates decline, and the borrower can obtain lower-cost money to pay off the debt. The Anheuser bonds cannot be redeemed prior to July 2, 1998, if the company raises the funds from a new issue with an interest cost lower than 10%. There is nothing to prevent the company from calling the bonds within the ten-year refunding protected period from debt sold at a higher rate (although it normally wouldn't do so) or, as we shall see, from funds obtained through other means.

Some prospectuses specifically clarify refunding and redemption. For example, Cincinnati Gas & Electric Company's prospectus for the 15 ¾% First Mortgage Bonds due in 1992 states,

> The New Bonds are redeemable (though CG&E does not contemplate doing so) prior to July 1, 1987 through the use of earnings, proceeds from the sale of equity securities and cash accumulations other than those resulting from a refunding operation such as hereinafter described. The New Bonds are not redeemable prior to July 1, 1987 as a part of, or in anticipation of, any refunding operation involving the incurring of indebtedness by CG&E having an effective interest cost (calculated to the second place in accordance with generally accepted financial practice) of less than the effective interest cost of the New Bonds (similarly calculated) or through the operation of the Maintenance and Replacement Fund.

Refunding means to replace an old bond issue with a new one, often at a lower interest cost. In the Florida Power & Light case the judge said:

> The terms "redemption" and "refunding" are not synonymous. A "redemption" is simply a call of bonds. A "refunding" occurs when the issuer sells bonds in order to use the proceeds to redeem an earlier series of bonds. The refunding bond issue being sold is closely linked to the one being redeemed by contractual language and proximity in time so that the proceeds will be available to pay for the redemption. Otherwise, the issuer would be taking an inordinate risk that market conditions would change between the redemption of the earlier issue and the sale of the later issue.[9]

Corporations generally prefer to issue callable bonds for the flexibility they offer in financial management. If interest rates decline or other circumstances change, they can get out of the debt contract with minimal cost. On the other hand, investors prefer noncallable bonds for their guarantee of certain cash flow for a fixed period; this allows them to plan accordingly. But borrowers and lenders often must compromise; thus, we get the bond that is noncallable or nonrefundable for only a part of the issue's promised life span. In the early sixties, electric utilities offered issues with five years refunding protection at rates of 15 to 25 basis points less than issues with no refunding protection, all other factors being the same. Investors were willing to reduce their yield for the additional protective feature.

Beginning in early 1986 a number of industrial companies issued long-term debt with extended call protection, not refunding protection. A number are noncallable for the issue's life such as Dow Chemical Company's 8 5/8% debentures due in 2006 and Atlantic Richfield's 9 7/8% debentures due in 2016. The prospectuses for both issues expressly prohibit redemption prior to maturity. These noncallable-for-life issues are referred to as "bullet bonds" in Wall Street. Other issues carry 15 years of call protection such as Eastman Kodak's 9.95% Debentures due July 1, 2018, and not callable prior to July 1, 2003.[10] According to *Standard & Poor's CreditWeek*, "The first wave of noncall long-term bonds gave issuers 20 to 25 basis points savings on their financing costs. . . . Now companies are lucky if investors give up 10 to 15 basis points for a noncall feature."[11] Of course, interest rates dropped considerably in early 1986. Call protection is a more valuable option when interest rates are high, which is precisely when lenders prefer noncallable issues. When interest rates are low, call protection is less meaningful, making fully call-protected bonds less attractive to investors.

Redemption dates are usually stated as "on or after" a certain date. In some cases, however, the bonds may only be redeemed on certain dates, often the interest payment dates. Prior notice must be given—usually 30 to 45 days preceding the redemption date. Of course, if the bonds are listed on a securities exchange, the exchanges must also be notified. For a fully registered bond, the redemption notice is sent directly to the registered holders; a printed notice in the financial press is not required, although it would aid market participants. If the bonds are in coupon form, a printed notice in the financial press listing the serial numbers of the bonds to be called is necessary.

Bonds can be called in whole (the entire issue) or in part (only a portion). A few issues, such as the Alaskan Housing Finance Corporation, permit optional redemption only in whole. The method of redemption is usually stated as "by such method as it shall deem fair and appropriate" or "fair and equitable," and is left to the discretion of the trustee. Most directly or privately placed and unregistered issues provide for pro rata redemption in case of partial calls. This means that all holders will have the same percentage of their holdings redeemed (subject to the restrictions imposed by the minimum denominations). Very few publicly issued bonds have pro rata redemption features; rather, the redemption is done "by lot." This is, essentially, the random selection of bonds through the use of computer programs.[12] One public issue with a pro rata redemption feature is Equitable Life Leasing Corporation's $100 million of 9 1/8% Senior Notes due 1990. The prospectus says, "The Notes are subject to redemption semi-annually on each December 4 and June 4 commencing on December 4, 1988 in $20,000,000 equal aggregate principal amounts. The Notes will be redeemed pro rata among the holders of Notes to the extent practicable and otherwise by lot. The Notes will be in fully registered form and will be in denominations of $1,000 or integral multiples thereof."

Often, the documentation states that the redemption is subject to the deposit of the redemption monies with the trustee on or before the redemption date. If funds are not at hand, the redemption notice becomes void and has no effect. An announcement of the intention to redeem debt also has no effect until an official notice has been issued and the funds given to the trustee. In March 1987, Wickes Companies announced plans to redeem in December $200 million of 12% sinking fund debentures. Subsequently, interest rates climbed and bond prices fell so that at the end of September it withdrew the redemption plans; market conditions made it undesirable for the company to proceed with the redemption.

According to the New York Stock Exchange, trading in nonconvertible bonds that have been called in whole ceases when funds are available for payment with the trustee. In the case of a partial call, bonds which have been called for redemption are no longer "good delivery" for the settlement of trades. The exception is when trades are specifically in the called bonds. Once a bond has been called, the few that do trade are, in effect, substitutes for short-term paper. Active bond portfolio managers should be alert as to which of their bonds have been called so that trades settle promptly and without any problems caused by the delivery of "bad" bonds.

Refunding is the primary cause of bond redemptions, as companies can increase shareholders' wealth by substituting lower-cost debt for higher-cost debt. There are many different ways in which issuers estimate the savings which can be achieved through refunding, but refunding is basically a capital budgeting procedure. One calculates, on an after-tax basis, the net present value of the expected savings over the life of the issue to be refunded and subtracts from that figure the costs of the transaction to obtain the net advantage for the refunding. The discount rate used is the after-tax yield on the new debt based on semiannual payments (assuming a conventional bond). It should be noted that the issue's call premium and related expenses are deductible from the current year's income taxes, thus reducing the cost of the refunding. Expenses associated with the new or refunding issue must be amortized over the issue's life. If the net advantage of the refunding is greater than zero, a refunding opportunity exists.[13]

Because the call premium and certain other costs are written off for financial purposes in the year incurred, the transaction may result in a loss for reported net income purposes. But that should not override the economics of the transaction. Many utility companies have been urged by their regulators to use all available means for reducing their interest costs. As further encouragement, the companies should be assured that they will not have to absorb the loss on the transaction in the year incurred, but can amortize it and other related costs (net of the tax benefits) over the new securities' lives for rate-making and reporting purposes. However, as a member of the staff of the Public Utilities Commission of the State of California stated in 1983, "if there is a clear-cut opportunity for a utility to effect substantial interest savings through refinancing and it fails to act promptly, there is ample justification for a ratemaking adjustment imputing a lower interest rate as a penalty."[14]

The optimal timing of a refunding may be difficult, for once done the opportunity to achieve further savings is gone; the issuer will have given up the call option. An issuer should decide whether to refund now or wait until rates are lower. If rates are expected to be lower, the issuer must determine whether they will be low enough to make the delay worthwhile. If a refunding is done now, the costs of the new bond issue are locked-in until the new refunding or call-protected period has expired.

The refunding of high-cost debt in a lower interest rate environment should come as no surprise to any investor. Any one who faithfully reads the financial press ought to be aware of current interest rate levels compared to those on the bonds he owns. Also, some companies have issued press releases and other reports discussing vulnerable issues. On March 18, 1986, Public Service Electric and Gas Company issued a release, "PSE&G Announces Potential Redemption of High Interest Rate Debt Issues." Listing seven high coupon issues (12% and higher) with a total outstanding principal amount of $482.28 million and the dates on which they are eligible for redemption, the release said, in part,

> The Company estimates that $132 million of interest costs would be saved through these refundings over the remaining lives of the redeemed bonds ($38 million on a 'present value' basis) based on a 9% refunding rate. Another benefit would be a reduction in the embedded cost of long-term debt by about 65 basis points. The interest coverage ratio would also be improved, thereby enhancing the credit standing of the Company.

Outright Redemptions

For want of a better term we will use *outright redemptions* to mean the retirement of debt at the general redemption price. The proceeds for the outright redemption need not come from lower cost borrowings, nor is the redemption triggered by the maintenance and replacement fund, the sinking fund, or the release and substitution of property provisions found in bonded debt. Outright redemptions are also known by some as "cash calls," but this term could also be applied to other types of debt calls. The point to remember is that they can occur at any time unless there are call prohibitions; investors should not be lulled by a nonrefunding provision.

In 1973 Bristol-Myers Company redeemed at 107.538 $25 million of its 8 5/8% debentures due 1995. Issued in 1970, they traded as high as 111 in 1972 and were about 108-109 when the call was announced. A number of holders, including institutional investors and at least one Wall Street corporate bond dealer, were confused by the call, having mistaken "nonrefundable" for "noncallable." The bonds were nonrefundable for 10 years but were currently callable. In 1977, N.C.R. Corporation redeemed all of its 9 3/4% debentures due 2000 at 107.88. Still within the ten-year nonrefunding period, the bonds were trading at 111 to 111.5 at the time the call was announced. NCR was in a strong cash position, with projected cash flow substantially in excess of expected capital spending plans. This redemption helped to improve NCR's balance sheet and reduced leverage. In the opinion of these companies' management, their debt offered them better returns than investment in plant and equipment.

Archer-Daniels-Midland Company (A-D-M) presents an interesting case. On May 12, 1981, the company sold $250 million of 7% debentures due May 15, 2011, and $125 million of 16% sinking fund debentures, also maturing on May 15, 2011. Both issues were currently callable, the 7% original issue discounts at par and the full coupon 16s at a premium. The 16% debentures also had the standard 10-year prohibition against lower-cost refunding. Subsequent to these offerings A-D-M raised money in 1982 and 1983 through lower-cost borrowings. It also sold common equity on January 28, 1983, raising more than $131 million, and again on June 1, 1983, raising another $15.45 million. Approximately at 6:19 P.M. on June 1, 1983, the Dow Jones Capital Markets News Wire Service announced that the company would redeem on August 1, at 113.95 plus accrued interest of $33.78, all of the outstanding 16% sinking fund debentures due May 15, 2011.

The corporate bond market was in an uproar. This call was well within the 10-year refunding protected period. One investment banking firm sued to bar the redemption, claiming that "investors expected the debentures to continue on the market until 1991 (which) kept the trading value of the debt at about $1,250 per $1,000 face value and misled investors into believing the debentures would continue to be traded . . . it wouldn't have purchased the debentures if it believed Archer-Daniels would redeem the bonds so soon."[15] People don't often sue in debt redemptions unless they stand to lose money. Here, the plaintiff lost money. Several weeks before the call, it purchased $15,518,000 face amount of the debentures at 125.25 each, and the day before, another $500,000 principal amount at 120.[16] If these bonds were held to the call date, the principal loss would have been nearly $1,784,000.

The company said that the proceeds for this redemption came from the sale of the common stock. The shelf registration prospectus dated March 22, 1983, may have indicated that the high-coupon debt might be in jeopardy when it said in the use of proceeds section, "The proceeds will be used, as required, for general corporate purposes, including working capital, capital expenditures and possible acquisitions of, or investments in, businesses and assets, *and the repayment of indebtedness originally incurred for general corporate purposes*" (emphasis added). The debenture prospectus said that "The proceeds will be used, as required, for general corporate purposes." This is part of the standard boilerplate found in many financing documents. The plaintiff claimed that A-D-M was not allowed, by the issue's terms, to call the bonds from lower-cost funds and it pointed to the 1982 and 1983 debt financings. It contended that the money raised from the common stock sales was little more than a subterfuge for circumventing the refunding protection provided in the indenture. It also alleged securities fraud by A-D-M, as the company did not reveal its own interpretation of the redemption language and would contemplate redemption if it felt that doing so was in its own best interests.

The court upheld A-D-M's right to call the sinking fund debentures with the proceeds from the sales of common shares saying the redemption was within the company's legal rights and in accordance with the indenture. It pointed to the strict "source" of funds argument which came up several years earlier in the case of the redemption of preferred stock with the proceeds of common stock.[17] The Archer-Daniels decision was an important event in modern corporate bond world, as it substantially eroded the effectiveness of standard refunding provisions.

The story didn't end with the 1983 call. Investors don't readily forget the times that they lost money, especially if they felt that they might have been "bamboozled." One year later, on August 6, 1984, A-D-M sold $100 million of 13% sinking fund debentures due August 1, 2014, at a price of 97.241. The new bonds, also with the standard ten-year refunding protection, were not well-received as only about 70% of the issue was sold by the underwriters at the original offering terms. When the managing underwriter terminated syndicate underwriting restrictions, the bonds immediately sold off. As *Bondweek* (August 13, 1984) said, "A-D-M Re-enters Market With a Thud," and " . . . the offering never really got off the ground. Street officials said that without a doubt A-D-M's controversial move last year was a factor in the poor reception of its issue last week in the midst of an otherwise bullish market."

On January 9, 1986, A-D-M sold $100 million of 10 ¼% debentures due January 15, 2006. The price the company paid to reenter the corporate bond market and the good graces of institutional investors was that these bonds were noncallable for life. In April, 1986, the company attempted to rid itself of the then high-coupon 13s. Instead of calling the bonds at below-market prices as it had nearly three years earlier, it tendered for them with a bid above the market. Archer-Daniels probably had enough of Wall Street lawyers for awhile.

Sinking and Purchase Funds

A sinking fund is a provision allowing for a debt's periodic retirement or amortization over its life span. It can also require the periodic deposit of funds or property into a reserve for the loan's eventual retirement or the maintenance of the value of the collateral securing it; this is called an *improvement fund* or a *sinking and improvement fund*. It is more common to have the sinking fund applied to the current extinguishment of debt and not to have the funds build up for use at maturity.

Were debt viewed as permanent, sinking funds would not be needed. Thus the huge United States Government debt does not have any sinking fund. Of course, some might say that with Treasury bills rolling over every week and the frequent note and bond maturities, a sinking fund, even if desirable, would be unnecessary. To reduce debt, the Treasury would only have to sell a smaller amount at each auction. However, much corporate debt generally has been viewed as less than permanent. Early U.S. railroad issues came with sinking funds, but in the last half of the nineteenth century, railroads sold many secured and very long-term issues with no sinking funds. Railroad promoters, financiers and investors apparently viewed the properties as lasting forever. But starting in the early twentieth century, as industrial corporations became more prominent with unsecured debt financing, the importance of sinking funds increased. Investors thought that provision for the periodic retirement of debt before the assets became economically worthless would be preferable to nonamortizing issues. This could strengthen an issuer's credit by prohibiting an unwieldy sum to become due and payable all at once at maturity. This final payment is called a *balloon*. The security provided by tangible assets was less important as investors realized that much property depreciates, deteriorates, depletes and becomes obsolete. Debt service and security would be better provided from cash flow and operations, or, in some cases, from the pledging of unfunded property in lieu of the debt retirement.

Sinking funds in various forms have probably existed for as long as people have borrowed money from one another and worried about the ultimate repayment. A sinking fund was proposed for government debt during the reign of England's William the III in the late seventeenth century.[18] References to measures for reducing the Crown's public debt are found in Mackay's narrative of the South-Sea Bubble scandal:

> Upon the 22d of January, 1720, the House of Commons resolved itself into a committee of the whole house, to take into consideration that part of the king's (George I, the Elector of Hanover) speech at the opening of the session which related to the public

debts, and the proposal of the South-Sea Company towards the
redemption and sinking of the same.[19]

In George Washington's administration, Alexander Hamilton, the
first Secretary of the Treasury, developed a plan for the reduction
of the country's debt. But many government attempts at using sinking funds for debt reduction purposes fell short of the goals.

A variety of sinking fund types may be found in publicly issued
debt. The most common is the *mandatory specific sinking fund* requiring the periodic redemption of a certain amount of a specific debt
issue. This type is found in most longer-term industrial issues and
some electric utility bonds. Bell System debt has no sinking funds.
The May Department Stores Company Debentures due 2018 has a
typical mandatory specific sinking fund as follows:

> The Company will provide for the retirement by redemption of
> $12,500,000 of the principal amount of the Debentures Due 2018
> on June 15 of each of the years 1999 to and including 2017 at the
> principal amount thereof, together with accrued interest to the
> date of redemption. The Company may also provide for the
> redemption of up to an additional $25,000,000 principal amount
> . . . annually, . . . such optional right being non-cumulative. The
> Company may (1) deliver outstanding Debentures Due 2018
> (other than Debentures Due 2018 previously called for redemp-
> tion) and (2) apply as a credit Debentures Due 2018 which have
> been redeemed either at the election of the Company or through
> the application of a permitted optional sinking fund payment, in
> each case in satisfaction of all or any part of any required sink-
> ing fund payment, provided that such Debentures Due 2018
> have not been previously so credited.[20]

The above tells us that for the Company must retire 5% of the
$250 million issue each year starting June 15, 1999 (one year after
the refunding protection expires). Four or five percent is customary
for longer-term industrial bonds. With bonds of shorter maturities,
sinking funds, if provided, may retire a greater percentage of the
issue on each sinking fund date. Owens-Corning Fiberglas
Corporation's 11 ¾% Senior Subordinated Debentures due 2001
have an annual 20% sinking fund requirement starting in 1997.
(Utility issues often have smaller sinking funds.) The May Com-

pany payments retire 95% of the issue prior to maturity, leaving $12,500,000 as the final amount due on June 15, 2018. Many investors erroneously call this a 100% sinking fund, implying that the entire issue is retired prior to maturity. However, the required sinking fund sinks only 95% of the issue, leaving a $12,500,000 balloon payment. The company has the right to increase sinking fund payments by another $12,500,000, a so-called "double up" option. Some issues allow the retirement of up to 200% or more of the minimum required amount. For example, the $100 million Kimberly-Clark Corporation 9 ½% Sinking Fund Debentures due 2018 has an annual sinking fund requirement of $5 million, with a noncumulative option allowing the redemption of up to $15 million. Usually the issuer may deliver debentures acquired by it instead of paying cash and calling the required bonds at par. In high interest rate periods, when the bonds are trading below par, companies would normally prefer to buy the bonds through open market purchases instead of calling them at the higher price; this can lend price support to the bonds. In times of lower interest rates, open market purchases are costly and unnecessary. The company can merely deposit cash with the trustee for a par call; this could depress the bond's price. Thus, depending on the coupon rate relative to the current market rate, a sinking fund may have varying affects on the bond's price and liquidity.

Over the years, a number of institutional investors have played "the sinking fund game": these have become known as "sinker sockers." In this scheme, one or a few investors attempts to control or corner an issue, i.e., buy up the available floating supply of a deep discount bond with a currently operating sinking fund or with one due to start within a couple of years. This does not mean that they must own 100% of the bonds, only a substantial portion of the available supply. Many bonds may be "locked up" in certain investment accounts due to restrictions on their sale at prices lower than their cost. These investors have often purchased the bonds at the time of the original offering at much higher prices. Even if the sinking fund collectors do not control every outstanding bond, they can make life difficult for corporate financial managers. After a company has cleared the market of tradable bonds for the sinking fund, the only remaining ones are those held by the sinking fund collectors. Therefore, the company needing bonds to satisfy the sinking fund must strike a bargain with the bonds' owner at a price at or close to the sinking fund call price. Thus, the investor stands to reap an extra reward.

Of course things can go wrong. Investors may have to sit with an underperforming asset for several years until its scarcity value becomes known. During that time, the credit quality may decline or the investor's objectives may have changed. One portfolio manager with a major eastern trust bank reportedly tried to corner some bonds of a steel company. However, the steel company, an important client of the bank, became aware of the plan and was perturbed; it stopped doing business with the bank. A number of companies have become painfully aware of sinking fund collectors and, as a result, try to keep their sinking fund activities and information (amounts outstanding and to be retired) as secret as possible.

There is also the *nonmandatory specific sinking fund*, the most prevalent type in electric utility company issues. The $100 million 12 1/8% bonds of Public Service Electric and Gas Company due on December 1, 2012, require the retirement of $1 million principal amount of bonds each December 1, 1983, through 2011. The company may satisfy the sinking fund, in whole or in part, by delivering bonds acquired through open market purchases or other means, by paying cash to the trustee who will call bonds for redemption at 100, or by the utilization of unfunded property additions or improvements at 60% of their cost. Property credits so utilized cannot be further employed under the mortgage.

Utilities are usually considered consumers of capital, for they engage in large, ongoing construction projects. As they need to borrow fairly regularly, the application of property credits helps to reduce the demands on the capital markets. (It makes no sense to pay off debt on the one hand only to have to go back to the market to raise the money that was just paid out.) Utilization of property credits conserves cash and still helps to maintain the integrity of the collateral behind the bonds. In some cases, a company may be able to authenticate and simultaneously cancel new bonds specifically authorized for this purpose. This usually is done against unfunded property additions and thus reduces the amount of new debt the company can issue.

A slight variation of the property sinking fund is found in the indenture of Continental Telephone Company of California's 7 5/8% first mortgage bonds due December 31, 1997. The requirement is 1% annually of each outstanding series of bonds. The funds must be held by the trustee as part of the mortgaged property and paid back to the company as reimbursement for 100% of the amount of available net property additions. If not paid out, the funds may be used to repurchase or call bonds. Any funds remaining in the trust after five years must be used to retire debt.

One cannot always rely on what is stated in a company's financial reports. In May, 1977, some holders of New England Power Company's 10 7/8% bonds due 2005 were surprised when the company announced the redemption on the following July 1 at 101.55, of $2.4 million of the outstanding $80 million issue. The bonds had the usual utility sinking fund provisions, namely, 1% annually, cash, bonds or property credits at 60%. The indenture also provided that an additional 2% ($1,600,000) could be retired. Surprised investors, having read the company's 1976 annual report, would have concluded that property credits would be used and bonds would not be called. A footnote to the financials said that "the company may elect to satisfy its annual sinking fund obligations of $3,850,000 ... by evidencing to the Trustee net additional property in amounts not less than $6,417,000 in 1977. . . . For the sinking fund requirement due in 1977 the company intends to so elect." Because of declining interest rates, the company did a complete about-face in less than a matter of weeks after the annual report was issued. Thus, the sinking fund obligation was satisfied with the high coupon bonds and property additions. In 1978 the company also retired $2.4 million of the 10 7/8s. High-coupon bonds in a lower interest rate environment are vulnerable to call even if the issuer promises not to do so.

Specific sinking funds apply to just the named issue. There are also *nonspecific sinking funds* of both the mandatory and nonmandatory variety. The nonspecific sinking fund, also known as a *funnel, tunnel, blanket,* or *aggregate* sinking fund, is based on the outstanding amount of a company's total bonded indebtedness. If mandatory, the sinking fund must be satisfied by bonds of any issue or issues selected by the company. If nonmandatory, the company may utilize certain property credits in fulfilling the sinking fund requirement. Nonspecific sinking funds are found in the indentures of 17 companies. Three of these—Baltimore Gas & Electric, Ohio Edison, and Pacific Gas & Electric—have mandatory funnel sinking funds. The other 14, including the subsidiaries of the Southern Company and Northeast Utilities, have nonmandatory funnel sinking funds.

In most cases the redemption price for bonds called under the funnel sinking fund is par, but Pacific Gas & Electric's and Southern California Edison's operate at the general or regular redemption prices. Pacific Gas has usually chosen to retire its low-coupon issues trading at discounts. The funnel sinking fund may be deceptive. Usually 1% of all bonds outstanding, this can amount to a large requirement, especially if the total amount is applied against a single issue. For example, if bonded debt of $3 billion consists of issues ranging in size from $50 million to $200 million, the annual funnel requirement is $30 million; this equals 15% to 60% of any one issue. When interest rates and cash needs are high, companies normally utilize unfunded property additions if they are able to do so. But actual bond retirement provides a way to redeem high coupon debt (usually at par) when interest rates are down. In some cases, however, a maximum of 1% of a specific issue may be retired in any one year if the call is within five years of issuance (the refunded protected period). The Southern Company (among others) had to place this restriction in its subsidiaries' indentures after the funnel calls of the early 1970s. Thus, while there is a limit on the amount of the bonds that can be redeemed in the first five years, once that period has expired, investors should be careful. An issuer could apply the maximum amount possible to the retirement of the bonds at par and then call any remaining ones at the regular redemption prices.

Most sinking funds operate annually, but some, such as Pacific Gas & Electric's are effective semiannually. Again, most sinking funds are based on a specific percentage of the original amount issued, or a fixed amount of bonds which remains the same until the entire issue is retired. But other issues' sinking fund payments may increase periodically. Each payment may be higher than the preceding one, or payments might be level for several years, then step up for another few years, and so forth. There are even some sinking funds that increase for several years and then decrease for a few more years.

Because of the risk of exhausting gas supplies, some gas pipeline company indentures provide for the acceleration of the sinking fund in the event that estimates of the reserve lives of the companies' proven gas reserves decline. ANR Pipeline Company (formerly Michigan Wisconsin Pipe Line Company) has such a provision. The prospectus for the 10 ⅝% First Mortgage Pipe Line Bonds due April 15 1995, states,

> Indenture will provide in substance that in the event that an independent engineer's certificate of reserve life, which the Company is required to file with the Trustee prior to May 1 of each year, shows a reserve life for the Company's controlled proven gas reserves of less than eight years and a date of exhaustion of reserve life earlier than any sinking fund payment date then in effect, the next two sinking fund installments shall each be increased. . . . However, if the reserve life shown in any such certificate is less than four years, all sinking fund installments falling due subsequent to the year in which such certificate is filed shall become payable on December 31 of such year.

Thus, the sinking fund payments can be increased, but if future certificates subsequently show an improvement in the gas supply, the sinking fund will be adjusted once again. Transcontinental Gas Pipe Line Corporation was required to accelerate the sinking funds of at least five of its mortgage bond issues and one debenture issue in the 1970s for at least five years in a row.

There are other types of sinking funds but they are seldom encountered in public U.S. corporate debt. Sinking funds can be on a contingent basis, i.e., based on a certain level of corporate earnings or expressed as a percentage of earnings or cash flow. This type may be found in some of the financially weaker companies (such as one emerging from bankruptcy or reorganization), requiring that part of the cash flow be directed towards debt retirement. If there are no earnings or a lack of adequate cash flow, there is no sinking fund requirement. Missouri-Kansas-Texas Railroad Company's 5% Prior Lien Series E bonds due 1990 has a 1% sinking fund with the deposits to be made from earnings in excess of $1 million. That company's 5½% Subordinated Income Debentures due in 2033 have a noncumulative sinking fund payable from available income, if any.

Another type of sinking fund found in Canadian provincial debt issues sold in the United States is called the *invested* or *Canadian* sinking fund. This is really a fund of cash and securities set aside to provide monies for debt retirement at maturity. Usually the funds can be invested in the same bonds, other bonds of the issuer, Canadian government bonds, and certain other permitted investments. Some issuers have utilized this type of fund to help support the market for existing bonds at the time of a new issue's sale by purchasing the outstanding bonds from holders at an attractive yield spread from the new issue if the proceeds were used to buy the new bonds.

A few issues may have a *purchase fund*. In some cases, it may operate prior to the start of the sinking fund; in others, there may be no sinking fund. Although the purchase fund may seem like a sinking fund, it does not operate when the debt's market price is above par. The purchase fund may require that the issuer, through its agent, attempt, on a best efforts basis and in good faith, to purchase each year a certain amount of bonds at par or less, in public and private transactions. This may lend market support to the bonds and encouraged some investors to buy the bonds who ordinarily might not do so.

One such purchase fund, found in Harnischfeger Corporation's 15% Notes due April 15, 1994, requires an annual purchase fund of 5% of the original issue in the event the notes' market price is less than par for 60 consecutive calendar days. This purchase fund is cumulative and remains in effect until satisfied, but there may be no more than one such purchase obligation in any one year. The prospectus says:

> The purchase agency arrangements have been designed to provide a limited measure of market liquidity for the Notes and in certain circumstances to result in the retirement prior to stated maturity of a portion of the outstanding Notes. There can be no assurance that such arrangements will, in fact, support market liquidity for the Notes or result in the retirement of any Notes.

The purchase agency arrangements are not equivalent to a sinking fund, mandatory redemption feature or similar provision . . . In the event that the market price of the Notes is equal to or greater than 100% of the principal amount thereof for even one day within each 60 consecutive calendar day period, the purchase agency arrangements of the Note Indenture will not become operative. Prospective purchasers should be prepared to hold any Notes to be purchased by them until maturity in 1994, optional redemption, if any, by the Company or sale in the open market or otherwise.

In 1986 the *annuity note* appeared. Basically a level debt service arrangement similar to a home mortgage, each periodic payment is applied to interest and principal. Ford Motor Credit Company issued Series 1 of its Annuity Notes in September 1986. The minimum denomination was $100,000, repayable in 20 equal quarterly installments of $5,933.28 each March 1, June 1, September 1, and December 1, starting December 1, 1986. The first installment consisted of $1,791.45 of interest and $4,201.83 of principal. The last installment, on September 1, 1991, will consist of only $105.47 of interest and $5,887.81 of principal. This type of security eliminates any large balloon payment at maturity and helps the Company to better match its liabilities with its automobile receivables. Some investors needing periodic return of principal, especially those pension funds with heavy payments to retired beneficiaries, have been thought to be among the purchasers of these notes.

Maintenance and Replacement Funds

Until March 23, 1977, hardly anyone in the investment community knew—or cared—what a maintenance and replacement fund (M&R) was. On that date the exact nature of this little known, never used, but standard provision was made abundantly clear when Florida Power & Light Company announced its intention to deposit $64.8 million of cash with the trustee of its 10⅛% bonds due March 1, 2005 (issued March 13, 1975) to satisfy the maintenance and replacement fund requirement. (The maintenance and replacement fund is also known as the maintenance and renewal fund, the maintenance fund, and the replacement fund.) The cash was used for the September 2, 1977, redemption of $63.7 million of the out-standing $125 million bond issue at the special redemption price of 101.65. The regular redemption price at that time was 110.98, and the refunding-protected period would not expire until March 1, 1980, when the regular redemption price would be 109.76. Prior to the March announcement, the bonds were trading around 111; afterwards, they fell immediately to 101.

The M&R provision was first placed in bond indentures of electric utilities subject to regulation by the Securities and Exchange Commission under the Public Utility Holding Company Act in the early 1940s. It remained in the indentures even when some of the companies no longer were subject to regulation under the act. Property is subject to wear and tear, and the replacement fund supposedly helps maintain the integrity of the property securing the bonds. One writer said, "A replacement fund is designed to force actual annual expenditures for new property or the reduction of bonded indebtedness."[21] It differs from a sinking fund in that the M&R only helps to maintain the value of the security while a sinking or improvement fund is designed to improve the security behind the debt. It is similar to, but more complex than, a provision in a home mortgage requiring the home owner to maintain his property in good repair.

A maintenance and replacement fund requires a company to annually determine the amounts needed to satisfy the fund and any shortfall. (Not all utility indentures provide for them, and some companies have eliminated or sharply modified them in recent years.) The requirement is based on a formula, usually 15% or so of adjusted gross operating revenues, but some are based on a much smaller percentage (such as 2% to 2 ½%) of depreciable mortgaged property or a percentage of bonded debt. The difference between what is required and the actual amount expended on maintenance is the shortfall. The shortfall is usually satisfied with unfunded property additions, but it can be satisfied with cash or, in some cases, maintenance and replacement fund credits from prior years. The cash can be used for the retirement of debt or withdrawn upon the certification of unfunded property credits.

Inflated fuel costs in the 1970s increased the M&R requirements of those funds based on a percentage of revenues beyond what normally was previously adequate. In some cases, unfunded property additions might be insufficient to satisfy the shortfall. Companies may be unable to obtain the necessary operating permits and other licenses for some nuclear plants, which would make such property ineligible for use as unfunded property. Also, the amount of available property additions may be inadequate due to declining construction outlays resulting from reduced demand for electric power. But the M&R certainly grants most companies the right to retire debt. Some issues restrict the amount of bonds that may be redeemed through the M&R fund. Investors should be skeptical of companies saying that they have no intention of retiring debt through the M&R provisions—they may be forced to do so by the economics of the situation, as Florida Power & Light was. Of course, the company's cash position is an important determinant of whether or not it is financially able to call the bonds. As we have seen, cash can be raised if doing so makes sense, and refunding limitations almost always relate to redemptions at the general, not the special, redemption prices. Also, some companies may be reluctant to utilize an M&R call for fear of angering their investors. But again, if the company is pressured by regulatory authorities, it may have no choice but to comply. Also, the initial trauma of the M&R calls of the late 1970s is over; investors today are more aware of the possibility of such calls and can usually position themselves accordingly.

What caused Florida Power & Light to resort to a maintenance and replacement fund call? In January 1977, the public service commission began rate hearings as it was interested in FP&L's cost of debt and ways to reduce it. It was suggested by the company's financial people that a debt retirement through the maintenance and replacement fund was one way to reduce interest costs. This testimony was given on March 23 and a press release issued, but the right not to redeem the bonds was reserved. In June, the commission issued an order granting FP&L a $195.5 million rate boost, based on the assumption that half of the 10 ⅛s would be retired and substituted a 9% rate. It projected that annual interest savings of more than $500,000 would be passed through to customers. "Once the Florida Public Service Commission factored these retirements into its cost of capital calculations, the company had little choice, but to go ahead and exercise the special redemption option."[22] The 1983 court decision said that all the benefits from the redemption would be passed through to the ratepayer whether or not the bonds were called. The company's shareholders received none of the savings.[23]

Florida Power and Light's redemption broke the ice. Several others followed, most notably Carolina Power & Light Company. In 1977 and 1978, Carolina deposited with its trustee nearly $79 million under similar M&R provisions. In June 1978, it called for redemption $46 million of the privately held 11 1/8% bonds due 1994 and $32.7 million of the publicly held 11s of 1984 at par, the special redemption price. Carolina was sued by its bondholders, including an insurance company which negotiated the first Carolina Power & Light Mortgage dated May 1, 1940; it contained an improvement fund and a maintenance and renewal fund that could be satisfied with fundable property or bonds. The courts have upheld the issuers' rights to redeem debt through such provisions. But companies should ensure that their offering documents clearly spell out special redemption features to avoid accusation of concealing important information. It is also incumbent upon bond buyers to know the terms of the issues they own. "Investors beware! We have the right to redeem our debt in any way that our contract allows. We will do it the cheapest way in order to benefit our ratepayers and shareholders."

After the 1977 to 1978 period, maintenance and replacement fund calls receded into the background as interest rates rose. It wasn't until 1985 that these redemptions again occurred to any noticeable degree. By that time investors should have been at least somewhat familiar with these provisions even though they still disliked them. The legal considerations were out of the way, and the provisions have become a fact of life. But par calls are especially painful as the following two examples show.

On May 5, 1986, Houston Lighting & Power Company redeemed $117,056,000 of its 12 3/8% first mortgage bonds due March 15, 2013, through the replacement fund provisions, leaving about $8 million outstanding. The call price was par but the bonds were trading at 115 or so just before the redemption was announced in early April.

On May 31, 1988, Central Maine Power Company redeemed at par $25.5 million of its Series F 12 ¼% General and Refunding Mortgage Bonds due May 1, 2013, under the renewal and replacement fund covenant. The sad part about this story is that many investors complained that they did not realize this issue was subject to the covenant as they assumed that the First Mortgage Bonds were still outstanding. After all, the prospectus for the subject 12 ¼s said that "The maintenance covenant contained in the First Mortgage . . . will remain in effect until the First Mortgage is discharged, and upon such discharge the renewal and replacement fund provisions of the General Mortgage will become effective." If the investors, especially those with fiduciary responsibilities, had done a responsible job of proper research, something as elementary as looking at the annual report each year, they would have known that the First Mortgage Bonds no longer existed. The annual report for the year ended December 31, 1986, stated: "The First and General Mortgage dated June 1, 1921, was discharged in December, 1986 in connection with the call for redemption of all outstanding bonds thereunder. Upon such discharge, the General and Refunding Mortgage succeeded the First and General Mortgage as the senior general lien on substantially all of the Company's properties and franchises." It goes on to say, in referring to the General and Refunding Mortgage Bonds, "Bonds may also be redeemed under certain conditions by means of cash deposited with the trustee under various provisions of the mortgage indenture."[24]

Redemption Through the Sale of Assets and Eminent Domain

Bondholders want the borrower to maintain and preserve the value of the collateral securing the debt. The fact that the debt may be overcollateralized does not necessarily mean that management has free rein over the use and disposition of the excess collateral and any proceeds therefrom. But the lender has no right to impose undue restrictions on the borrower's ability to sell plant and property if doing so is deemed desirable from the standpoint of sound business practices. The secured lender has the right to adequate protection. If a company has $100 million of bonded debt outstanding secured by $200 million of plant, property and equipment, the $100 million surplus collateral provides additional protection for the bond owner. If the company feels that it is prudent to sell some of the property securing that debt, it should be allowed to do so (release the property from the mortgage lien) and substitute either cash or other property so that the total value of the collateral will not be reduced. The cash can be used to retire bonds or buy additional collateral. This type of situation is covered by *release and substitution of property clauses.*

The release and substitution of property clause of Arizona Public Service as described in its prospectuses is fairly clear.[25]

> When not in default under the Mortgage, the Company may obtain the release from the lien thereof of (a) property that has become unserviceable, obsolete or unnecessary for use in the Company's operations, provided that it replaces such property with, or substitutes for the same, an equal value of other property and (b) other property that has been sold or otherwise disposed of, provided that the Company deposits with the Trustee cash in an amount, or utilizes as a credit net Property Additions acquired by the Company within the preceding five years and having a fair value (not more than Cost), equal to the fair value of the property to be released.

Arizona has utilized this method of debt redemption a couple of times. In late 1984, it retired $100 million of its 16% First Mortgage Bonds due 1994 at 100, with the proceeds from the sale of its gas distribution assets. In early 1987, it redeemed $150 million of its 11 ½% First Mortgage Bonds due June 1, 2015, also at par. The proceeds for this redemption came from the sale and leaseback of its portion in the Unit #2 of the Palo Verde nuclear power plant. These bonds had been issued only in June of 1985.

There have been cases in which companies sold plant, deposited the funds with the trustee, and then later decided not to redeem debt. In March 1984, Georgia Power Company sold some property and deposited funds with the trustee. It could have used the funds to purchase or redeem bonds or could have withdrawn them against delivery of bonds or shown that unfunded property additions existed after withdrawal. The fear of high-coupon bond redemption hung over the market for a couple of months until, on May 31, the company said it would not redeem any debt. Georgia decided against the call because of uncertainties in the financial markets. It pointedly stated that if it had future asset sales, its options regarding the funds would remain open.

Of course, investors are hurt most when their high-yield, premium-priced bonds are called at par or the special redemption price, and most electric utility mortgage issues use the special redemption price for these special calls. A few provide for the regular redemption prices including Florida Power & Light Company, Duke Power Company and Southern California Edison Company, among others. System Energy Resources 14% First Mortgage Bonds due November 15, 1994, are not optionally redeemable by the Company but they are redeemable with the proceeds of released property at 125% of their principal amount, a rather high call premium which should ease any investor ill-will in case the bonds have to be called. Of course, par is the price for certain other redemptions. The Company has also used the par price for released property redemptions of other high-coupon issues such as its 16% and 15⅜% First Mortgage Bonds due 2000. Because the redemption prices used in any special redemption may vary between issues of the same company, prudent investors should carefully review the bonds' documentation to ascertain the call prices and the issues' vulnerability to special call.

Unsecured debt usually has no special redemption prices or requirements for prepayment in the event of asset sales. However, there may be exceptions, especially in the case of some sub investment-grade debt. Remember, do not confuse call protection with refunding protection. Redemptions of unsecured debt do occur within the refunding-protected period where the funds came from the sale of assets. In December 1983, Internorth, Inc. announced a February 1, 1984, call of $90.5 million out of $200 million of its 17½% debentures due August 1, 1991, at the regular redemption price of 112.32. The refunding-protected period ran until September 30, 1988. However, the proceeds were obtained from the sale of its Northern Propane Gas Company unit. On October 1, 1984, it redeemed another $23,875,000 of these 17 ½% debentures at 109.86 with funds obtained from the 1983 sale of two tanker ships.

The sale of assets to an affiliated company will not prevent debt redemption through the release clauses. Wisconsin Michigan Power retired $9.9 million of its 9 ¼% bonds due 2000 in February, 1977, at 100.97. On June 30, 1976, the company sold its gas business for $16.9 million to Wisconsin Natural Gas Company, an affiliate. The gas company got some of the money through bank borrowings. Of the proceeds, $16.5 million was deposited with the trustee under the release and substitution of property clause and a portion of the funds released to the company against certified property additions. The balance was used to redeem the high-coupon 9 ¼s, as interest rates had declined to the point where management thought it was in the company's best interest to do so.

Another similar transaction between affiliates occurred eight years later. This resulted in South Carolina Electric and Gas Company's (SCE&G) redemption of its 16% First Mortgage Bonds due June 1, 2011, at par on March 1, 1985. At the end of 1984, a new holding company called SCANA was formed that had two subsidiaries, SCG&E and the South Carolina Generating Company. SCG&E sold a coal-fired generating plant to its affiliated generating company for $80 million. It used these funds to par call the 16% bonds, which recently had been trading at 116. Some have called this unfair dealing and even a sham transaction. The lesson for investors is to be wary of debt redemption in times of lower interest rates.

Many utility bond issues contain provisions regarding the taking or confiscation of assets by a governmental body through its right of eminent domain or the disposition of assets by order of or to any governmental authority. In a number of cases, bonds must be redeemed if the company receives more than a certain amount in cash. Washington Water Power Company must apply the proceeds of $15 million or more to the retirement of debt. The redemption price may be either the special or regular, depending on the issue. In 1984, Pacific Power & Light Company sold an electric distribution system to the Emerald People's Utility District for $25 million. It applied these proceeds to the redemption of half of the outstanding 14 ¾% Mortgage Bonds due 2010 at the special redemption price of 100. This issue was not the highest-coupon bond outstanding in the company's capitalization. There were some 18s of 1991, but these were exempt from the special provisions for the retirement of bonds with the proceeds from property sold to governmental authorities. More recently, in April 1988, Utah Power & Light Company retired some 13% bonds due 2012 with funds obtained from the condemnation of some of its property in Kaneb, Utah, and the sale of electric assets to a couple other cities.

Net Worth, Merger, and Other Redemptions

The great increase in merger and acquisition activity, including leveraged buyouts and other corporate restructurings, has caused some companies to include other special debt retirement features in their indentures. For example, *the maintenance of net worth clause* is included in the indentures of many lower-rated bond issues of the 1980s. In this case, an issuer covenants to maintain its net worth above a stipulated level. If its net worth falls below that specified amount for a certain period (usually two consecutive quarters), the company must begin redeeming its debt at par. The redemptions, often 10% of the original issue, are mostly on a semiannual basis, and must continue until the net worth recovers to an amount above the stated figure. In many cases, the company is only required to "offer to redeem" the stated amount. An offer to redeem is not mandatory on the bondholders' part; only those holders who want their bonds redeemed need do so. In a number of instances in which the issuer is required to call bonds, the bondholders may elect not to have bonds redeemed. This is not much different from an offer to redeem. It may "protect" bondholders from the redemption of the high-coupon debt at lower interest rates. However, if a company's net worth declines to a level low enough to activate such a call, it would probably be prudent to have one's bonds redeemed.

The minimum net worth requirement varies from approximately 45% to 65% of the issuer's net worth at the time the debt was issued, depending on the company. The definition of net worth, or net tangible assets, will also vary among issuers. The prospectuses talk about generally accepted accounting principles and frequently include only common shareholders' net worth, but some also include preferred stock. Intangible assets, such as goodwill, patents, trademarks, and unamortized deferred charges, normally are excluded from the calculation of tangible net worth. But again, definitions vary among issues. The prospectus for Coastal Corporation's 11 ¾% Senior Debentures due June 15, 2006, defines consolidated net worth as:

> . . . the total consolidated stockholder's equity (exclusive of any Mandatory Redemption Preferred Stock) of such person and its subsidiaries determined on a consolidated basis in accordance with generally accepted accounting principles, except that there shall be deducted therefrom all intangible assets (determined in accordance with generally accepted accounting principles) including, without limitation, organization costs, patents, trademarks, copyrights, franchises, research and development expenses, and any amount reflected as treasury stock; provided, that goodwill arising from acquisitions and unamortized debt discount and expense, whether existing on the date of the indenture or arising thereafter, shall not be deducted from total consolidated stockholders' equity.

Obviously the definition is very important, and one cannot always rely on the prospectus since it may include no definition or only an incomplete one. This was important for the holders of Minstar Inc.'s 14 ⅞% Senior Subordinated Notes due 1995. The $300 million issue was publicly sold in April 1985, and one year later the company announced the call of $30 million at par due to the net worth clause (they were otherwise not callable until April 1, 1990). The notes were trading around 113 ($1,130 each) prior to the call announcement. Minstar subsequently redeemed another $30 million in September 1986 and purchased an additional $126.6 million of notes in the open market, recording an extraordinary loss of $13.5 million on the debt extinguishment. Also, in the annual report for the year ended December 31, 1986, the company recorded as current maturities of long-term debt $60 million of notes subject to this mandatory redemption in 1987. Here again an indenture provision was used to retire some high-cost debt and caught investors off guard. Analysts and investors relying on the prospectus could come up with no close approximation of tangible net worth. The prospectus stated: "Tangible Net Worth generally means consolidated shareholders' equity, less, among other things, goodwill, patents, trademarks, service marks, trade names, copyrights, organization or developmental expenses and other intangible items."

The indenture for the notes defines tangible net worth as follows:

> *Tangible Net Worth* means the consolidated equity of the common stockholders of the Company and its consolidated subsidiaries less their consolidated Intangible Assets, all determined on a consolidated basis in accordance with generally accepted accounting principles. For purposes of this definition "Intangible Assets" means the amount (to the extent reflected in determining such consolidated equity of the common stockholders) of (i) all write-ups (other than write-ups resulting from foreign currency translations and write-ups of tangible assets of a going concern business made within twelve months after the acquisition of such business) subsequent to December 31, 1984 in the book value of any asset owned by the company or a consolidated subsidiary, (ii) all investments in unconsolidated subsidiaries and in persons which are not subsidiaries, and (iii) all unamortized debt discount and expense, unamortized deferred charges, goodwill, patents, trademarks, service marks, trade names. Copyrights, organization or developmental expenses and other intangible items, all of the foregoing as determined in accordance with generally accepted accounting principles.[26]

Note item (ii) above and the reference to investments. Minstar had substantial investments in marketable equities with value, yet the indenture was written so as to make then valueless. They had to be eliminated in the calculation of tangible net worth. It is interesting to note that the use of proceeds section of the prospectus stated that the monies "will be added to the Company's general funds to be used for acquisitions, investments and general corporate purposes." It said that the company "makes significant investments in securities of other companies." Thus, investors who initially purchased the bonds were effectively reducing tangible net worth to the extent that investment securities were purchased with the proceeds. Also, this could allow a company with a similar definition and operations to rid itself of some high-coupon debt at par just by making more investments! Of course, Minstar's published annual report made no mention of what tangible net worth amounted to according to the indenture's definition at December 31, 1985.

There are a few other ways companies can (or must) extinguish debt prior to maturity. The issues of some finance companies and others with a considerable amount of accounts receivable have provisions allowing the issues to be redeemed if the receivables decline below a certain amount. While not mandatory, this provision can protect debtholders from a weakening of credit due to a substantial decline in the issuer's asset base. It allows the issuer to reduce its debt burden, assuming that it still has the wherewithal to do so. Of course, if the company elects to redeem debt, it will most likely choose from the higher-coupon issues. This provision has been infrequently invoked—if ever—by major debt issuers. A call could occur if there were a serious recession and receivables declined by a substantial amount. It could also be activated if a company sold or transferred receivables to another corporation as part of a reorganization, restructuring or liquidation.

The debt of some foreign companies sold in the United States may be subject to premature redemption in the event of certain situations that normally would not affect conventional domestic issues. In December 1983, The Swan Brewery Company Limited sold US$135 million of 14 7/8% Limited Subordination Debentures due December 15, 1998. The issue requires Swan to redeem a specific percentage of the outstanding debentures (subject to certain credits) if the average of the U.S. dollar noon buying rates for Australian dollars over certain six-month periods is less than those stated in the prospectus. The redemption is on a pro rata basis, but holders may elect not to have their bonds redeemed. Another provision, also subject to election by the debtholder, allows the company to offer to redeem the entire issue if the Australian government requires the withholding of taxes and other governmental charges from payments to the debenture holders.

Tenders

A more pleasant debt retirement method, at least for the bondholders, is the tender. While it may be more costly for the borrower than a straight cash call, it allows debt to be retired even if it is noncallable. Also, tenders don't force the holder to give up the bonds. To encourage holders to tender their bonds, the issuer must offer a price above what others are willing to offer, namely a buyback price above the market. The premium which Mountain States Telephone & Telegraph Company offered for its 11 5/8% Debentures in the March 1986 tender "was determined by calculating the tender price that would provide a yield-to-first-call comparable to the yield an investor could realize by investing in U.S. government agency issues over the same time horizon."[27]

Tenders are not limited to only issues selling above par. In 1983, Diamond International Company tendered for its 8.35% debentures due in 2006 at 77 1/2, and Black & Decker Manufacturing Company tendered for its 8.45% notes due 1985 at 98. In 1985, Burlington Northern Railroad Company made an unsuccessful tender at 53 1/2 for Northern Pacific Railway Company's 4% Prior Lien Railway and Land Grant Gold Bonds due 1997, and at 39 for Northern Pacific's 3% General Lien Railway and Land Grant Gold Bonds due 2047. The bonds, issued in 1896, are not callable for life. The mortgages do not provide for their modification or for the release of certain collateral, namely some valuable natural resource-laden properties Burlington Northern wanted to commercially develop. The tender was part of a plan to obtain the release of the property by substituting government bonds in a trust to ensure the payment of principal and interest when due for the remaining untendered bonds; this is an in-substance defeasance (discussed shortly). Bondholders sued, as they thought a higher price should have been offered. A federal judge barred Burlington from proceeding, and the company withdrew the offer. Burlington subsequently ne-gotiated a settlement (effective in early 1988) with the bondholders and paid them what some called a "hold-up" premium of $147.50 per $1,000 1997 bond and $456.30 per 2047 bond. In return, the bondholders release from the lien of the mortgage millions of acres of land and mineral rights.

Each summer the Baltimore Gas & Electric Company asks for tenders for the funnel sinking fund on its mortgage bonds. In some cases the tenders are accepted and in other cases it is more advantageous for the company to repurchase bonds in the open market, or to even have the trustee call the bonds at the special redemption prices.

A tender allows a company to retire debt at a predetermined price, and rather quickly since tenders are usually open for only a limited time. A simple open market purchase of bonds usually occurs over a longer period, leaving the purchaser subject to changes in market conditions. This may prove cheaper than a tender offer if interest rates rise and prices decline, but it is less likely to permit the company to achieve its debt retirement goals. Of course, the market can also go against the company using a tender offer, with the result that few bonds will be repurchased. As with cash calls, net present value savings are made under successful tenders, the average coupon of the outstanding debt is reduced, and certain expenses are currently deductible for income tax purposes. But like other debt retirement transactions, tenders may result in accounting or financial reporting losses.

With the Dutch auction tender, the sellers rather than the buying company set the prices they wish to receive. At the end of the tender period, the buyer reviews all of the tenders received and determines the highest price it is willing to pay. It then buys all of the bonds tendered at and below the maximum acceptable tender price. The Dutch auction allows the market to set the tender price.

Proceeds for a tender can come from any source. On December 3, 1986, The May Department Stores Company sold $150 million of 9 1/8% debentures due 2016. The use of proceeds section says that the new funds would be used to retire some short-term debt that had a weighted average interest cost of 5.8% and matured before January 1, 1987. Yet, on December 11 the company announced the tender for $100 million of its 11 7/8% debentures due April 15, 2015, at 112.04. Holders need not tender their bonds, and the company is within its rights to offer to repurchase them even within the refunding-protected period.

In general, it makes good sense for investors to consider tender offers because if enough bonds are repurchased, the few remaining could very well become virtually unmarketable, or at least, very illiquid. If listed, they could be delisted. Traders will not ordinarily take into their positions bonds which can't be readily resold. Also, with fewer bonds outstanding the holder is more likely to lose a greater percentage of its holdings through the sinking fund. In September 1983, Northern States Power Company (Minnesota) received tenders at 119.75 for about $65.6 million out of $75 million of its 15¾% mortgage bonds due 2011. Some $9.4 million remained in public hands. The sinking fund was 1% or $750,000 each year, cash, bonds or property additions. On October 31, 1983, the company called for the December 1 sinking fund—$750,000 of the bonds, or nearly 8% of the then outstanding amount. Thus, in less than two months holders lost some 19¾ points—the difference between the tender price and the sinking fund call price. Similar amounts were retired in subsequent years at par and the remaining balance was retired on December 1, 1986, at 112.21.

Defeasance

Defeasance is included as a type of debt extinguishment even though the bonds remain outstanding. There are two types of defeasance transactions. One is called *economic* or *in-substance defeasance* and the other is *legal defeasance* or *novation*. Until the early 1980s, defeasance was rarely used for public corporate debt. There had been cases of privately placed debt in which the issuer reached an agreement with all of the lenders under which they would release the borrower from the indenture in return for ample consideration, typically an acceptable package of securities. A corporation with public debt could do little to defease its obligations, although municipal obligations provided for legal defeasance for a number of years.

In 1983, the Financial Accounting Standards Board (FASB) narrowly approved the *Statement of Financial Accounting Standards No. 76* "Extinguishment of Debt, An Amendment of APB Opinion No. 26," providing for the defeasance of corporate debt.[28] Effective for transactions entered into after December 31, 1983, it applies only to debt with specific maturities and fixed interest rates. In this type of defeasance, an irrevocable trust is established to service the principal and interest payments on the debt issue being defeased. The assets of the trust must consist of essentially risk-free monetary assets in the currency in which the debt is denominated and with a cash flow timed to very closely match that of the defeased obligation. For U.S.-dollar payable debt, these qualified assets include cash, direct obligations of the U.S. government, debt guaranteed by the U.S. government, and securities that are backed by U.S. government obligations as collateral under an arrangement in which the collateral's interest and principal payments flow directly to the security holder. As some securities can be paid prior to the stated maturity or have partial principal payments that may be paid before the final maturity, they are not essentially risk free from a timing standpoint and thus are not eligible for inclusion in the trust assets. Many issues of U.S. Government sponsored corporations (also known as agencies) also are ineligible, as they are not guaranteed by the United States. The debtor must be virtually assured that it will not be required to make any future payments in regard to the defeased debt.

An economic defeasance removes the debt from the corporation's balance sheet but leaves the borrower still liable under all of the indenture provisions until the debt is actually extinguished. It must abide by any covenants, as economic defeasance is not provided for in indentures. Because of the debtor's continuing obligation under the indenture, the transaction must be disclosed in the notes to the financial statements for as long as the debt remains outstanding. The debtor remains liable for tax reporting purposes since it pays income taxes on the income of the trust and takes a deduction for the interest expense. Also, when the trust terminates at the defeased debt's maturity, taxes also must be paid on the increase in value between the cost of the trust's assets and the maturity value. But any fees paid to investment bankers for advice and any trustee fees normally will be considered tax deductible expenses at the time they are incurred.

A novation, or legal, defeasance removes the debt from the balance sheet for financial reporting purposes, frees the corporation from any indenture terms (with a few minor exceptions), and eliminates any further tax consequences. In order to obtain this, the indenture must make provision for legal defeasance. In January 1981, Union Carbide Corporation registered a proposed $200 million offering whose indenture contained such a provision. The issue never came to market as investors, being overly wary, thought this was another method by which a company could prematurely retire debt. However, after in-substance defeasance got the nod of approval from the Securities and Exchange Commission in 1983, most indentures of publicly offered corporate bonds included legal defeasance language.

For several years, the defeasance provision was viewed as a pledge rather than a sale or exchange of property and thus a transaction was not taxable. More recently, the indenture language was modified to take note of regulations treating defeasance as a debt redemption prior to maturity in exchange for property deposited in a trust, a transaction subject to federal income taxes. Defeasance sections of prospectuses have thus been modified. The following from the May 5, 1989, prospectus for General Motors Corporation 9 ¾% Notes due May 15, 1999, is one such example.

> The Corporation, at its option, (i) will be discharged from any and all obligations in respect of the Notes (except for certain obligations to register the transfer or exchange of Notes, replace stolen, lost or mutilated Notes, maintain paying agencies and hold monies for payment in trust), or (ii) will not be under any obligation to comply with certain covenants applicable to the Notes . . ., if the Corporation deposits with the Trustee, in trust for the holders of the Notes, (A) money or (B) obligations issued or guaranteed by the United States of America which through the payment of interest thereon and principal thereof will provide money, in each case in an amount sufficient to pay all the principal of (and premium, if any) and interest on the Notes on the dates such payments are due in accordance with the terms of the Notes. To exercise the option described in (i) above, the Corporation is required among other things, to deliver to the Trustee an opinion of nationally recognized tax counsel to the effect that holders of Notes will not recognize income, gain or loss for Federal income tax purposes as a result of such deposit and discharge and will be subject to Federal income tax on the same amounts and in the same manner and at the same times as would have been the case if such deposit and discharge had not occurred.

Section (i) above is often called "defeasance and discharge" while section (ii) is referred to as "covenant defeasance." It is important to note that provisions may vary among issues and a few do not provide for tax opinions as the General Motors issue. In such cases where a defeasance transaction occurs, the result would be a taxable transaction under current rules and regulations. Investors subject to Federal income taxes should consult with tax counsel if purchasing or trading defeased bonds to see if there might be a tax liability.

While the trusts are irrevocable they are not inviolable, as a considerable number provide for the withdrawal and substitution of collateral sufficient to satisfy the payment obligations. It was reported that withdrawals were made in 1986 when some companies bought back and retired portions of their defeased debt and sold a corresponding share of the Government securities withdrawn from the trusts. This was an economic way of taking advantage of the tax laws, which would shortly change. The loss taken on the repurchase would be partially offset by the high 46% income tax rate, while the capital gain on the sale of the Treasuries would be taxed at 28%. This caused some accounting experts to consider whether the whole issue should be reexamined. The initial FASB bulletin took into account the possibility of the repurchase of defeased debt and said that it should be viewed as though "the debtor is making an investment in the future cash flows from the trust and should report its investment as an asset in its balance sheet. The debtor should not be considered to be reextinguishing its debt. Thus, no gain or loss should be recognized from such purchase of those debt securities."[29] It did not consider that the "irrevocable" trusts could be violated even if provided for.

In 1982 there were several economic defeasance transactions. Kellogg Company defeased its 9 5/8% Notes due October 1, 1985, by paying $65.6 million in cash to the Morgan Guaranty Trust Company, which arranged for a group of companies to assume the principal and interest payments for the $75 million issue. The transaction was also guaranteed by a Morgan Guaranty letter of credit. Exxon Corporation defeased its 6% debentures due 1997 and the 6 1/2% debentures due 1998. The trust portfolio consisted of federal government and agency securities. These transactions were allowed to stand as economic defeasances, since they occurred before FASB No. 76 took effect. Since the beginning of 1984 a number of other companies defeased debt including Atlantic Richfield Co., The Cincinnati Gas & Electric Company, and City Investing Company.

Normally, defeasance transactions occur when interest rates are high, a company has lower-coupon debt outstanding, the prices of Treasury securities are depressed, and the issuer is in an ample cash position. Also, the benefits of investing in a trust of Treasury securities should outweigh investment in new plant and equipment. Among the advantages of defeasance is the boost it can give to reported earnings due to the difference between the par value of the defeased bonds and the cost of the trust assets. United States Steel Corporation (now USX Corporation) issued an earnings release on July 30, 1985, stating that it retired $192 million of debt in the first half of the year, including defeasing $168 million of the 4 5/8% subordinated debentures due 1996. The total extinguishment resulted in an extraordinary gain of $38 million net of income tax of $32 million. These earnings are "below the line" and should not be used in calculating the financial ratios popular with corporate bond analysts; they are nonoperating, noncash, and nonrecurring.

The debt is also removed from the books, leverage should decrease and other debt-related measurements should show improvement. This could lead to a better credit evaluation of the company, especially if it is a novation. The repayment risk that had been associated with the predefeased debt is, to all intents and purposes, eliminated. Defeasance reduces the chance of the issue's price being run up in a repurchase program, but at times it may be more expensive. Obviously, it should be undertaken only after all alternative methods of debt redemption have been analyzed. The benefits to the balance sheet and income statements are one-time occurrences. Finally, with an in-substance defeasance, nothing really has changed as the company is still legally liable for the debt.

How have the rating agencies reacted to defeasance transactions? When the previously mentioned Union Carbide issue was proposed, Moody's Investors Service in its *Bond Survey* of February 2, 1981, stated, "When and if such a transaction (defeasance) occurs, payment of the bonds becomes assured, Moody's would raise the rating for these debentures from Aa to Aaa." Standard & Poor's Corporation commented that it would rate legally defeased issues AAA in consideration of the quality of assets in the trust and the matched flow of funds to debt service requirements. Examples of

legally defeased issues raised to the S&P "AAA" rating category
include Cameron Iron Works Inc. 11 ½% Notes due 1991 (formerly
rated "BB+") and Leaseway Transportation Corporation's collateral
trust notes ("B+").

Obtaining the highest rating for an in-substance defeased issue
requires overcoming some concerns about bankruptcy and the effects on the trust estate pledged to service the debt. Standard &
Poor's commented:

> Therefore, in order for S&P to rate in-substance defeased debt
> 'AAA', opinions of counsel are required indicating that:
>
> — The automatic stay provisions of the Bankruptcy Code (Sec-
> tion 362 (a)) would not apply in the event of the company's
> bankruptcy.
>
> — Section 549 of the code, which could void or impair the
> timely use of escrowed funds to pay debt service, would not
> apply in the event of the company's bankruptcy.
>
> — Deposit of assets into the escrow account will not constitute a
> preference with respect to the company in the event of the
> company's bankruptcy within 90 days after such deposit.

In addition, S&P must be assured that the defeased debt will be
free from any risks associated with cross-default provisions that
would tie the default and acceleration of the defeased issue to a
default on other debt of the company.[30]

Conclusion

The level and trend of interest rates are among the more important
factors in a company's decision whether or not to retire its debt, be
it through a sinking fund, refunding or defeasance. An issuer will
redeem its debt when it is to its own advantage, not the
debtholder's. If necessary, the issuer may use the protective provisions of the indenture against the bondholder. Other factors considered are the company's cash position and ability to raise the needed
cash, its future cash requirements and financing plans, and, in the
case of some utility companies, its ability to certify property additions or specifically authenticated bonds as credits for certain re-

demptions. Of course, we must not leave out the tax factor as another important consideration. Issuers must consider the impact of any redemption on its relationships with creditors, the investment community, the regulatory authorities and, most important, its shareholders and customers. Circumstances and attitudes do change. Just because a firm has established a pattern for the satisfaction of sinking fund and other indenture provisions, and may have waited until the refunding-protected period passed, does not mean that it will continue to follow these patterns and methods. The greater the difference between the interest costs on the outstanding debt and the present level of interest rates (and the savings to be achieved), the more a company is compelled to use whatever means it can to retire debt.

Finally, the reader may find these definitions about call and redemption of interest.

> "*Call feature*: A device that allows the only good bond you ever owned to be taken away from you.
>
> *Call protection*: Something that exists only in the mind of the naive investor."[31]

Notes

[1] "The Lessons of a Bond Failure." The *New York Times* (August 14, 1983).

[2] Samuel Lucas, et. al., Plaintiffs, v. Florida Power & Light Company, Defendant. Final Judgment, 77-4009-Civ-SMA, United States District Court, Southern District of Florida, October 31, 1983.

[3] Judgment, Harold Harris, Continental Casualty Company and National Fire Insurance Company of Hartford, etc. Plaintiffs-Respondents, v. Union Electric Company, Defendant-Appellant, St. Louis Union Trust, et al., Defendant-Cross Appellant. Missouri Court of Appeals, Eastern District, June 16, 1981.

[4] Charles A. D'Ambrosio, "When's the Last Time You Read a Prospectus?" *Financial Analysts Journal* (September-October 1983), p. 10.

5 James Grant, *Bernard M. Baruch, The Adventures of a Wall Street Legend* (New York, NY: Simon and Schuster, 1983), p. 55.

6 W. Braddock Hickman, *Corporate Bond Quality and Investor Experience* (Princeton, NJ: Princeton University Press, 1958), p. 87.

7 On May 8, 1969, the Securities and Exchange Commission issued a release which modified its policy regarding refunding protection provisions for first mortgage debt of companies subject to its jurisdiction under the Public Utility Holding Company Act of 1935. Prior to that date, those subject issues had to "be redeemable at the option of the issuer at any time upon reasonable notice and with reasonable redemption premiums, if any." The modification allowed issuers to include in their indentures provisions prohibiting the refunding of those new bonds with the proceeds of lower cost debt securities for a period of not more than five years. These companies had to pay higher interest costs than other utility companies due to the lack of refunding protection. This SEC modification placed the utility holding company subsidiaries on a more equal footing with other non-holding company operating utilities. The release also stated:

> Heretofore, the general redemption prices of first mortgage bonds have been considered reasonable . . . whenever such redemption prices commence, immediately following the issuance of such bonds, at an amount equal to the sum of the coupon rate plus the public offering price and decline each year thereafter by equal amounts to the principal amount at the beginning of the last year prior to maturity. No change in this policy is authorized. Therefore, when the five-year period of nonrefundability authorized herein expires, the general redemption price at which the bonds may then be called will be the same as it would have been if there had been no restriction on refundability.

8 Arleigh P. Hess, Jr. and Willis J. Winn, *The Value of the Call Privilege* (Philadelphia, PA: University of Pennsylvania, 1962), p. 24. The publication presents an interesting historical background of bond calls, including corporate, government and municipal.

9 Lucas et al. v. Florida Power & Light Company, Final Judgment, paragraph 77.

[10] The call pricing formula for this issue is not the usual par plus the coupon on a sliding scale but a so-called make-whole premium. The debentures are callable on July 1, 2003, and any interest payment date thereafter "at a redemption price equal to the greater of (i) 100% of their principal amount and (ii) the sum of the present values of the remaining scheduled payments of principal and interest thereon discounted to maturity on a semi-annual corporate basis at the Treasury Yield. . . ." The Treasury yield is the semi-annual equivalent yield to maturity of the Treasury 9 1/8% Bond due May 15, 2018, priced on the third business day prior to the redemption date. Thus, the lower the Treasury bond's yield, the greater will be the call premium to the investor. This is reasonable as the investor will have to reinvest the redemption proceeds in a lower interest rate environment.

[11] "'Vanilla' Bonds Suit Investor Tastes." *Standard & Poor's Credit-Week* (August 4, 1986), p. 16.

[12] Descriptions of the bond selection process may be found in Robert I. Landau; *Corporate Trust Administration and Management* (New York, NY: Columbia University Press, 1985), pp. 161-163, and *Commentaries on Indentures* (Chicago, IL: American Bar Foundation, 1971), pp. 497-499.

[13] A comprehensive review of debt retirement and the analytical framework are found in John D. Finnerty, Andrew J. Kalotay and Francis X. Farrell, Jr. *The Financial Manager's Guide to Evaluating Bond Refunding Opportunities* (Cambridge, MA: Harper & Row, 1988). This book covers discounted cash flow methodology, tax and accounting considerations, refunding of premium and discount debt, sinking fund issues, tenders, exchange offers, defeasance and the refunding of preferred stock.

[14] Letter dated June 13, 1983, to Members and Conferees, National Association of Regulatory Utility Commissioners (NARUC) from John J. Gibbons, Chairman NARUC Staff Accounting Committee. Mr. Gibbons was also the Assistant Director and Chief Accountant, Revenue Requirements Division of the California Commission.

[15] "Morgan Stanley Sues Over Archer-Daniels' Plan to Redeem Debt." *The Wall Street Journal* (July 11, 1983).

[16] Morgan Stanley & Co., Incorporated, Plaintiff, v. Archer-Daniels Midland Company, Defendant. Opinion 83 Civ. 5113, United States District Court Southern District of New York, July 29, 1983.

[17] The Franklin Life Insurance Company v. Commonwealth Edison Company, United States District Court, Southern District of Illinois, May 19, 1978.

[18] F. Corine Thompson and Richard L. Norgaard, *Sinking Funds: Their Use and Value* (New York, NY: Financial Executives Research Foundation, 1967).

[19] Charles Mackay, *Extraordinary Popular Delusions and the Madness of Crowds* (New York, NY: L. C. Page & Company, 1932 reprint), p. 49. Originally issued in 1841, this book became popular after being recommended by Bernard M. Baruch nearly 60 years ago. In discussing the speculative madness of the time, Mackay comments on one of the "bubbles" as follows:

> But the most absurd and preposterous of all, and which shewed, more completely than any other, the utter madness of the people, was one started by an unknown adventurer, entitled, '*A company for carrying on an undertaking of great advantage, but nobody to know what it is.*' (p. 55).

This appears to be similar to the blind investment pools of the mid-1980s.

Mackay also wrote something which sounds as though it could appear in today's financial press after the insider trading scandals.

> The public mind was in a state of unwholesome fermentation. Men were no longer satisfied with the slow but sure profits of cautious industry. The hope of boundless wealth for the morrow made them heedless and extravagant for today. A luxury, till then unheard of, was introduced, bringing in its train a corresponding laxity of morals. The overbearing insolence of ignorant men, who had arisen to sudden wealth by successful gambling, made men of true gentility of mind and manners

blush that gold should have power to raise the unworthy in the scale of society. The haughtiness of some of these 'cyphering cits,' as they were termed by Sir Richard Steele, was remembered against them in the day of their adversity. In the parliamentary inquiry, many of the directors suffered more for their insolence than for their peculation. One of them, who, in the full-blown pride of an ignorant rich man, had said that he would feed his horse upon gold, was reduced almost to bread and water for himself; every haughty look, every overbearing speech, was set down, and repaid them a hundredfold in poverty and humiliation. (pp. 71-72).

[20] Prospectus for The May Department Stores Company's $250 million of 10 ¾% Debentures Due 2018, dated June 8, 1988.

[21] John M. Stuart. "A Re-examination of the Replacement Fund." *Public Utilities Fortnightly* (May 23, 1968), p. 3.

[22] "Early Redemption of Outstanding High Coupon Bonds—A Welcome Relief for Ratepayers." (Speech by William D. Talbott, Director, Accounting Department, Florida Public Service Commission, presented at the Fifth Institutional Investors Bond Conference, New York, October 21, 1977.)

[23] Lucas et al. v. Florida Power & Light Company, Final Judgment.

[24] See *Bondweek*, Vol. IX, No. 14, April 11, 1988, for more flavor about this redemption. The replacement fund call was only part of the total redemption that May 31. The Company also offered to repurchase up to $34 million of the bonds through a Dutch auction procedure; it repurchased $18.8 million at 103.98% of par. The Company's treasurer said, "We want to give holders an option without alienating them." The tender and the possibility of the replacement fund redemption was announced in March. The bonds fell to par from about 109 to 109 ½ before getting back to 104 to 105. One manager was quoted as saying that "It caught all holders by surprise. No one really knew they were eligible to be taken out at par." This is just another example disproving the notion many have that bond investing is easy, a "no-brainer." Proper bond investment requires continual research, an inquiring mind, and common sense.

[25] Prospectus for $100,000,000 of Arizona Public Service Company First Mortgage Bonds, 11½% Series due November 1, 2015, dated November 21, 1985.

[26] Minstar, Inc. $300,000,000 of 14⅞% Senior Subordinated Notes due 1995, *Indenture*, dated as of April 1, 1985, Norwest Bank Minneapolis, N. A. Trustee.

[27] See Finnerty, Kalotay and Farrell, *Evaluating Bond Refunding Opportunities*, p. 38.

[28] *Statement of Financial Accounting Standards No. 76*, "Extinguishment of Debt, An Amendment of APB Opinion No. 26." November 1983. This statement was approved by only a four-to-three vote. The three dissenting members said:

> . . . they do not believe the extinguishment of debt accounting and resultant gain or loss recognition should be extended to situations wherein the 'debtor was not legally released from being the primary obligor under the debt obligation.' They believe . . . that 'a liability once incurred by an enterprise remains a liability until it is satisfied in another transaction or other event or circumstance affecting the enterprise.' . . . Dedicating the assets might ensure that the debt is serviced in timely fashion, but that event alone just matches up cash flows; it does not satisfy, eliminate, or extinguish the obligation. For a debt to be satisfied, the creditor must be satisfied. (p. 5).

[29] *Statement of Financial Accounting Standards No. 76*, p. 14.

[30] Roy Taub and Neil Baron. "Bond defeasance nears FASB approval." *Standard & Poor's Credit Week*, November 28, 1983, p. 550.

[31] Maurice Joy, *Not Heard on the Street* (Chicago, IL: Probus Publishing Company, 1986), p. 17.

Chapter 6

CONVERTIBLE BONDS

Convertible bonds are debt instruments with an embedded equity participation feature. They allow investors to participate in both interest rate and stock price movements, although the latter may have a greater price influence. As with the case of conventional debt securities, the term "bonds" is used in its generic sense. There are few true convertible bonds outstanding as most are notes and debentures. We will use bond interchangeably with note and debenture. This chapter explains many of the special features of convertibles. The option's approach to convertible bond evaluation is discussed in Chapter 13 of Section II.

What Is a Convertible Bond?

A convertible bond can usually be exchanged or converted at the option of the holder into a fixed number of shares of common stock (and sometimes other securities).[1] Price appreciation in the underlying common stock will usually be reflected in the market price or value of the convertible. Referred to as hybrid securities, they combine elements of senior securities with those of junior equity. While of primary appeal to common stock buyers, at times traditional fixed income investors may also be interested in convertibles. Being equity substitutes, they are more affected by individual company news and events than by interest rate and economic factors.

Convertibles are not new to the twentieth century. Dewing notes that convertibles of one type or another have been around since at least the seventeenth century.[2] In our corporate history they were used by some infamous characters such as James Fisk, Jr., Daniel Drew and Jay Gould in their battles for the Erie Railway with Commodore Cornelius Vanderbilt in the 1860s.[3] Most often convertible bonds have been for legitimate corporate purposes by sound companies. Many well-known corporations have utilized this form of financing including American Telephone and Telegraph Company, Eastman Kodak, International Business Machines, Greyhound Corporation and Union Pacific Corporation, among others.

The size of the outstanding publicly issued convertible market can only be estimated. *Moody's Bond Record* for April 1989 carried details about 674 issues of domestic convertible bonds. The outstanding par value of these issues was approximately $36.5 billion but many had less than $10 million principal amount outstanding. Eliminating all the issues under $10 million reduces the estimated number of converts as candidates for purchase to 501 with a par value of $35.9 billion. Included in the *Moody's* listing are issues that were once convertible into common stock but now are convertible into cash or other securities.

At about the same time the Merrill Lynch Capital Markets' convertible bond indices data base was comprised of 332 domestic issues with a total par value of nearly $32 billion. Each issue had to have at least one year remaining to maturity with an outstanding par amount of $25 million or more. Excluded were issues of bankrupt companies and those convertible into preferred stock, cash, or bonds. Table 6–1 gives the breakdown of the indices weighted by market value and par value. Convertible bond financing volume has fluctuated over the years as shown in Table 6–2. These data from the Securities and Exchange Commission point out that 1987 was a record year for proceeds from convertible debt financing activities. Only a decade earlier volume was but $407 million issued. Manufacturing companies have been the largest convertible bond issuers followed by the commercial and other category. Electric and gas utilities have not been much of a factor.

Table 6–1 Characteristics of the 332 Domestic Convertible Bonds Included in the Merrill Lynch Capital Markets Convertible Indices at May 31, 1989

	Total Issues	Rating Grade Status			Maturity (Years)		
		Investment	Speculative	Not rated	1-9.99	10-14.99	15 + years
Market Value Weighted							
# of Issues	332	89	226	17	13	33	286
Value ($ millions)	24,883.82	11,135.86	13,242.62	505.34	571.67	2,515.38	21,796.77
Coupon (%)	6.660	6.171	7.041	NA	5.806	4.813	6.895
Years to Maturity	19.793	19.733	19.869	NA	7.785	12.455	20.955
Yield to Maturity (%)	7.791	6.623	8.719	NA	6.988	7.098	7.892
Average Quality	BB1	A3	B1	NR	BB3	BB1	BB1
Par Value Weighted							
# of Issues	332	89	226	17	13	33	286
Value ($ millions)	31,514.06	13,843.86	17,074.25	595.95	613.01	3,473.61	27,427.33
Coupon (%)	5.630	4.741	6.280	NA	5.803	3.918	5.843
Years to Maturity	19.417	19.475	19.394	NA	7.710	12.666	20.533
Average Price*	78.961	80.439	77.559	NA	93.256	72.414	79.471
Yield to Maturity (%)	8.294	6.689	9.453	NA	7.460	7.520	8.4107
Average Quality	BB1	A3	B1	NR	BB3	BB2	BB1

Note: NA = not available. NR = not rated. * = excluding accrued interest.

Source: Derived from "Convertible Securities, Convertible Indices–May," *Merrill Lynch Capital Markets, June, 1989.*

Table 6-2 Gross Proceeds From Primary Public Convertible Bond Offerings by Industry 1978–1988 ($ millions)

	Total Business	Manufacturing	Extractive	Electric Gas and Water	Transportation	Communication	Sales and Consumer Finance	Financial and Real Estate	Commercial and Other
1988	$2,106	$ 505	$340	$ 75	$ 0	$350	$ 0	$ 214	$ 542
1987	9,607	5,503	372	393	20	344	0	883	2,092
1986	8,950	3,586	258	110	365	410	0	1,395	2,826
1985	8,018	2,678	25	291	540	130	0	2,396	1,958
1984	3,408	1,247	5	280	110	70	1	433	1,262
1983	5,871	1,958	217	256	425	400	0	811	1,804
1982	2,915	905	4	0	300	549	0	489	668
1981	4,271	2,309	211	77	0	226	0	411	1,037
1980	4,665	2,558	490	140	344	135	0	607	392
1979	2,229	325	85	0	200	0	200	1,384	35
1978	407	271	12	0	0	10	0	69	45

Note: Figures may not add due to rounding

Source: U.S. Securities and Exchange Commission, "SEC Monthly Statistical review," various issues.

Convertible Bond Provisions

As with any security, investors should analyze the terms of the convertible in which they are interested, especially before the investment is made rather than when trouble looms. There are always exceptions to general statements and a knowledge of these exceptions may mean the difference between profit and loss. While the indenture may be the best source of information about the terms of the issues, they may not be readily available. Therefore, prospectuses will have to do even though they are summaries of the indenture and do not profess to be complete. The statements are qualified in their entirety by reference to the indentures.

The first part of the security description gives the maturity, interest record and payment dates, the issue's size, denominations and similar information. The next section discusses the status or ranking of the security. Convertible debentures are mostly subordinated in the right of payment to the senior debt and are designated with subordinated in the bond's title. Seldom will the most senior level of debt in the capitalization structure include a convertible issue. One exception is Dana Corporation's 5 7/8% Convertible Debentures due in 2006. Some companies might have issued convertible debentures or notes, but upon closer inspection they will have been found to be junior to other issues.

The next section of the offering circular covers conversion rights, giving the price and number of shares into which the security is convertible, and the procedure for converting or exchanging the bonds. The conversion price for a majority of new issues is usually set at 15 to 25% above the common's closing price on the day the offering was priced. Some issuers have the right to lower the conversion price to induce the holder to convert. There have been issues in which the conversion price increases during the life of the conversion privilege. This is designed to encourage early conversion if the stock's price increases. If the security is convertible into a fraction of a share, cash is normally paid instead of issuing fractional shares.

In most cases the bondholder receives common shares of the issuing company, but some convertible debentures are *exchangeable* into common shares of another company. The shares received may be those of the parent company such as Ford Motor Credit's bonds exchangeable for the shares of Ford Motor Company, or the shares may constitute an investment for the issuer. An example is Allegheny Corporation's 6 ½% Subordinated Exchangeable Debentures due June 15, 2014, exchangeable at $43.70 into 22.8833 shares of American Express Company. Any regular cash dividends paid on the underlying stock belong to the issuing company as long as it is the owner of the underlying shares. However, certain types of special or liquidating dividends and distributions remain with the associated shares and are distributed when an exchange occurs. The shares are held by an escrow agent who also acts as agent for the exchange of the debentures.

An investor must be concerned about two companies covered by one investment. These are (a) the issuing company which has the responsibility of servicing the debt and (b) the company into which stock the security is exchangeable. You want both to remain healthy and to prosper so there is little chance of the interest or dividend not being paid on a timely basis and the market value of the underlying equity increases so to make the exchangeable senior security more valuable. If the issuing corporation fails to meet its obligations, default and bankruptcy may follow. The exchangeable security holder is left in a subordinated general unsecured creditor status even though the underlying stock might be of a very sound company. The exchangeable holder does not have the right to these shares. The shares may be considered impaired and are likely to be deemed assets of the bankrupt's estate, which, along with the corporation's other assets, may be used to satisfy general creditors' claims.

When some convertibles are exchanged or turned in for the underlying stock of a different company, a taxable event occurs. When the Allegheny Corporation bonds are exchanged for American Express shares, Allegheny will be liable for income tax on the gain realized from the exchange. It is also a taxable event for the bondholder with the gain or loss being the difference between the fair market value of the American Express shares at the time of the exchange and the holder's tax basis in the surrendered bonds. It is best to consult the prospectus of the exchangeable issue to see if the counsel states that taxes will have to be paid. Since changes in regulations may occur from time to time, advice of your tax advisor is also recommended.

The conversion section provides information about the adjustment of the number of shares that are issued upon conversion or exchange in cases of stock splits, dividends, reverse splits, recapitalizations, issuance of warrants, assets and other securities. Without anti-dilution provisions, only the naive would buy convertibles as a company may split its stock and the convertible holder would receive only the old number of shares upon conversion. The Allegheny prospectus states: "If the American Express Common Shares shall be increased by a stock split or reclassification or by way of a stock dividend, or if American Express shall effect a combination . . ., the exchange rate will be proportionately adjusted."

If the conversion occurs after the interest payment date and before the record date, adjustments are not made for the accrued interest. Due to this, the conversion price of the underlying stock may be greater than is first apparent. Convertible bonds trade like other bonds, namely at a certain price plus accrued interest to the settlement date. If you sell the bond in the open market you get the accrued interest, but if you convert you lose the accrual.

However, if an investor converts between the interest payment record date and the end of the day before the payment date, he may or may not have the right to the interest payment due on the payment date; it all depends on the terms of the particular issue. Often, securities surrendered for conversion during those dates must be accompanied with a check for the full amount of the interest to be received on the payment date. In some other cases, the interest will be paid to all holders of record even if they had converted prior to the payment date.

Most issues allow conversion to begin immediately after issuance but, from time to time, one runs across a bond with a delayed conversion feature. Most conversion rights expire at or just before the maturity or redemption date, but a few lose the conversion privilege several years before maturity. Dana Corporation's 5 7/8% debentures of 2006, lose their convertibility on December 15, 1993. After that date the bonds will be just straight debt securities. Failure to convert when the issue has been called may mean a large loss but time and again investors fail to convert when it is in their interests to do so. Bond investment is not a passive activity; it requires investors to remain alert to market events which may have an impact on their portfolios.

As with straight debt, an increasing number of convertibles issued in the late 1980s grant put options to the holders. Some issues provide that instead of paying cash for the put, the company may issue other securities. NeoRx Corporation's 9 ¾% Convertible Subordinated Debentures due 2014 has a change of control put option applicable before June 1, 1994. If a change of control (as defined) occurs the bonds may be put back to the issuer for $1,000. The company may, at its option, instead of paying cash, pay the repurchase price in common shares valued at 95% of the average trading price for a specific period before the repurchase date. The terms of the put features are spelled out in the issuing documents. The put is a valuable feature allowing the holder to get out whole if the conversion privilege doesn't turn out to be as profitable as thought when the bonds were first purchased. The put, especially one exercisable only for cash, will act as a floor for the market price of the security.

Until the early 1980s most convertible bonds lacked call protection, that is, they could be redeemed at any time at the issuer's option. Early in the decade some companies called their convertibles within a year after they were issued. A few were redeemed even before the first interest payment date. Some observers suggested that these early redemptions were "scams" in that the companies paid out little interest and through the forced conversions effectively sold common stock 15% to 25% above the market when the convertibles were first sold. On the other hand, if the issuing companies prospered from the good markets, so did investors. They had a higher yielding debt substitute for the equity providing some degree of market protection. While the bonds were called with large gains for the investors, they did not profit as much as the common shareholders. Nonetheless, gains were achieved with less risk than an alternate investment in the underlying shares. The gains probably came sooner than investors first thought when the convertibles were purchased. These earlier than expected riches increased the per annum rates of return. Certainly, investors would like to have such profitable "scams" day in and day out.

Since investors demanded some type of protection against early call, issuers began to add delayed redemption features to new convertible issues. Some have absolute redemption bars for a certain period of years, but many come with conditional redemption protection. In the latter case, the issuer agrees that the bonds won't be called in the first two or three years *unless* the common stock trades at 130% to 150% of the conversion price for a certain period of time (often 20 trading days) before the redemption date. Thus, an early call ought not to harm the investor as the converts would be trading at good premiums over the redemption price. If the bonds were not called, it would normally mean that the underlying stock had not performed as well as anticipated.

Corporations usually call their converts to force conversion and not to redeem the securities for cash. There are times, such as the low interest rate period of 1985 to 1986, when cash calls occur. In these cases, some companies want to pay off their more costly securities. However, one study said "refinancing did not seem to be a motive behind these out of money convertible debt calls" in 1980 to 1984.[4] Investors usually have at least 30 days in which to convert their bonds after a redemption announcement. If a forced conversion, investors can convert into common stock but they normally lose the accrued interest. Investors can sell the converts, in which case the accrued interest is theoretically paid. The bid will be higher than the call price or the conversion value less the accrued interest. In such instances the buyers (usually arbitrageurs) adjust. Bids are reduced since they are not receiving the accrued interest even though they must pay it when purchasing bonds. Participating in the market to buy and convert the bonds and selling the resulting shares, they lock in a small but sure profit. Another course is to take the cash redemption price. This is done only if the call price plus the accrued interest is more than what investors would receive upon conversion or sale.

Convertibles can also be redeemed to satisfy sinking fund requirements. This can be a valuable feature when the issue is selling at a discount. It is a negative when the convertible is trading above the call price. Usually, the sinking fund can be satisfied with bonds previously redeemed or converted but not yet credited for sinking fund requirements. If these credits are not available, the company must purchase the requirement in the open market or call the securities.

Convertible Bond Concepts and Investment Characteristics

Many years ago we heard the saying that one should never buy a common stock without checking to see if a convertible was available. Upon investigation the convertible might be a better alternative to an investment in the common shares. However, they often will not provide as much appreciation potential as the underlying common stock, but they may have a greater current return than the common. Also, the credit risk of a convertible bond is less than the junior common shares. Some institutional investors are barred from investing in common stock; purchase of convertible debentures is one way around this prohibition. At times, when the bonds are selling near their theoretical investment value as a debt instrument, they may be viewed as near substitutes for straight corporate debt (with a long-term option on the underlying common shares costing little or nothing).

Let's look at some of the terminology used in the convertible world along with an issue's details for illustrative purposes. We will use United States Steel Corporation's convertible subordinated debentures with data from Tables 6–3 and 6–4.

Conversion price is the price of the common stock at which the debenture is convertible: $62.75 per share. It is also called the *par conversion price.*

Conversion ratio is the number of common shares that the bondholder receives from exercising the call option of the convertible or exchangeable bond. It is obtained by dividing the par value of the bond by the conversion price, thus: $1,000/$62.75 = 15.936 shares per $1,000 debenture.

Conversion parity price, also known as the *market conversion price,* is the market value of the convertible security divided by the number of shares into which it is convertible. Market conversion price is the effective conversion price for a buyer of the bond in the secondary

Table 6-3 USX Corporation
5 3/4% Convertible Subordinated Debentures due July 1, 2001

Issue date: June 22, 1976   *Ratings:* BB (Fitch) Ba2 (Moody's) BB+ (S & P)

Interest payment dates: January 1 and July 1

Amount issued: $400,000,000   *Amount outstanding* (12/31/88): $214,000,000

Redemption: Currently callable at 102.02 through June 30, 1990, then at 101.73 through June 30, 1991, and at prices declining by about .29 annually to 100.00 on and after July 1, 1996.

Sinking fund: $20 million each July 1, 1987, through July 1, 2000, will retire 70% of the issue prior to maturity. Credit may be taken against the sinking fund obligation for debentures previously acquired, converted, or redeemed other than through the sinking fund, and the company has the noncumulative option to double payments.

Conversion: Convertible at $62.75 into 15.936 shares of common stock. The conversion privilege is protected against dilution as defined, and adjustments are made for cumulative changes of at least 1%.

Listed: New York Stock Exchange   *Quotron Symbol:* XJJ.F

Table 6–4 USX Corporation
Price Data and Dividend History

	Common Stock			5 3/4% C.S.D. 7/1/2001		
	Price	Indicated Dividend	Current Yield	Price	Yield to Maturity	Current Yield
12/31/83	30 3/8	$1.00	3.29%	63 3/4	10.25%	9.02%
12/31/84	26 1/8	1.00	3.82	57 1/4	11.63	10.04
12/31/85	26 5/8	1.10	4.13	68 7/8	9.64	8.35
12/31/86	21 1/2	1.20	5.58	63 1/2	10.78	9.06
12/31/87	29 3/4	1.20	4.03	71 7/8	9.49	8.00
12/31/88	29 1/4	1.40	4.79	70 3/8	9.94	8.17
6/30/89	34 1/2	1.40	4.06	76	9.07	7.57

market. Viewed as a breakeven point, it is the price at which the common stock must trade in order for the conversion value to equal the market price of the convertible. Thus $760/15.936 equals a conversion parity price of $47.69. The common stock must trade at $47.69 in order for the total value of the underlying shares to be worth the convertible's current market price.

Conversion value is the market price of the common stock multiplied by the conversion ratio. Therefore, 15.936 shares times the market price of 34 ½ equals a conversion value of $549.79.

Conversion premium or market conversion premium is the market price of the convertible minus the conversion value. This may also be expressed in percentage terms with (a) the conversion premium divided by the conversion value or (b) the market price divided by the conversion value. Calculated on a per share basis, it is the market conversion price (conversion parity price) less the current market price of the stock. These values are calculated below for the USX convertible:

	Per Bond		Per Share
Market price of debenture	$760.00	Market conversion price	$47.69
less: Conversion value	549.79	less: current market price	34.50
equals: premium	$210.21	equals: market premium	$13.19
(a) $210.21/549.79 = 38.24%		$13.19/34.50 = 38.24%	
(b) $760.00/549.79 =138.24%		$47.69/34.50 = 138.24%	

The investor is paying a premium of $210.21 per bond ($13.19 per share) over the bond's conversion value (current market price per share) for the right to convert into common stock. This is a premium of 38.24%. In other words, the bond is selling at 38.24% above its conversion value.

Premium recovery period (also known as *premium payback period* or *break-even time*) is the length of time required to recover the dollar conversion premium through the difference between the higher income generated by the convertible and the dividend income on the underlying number of shares which could be purchased for the same cost as the convertible. This dollar-for-dollar calculation is important for determining the relative attractiveness of a convertible issue compared with the common stock. Usually, the higher the premium recovery period, the less attractive the convertible. Many investors view a recovery period of three years or less as most desirable, purchasing the convertible when the premium recovery period is under three years and buying the stock when it is greater than three years. However, there could be other attractive convertibles with longer premium recovery periods. Each issue must be carefully analyzed within the context of the goals, objectives and risk parameters of the investment portfolio. The premium payback period does not consider the time value of money.

For the cost of the convertible bond ($760) an investor could buy 22.03 shares at the current market, ignoring commission charges.

Market price of convertible	$ 760.00
Divided by: market price of common	34.50
Equals: Number of shares that could be purchased for the cost of one bond	22.03
Annual income from convertible	$57.50
Annual income from investment in common stock (dividend $1.40 per share)	$1.40 × 22.03 = $30.84
Difference in income	$26.66
Premium recovery period:	$210.21 / 26.66 = 7.88 years

Another calculation method uses the percentage premiums and yields. Thus, for the convertible debenture the formula is:

$$\frac{\text{(Percentage premium)} / \text{(Premium} + 100)}{\text{Yield Differential}} \times 100 = \text{Premium recovery period}$$

$$\frac{(38.24\%) / (38.24\% + 100.00)}{(7.57\% - 4.06\%)} \times 100.00 = \frac{0.27662}{3.51} \times 100 = 7.88 \text{ years}$$

A few convertible traders use a different formula taking into account the conversion ratio. It can be calculated either on a per share or per bond method. The per share method divides the market conversion premium ($13.19) by the favorable income differential ($2.21) resulting in the break-even time of 5.97 years. The $2.21 favorable income differential is obtained by (i) subtracting from the dollar interest income ($57.50) the product of the conversion ratio (15.936) and the dividend per share ($1.40) divided, and (ii) dividing the result by the conversion ratio to get the per share favorable income differential.

Thus, we have:

$$\frac{\$57.50 - (15.3936 \times \$1.40)}{15.936} = \$2.21.$$

The conventional formula based on the par conversion ratio is less precise and conservative than the dollar-for-dollar method.

Investment value is the theoretical price the convertible bond would trade if it were a nonconvertible security of the same capitalization ranking, taking into account the rating, redemption features and sinking fund provisions. It is also called the *straight bond value*. The premium over straight or investment value is obtained by dividing the convertible's market price by its straight bond value. As interest rates change, so will the bond's straight value.

If a high premium recovery period makes an issue unattractive for the normal convertible buyer, who else might buy the bond and why? A traditional straight bond investor might find the USX Corporation convertible debenture attractive if it were selling close to or at the yield level a regular nonconvertible subordinated issue of similar quality standing and features might trade. Bonds with large premiums over conversion value ("out-of-the-money") selling at or near theoretical straight investment values are known as "busted converts."

At the end of June 1989, Merrill Lynch Capital Markets gave an investment value of 59 to the USX 5 ¾% convertibles. This is a yield to maturity of 12.41% and a current yield of 9.75%. The bonds were trading around 76 for a 7.57% yield to maturity and a 9.07% current yield. These converts are not properly "busted converts" as they are trading 17 points (29%) over investment value and 21 points or 38% over conversion value. If the stock market turns down and USX common shares decline, there would be little support from the investment value. The bonds would likely decline in price as convertible as well as straight bond investors find little attraction at those higher levels. The bonds' drop could be less as support may develop if interest rates were to decline sharply causing an increase in the perceived investment value. A 12% yield would give a value of about 60 ¾, an 11% maturity yield results in a value about 65 ½, and a 10% yield gives a 70 ⅝ valuation.

However, while the theoretical investment value can offer some protection against price declines under certain conditions, there may be times when convertible prices go through these support levels "as a hot knife goes through soft butter." The late winter and early spring of 1966 was one of these periods when investment support levels didn't mean much. At that time interest rates were rising and stock prices plummeting. Commercial banks were under pressure from the Federal Reserve System to reduce their lending for speculative activities. Many banks withdrew their lines of credit to convertible bond speculators while others sought more collateral value to support the loans. At that time loans up to 90% and more were made against the market value of convertible bonds. There were declining investment values due to rising interest rates; declining conversion values due to lower stock prices; decreased speculative interest because of the previous two factors; a drying up of the source of funds to fuel speculative purchases, and increased selling pressure as banks called in many of their loans and speculators sold to satisfy the margin calls. It was an unpleasant time to be in the convertible bond market, especially for brokers, traders and speculators.

Price Risk

We have reviewed the type of price risk caused by a sharp decline in the price of the underlying common stock and where the bond is selling above conversion *and* investment value. Another type of price risk is due to the risk of call and the consequent forced conversion. The USX debenture has little risk of call now since it is selling about 26 points below the 102.02 call price and the conversion value is only around 55. As the bond price rises above the par level, the risk of call and forced conversion increases. This is one reason conversion premiums tend to diminish, often being quite nominal or nonexistent beginning around the 115 to 125 price level. The investor's risk at these levels in cases of a forced conversion is the amount of the conversion premium and accrued interest, if any.

Another type of price risk touched upon earlier in this chapter and not caused by a drop in the common stock or forced conversion, is due to the issuer's voluntary redemption of the bonds. The driving force behind this type of call is the same as with straight senior securities, i.e. the desire to remove costlier securities from the balance sheet to enhance shareholders' wealth. Conversion isn't forced as investors would gain more by taking the redemption price than by exchanging the convertible for shares with a market value less than the redemption price. Admittedly, such redemptions are not all that common but they have caught many investors unaware. They just couldn't imagine a call when the conversion value was less than par value. Such an act would not force conversion.

The spring of 1986 saw several redemptions of this type. National Medical Enterprises had an issue of $124 million of 12 5/8% Convertible Subordinated Debentures due November 15, 2001. Convertible into 27.72 shares at $36.06, the bonds were trading on the New York Stock Exchange on April 8 at 114, and the common was selling at 24 1/2 per share. The conversion value was $679.14 and the conversion premium $460.86 or 67.9%. Currently callable at 100, the convertibles were at a 14% premium over the redemption price. Before the next day's trading opened, the company announced the bond's call at 100 plus accrued interest on May 15. The stock closed on April 9 at 24 5/8; it did not decline in price as there was little chance of the bonds being converted resulting in more shares in the market. However, the premium disappeared. On that day the converts traded between 100 and 101 and closed at 100, down 14 points overnight. The 14 point decline ($140 per $1,000 bond) meant that investors lost a grand total of $17,360,000 on the issue.

Liquid Yield Option Notes

In 1985, Wall Street investment bankers added another "animal" to the menagerie of investment products. Liquid Yield Option Notes, known as LYONs (registered trademarks of Merrill Lynch & Co., Inc.), joined their fellow CATS, TIGRs and other feline zero coupon investments. LYONs are zero coupon convertible securities combining a convertible feature with a put or series of puts. By June 1989, 17 issues with a par or face value of $9.833 billion had been sold in the public market raising $2.532 billion before underwriting fees and expenses. The securities met with favorable response from many different types of investors including foreigners, pension funds and other tax-favored entities including individual retirement accounts.

From the issuers' viewpoint, LYONs provide a favorable long-term rate which is a less costly source of funds than regular convertible and zero coupon debt. There is no cash outlay for interest charges but the companies can take a tax deduction for the original issue discount, thus aiding cash flow. Underwriting discounts charged on these issues (before deducting expenses paid by the issuer) range from 0.5625% to 0.925% of the principal amount due at maturity (but payable when the payment is received from the buyers). Based on the lower discounted price to the investor, the underwriting fees are at a higher rate ranging from 2¼% to 3½%. Underwriting fees on investment grade conventional convertible debt may range from 1% to 2% of the principal amount, with higher rates for more speculative issues. However, if the issuers viewed the underwriting fee as excessive, then they would have sought a less expensive way to raise capital.

None of the issues has a sinking fund but they all have deferred call protection for approximately the first two years after issuance. However, if the market price of the common exceeds 50% to 73% (depending on the issue) of the initial conversion price for a specified period before the start of the regular redemption, the securities may be called. The call schedule for the earlier issues is the original offering price plus the redemption premium (initially at the offering yield scaled down annually to zero ten years after issuance) plus the accrued original issue discount. Newer issues offered in 1988 and 1989 do not contain any redemption premium. The call price is just the original offering price plus the accrued interest computed at the original issue discount to the call date.

Holders have the right to require the issuer to redeem the LYONs at the holders' option. Most of the seasoned issues provide for annual puts after a delayed starting date. These puts require several months' prior notification to the issuer. The initial yield to the holders' put is several percentage points lower than the purchase yield but it increases each year by one percentage point until the original purchase yield is reached. This is similar to the redemption provisions of United States Series EE Savings Bonds. The put feature provides some protection to the bondholder in case of a rise in interest rates or a sharp decline in the stock's value. As explained in Chapter 10, zero coupon bond prices are much more volatile than the prices of coupon debt instruments and the put provides a floor for the investor. However, the put can come at an inopportune time when the issuer would rather not pay out the cash. This may be due to its poor financial condition. Maybe the issuer would rather retain the monies for other corporate purposes. Failure to make payment on a put is an event of default and, if not cured, may lead to bankruptcy proceedings. However, no payment under the put provisions may be made by the issuer if an event of default has occurred and has not been cured.

To get around some of the problems with an annual put payable in cash, most of the recent issues provide for only one put date prior to maturity with the price payable in cash, shares or notes. The put price does not include a premium but is only the original offering price plus the accrued original issue discount. The notes are interest bearing with a principal amount equal to the amount due at the put date; most have a maturity the same as the LYON. The interest rate on the notes is to be set at a rate determined by the underwriter necessary for the notes to have an initial market value at or as near as possible to par. Of course, no assurance can be given the note will sell at such a price. If an issuer could not afford to pay cash on the exercise of the put, why would one want to take some more funny money of an obviously weak and suspect firm? Maybe one should consider the LYON's sale.

The conversion rate is subject to the normal adjustment in cases of stock dividends, combinations, subdivisions and reclassifications. However, upon conversion, no adjustment is made for accrued interest or original issue discount as it is deemed to have been paid by the common stock received upon conversion. It is effectively lost. Therefore, while the number of shares into which the LYON may be converted is fixed, the conversion price slowly and steadily increases. Let us look at Hecla Mining Company which issued some LYONs in June 1989. Maturing June 14, 2004, they are convertible into 20.824 shares per note. The initial offering price of $308.32 results in a conversion price of $14.81. This security accretes interest and doesn't pay it out. Issued at an 8% yield to maturity, it would be worth $333.58 a year after issuance, $360.69 two years after issuance, and $1,000 at maturity. The conversion price thus rises to $16.01 at the end of the first year, $17.32 at the end of the second year, $18.73 at the end of the third year, and to $48.02 on June 14, 2004. On the June 14, 1994, put date the implied conversion price is $21.92.

When analyzing LYONs for possible purchase, the conventional premium recovery period method is useless as the bonds do not pay interest. One has to look at the conversion premiums to decide whether or not the LYON should be purchased. Keep in mind that if the stock does not move then the conversion premium is steadily increasing. It is for this reason that some convertible analysts feel that potential share dilution is limited. As time passes there is increasingly less incentive for holders to convert.

Usable Securities

Usable bonds are not convertible securities in the traditional sense discussed in the preceding sections. Instead, when combined with certain warrants, they become what are known as "synthetic convertibles."

A *warrant* is a longer term option giving the holder the right to buy shares of stock at a fixed price for a certain period. The length of the period differentiates a warrant from a common stock option.

An option has a life of under one year and is usually measured in months. On the other hand, a warrant's life is longer and is measured in years; in a few cases a warrant may be without any terminal date and is called a *perpetual warrant*. Atlas Corporation has perpetual warrants listed on the American Stock Exchange that give the holder the right to purchase common stock at $31.25 a share.

Warrants have been created out of corporate bankruptcy and reorganization, being given as part of the new company's securities in a recapitalization. Some have been issued with straight bonds as a "sweetener" to reduce the issuer's cost of capital. When issued with other securities, the package is called a *unit*. After issuance the warrants may be detached from the other part of the unit and both traded separately. A bond which can be used instead of cash upon the exercise of the warrant is known as a usable security.

The conventional convertible bond combines into one instrument a straight fixed income obligation and a long-term option to buy stock. A synthetic convertible allows the two parts to be separated and freely traded, each on its own merits. As with a convertible bond, the warrant allows a delay in the issuance of the common shares from the time the warrant is issued to the time of exercise. The exercise of a warrant does not mean that debt is reduced. If the exercise price is paid in cash, the associated debt remains outstanding.

A usable security trading below par effectively reduces the exercise price of the warrant. For example, if a warrant has an exercise price of $10 per share, the exercise of 100 warrants to purchase 100 shares of common stock would require $1,000 in cash. If the terms of the warrant provide for the exercise price to be paid in usable debt instead of cash, an investor would use the usable security as long as it is selling below par value (taking into account any accrued interest). A usable bond trading at 80 reduces the exercise price from $10 to $8; in effect the investor is paying for his stock with a security worth 80 cents on the dollar.

Due to this usable feature, lower coupon discount issues might trade at lower yields to maturity than would otherwise be the case if it were an ordinary straight issue. The premium over the normal pricing or valuation, or the demand for the usable bond, depends on several factors including the likelihood of the warrants being exercised and the time to the expiration of the warrants. The more likely the exercise of the warrants and the closer to their expiration, the greater the demand may be for the bond. Demand for the bond normally increases as the warrants' expiration date approaches assuming that the warrants will have value and thus will be exercised.

Another important factor is called "availability." This is the relative amount of bonds outstanding compared with the amount of bonds needed to exercise all of the warrants. Early in 1986 American Airlines, Inc. issued $200 million of 6 ¼% Subordinated Debentures due March 1, 1996, with 200,000 warrants to purchase 16.19 shares of AMR Corporation at $61.766 a share. If all warrants were exercised before the expiry date of March 1, 1996, AMR Corporation would issue 3,238,000 shares of common stock. The cost of these shares is $199,998,310 (in effect, $200 million). The warrant exercise terms allow the payment to be made in cash, check or "by the tender of the Debentures or by any combination thereof. For purposes of paying the exercise price of Warrants, Debentures will be valued at their principal amount, without credit for accrued interest, and applied only in integral multiples of $1,000 up to an amount not exceeding such exercise price."[5] Thus, $100,000 principal amount of debentures will pay the cost of 1,619 shares of common upon the exercise of the warrants. If the common price rises, the warrants would more than likely be exercised. As long as the bonds trade below par a wise speculator would use the bonds instead of cash. At a bond price of 80 the exercise price of the warrants is effectively reduced from $61.77 to $49.41 a share.

This potential demand for the bond may be viewed as an opportunity for the bondholder to redeem it early and thus increase the yield. Assume that these bonds have nine years remaining to maturity and are trading at 85 for a yield to maturity of 8.39%. Also, that the stock turns out to be a big winner and the warrants get exercised by 1992 so the bonds would then be worth par (assuming that all the bonds are used to pay the exercise price). Therefore, the effective yield from 85 to the 1992 redemption price of par is 10.37%, nearly 200 basis points more than to the 1996 maturity. The warrants are subject to redemption on and after March 1, 1988, if the stock price equals or exceeds 115% of the effective exercise price for a certain period before the date of the redemption notice, thus further adding to the near term demand for the bonds.

In 1983, Pan American World Airways, Inc. issued $100 million of 13 ½% Senior Debentures due May 1, 2003, with warrants to purchase 10,000,000 shares of common at $8 per share. The warrants expire on May 1, 1993, and are subject to early redemption on May 1, 1986. To exercise all the warrants would require only $80 million face amount of the Debentures, or 80% of the issue. Thus, the amount of the bonds outstanding exceeds by 25% the amount needed for the exercise of all the warrants. Since the amount of bonds needed to exercise the warrants in full is less than the amount of bonds outstanding, the potential demand from warrant holders will not be as great; and, it is less likely that this issue would get overvalued based solely on this demand factor.

There are cases where there are not enough bonds outstanding to satisfy potential demand from warrant holders. In 1983 Western Air Lines, Inc. sold 90,000 units consisting of $90,000,000 10 ¾% Senior Secured Trust Notes due 1998, with 3,240,000 shares of common stock and warrants to purchase 9,000,000 shares of common. The warrants, exercisable at $9.50 (the Notes may be used instead of cash), expire June 15, 1993, and are currently callable. Therefore, at issuance the availability factor was 95%. The principal amount of Notes outstanding exceeded the exercise price of the warrants by $4.5 million. In 1985 the Company repurchased $13.9 million face amount of the Notes, reducing the outstanding amount to $76.1 million. Now the availability factor changes for the better to 112.4%. There are not enough bonds outstanding to satisfy the potential demand if all the warrants were exercised. Thus, any price up to a fraction below par (leaving out consideration of accrued interest) should gladly be paid for the bonds by warrant holders wishing to exercise their rights.

Traditional Convertible Strategies

The Hedge

Convertibles are purchased by investors as alternatives to common stock when they have a positive outlook for the market and the shares. However, there are times when one may be bearish on the market in general and certain stocks in particular; short positions may then be justified. A short sale involves the sale of stock which is not owned in the hopes of buying back the shares (or covering) at some future date at lower prices. When stock is sold short, the shares must be borrowed from another owner to make delivery to the person who purchased the shares. To cover one's position and close out the short sale, the stock must either be purchased in the open market or obtained through the conversion of a convertible. As we mentioned, that one should not buy a common stock without first seeing if there is a good convertible substitute, one should not short common stock without first checking if there is also a convertible for it. If the stock sold short also has a convertible, then investigate the convertible hedge for reducing the risk of having the market move against the short position, i.e., go up above the sales price.

A convertible hedge involves a long position in the convertible security and a short position in the shares into which it is convertible. The hedge's purpose is to reduce or eliminate the loss if the common stock price goes up instead of down. For a convertible to be a candidate for the long side of a hedge it should be trading close to or at its conversion value, ideally just at that point in the 115 to 130 price range where the conversion premium all but disappears. It should provide a greater yield than the underlying common so the interest income may be used to pay dividend payments on the shorted shares. Also, the greater the volatility of the shorted shares, the greater the chance for profit.

If the price of the underlying stock declines, the profit from the hedge will come primarily from a widening of the conversion premium. If the price of the underlying stock rises, the loss on the short position will be offset by the gain or the narrowing of the conversion premium on the long position in the convertible. Various names are given to convertible hedges depending upon the balance or imbalance between the common share equivalent of the long position and the common shares on the short side. A full hedge is where the long and short sides are equally matched. If the common stock moves up in price, it will be more or less evenly offset by the expected increase in value of the convertible. Table 6–5

gives some details of a hypothetical convertible issue that we will
use for illustrative purposes.

**Table 6–5 XYZ Company 8.00% Convertible Subordinated
Debentures due June 1, 2009
Convertible at $50 into 20 shares of common stock**

Price of common:	$62.50
Price of convertible	$1,250
Conversion value:	$1,250
Conversion premium:	$0
Dividend per common share:	$2 per annum

In a full hedge the long and short side is in balance. Thus we

Buy $100,000 par value 8% Convertibles at 125   cost $125,000

Short 2,000 common shares at 62 ½   proceeds $125,000

If the stock rises to 90 (an increase of 44%) in six months' time,
we would get a loss on the short position of 27 ½ points a share for
a total amount of $55,000. The bonds have to be worth a minimum
of 180 (20 shares times $90) producing a profit of $55,000 which
offsets the loss. In addition, we would have had to pay two quarterly dividends of $0.50 each or a total of $2,000 to the lenders of
the stock which we shorted. However, we would have also received
six months' interest, or $4,000 on the bonds thereby producing an
overall profit of $2,000 on the hedge. Had the hedge been entered
into when there was still some slight conversion premium on the
bonds, the gain on the bonds would have been reduced to the extent of that premium.

What would happen if the common stock declined? Again, assume the stock dropped to 35, a decline of 27 ½ points over a six-
month period. We have a gain on the short position of $55,000. The
bond would also drop in price, but most likely not as much as the

common. The conversion premium would start to reappear as the common declined. Let us assume that the bond dropped to 90. At this level the premium over conversion value is $200 ($900 – $700) or nearly 29%. In addition, suppose the premium recovery period is seven years. At 90 we have a loss of 35 points in the bonds for a total of $35,000. Thus, the hedge produced a net gain of $20,000 (without much risk) before commissions, interest received and dividends paid out. A speculator engaging in these hedges only has to put up funds equal to the long position. Common stock can be shorted without any additional margin being required as long as the portfolio holds securities convertible into at least an equal amount of the stock sold short.

The full hedge produced profits on the downside with little risk. There are also partial hedges in which the two sides are not in balance. A half hedge with the hypothetical issuer would have involved the shorting of 1,000 shares and a quarter hedge the shorting of 500 shares, at the same time being long 100 bonds. The partial hedge may also produce profits on the downside, depending on where the long position starts to develop a premium over conversion value. It may also produce profits on the upside with reduced risk. Let us run through the numbers with a half hedge assuming that we are not as bearish as the fully-hedged investor. A rise in the stock to 90 produces a loss on 1,000 shares of 27 ½ points or $27,500. On the long side, the 100 bonds at a cost of 125 produces a $55,000 profit for a net gain of $27,500. On the downside, the short position of 1,000 shares shows a profit of $27,500. With a loss of $35,000 on the bonds, a net loss of $7,500 would result.

Actually, many speculators might start with a half hedge and adjust the long and short sides depending upon market conditions and movement. For example, as the stock declined the short position might have been gradually increased or the long position decreased resulting in a more fully hedged and profitable situation. There are many variations that can be produced with a convertible hedge. Investors should be alert to the opportunities for profitable trading with reduced risk as they arise.

The convertible hedge was used in the 1940s and 1950s by an investment company managed by the gurus of security analysis, Benjamin Graham and David L. Dodd. Reviewing the annual reports of the Graham-Newman Corp. for the fiscal years ended January 31, 1950, to January 31, 1957, the year the company was liquidated, reveals several convertible hedges, both full and partial, throughout this period. We don't know how profitable they were nor what activity occurred between the reports but it interesting that sophisticated investors such as these used the technique. Hedges included securities of companies such as Avco Manufacturing, Fedders-Quigan Corp., Gar Wood Industries, Tung-Sol Electric, Inc., Crucible Steel Co. of America, Allegheny Corp., American Airlines, American Cyanamid, Dow Chemical, National Container, Olin Mathieson Chemical, Pfizer & Co., Inc. and Granite City Steel. Some positions appeared on only the financial statements for one year while other positions were carried for more than five years. We believe that all the short positions involved hedges to some degree.

The prospectus for the Ellsworth Convertible Growth and Income Fund, Inc., dated June 20, 1986, mentions that the fund is allowed to "make short sales of securities which it owns or which it has the right to acquire through conversion or exchange of other securities." It goes on to say that it "may make a short sale in order to hedge against market risks when it believes that the price of a security may decline causing a decline in the value of a security . . . convertible into or exchangeable for such security. . . . The extent to which . . . gains or losses are reduced will depend upon the amount of the security sold short relative to the amount the Company owns, either directly or indirectly, and, in the case where the Company owns convertible securities, changes with the convertible premiums."

Convertible hedging is an appropriate technique for equity speculators engaging in short selling. It can reduce the risk of loss if the stock goes up and not down. It is important to act without emotion and to map out the upside and downside projections for both the long and short positions. A good chart of the historical prices and relationships of the convertible and the underlying stock is a valuable aid to convertible hedgers. It allows them to see where the securities have been so they can project where they might go in the future. It can also assist more active speculators as they vary the degree of the hedge.

Writing Covered Calls

Another convertible strategy is to use convertibles in a program of writing covered call options. A call option is a right to buy common stock at a predetermined price for a certain period, usually under one year. The issuer or writer of the call option is obliged to sell the underlying shares at the exercise price during the option period. This obligation terminates when the option expires or when the call is covered, i.e., repurchased. Few calls are exercised, as call owners usually sell profitable calls in the market. For writing the call option, the buyer pays the seller or writer a premium that is determined in part by the remaining life of the option, the exercise price in relation to the common's price, and the volatility of the underlying stock. A covered option means that the option writer has the shares or securities convertible into the shares held in his account or portfolio. The options are written on the underlying common shares and not on the convertible securities.

Writing covered call options is done to enhance overall portfolio returns, not to maximize profits on individual issues. Better results are obtained in stable or rising equity markets than in declining markets. However, in a rising market calls may be exercised, thus restricting profit opportunities. This is offset, to some extent, by the option premiums received. To determine the number of convertible bonds needed to write calls, divide the number of shares to be received upon conversion of one bond into the number of shares for which the call option is being written. In the example in Table 6–5, each bond is convertible into 20 shares. To write one covered call option for 100 shares, we need five bonds, and for 2,000 shares we need 100 bonds. As the bonds are selling at the conversion value of 125, any rise in the stock price should be fully reflected in the bond's price. On the downside, we expect the conversion premium to reappear, thus reducing our loss. The bonds normally would decline at a slower rate than the underlying common. In addition, they offer a greater current yield than the stock, another advantage of many convertibles.

Therefore, for our 100-bond long position we can write 20 covered call options. Suppose a six-month option exercisable at 65 with the stock at 62 ½ has a premium of $375 per 100 shares.[6] Let us look at the possible results of writing covered call options against the convertible and the underlying shares of our hypothetical company. Table 6–6 shows that using convertibles instead of the underlying common stock in a program of writing covered call options may lead to better investment results. In this case there were smaller losses on the downside and greater gains when the stock rises.

Of course, the final results of covered call writing strategies depend on several factors including the income differential between the convertible and the common, the premium received for writing the call, the conversion premium, and the price action of the securities. This is a passive example. In actual practice, some investors might wish to limit their losses or take their gains at certain predetermined price levels by closing out or repurchasing the calls they had written.

Before attempting any covered call writing program, investors should go through simulations to see what the results might look like. Price history charts should be studied to get an idea of the past and a glint of future relationships between the common, the convertible and the option. There are investment services to assist investors in their call writing activities.

Convertibles are wonderful securities for investors who lack perfect foresight. If our crystal ball worked, we would only go with the investments that would be profitable; we would not need securities that provide some degree of downside protection. Few of us are perfect investors—and thus the need for convertible securities.

Table 6-6 XYZ Company
Covered Call Option Data at Expiration Date
(Option is Exercisable at 65)

Common Price	$35	$50	$62 ½	$75	$90
Convertible Price	$900	$1,100	$1,250	$1,500	$1,800
Option value	$0	$0	$0	$10	$25

Cost of 100 Convertibles		$125,000
less Option premium received		7,500
Net cost of convertible position		$117,500

Profit (loss) on:

convertible	($35,000)	($15,000)	0	$25,000	$55,000
option	7,500	7,500	$7,500	(12,500)	(42,500)
Profit (loss)	(27,500)	(7,500)	7,500	12,500	12,500
Interest income	4,000	4,000	4,000	4,000	4,000
Net profit (loss)	($23,500)	($3,500)	$11,500	$16,500	$16,500
Rate of return on investment	(18.8%)	(2.8%)	9.2%	13.2%	13.2%

Cost of 2,000 shares of stock		$125,000
less Option premium received		7,500
Net cost of stock position		$117,500

Profit (loss) on:

stock	($55,000)	($25,000)	0	$25,000	$55,000
option	7,500	7,500	$7,500	(12,500)	(42,500)
Profit (loss)	(47,500)	(17,500)	7,500	12,500	12,500
Dividend income	2,000	2,000	2,000	2,000	2,000
Net profit (loss)	($45,500)	($15,500)	$9,500	$14,500	$14,500
Rate of return on investment	(36.4%)	(12.4%)	7.6%	11.6%	11.6%

Notes

[1] While most convertibles may be exchanged for common stock, there are issues convertible into straight debt, cash and/or other securities; most of these have been created out of mergers and acquisitions. One such example was Avco Corporation's 5.50% Convertible Subordinated Debentures due November 30, 1993, convertible originally into 18.52 shares of common stock at $54 a share. In 1985 Textron acquired Avco for $50 per share and the terms of the outstanding convertibles were changed so the bonds were entitled to receive the cash value offered for the underlying security, namely $50 times 18.52 shares or $926 per bond.

[2] Arthur Stone Dewing, *The Financial Policy of Corporations* vol. 1, 5th ed. (New York, NY: Ronald Press Company, 1953). He states:

> Conversion from one type of security into another has existed in England for a long period of time. Scott mentions the case of an early London Water Company in which King Charles I was allowed to convert his stock into bonds.

[3] George Wheeler, *Pierpont Morgan and Friends: The Anatomy of a Myth* (Englewood Cliffs, NJ: Prentice-Hall, Inc., 1973). In discussing Daniel Drew's three methods of twisted finance, Wheeler describes the first method, which consisted of violations of the New York State railway act, as follows:

> That law permitted the roads to issue bonds to raise money 'to complete, equip and operate' the line. To help sustain the value of the bonds, a 'sweetener' was allowed in which the buyer could convert the bond into a share of common stock. The theory was that the buyer would pay a better price for the bond and thus maintain its value if he knew that later, when the stock rose above par, he would have an additional profit through the conversion feature. But Drew had his own theories. He had the company issue the bonds in violation of the legislative provisions that they were only to be brought out for the specific purposes cited, and he immediately used the convertible feature despite the fact that the stock was far below par value.

[4] Sankarshan Acharya and Puneet Handa. "Early Calls of Convertible Debt: New Evidence and Theory." Working Paper Series Number 477, June 1988, Salomon Brothers Center for the Study of Financial Institutions. The study concludes:

> A significant percent (about 32%) of all the convertible bond calls [230], during 1980-1984, were made when they were out of money. The median firm in the sample . . . called when the conversion value was 48.5 percent below the call price. We considered an economic setting in which the manager, who was assumed to maximize the value to common stockholders, did not find it optimal to call the out of money convertible bonds if he was no more informed than the outside investors in the stock market. In the same setting we considered an asymmetry of information between the manager and the investors and showed the existence of an equilibrium in which the common stockholders' wealth could be improved by calling an out of money convertible bond if the manager's private message indicated good future prospects of the firm. In this equilibrium, the stock price jumped upward on the announcement of call of an out of money convertible bond.

[5] Prospectus for 200,000 Units of American Airlines, dated March 7, 1986, pp. 15-16.

[6] Factors that determine the option premium are discussed in Chapter 12.

Chapter 7

SPECULATIVE-GRADE BONDS

Today's speculative-grade bonds are an investment area that can be quite rewarding and yet fraught with risk. Many debt issuers may end up bankrupt during the next economic downturn and seek the protection of the courts under the Bankruptcy Reform Act of 1978 ("the Act"). Some may try to reorganize under Chapter 11 of the Act, but others may be unable to satisfy claimants and will be forced into liquidation under the Act's Chapter 7 provisions. Thus the discussion of speculative-grade bonds in this place of Section I. Again, we will use "bond or bonds" in the generic sense.

What Are Speculative-Grade Bonds?

Speculative-grade bonds are those rated lower than investment grade by the rating agencies, i.e., BB+ and below by Fitch Investors Service, Inc. and Standard & Poor's Corporation, and Ba1 and lower by Moody's Investors Service, Inc. They may also be unrated, but not all unrated debt is speculative. Also known as junk bonds, promoters have given these securities other euphemisms such as high-interest bonds ("HIBS"), high-opportunity debt, and high-yield securities.[1] While some of these terms may be misleading to the uninitiated, they are used throughout the investment world. Speculative-grade bonds may not be high-yielders at all as they may not be paying any interest, and there may be little hope for the resumption of interest payments; even the return expected from a reorganization or liquidation may be low. Some high-yield instruments may not be speculative-grade at all as they may carry investment grade ratings. The higher yields may be due to fears of premature redemption of high-coupon bonds. The yields may be caused by a sharp decline in the securities markets which has driven down the prices of all issues including those with investment merit. Using the term "high-yield securities" may be an attempt to whitewash the risks associated with these securities.

On the other hand, although the term "junk" tarnishes the whole less-than investment-grade spectrum, it will be used occasionally. Junk bonds are not useless stuff, trash or rubbish as the term is defined. Many investors overpay for their speculative-grade securities at times, so they feel that they may have purchased junk or worthless garbage. But isn't this also the case when they have overpaid for high-grade securities? There are other times when profits may be made from buying junk bonds; certainly then, these bonds are not junk but something that may be quite attractive. Also, not all securities in this low grade sector of the market are on the verge of default or bankruptcy. Many issuers might be on the fringes of the investment grade sector. Market participants should be discriminating in the choice of their terminology.

Several types of issuers fall into the less-than-investment-grade category including the following:

Original issuers. These may be youthful and growing concerns lacking the stronger balance sheet and income statement profile of many established corporations, but often with lots of promise. Also called growth or emerging companies, the debt is often sold with a story projecting future financial strength. There are also the established operating firms with financials neither measuring up to the strengths of investment-grade corporations nor possessing the weaknesses of companies on the verge of bankruptcy. Subordinated debt of investment grade issuers may be included here. Bonds in this latter category are often called "businessmen's risk" issues. Many of these companies formerly had their financial needs satisfied by commercial banks and finance companies.

Fallen angels. Formerly companies with investment-grade rated debt that have come upon hard times with deteriorating balance sheet and income statement financial parameters are included in this category. They may be in default and near bankruptcy. In these cases, investors are interested in the workout value of the debt in a reorganization or liquidation, whether within or without the bankruptcy courts. Some refer to these issues as "special situations." They have fallen on hard times over the years; some have recovered and others have not. A few examples of fallen angels are Navistar International Transportation Company (formerly International Harvester Company), Chrysler Corporation, some of the steel and metals companies, a few utilities including Long Island Lighting Company and Gulf States Utilities Company, among others.

Restructurings and leveraged buyouts. These are companies which have deliberately increased their debt burden with a view towards maximizing shareholder return. The shareholders may be the existing public group for which the company pays a special extraordinary dividend with the funds coming from borrowings and the sale of assets. In any case, cash is paid out, net worth decreased and leverage increased, and ratings dropped on existing debt. Newly issued debt gets junk bond status because of the company's weakened condition. In 1988, The Kroger Co. declared a dividend of about $3.2 billion in cash and junior subordinated discount notes. Funds were obtained through bank borrowings with repayment to be made from asset sales and retained future cash flow. The proceeds did not go towards building the company, but towards its weakening and dismantling, at least over the intermediate term.

In a leveraged buyout (LBO), a new and private shareholder group owns and manages the company. The debt issue's purpose may be to retire other debt from commercial and investment banks and institutional investors incurred to finance the LBO. The debt to be retired is called bridge financing as it provides a bridge between the initial LBO activity and the more permanent financing. One example is Ann Taylor, Inc.'s 1989 debt financing for bridge loan repayment. The proceeds of BCI Holding Corporation's 1986 public debt financing and bank borrowings were used to make the required payments to the common shareholders of Beatrice Companies, pay issuance expenses, retire certain Beatrice debt, and for working capital.

The Market

The outstanding amount of publicly traded lower rated bonds is quite sizeable and expanding. The junk market's size varies depending on one's source of data. The General Accounting Office in its March 2, 1989, report to Congress on high-yield bonds estimated that ". . . the amount . . . outstanding rose from about $9 billion in mid-1977 to about $159 billion in mid-1988." In August 1989, Moody's said that it rated about $210 billion of speculative-grade corporate debt, approximately 25% of all of its rated corporate debt. This compares with $23 billion at the end of 1981, equal to only 6.5% of Moody's rated debt.

While new issue activity has peaked from the high level of 1986, it is still large. Depending on one's definition and source of data, new issue volume will vary. Table 7–1a shows that the total amount of junk bonds issued in only 1986, 1987 and 1988 amounted to 65.6% of the total new issue junk bond volume for the twelve years from 1977 to 1988. This includes split-rated issues where either Moody's or Standard & Poor's gave the issue an investment-grade rating while the other had a lower, speculative rating assigned to the paper. To these figures must be added debt issued in exchanges, bonds created from bankruptcy and other reorganizations.

The inception of the modern day speculative-grade bond market was in the late winter and early spring of 1977. While below-investment grade new corporate debt issues were sold or underwritten by investment bankers from time to time before 1977, it was then that prestigious investment banking firms got into the act. Lehman Brothers underwrote three "single-B"-rated issues in March, raising $178 million. In early April, Drexel Burnham Lambert underwrote $30 million of subordinated debentures for Texas International Company. Over the next several years volume ranged between $1.2 billion and $1.5 billion. New issuance jumped 67% in 1982 compared with 1981 and nearly tripled in 1983. It rose another 93% in 1984, and a modest 9.2% in 1985 to $16 billion. Fueled by investor demand and increased speculation, among other things, volume more than doubled to 1986's peak of $34.2 billion.

The quality makeup of this new issue volume is interesting as shown in Table 7–1b. Nonrated issues and those with single-B and lower designations accounted for 53.7% of 1977's volume, rising steadily to 69.3% in 1980 before declining to 48.2% for 1984. The average quality continued to decline with the lower-rated junk reaching nearly 86% of 1988's speculative debt offerings. In the twelve-year period through the end of 1988, more than 71.5% of the new junk bonds were rated highly speculative.

The large increase in the lower orders of corporate debt has led some to wonder if junk bond market participants perhaps have lost track of their senses. Creditors become less wary as the business cycle expansion moves along—in fact, they become more optimistic when they should become more cautious. Banks become less selective as to whom they lend, and the terms of loans become less restrictive. Investment banking firms become less selective about their underwritings, they just want to get deals done. After all, they want to maintain or even increase their market share. One way to do it is to finance every cat and dog that wants to come to market. The good, solid long-term investment banking and client relationships, long the mainstay of the investment banking industry, get shunted aside for shorter-term accommodations. Their investor customers will often buy what they have to offer without too much of a discerning eye.

It has even been suggested that some investment banks have certain clients "in their hip pocket." These clients have a very close relationship with their investment bankers and participate in each others' new issues. It is sort of like "you scratch my back and I'll scratch yours." With the decline in interest rates over the past few years, investors wanting higher yields have to go to lower-rated securities. Not satisfied with the yields of government bonds and investment-grade corporates, they want the higher yields offered by speculative-grade bonds (and the higher the yield the better). Above average yields usually denote above average risks, but many investors apparently do not care. And yet, there is no such thing as a free lunch. In return for high yield the investor assumes above average risk whether he accepts the fact or not. High yield to maturity or high current return may become no yield or return at all. Maybe the appropriate measurement should be "yield to default" or "yield to reorganization." In the 1984 to 1988 period, the market for speculative-grade debt was such that investors bought issues that probably would have never reached the marketplace a decade

Table 7–1a Speculative-Grade New Issue Activity 1977 to 1988 ($ millions)

	Total	Baa/BB Ba/BBB	Ba/BB, Ba/NR NR/BB, Ba/B, B/BB	B/B, NR/B B/NR	Caa/CCC, Caa/NR, NR/CCC, B/CCC Caa/B, Caa/D, NR/CC, NR/C	NR/NR
1988	$27,670.5	$2,002.0	$1,875.0	$18,254.5	$5,539.0	$ 0.0
1987	28,576.0	1,113.0	3,734.5	18,502.5	4,886.0	340.0
1986	34,197.7	2,480.0	7,318.3	17,490.4	6,224.0	685.0
1985	16,040.9	510.0	5,544.4	6,361.1	2,236.3	1,389.1
1984	14,687.8	3,540.0	4,072.0	5,183.7	755.1	1,137.0
1983	7,614.0	1,060.0	2,737.5	2,574.0	495.0	747.5
1982	2,548.0	50.0	1,205.0	1,058.0	40.0	195.0
1981	1,523.6	100.0	290.0	939.6	—	194.0
1980	1,351.1	165.2	250.0	827.5	25.0	83.4
1979	1,240.5	—	323.0	903.5	14.0	—
1978	1,463.8	40.0	427.8	984.0	12.0	—
1977	952.5	70.0	371.5	498.0	13.0	—
Total	$137,866.4	$11,130.2	$28,149.0	$73,576.8	$20,239.4	$4,771.0

earlier. By mid-1989, there were signs that the market was beginning to take heed over junk bond quality. Some new issues were postponed or withdrawn, and the prices on many outstanding bonds declined in the face of several defaults and concern over the ability of the economy to avoid a recession. Hickman says:

> . . . the trends in default rates are roughly comparable with trends in net and gross new financing, default rates tending to be high on securities issued during years of high financial volume and vice versa. . . . This would seem to suggest that some issues, perhaps those of marginal quality, can find a ready market only when the market is buoyant, and that in periods of market pessimism only the top grade issues can be placed. . . .[2]

Table 7-1b Speculative-Grade New Issue Activity 1977 to 1988 (% Distribution)

	Total	Baa/BB Ba/BBB	Ba/BB, Ba/NR NR/BB, Ba/B, B/BB	B/B, NR/B B/NR	Caa/CCC, Caa/NR, NR/CCC, B/CCC Caa/B, Caa/D, NR/CC, NR/C	NR/NR
1988	100.0%	7.24%	6.78%	65.97%	20.01%	—
1987	100.0	3.90	13.07	64.75	17.10	1.18%
1986	100.0	7.25	21.40	51.15	18.20	2.00
1985	100.0	3.18	34.56	39.66	13.94	8.66
1984	100.0	24.10	27.72	35.29	5.15	7.74
1983	100.0	13.92	35.95	33.81	6.50	9.82
1982	100.0	1.96	47.29	41.52	1.58	7.65
1981	100.0	6.56	19.03	61.67	—	12.74
1980	100.0	12.23	18.50	61.25	1.85	6.17
1979	100.0	—	26.04	72.83	1.13	—
1978	100.0	2.73	29.23	67.22	0.82	—
1977	100.0	7.35	39.00	52.28	1.37	—
Total	100.0%	8.07%	20.41%	53.37%	14.68%	3.47%

Source: Derived from data in *High Yield Handbook*, February 1986 and January 1989, published by The First Boston Corporation.

High-Yield Bond Performance and Default Rates

Without question, there have been disasters in the high-yield bond market as there have been crashes in the equity markets. Prices of bonds have suffered great declines as issuers have gone bankrupt, defaulted or as they tried to reorganize outside of the bankruptcy court. These actions do not mean that all is lost, as we shall see later. The investor holding Republic Steel, McLean Industries, Western Union, and Zapata Corporation debentures in mid-July 1986 would have felt as though all *was* lost. In the two-week period ending July 25, prices of these bonds dropped like a lead balloon after LTV's announcement that it would seek protection from creditors under the Federal bankruptcy laws. Republic Steel (now J&L Steel) was carried down by the bankruptcy of the LTV group of companies. The decline in the other issues were due to the marginal nature of their operations and investors' perceptions that they might have to file for bankruptcy. The Republic Steel 12⅛s of 2003 dropped from 58⅝ to 18⅞, a decline of 68%, not including approximately $15 of accrued and unpaid interest. The Western Union 16s of 1991 went from 100 to 49½ before closing at the end of the period at 67, a price erosion of 33%. The Zapata 10⅞s of 2001 fell only 18 points from 50 to 32, and the McLean Industries 12s of 2003 went from 70⅞ to 40.

More recently, the summer of 1989 saw similar price action in the debt of Integrated Resources Inc. Table 7-2 shows the price declines came at two distinct times. The first shock was on June 14 when the company announced that its commercial paper dealers could no longer refinance or roll over maturing paper due to a lack of buyers and its bankers wouldn't extend new credit. On June 15 it defaulted on close to $1 billion of short-term debt. It offered to exchange new secured debt with a longer maturity for this short-term paper but found no takers. The securities had been on Standard & Poor's *CreditWatch* list since January 2, 1989, with developing implications; it changed to negative on June 5. On June 14, S&P lowered the senior debt ratings from "BBB" to "BB–," the subordinated debt from "BBB–" to "B," and the commercial paper from "A-2" to "B." By the end of the week the senior debt was further downgraded to "CCC+," the subordinated to "CCC–," and the commercial paper to "D." The week-to-week declines were impressive, both absolutely and relatively, with the largest percentage losses occurring in the subordinated debt. Investors who had done their homework on the company more than likely would not have been caught holding this high-yielding junk; only the greedy or those with hope in their hearts.

The story doesn't end at the end of June as there was an aftershock. Following the initial default, prices gyrated up and down as spec-ulators awaited news of restructuring plans. One plan would give senior creditors about 80 cents on the dollar in cash and securities. In mid-August, management cut the value of its assets and proposed a less attractive plan. Debt prices fell again as investors believed a bankruptcy filing was becoming increasingly certain

Table 7–2 Price Activity of the Bonds of Integrated Resources Inc. Listed on the New York Stock Exchange, weeks ended June 23 and August 18, 1989

| | Week of June 19-23 | | | | | Week of August 14-18 | | | | |
| | | | | Week-to-Week | | | | | Week-to-Week | |
Issue	High	Low	Last	Price Change	Percent Decline	High	Low	Last	Price Change	Percent Decline
Senior Debt:										
10% 5/1/90	59	41.2	57.2	-42.2	-42.5	46	37	38	-9	-19.1
10 3/4% 5/1/92	66.3	37.4	57.2	-37.2	-39.4	46	36	37.3	-1.5	- 4.2
11 1/8% 5/1/94	70	40.1	55.2	-37.5	-40.5	45.4	36.2	37.1	-7.7	-17.5
Subordinated Debt:										
8 5/8% 4/15/97	26	26	26	-30	-53.6	14	11	11	-7	-38.9
13 1/8% 7/15/95	45	24.1	29	-43	-59.7	16.4	8.4	8.6	-7.2	-45.3
10 3/4% 4/15/96	35	20.6	26.3	-34.5	-56.8	16.2	9	9	-6.5	-42.4
12 1/4% 8/15/98	33	22	26	-39.7	-60.5	15.2	7.4	9	-6.6	-42.9

Note: Prices are expressed as a percentage of par with fractions expressed as the number of eighths of a percent after the decimal; hence 98.3 equals 98 3/8.

with each passing day. Under such circumstances, Integrated's business could continue to deteriorate with creditors recovering even less. This August aftershock reduced the prices of some subordinated debt issues more than 40% to single-digit prices. At that time speculation was that senior creditors might recover about 70% of their claim and subordinated creditors about 30% within three years. Again, depending on economic conditions, it is difficult to estimate the real value of these assets.

Adverse selection could lead many investors to forgo the junk markets. However, most proponents of high-yield bonds feel that looking at the total picture instead of a few isolated cases gives a truer view of the merits and returns available from speculative grade bonds.

Several major investment banking firms active in the high-yield market have indices measuring market performance. Table 7–3 compares the total returns for the *First Boston High Yield Index*™ to the ten-year Treasury bond, the popular Shearson/Lehman Corporate Bond Index, and the Standard & Poor's 500-Stock Index. Total return includes interest income, principal gain or loss, and reinvestment of interest received.

The eight-year performance has been pretty impressive, especially considering a large increase in new issue supply (many from untested companies and structures), adverse publicity concerning some of the leaders in the industry including scandals and admission of criminal and unethical behavior, and a stock market crash. In 1981 and 1987, high-yield bonds turned in the best total return of the four measures. Junks outperformed the stock market in four of the eight years, had better returns than Treasuries in four years, and beat the corporate bond index in five years. Benefitting the returns is the higher coupon income received and reinvested from junk bonds. One hundred dollars invested in the index at the end of 1980 would have grown to $328.18 at the end of 1988, an annual compounded rate of return of 16.01%. This was 171 basis points better than the second place corporate bond index. Further, the returns came with less volatility than the other sectors. This suggests that higher grade markets may be more treacherous than the junk market, at least for the period under review.

Table 7-3 Comparison of the Total Rates of Return for the High-Yield Market to Selected Market Indices (1981-1988)

	First Boston High-Yield Index^{TM}	10-Year Treasury Index	Shearson/Lehman Corporate Bond Index	Standard & Poor's 500 Stock Index
1988	13.65%	6.11%	7.59%	16.44%
1987	6.54	- 2.79	2.55	5.23
1986	15.63	20.15	16.52	18.60
1985	24.93	26.31	24.05	31.70
1984	10.69	12.93	16.62	6.20
1983	13.91	3.50	9.27	22.60
1982	26.57	32.02	39.20	21.60
1981	8.96	4.85	2.95	- 5.00
Volatility of annual returns	9.21%	11.42%	11.51%	11.00%
Growth of $100 over 8 years	$328.18	$253.27	$291.24	$287.86
8-Year compounded growth rate	16.01%	12.32%	14.30%	14.13%

Source: *High Yield Handbook*, January 1989, High Yield Research Group, The First Boston Corporation.

Total returns are one measurement in the evaluation of portfolio performance. They should not be used as a short-term measurement or timing device. Many investors use yield spreads ("risk premiums") as a guide to relative valuation in both the high-grade and speculative areas of the market. Spreads can help them answer such questions as: Should we increase our participation in the speculative-grade market and reduce holdings of higher grade issues? Is the market paying us enough to justify the additional risk of more speculative-grade issues? Spreads are affected by many factors including perceived credit risk, bond characteristics, and market conditions. Spreads between high-grade and low-grade bonds usually increase when interest rates are rising and during economic recessions. They also increase when investors are fearful and move towards the haven of less credit risk investments. Recent occurrences were in 1986 when LTV filed for bankruptcy, when the insider trading scandals came to light later that year, and when the stock market collapsed in October 1987 and October 1989. During recessions, investors opt for stronger credits, bidding up their prices (lowering yields) while avoiding more risky debt issues.

Barron's publishes a Treasury-Junk Bond Spread. The spread is the "Difference in yield between Donaldson, Lufkin & Jenrette's index of actively traded, liquid high-yield bonds and seven-year Treasury notes. A lower spread implies greater investor confidence in junk bonds." The spread rose from about 350 basis points in the first quarter of 1989 to more than 700 in the fourth quarter.

If one achieves 300 to 500 basis points more return each year through a diversified portfolio of lower-rated bonds compared with higher-grade issues, the additional dollars would certainly add up over the years, especially through the miracle of compounding. However, this spread is an indication of the risk; it is additional payment (such as an insurance premium) for the investor to absorb such greater risk. Thus, if the yield spread averages 400 basis points and the default rate is 175 basis points, the excess return is 225 basis points, i.e., one gets an additional 225 basis points more in yield for accepting greater risk after considering default losses. Data from The First Boston Corporation's *High Yield Handbook* (January 1989) show that the excess returns ranged from 50 basis points in 1977 to 315 basis points in 1988, averaging 232 basis points. Some reasons for these excess returns are suggested in a 1989 General Accounting Office report including:

- The market has been mispricing the bonds; in other words, it has been inefficient.

- The demand for high yield bonds has been artificially reduced because some classes of institutions, such as commercial banks, are restricted from investing in them.

- The high yield market is young compared to the market for investment grade bonds and must offer very attractive yields to secure capital.

- The yield spread includes a premium for liquidity risk.

- A portion of the yield probably reflects some expected future decline in the economy.

- Issuers have been optimistic about what they could earn on their investments, especially LBOs, and have been willing to pay relatively high rates.[3]

It is this optimism that allows them to obtain the funds for their speculative ventures. In August 1989, Resorts International Inc. said it would stop paying interest to its bondholders and that it would submit a debt rescheduling or recapitalization plan to bondholders the next month. Management miscalculated, it was too optimistic as to what it could do. The *New York Times* quoted Merv Griffin who purchased the company in November 1988 as saying, "Operating cash flows have been less because we underestimated the time and capital expenditures it would take to turn around the company's operations to generate increased profits. It has taken the company longer to sell nonoperating real estate assets than originally expected." The president of Resorts said that the problems the company had when it was purchased were more than they expected. "It turned out to be something different than Merv envisioned he was buying. . . . I will say that knowing what we now know, we wouldn't do the same deal. We discovered a lot in the way of problems after we got here."

Of course, unwarranted optimism can lead to destruction. For example, Resorts International Financing's B3-rated 16 5/8% Subordinated Debentures due September 1, 2004, were trading at 96 1/2 at the end of 1988, a 17.27% yield to maturity and a 17.23% current yield. Nine months later they hit 30 before bouncing back to 34, were trading flat (without accrued interest) without a current or maturity yield, and rated Ca. Even well-intentioned and knowledgeable professional investors can be too optimistic at times. One junk bond research firm expressed its good feelings about these bonds in its year-end 1988 review.

The report mentioned the analyst's optimism about management's ability to improve operating results. The company could also fund cash flow deficiencies through the sale of non-operating assets. It was the belief that Griffin had no incentives to default on this debt. Finally, as the bonds were trading at a 350 basis point premium over newly issued Griffin debt, this spread made the bonds attractive.

In retrospect, this turned out to be a bad call. The Resorts' bonds declined to 34 by the end of August, a drop of only 64.8%. The Griffin Resorts 13½% First Mortgage Bonds due November 15, 1995, and the 13⅞% Senior Secured Notes due May 1, 1998, suffered smaller losses. Both issues traded around 100 at the end of 1988. At the end of August, they were 70 and 67, respectively, down a modest 30% and 33%. Junk is perfidious, requiring diligent research on the part of investors. One should always be skeptical, but more about this later when we discuss ways to reduce the risks of investing in junk.

There have been many studies on junk bond default rates and mortality experience, especially by Professor Edward I. Altman of New York University.[4] Altman defines the default rate as the dollar amount of defaulting bonds divided by the amount of junk debt outstanding. His figures exclude convertible bonds and distressed debt exchanges. During the 1970 to 1988 period, the default rate has ranged from a low of 0.156% in 1981 to a high of 11.388% in 1970. The average default rate for 1978 to 1988 was 1.875% and for 1970 to 1987, 2.378%. Excluding Texaco, the average default rate drops to 1.5% and 2.195%, respectively.

Table 7–4 presents Altman's and Moody's default rate data. The Moody's study includes distressed debt exchanges. Altman weighted his statistics by the par value of defaulted debt while Moody's assigned equal weight to each issuer. Altman's 1987 default rate of 5.466% is lowered to 1.34% if the special default of Texaco, Inc. and affiliated companies is excluded. The Moody's default rates for 1986, 1987 and 1988 would be 5.3%, 2.9% and 2.8%, respectively, excluding special events. The 1970 to 1988 average is reduced to 3.06% from 3.30%. Moody's defines special events as:

> . . . rapid changes in a company's prospects or financial position that (a) result in a sudden shift in credit quality but (b) the pre-

cise timing and nature of which could not have been predicted by the normal tools of fundamental credit analysis. Examples include mergers, acquisitions, takeovers, divestitures, capital restructurings (many due to leveraged buyouts), and filing for bankruptcy protection as a defense against litigation.

Debt mortality studies look at default rates as bonds age, similar to the way insurance actuaries look at human mortality. Altman's mortality study covering new issues from 1971 through 1987 and based on the initial bond rating shows that defaults increase as the credit rating declines. Investment-grade issues had a ten-year cumulative mortality rate of 0.13% for issues originally rated AAA, 2.46% for AA-rated bonds, 0.93% for A-rated debt, and 2.12% for issues initially in the BBB category. In the speculative-grade sector BB-rated bonds had a ten-year cumulative mortality rate of 6.64% and single-B issues a mortality rate of 31.91%. Ten-year results were not available for CCC issues. The five-year mortality figures were 1.84% for BB debt, 11.53% for B-rated bonds, and 31.17% for CCC junk.

Another mortality study which caught the attention of the financial press in 1989 was written by three faculty members of the Harvard Business School, Paul Asquith, David Mullins and Eric Wolff. Known as *The Harvard Study*, it is an aging analysis of 741 junk bonds issued in 1977 through 1986. If found that 33.92% of the bonds issued in 1977 and 34.26% of those issued in 1978 had defaulted by the end of 1988. Bonds issued in 1979 through 1983 had mortality rates between 19.21% and 27.56% and bonds issued in 1984, 1985 and 1986 had mortality rates of 9.38%, 3.53% and 8.14%, respectively.[5]

Care in the use of default and mortality rates must be exercised when examining the impact on a diversified portfolio. If the default rate is 5%, the portfolio's total return would not necessarily take a 500 basis point loss. A loss of that magnitude would mean that the bond was purchased at par and became completely worthless upon default; the portfolio manager could not salvage anything from it. Defaults do not mean that a bond's price goes to zero. The prices of the various LTV Corporation issues one week after the filing of bankruptcy in July 1986, ranged from 19 ½ to 63 ⅛ for a simple average of 38.33. The debt includes well-secured first mortgage bonds on a good steel plant to unsecured subordinated debentures. The average price one month before bankruptcy was 71.85 with a range of 56 to 90. Altman says the average retention or recovery rate on the bonds used in his study was 44.6% including Texaco, and 39.2% without Texaco. The loss on a portfolio depends on the actual loss incurred or reported. Not everyone buys bonds at par. Of course, to this must be added the loss in accrued coupon income; one assumes slightly less than six months interest on average but it would vary depending on the time of the last interest payment date and the coupon rate. Thus, the default loss to investors would be (i) the default rate, times (ii) the loss of principal, plus (iii) the loss of coupon or accrued interest. For 1988, the default rate of 1.986% results in a default loss of 1.193% using the weighted average price after default of 45.9 (average loss of 54.1) and the weighted average coupon of 11.97%.

Default rate	1.986%
× Loss of principal	0.541
= Loss from principal	1.074
+ 1/2 Coupon × default rate (.1197/2 × 1.986)	0.119
Default loss for 1988	1.193%

Hickman had several qualifications about the higher returns available from low grade issues that bear repeating. He states:

> The major conclusion that investors obtained higher returns on low-grade issues than on high grades should not be accepted without proper qualification. For it cannot be emphasized too strongly that this finding emerges only when broad aggregates of corporate bonds are considered over long investment periods, and given the price and yield relationships that existed during these periods. In effect, the aggregate results reflect the experience of all investors over long periods, rather than that of any particular investor over any given short period.
>
> Another qualification is that realized yields and loss rates were not nearly so regularly related to quality as were promised

Table 7–4 Historical Default Rates, 1970 to 1988

Year	Altman	Moody's
1988	1.986%	3.6%
1987	5.466	3.9
1986	3.394	5.7
1985	1.679	4.4
1984	0.825	3.2
1983	1.066	3.4
1982	3.115	3.4
1981	0.156	1.0
1980	1.482	1.5
1979	0.187	0.4
1978	1.265	1.8
1977	4.488	1.9
1976	0.368	1.4
1975	2.644	2.3
1974	1.106	1.4
1973	0.607	1.4
1972	2.720	3.3
1971	1.234	1.6
1970	11.388	10.9

yields and default rates. Because of the disparity in the performance of low-grade bonds, small investors (and many large investors that may have been inhibited from practicing the broadest type of diversification) would frequently have fared best by holding only the highest grade obligations. This conclusion follows both from the higher average default rate on low-grade securities and from the wider scatter of realized yields obtained on them over given periods.

A third qualification is that realized yields were subject to extreme aberrations over time, since they reflected not only the risks of the business cycle but the state of the capital market as well. The average yields realized over selected periods of offering and extinguishment, or over selected chronological periods during which the issues were outstanding, indicate that the market usually overpriced low-grade issues (and underestimated default risks) at or near peaks of major investment cycles. As a general rule, low-grades fared better than high grades when purchased near troughs and sold near peaks of the investment cycle; but by the same token, losses were heavy on low grades purchased near peaks and sold near troughs. The same is true of investments in declining as against growing industries. Low-grade issues of a declining industry rarely worked out as well as high-grade issues.[6]

Who Owns the Junk?

Buyers of speculative-grade bonds run the full range of the debt investor category. At the end of 1988 it was estimated that insurance companies and mutual funds (including money managers of pooled assets) each owned about 30% of the outstanding high-yield bonds. Pension funds held 15%, foreign investors 9%, thrift institutions 7%, individuals 5%, corporations 3%, and securities dealers 1%.[7] Individuals are an important category, through both direct purchases and indirectly through mutual funds, unit trusts and the like. In some experts' opinions, individuals should not participate directly in this market to any extent. Many have individual retirement accounts and other self-directed pension plans that can build up interest income on a tax deferred basis until the plan is liquidated. Should these funds be used for speculation? Probably not, for it is retirement money with which little credit risk should be taken; appropriate investments would be higher-grade bonds. Further, to reduce the chances of adverse selection, diversification is a necessity. Most individual investors do not have portfolios large enough to permit adequate diversification of credit and market risk. Also, many individuals do not have the right attitude for dispassionate investing; they don't buy when they should and they don't sell when they should. How often do we hear the excuse, "I don't want to take the loss." It really doesn't matter—the loss exists whether or not it is taken, and without the particular investment position the investor perhaps may be better able to think more clearly, rationally and without emotion.

Further, many neither have the time nor the knowledge and experience to adequately analyze the market for speculative bonds. Besides reviewing the operations and credit status of the issuer, the terms of the issue have to be studied. It is not enough to look at an equity analyst's bullish opinion on a common stock of the company in question. If the investment is successful the shares can be worth many times the current price. Bonds on the other hand, cannot trade far above par, and at maturity will not be worth more than par. Many equity analysts are unfamiliar with the nature of debt and may not be qualified to aid fixed-income investors. This is not to say that they should be completely ignored; they will often have important information about a company and an industry that could be helpful for a bond investor. One must be careful not to get swept away in the analyst's euphoria.

Since most individual investors cannot achieve proper diversification, many turn to mutual funds instead. Mutual funds pool monies from many people and invest in securities. An open-ended fund normally must be prepared to buy and sell its shares when investors want to invest in or redeem their stock. Thus, the fund must usually keep some highly liquid investments on hand to meet normal redemptions. In times of higher than normal redemptions, they will have to sell investments. This can work to the investors' detriment as it will likely be the better junk the fund sells when under pressure—the more liquid issues—while retaining the weaker credits. A closed-end investment company does not face redemption pressures as it is not committed to buy and sell its shares. With a more stable capital structure there is little need for liquid reserves and a greater percentage of its assets can be working for the investor. In periods of poor junk bond markets and investors running for the exits, the additional selling pressure from mutual funds exacerbates an already weak situation resulting in lower prices and lower net asset values.

Despite some of the concerns people may have with junk mutual funds, the important fact is that they can achieve the diversification individuals must have and the portfolio is under constant professional management. Prospective investors must do their homework and check out the fund's record and philosophy. Is the fund investing in the better or more conservative junk or is it investing solely for high yield? In effect, is the dividend payment being paid only out of income or is it being maintained at the cost of principal? This research does not guarantee good results but it can reduce one's worry. Also, most funds provide for the automatic reinvestment of dividends into additional shares. This is another aid for the longer-term investor seeking to build assets through the periodic compounding of the reinvestment of dividends.

There are also unit investment trusts for high-yield bonds. A unit investment trust is another type of financial vehicle which invests in a fixed portfolio of securities. The advantage here is supposed to be professional selection of the initial portfolio along with diversification (although often not as broad as with some mutual funds) and monthly payment of interest. However, after the initial sale, management of the trust's holdings is usually less than with a continually managed mutual fund. The adverse financial condition of a portfolio investment may not require the sale of the security from the trust. The sponsor of the trust is usually empowered to direct the trustee to sell investments upon the occurrence of certain events such as default or decline in price due to market or credit conditions if the retention of the securities would be detrimental to the interest of the investors. Hopefully, the sponsor can or will act before "the horse is out of the barn."

In 1989, the risks of investing in unit trusts became apparent when Drexel Burnham Lambert ordered the liquidation of its *High Income Trust Securities* ("HITS"). Drexel decided to leave the retail securities business and wouldn't make a secondary market for the various units. Investors got *HIT* in several ways. They originally bought the units with a 4% sales charge. Then, the liquidation occurred before the bonds had a chance to mature and the sales were done in a less than robust junk bond market climate. With a forced sale, bidders either stayed away or submitted low bids for many of the less liquid issues. Some of the bonds did not receive any bids at all and final distributions on several trusts were delayed. Some of the units had defaulted bonds which, if the fund were actively managed, might have been sold before the default, not after. The trustee said that the liquidated trusts had annual returns from 1.7% for the Series 12 trust to 10.8% for the Series 1 trust. The rates of return on these liquidated trusts were certainly not what the investors expected when they bought this garbage.

Insurance companies are active in the junk bond market. In some cases, the portfolio holdings were once high grade but economic and business conditions caused the quality of the holdings to decline. More recently, they have participated in the craze for original issue junk. Big enough to achieve the broad diversification of credit and market risk, many have large staffs who can analyze and monitor the credits in the portfolio. Often, due to their investment in private placements, they have close relationships with the issuers. Also, they can further diversify some of the credit risk by buying securities of privately held companies (issues that are not available to most public bond buyers). Several state regulators have expressed concern over the rising use of high-yield bonds by insurance company portfolio managers. In 1987, New York State's Insurance Department issued rules limiting insurance company investments in junk bonds to a maximum of 20% of their assets. It said that the rules would allow the companies to pursue their investment strategies without putting their policyholders at undue risk. The head of a major life insurance trade group was quoted by *The Wall Street Journal*, "Setting a ceiling on those kinds of investments is reasonable, particularly if the investment goes sour. If a company becomes insolvent, insurance law requires the entire industry to participate in the rescue of that company's policyholders." As investors should review the policies of mutual funds, insurance policyholders ought to review the investment philosophy and practices of their insurance companies.

Pension funds are increasing their activity in the lower-grade sector but some observers feel that it is not enough. About 1% of pension fund assets were invested in junk bonds in mid-1989 and one pension fund consultant suggested that it should increase to 5%. With interest rates in the late 1980s considerably lower than at the start of the decade, these funds have to reduce quality for higher income. Some of the funds are so big that an investment, though large by most standards, might be rather modest to the particular fund. Again, pension funds can achieve the broad diversification necessary and they usually have professional management. Diligence must be exercised in selecting the securities. After all, who will pay for the manager's mistakes? Ultimately, it will be the beneficiaries; widows, orphans and retired folks who can least afford the possibility of reduced income.

Critics have attacked pension plans and their relationship with junk bonds. An article in The *New York Times*[8] discussed the problems that might arise from corporations terminating their pension funds to recapture excess assets. They would buy single-payment annuities from insurance companies. "Whom do these assets belong to anyway?" is a question some have asked. The article said that the annuity contracts were often purchased ". . . from those companies that offer the best price. Of course, the companies that offer the best prices are those that have invested heavily in high-yield bonds." Further, "these unsuspecting retirees and employees, who typically have no role in the bargaining and get none of the savings, are left to depend on an insurance company of uncertain worth." Obviously, this does not apply to all pension plan terminations, but we believe that plan sponsors must be careful when terminating plans and ensure that the annuity contracts later purchased are with reliable and strong insurance companies.

Another type of junk bond investor has raised the ire of financial critics; it is the savings and loan association. S&Ls are deposit-accepting financial institutions that traditionally invested in residential mortgage loans, commercial real estate mortgage loans, land loans and consumer and other loans. In the last decade they were allowed to expand their business activity to include the management of corporate debt and equity securities. Often these investments were not substantial but, in some, they loomed rather large. The General Accounting Office reported that as of September 30, 1988, 161 thrifts had invested $13.2 billion in high-yield bonds with 25 institutions owning about 91% of the total. The GAO's survey of 11 thrifts with significant junk bond investments showed that at March 31, 1988, their high-yield bond holdings amounted to $9.1 billion. Five of the eleven thrifts had junk bond investments amounting to 11.9% to 28.8% of their total assets. The book value of bonds in default was $184 million, or 2% of the junk portfolio.

Thrifts invested in these securities for the greater yield or potential rates of return than those offered by mortgages and other permitted investments. It allows them to be commercial lenders without the trouble and expense of establishing commercial loan departments. Commercial loans are not liquid and they allow diversification of assets into other geographic areas of the country.

The big question that arose in the thrift crisis of 1986-1989 was whether it was appropriate for a federally-insured thrift institution to play in the speculative bond market? Who would pay if defaulted junk bonds are a contributing factor in a savings and loan association's demise? The Federal Savings and Loan Insurance Corporation (now the Savings Association Insurance Fund) would end up bearing the cost; thus the burden eventually falls upon Mr. and Mrs. Taxpayer and the more responsible thrifts through increased deposit insurance premiums and taxes paying for the thrift bailout. The legislation passed in the summer of 1989 should render these points moot. Thrifts are now prohibited from directly investing in junk bonds and must phase out their holdings within five years. However, separately capitalized affiliates may hold and buy high-yield bonds.

Reducing Risk in a Speculative-Grade Portfolio

The 1989 General Accounting Office report on thrift junk bond investments said ". . . the high yield bond market, in its present size and form, has not been tested by a recession. A severe economic downturn might increase bond defaults, especially for those companies issuing bonds as part of leveraged buyouts."[9] Junk bond investors must realize there is default risk in holding these securities but it can be reduced and incremental yield obtained through careful selection of issues.

Adequate diversification is essential, and the lower down the quality ladder, the more diversified the portfolio should be. Table 7-5 shows the diversification guidelines established by Moody's Investors Service and Standard & Poor's Corporation for the 9 ⅜% Collateralized Notes due September 15, 1990, issued by Imperial Savings Association. The original issue size for any bond in the pool must be at least $100 million, but 20% of the speculative-grade sector may be from issues with an original issue amount of $50 million or greater. Note that the higher quality the collateral, the less diversification required. For example, bonds rated Ba/BB from any single issuer cannot exceed 4% of the market value of the pledged property, and no more than 12% of the portfolio can be from any one industry. In the single-A category, the single issuer limit increases to 10%, while the industry concentration is 33% to 40%, depending on the rating agency. Such diversification helps protect against adverse selection. Of course, one should not modify the guidelines just because there are not enough qualified issues available for investment; just make do with the issues that fit.

Investors should limit the amount of subordinated debt in the portfolio. Subordinated debt of financially strong companies may offer little concern but, as credit quality decreases, consideration should be given to senior versus subordinated debt. Investors may permit subordinated debt if it is rated no lower than the Ba/BB category, implying that the senior debt may be investment grade. This may reduce the universe of possible investment opportunities, but we should not lose sight that we are seeking to minimize risk while still trying to achieve a better return. We are not seeking maximum short-term income without regard to risk. Most senior unsecured issues have negative pledge clauses; most subordinated debt issues do not. If a company runs into financial difficulty and needs additional financing, banks might provide the funds only if the new loan is secured by accounts receivable, inventory or certain other assets. If senior debt has a negative pledge clause then it, too, would fall under the security umbrella; subordinated debt would normally be excluded.

In the fall of 1981, the public debt securities of International Harvester Company and its finance subsidiary (now Navistar International Transportation Corporation and Navistar Financial Corporation) were selling at distressed prices after a period of operating losses. The bonds traded at levels suggesting that the companies were about to file for bankruptcy. Locked out of the commercial paper and long-term debt markets, they relied on more costly bank financing. The companies successfully negotiated with their banks a debt restructuring extending the parent's short-term debt maturities by two years. As part of the agreement, the parent pledged its fixed

Table 7–5 Collateralization Guidelines
Imperial Savings Association
9 3/8% Collateralized Notes due September 15, 1990

Rating	Maximum Percent of Market Value of Pledged Property Issued By Any One Issuer (1)	Maximum Percent of Market Value of Pledged Property in Any One Industry Category (1)
Moody's		
Aaa	100.0%	100.0%
Aa	20.0	60.0
A	10.0	40.0
Baa	6.0	20.0
Ba	4.0	12.0
B	3.0	8.0
Standard & Poor's		
AAA	10.0%	50.0%
AA	10.0	33.3
A	10.0	33.3
BBB	5.0	20.0
BB	4.0	12.0
B	3.0	8.0

(1) The referenced percentages represent maximum cumulative totals for the related rating category and each lower rating category.

Source: Prospectus dated September 24, 1987.

assets including plants and certain other properties but excluding inventories and receivables. The finance subsidiary's bank loans were secured by self-liquidating accounts receivable. The senior debt of both companies became secured as they contained negative pledge covenants. The parent's subordinated debt lacked any negative pledge and remained unsecured. If the restructuring failed, the public senior debtholders would at least have bccn on a parity with the banks; the subordinated debtholders did not obtain any greater protection or security.

If an issuer has senior and subordinated debt outstanding, the senior should normally be preferred. The senior issue's priority ranking may mean less price risk in case of bankruptcy. If there are several issues of senior debt outstanding, the one with the lowest dollar price is to be preferred, but keeping in mind the accrued interest to be paid at purchase. The idea is to reduce the risk of loss in case something unexpected occurs, such as the bankruptcy of the LTV Corporation in July 1986. In bankruptcy, the claim of all the senior debt against the bankrupt's estate would be approximately the same, namely principal plus accrued interest to the date of the filing of the bankruptcy petition. LTV (the parent company) had publicly held unsecured senior and subordinated debt. For example, the three senior issues (9 ¼s of 1997, 13 ⅞s of 2002 and the 14s of 2004) traded on a yield-to-maturity basis before bankruptcy. On June 6, six weeks before the filing, the closing prices of the three issues were 70, 90 ⅛ and 92, respectively. The promised yields to maturity were 14.96%, 15.55% and 15.30%, and the current returns were 13.21%, 15.23% and 15.22%. At the end of August, some six weeks after bankruptcy, the issues were trading at 35 ⅜, 37 ⅛ and 35 ⅝, respectively, down 49.5%, 58.8% and 61.3%. These prices were about 37% to 39% of the debtholders' claim, taking into account the original issue discount. On June 6 the subordinated debt prices ranged from 58 for the 7 ⅞% Reset Notes due April 1, 1998, to 86 for the 5% Subordinated Debentures due January 15, 1988, a difference of 48.3%. On August 29 the prices of these issues were 21 ½ and 26 ½, a difference of 23.3%. Before bankruptcy the issues were selling at 97.5% and 91.5% of the claim value; after bankruptcy they sold at 36.1% and 27.9%.

Some investors think that a short maturity bond is safer than a long-dated instrument. They are willing to buy it on a yield-to-maturity basis instead of on a more realistic one. If the company does not go under, the short bond may provide a very attractive return. If the issuer defaults, there may be a big price drop. In 1985 and 1986, up to the date of LTV's filing, many market participants said they liked the LTV 5s due January 15, 1988—after all, the bonds had only a couple of years to go until maturity, and maybe the company would make a good exchange offer for them. Speculators thought nothing could happen to jeopardize their investment. Bankruptcy wasn't likely, as many expected industry conditions to improve over the next several years. The company was reducing operating losses from steel while its aerospace business was profitable. Were these speculators wrong! The bankruptcy filing struck like a bolt of lightning. The 5s of 1988 had a 15.12% yield to maturity on June 6, but investors didn't achieve it; the high yield caused by the short maturity lulled them into a quick loss.

If the issuer goes bankrupt, the chances of recovery of a larger amount of the claim are greater for senior debtholders than for holders of junior paper. We will look at some examples of what bankrupt companies have paid to their debtholders later.

Another rule to follow is to limit, if not restrict completely, bonds that do not pay interest in cash. These include zero coupon bonds, deferred coupon debt (also called zero/coupons) and coupon issues with the interest payable at the issuer's option in cash, common stock, debt or a combination. The later issues are also know as payment-in-kind bonds. A zero coupon bond does not pay periodic interest and is sold at a discount from face value. The return comes from the difference paid for the issue and what one gets at redemption; there is no cash return before the final payment date. A deferred coupon (or zero slash coupon) bond is a combination of a straight zero and a regular coupon issue. For a certain period (typically four to five years) it will not pay any interest but, at a specific date in the future, interest payments will accrue at a predetermined rate and paid semi-annually. An example is Ann Taylor, Inc's Senior Subordinated Discount Notes due July 15, 1999. Issued July 20, 1989, at 53.646% of par, interest does not accrue on the notes until January 15, 1994, payable starting July 15, 1994, at 14 3/8%.

Some financially weak companies have issued bonds permitting interest to be paid in shares of common stock. The shares delivered in place of cash are usually valued at between 75% and 90%, depending on the trading volume of the stock, of the average sale price of the stock for a specified period before the payment date. This provision helps companies conserve cash. They have been issued or proposed by such firms as Petro-Lewis Corporation, LTV

Corporation, Western Union Corporation, Sunshine Mining Company and Mesa Capital Corporation, among others. The bonds would normally trade with accrued interest if they have been paying cash interest; otherwise they trade flat, i.e., without accrued. Mesa Capital Corporation, for example, has an agreement with the New York Stock Exchange that its 12% Subordinated Notes due August 1, 1996, trade with accrued interest. Mesa may make payment in common stock only if it has given public notice at least 10 days before the start of the applicable interest period. If it pays stock interest, the notes would trade flat until the Exchange determines otherwise.

In speculative-grade bond investment, cash flow should come from the portfolio, not from bookkeeping accretions of invisible interest or blizzards of paper certificates. Investors should get some cash return out of the investment and decide where and when to reinvest the interest payments—an option that non-interest-bearing securities don't offer. Also, if a company is so strapped for cash as to be unable to pay interest in dollars, it is foolish to stay with the investment and take the big risk that the situation may not get any better.

Careful analysis is essential for reducing the risk of default in a speculative bond portfolio. The prospectuses of new issues must be diligently evaluated for the terms and nature of the issuer's business and industry. We trust that the underwriters have faithfully done their due diligence. Many new issue prospectuses, especially for lower-rated issues, have sections called "risk factors," "certain considerations," and "risk and special factors" that point out some of the possible risks to consider before making the investment. Sometimes these risks may be insignificant or just normal business hazards, but these sections often mention risks that some might not have considered. They are in prospectuses for a good reason and thus they should not be ignored.

Some of the risks mentioned in these special sections include the following:

1. The company might have a high debt-to-equity ratio. Often debt may be equal to eight, nine or more times equity. In a few cases, there might not be any equity. The large leverage

could impair the issuer's ability to obtain additional financing in the future. The issuer may be more vulnerable to interest rate changes than it had been historically.

2. Restrictions have been placed on the company by its senior creditors (such as banks) that may require the company to use proceeds from asset sales to repay them.

3. The company may have been experiencing operating losses. It may have a negative interest coverage ratio because earnings are inadequate to cover fixed charges. It is in a weak financial condition, and losses are expected to continue so long as depressed industry conditions persist. In addition to operating cash flow, the company may need additional funds in the future to pay the principal and interest on the securities being offered or outstanding. It may have to refinance its operations or sell some assets to meet these expected obligations. Based upon current operations and anticipated growth, the company does not expect that it will be able to generate sufficient cash from operations to make all payments under the credit agreements when due for the first two years following the leveraged buyout.

4. The subject issue is subordinated to other debt. Also, the issuer is a holding company and thus conducts its operations through subsidiaries. It relies principally on income from dividends from subsidiaries to supply the necessary funds for the payment of interest and principal on the outstanding debt. There might be restrictions on such upstreaming of dividends. Any right of the company or the debtholders to participate in the assets of any of the subsidiaries upon the subsidiaries' liquidation or recapitalization is subject to the claims of the subsidiaries' creditors and preferred shareholders.

5. There may be no public market for the securities and a warning that none may develop.

6. The impact of interest rate fluctuations on the profitability of the issuer must be considered; that future performance is

subject to prevailing economic conditions and business and financial factors, including those beyond control of the company.

7. The indenture does not restrict the payment of dividends in certain cases.

8. Nonrecurring income may have an adverse impact on the financial statement.

9. Operating restrictions have been imposed on the company by regulatory authorities.

10. There may be income tax deficiencies due the Internal Revenue Service.

11. There may be contingencies due to the bankruptcy of a subsidiary and possible payments due the Pension Benefit Guaranty Corporation.

12. There is the risk of fraudulent conveyance liability. If a court, in a lawsuit by an unpaid creditor, finds that the issuer did not receive fair consideration or reasonably equivalent value for incurring the new debt, and the issuer was (i) insolvent, (ii) was rendered insolvent by reason of such transaction, (iii) was engaged in a business or transaction for which the assets remaining in the company constituted unreasonably small capital, or (iv) intended to incur or believed it would incur debts beyond its ability to pay such debts as they mature, it could invalidate the issuer's obligation under the new debt securities. The court could also subordinate the securities to existing and future debt, or take other action detrimental to the holders of the debt.

In the fraudulent conveyance sections of prospectuses, there are statements similar to the following from the prospectus dated December 8, 1987, for The Southland Corporation.

The Company currently believes that, after giving effect to the Merger and the Financing, it will not be rendered insolvent. This belief is based in part on the Company's forecast . . . which reflects the current structure of the transaction, and in part on the estimates by . . . as to the "present fair saleable value" of the various business segments and assets of the Company, which . . . exceeded the Company's probable consolidated liabilities. . . . The Company believes that the assumptions underlying this belief are reasonable. There can be no assurance, however, as to what standard a court would apply in order to determine whether the Company was "insolvent" upon consummation of the Merger or that, regardless of the method of evaluation, a court would not determine that the Company was insolvent upon consummation of the Merger. However, the Company believes that, following the Merger, the Company will have sufficient capital for businesses in which it will be engaged.

Many new issues are from privately-held companies, that is, the common stock ownership is held by a few people and thus the shares are not traded on a national securities exchange or in the normal over-the-counter market. Some have been issued by firms engaged in leveraged buyouts. If the securities are held by 300 or more persons, the company is considered a reporting one by the Securities and Exchange Commission, and must submit certain reports to the SEC. The prospectus for Dart Drug Stores, Inc., 12.70% Senior Debentures due 2001, states that as it expects to have fewer than 300 debentureholders, it ". . . will not file reports with the Commission or furnish information to Debentureholders in accordance with the Exchange Act reporting requirements. . . . Pursuant to the Indentures, however, the Company must furnish annual and quarterly reports to Debentureholders containing financial statements and certain other information. . . ." Dart filed for bankruptcy in mid-1989.

Investors should make sure the indenture requires that quarterly financial statements with income statements and balance sheets and audited annual reports be sent to all debtholders of record. These statements should contain management's discussion of the operations and any other developments affecting the debtholders. They should contain a discussion of any of the financial ratios or tests that must be satisfied according to the indenture. These include information concerning redemption if net worth declines or the use of maintenance and replacement funds or certain coverage tests.

Often, bond investors don't even get these reports. Many publicly held companies have shareholder meetings, talks with analysts, and public affairs meetings where fuller discussions of the firm's operations and outlook take place. Many privately held companies release only the minimal amount of information necessary to satisfy the SEC, indentures and their lawyers; they don't have to respond to outside investor queries. A large institutional buyer is in a much stronger position to ask for information. The investment banker may arrange meetings between the issuer and its bondholders, but individual investors don't get invited. This is another reason why individuals should invest in speculative-grade debt through professional money managers.

There are the traditional issues of lower-rated publicly held companies—those not involved in the front page battles to avoid being taken over by financial wizards. These are the run-of-the-mill businessmen's risks mentioned earlier. The proceeds from the issues might be used for regular business purposes, such as financing plant, equipment, research and development expenses, rather than blind pools, which some companies use to play the acquisition game. According to The First Boston Corporation, 35.5% of 1988's new issue junk bond proceeds were for general corporate purposes. Traditional credit analysis can be used in these cases. Of course, leverage may be higher than with investment-grade issues (but probably lower than with leveraged buyouts), coverage of fixed charges may be lower, and many other financial measurements might appear weak. Investors can analyze the business, get some sense of the value or worth of the assets (real, not blue sky), even under a worst-case scenario, and come to a decision that it is or is not a viable entity and the risk is worth the potential reward. Such investigation is not one shot at the time of issuance or proposed purchase but continual. Investors should evaluate the fundamentals of the industry and the company, see where they are, and estimate where they might be in the future. They should look at cash flow and the firm's debt servicing ability.

After doing their preliminary work, investors must relate the value of the issue to other securities. Is the yield sufficiently high enough to compensate for the additional risk? Is it in line with comparably rated securities? If not, investors must find out why there is a difference. It could be that the market views the bond as better or worse than other similar issues.

Defaulted and Bankrupt Issues

A bankrupt issue may be more attractive than one that is not. Certainly issues of many marginal companies appear overpriced for the risks involved. These should be analyzed and periodically reviewed on both an operating and liquidation or bankrupt basis. Much of the analysis may involve educated guesswork as to what the assets might be worth in liquidation or reorganization. By so doing, investors will be prepared to step in or to avoid the issue if the company goes under. It is emphasized that this area of speculation is not for the faint at heart nor for the uninformed. To participate in distressed securities one must become familiar with the law and process of bankruptcy and creditors' rights. It is a complex area of the securities world.

When a company files for bankruptcy, many investors are forced to sell their positions. This is often the wrong time to do so. The market often cannot absorb the large amount of selling accompanying a bankruptcy filing. The securities may fall to levels far below what they are worth creating an opportunity for the knowledgeable speculator. Hickman says: "The conclusion appears unmistakable; on the average, investors who sold at default suffered unnecessarily large losses, and those who purchased obtained unusually large gains. It is unfortunate that many financial intermediaries were forced by their directors or by regulatory authorities to sell at that time." [10]

Purchasing a security of a company in bankruptcy is buying several uncertainties. You know your cost. You might have some idea of what your claim is against the bankrupt's estate. You do not know how long it will be before a distribution is made. A few companies come out of bankruptcy in less than two years, while others take considerably longer. Two years is not considered to be a long reorganization period. It all depends on such factors including the complexity of the case, the friction between the various classes of creditors and claimants, the status of the company's current operations, management decisions, and other lawsuits pending against the bankrupt. Time is money, and the longer before a distribution, the lower the rate of return on the invested funds. You also do not know the exact value of what eventually will be paid or the breakdown of the distribution between cash (if any) and new securities. Essentially, you have bought a non-income-producing bond with an unknown future value and an indeterminate payout date.

The amount of the claim for unsecured debt is the face value of the security (or accreted principal amount for debt with an original issue discount) plus accrued and unpaid interest to the date of bankruptcy. Claims for unmatured interest are disallowed, and interest stops accruing on the date of filing. Thus, two issues of equal ranking may have different claims depending on the amount of accrued interest and accreted original issue discount.

The courts may allow a well-secured or over-secured claim (the value of the collateral exceeds the amount of the debt) to accrue interest after bankruptcy is filed. This is supposed to give adequate protection for the interest of the secured creditor. Thus the claims of mortgage bonds that are well secured continue to increase until a settlement is reached. The first mortgage bonds and the general and refunding mortgage bonds of Public Service Company of New Hampshire had their interest payments reinstated within a few months of the bankruptcy. There is a question in some jurisdictions if under-secured creditors can claim adequate protection—that is, whether interest continues to accrue up to the value of the collateral even though the value is less than the full claim?[11] Where the collateral is worth less than the claim, the difference between the claim and the value of the collateral becomes a general unsecured claim against the bankrupt estate.

Let us look at the results of a few bankruptcies and what investors have received upon reorganization or liquidation. We will use four companies that had both senior and subordinated debt outstanding and see how bondholders fared. Two dates were used for pricing: the end of the month before the bankruptcy filing and the end of the month after it. There were eight senior debt and five subordinated debt issues for these companies. In some cases, the prices used were valuations or bid prices, not actual trades, and were those nearest the chosen dates. The senior debt had an average price of 47 7/8 the month before bankruptcy and a price of 32 1/2 the month after, a decline of about 32%. The five subordinated issues declined, on average, from 29 ⅞ before bankruptcy to 14 ¼ a month later, representing a 52% drop in price. Cases where the debt rises in price when a company files for reorganization are rare, but it happens at times. This might occur when the issue's price has been pounded down to below what it may truly be worth by sellers who fear holding the bonds if a bankruptcy occurs. Braniff International 9 ⅛s of 1997 is an example in which the price was higher a month after bankruptcy.

Table 7-6 summarizes the annualized returns of these securities from the date of theoretical purchase to the date of emergence from bankruptcy or the liquidation of the company. In most cases cash is only part of the total package distributed to debtholders with the remaining portion a combination of debt and equity securities. Senior creditors normally will have a greater portion of their distributions in cash than do subordinated creditors. W. T. Grant Company was liquidated and the total distribution was in cash. Braniff International paid part of the claim of its subordinated debtholders in discount travel scrip.

The data show that greater returns go to those who bought after, rather than before, the company filed for bankruptcy. The returns for pre-bankruptcy investment include accrued interest paid at the purchase date, except in those cases where there was an interest payment between the purchase and bankruptcy dates. Most of the prices of these securities reflected the companies' rather weak financial health just before bankruptcy. They were in the "twilight zone" of pricing, not high enough to create confidence that the issuers could survive and not low enough to reflect their possible rebirth. The high yields to maturity (an indication of expected return) pointed to the risks involved, yet many assumed those risks just at the wrong time. Also, most investors who purchased the senior debt after bankruptcy received greater returns than the subordinated debt buyers, as they had a greater portion of their claim against the bankrupt satisfied.

Summary

Investment in speculative-grade debt can provide a portfolio with incremental returns over those available from higher-grade issues despite the increased risk of default. Careful analysis is imperative. Remember, in general bonds are securities with limited upside potential. Bond selection and investment are a negative art. Diversification among issuers is very important to reduce the negative impact of default on the portfolio. Again, as quality declines, the risk of default naturally increases, and bond prices become more subject to equity related events than to interest rate developments. Of course, investors should be most concerned with the company's survival and ability to meet its debt obligations on a timely basis. While one cannot predict what havoc the next business downturn may wreak on the ranks of speculative-grade companies, with the increasing numbers of very highly leveraged corporations, the default rate is likely be higher than at any time in the postwar period. Investors and the financial markets cannot ignore the fundamental rules of finance for too long a period without suffering the consequences. The investment company approach is strongly recommended for most individual and small institutional investors. Here one gets ample diversification and professional management—two features critical for success in the high-yield world of bonds.

Table 7-6 Summary of Distributions upon Settlement of Bankruptcy

BRANIFF INTERNATIONAL CORP.
Bankruptcy petition filed: May 13, 1982
Reorganization confirmed: December 15, 1983
Distribution: February 16, 1984

Issue	Price 4/30/82	Y.T.M.	Annual Rate of Return	Price 6/30/82	Annual Rate of Return	Distribution per $1,000	Paid in Cash
10% Notes—7/1/86	$438.75	37.22%	33.76%	$382.50	55.94%	$807.62	22.16%
9 1/8% Debs—1/1/97	355.00	26.31	47.99	382.50	54.59	795.58	20.78
5% Sub Debs—12/1/86	290.00	40.27	-57.38	50.00	24.64	72.04	No cash

DAYLIN, INC.
Bankruptcy petition filed: February 26, 1975
Reorganization confirmed: October 20, 1976
Distribution: October 20, 1976

Issue	Price 1/31/75	Y.T.M.	Annual Rate of Return	Price 3/31/75	Annual Rate of Return	Distribution per $1,000	Paid in Cash
8.35% Debs—4/15/97	$700.00	12.32%	-18.44%	$500.00	2.11%	$516.56	31.53%
5% Sub Debs—3/21/89	220.00	25.77	-59.67	195.00*	-57.90	55.52	No cash

* Based on the price reported on 3/21/75. A bid of $40 was reported on 3/31/75 by the National Bond Quotation Bureau. The $40 price, if bonds could have been purchased, produces a 22.99% annualized rate of return to the distribution date.

Table continues

Table 7-6 Summary of Distributions upon Settlement of Bankruptcy (Continued)

W. T. GRANT COMPANY

Bankruptcy petition filed: October 2, 1975
Liquidation order issued: February 12, 1976
Adjudicated a bank: April 13, 1976

Issue	Price 8/31/75	Y.T.M.	Annual Rate of Return	Price 10/31/75	Annual Rate of Return	Distribution per $1,000	Paid in Cash
8.35% Debs—4/15/97	$360.00	18.35%	25.72%	$150.00	55.76%	$967.90	100.00%
4 3/4% Sub Debs—4/15/96	245.00	20.52	-3.29	55.00	17.24	190.00	100.00

Note: The date of the payment for the debentures is unclear, as the settlement offer was extended several times, but it was probably prior to January 1, 1980. The date of the distribution for the subordinated debentures was about April 29, 1983, after being extended several times. For purposes of the rate of return calculations, we have used these dates.

WICKES COMPANIES, INC.

Bankruptcy petition filed: April 24, 1982
Reorganization confirmed: January 26, 1985
Distribution: December 20, 1984 (cash); January 28, 1985 (securities)

Issue	Price 3/31/82	Y.T.M.	Annual Rate of Return	Price 5/31/75	Annual Rate of Return	Distribution per $1,000	Paid in Cash
8 1/4% Notes—7/1/84	$650.00	31.08%	10.02%	$350.00	41.04%	$886.51	16.70%
8 7/8% Debs—8/1/97	480.00	19.74	22.12	270.00	55.02	886.51	16.70

Issue	Price 3/31/82	Y.T.M.	Annual Rate of Return	Price 5/31/75	Annual Rate of Return	Distribution per $1,000	Paid in Cash
7 7/8% Debs—5/1/98	390.00	21.49	29.11	270.00	55.02	886.51	16.70
10 1/4% Debs—7/15/04	455.00	22.72	23.76	300.00	49.20	886.51	16.70
5 1/8% Sub Debs—5/1/94	300.00	21.68	21.86	200.00	47.26	570.15	8.77
9% Sub Debs—5/1/99	440.00	31.32	5.98	210.00	44.66	570.15	8.77

Note: For further details on the distributions to debtholders for the above issues see Richard S. Wilson, *Corporate Senior Securities: Analysis and Evaluation of Bonds, Convertibles and Preferreds* (Chicago, IL: Probus Publishing Company, 1987), Chapter 11.

Notes

[1] High interest bonds ("HIBS") was applied to this type of debt in 1986 by the financial writer Ira U. Cobleigh. "Junk" is not of recent vintage as it was used in an article called "The Big Money in 'Junk' Bonds" which appeared in *Forbes* magazine, April 1, 1974. It said in part:

> What makes an issue a junk bond? While there is no precise definition, they typically come out of mergers or exchange offers. Some traders extend this definition to include the bonds of highly leveraged companies whose bonds are of questionable quality.

Columnist Ben Weberman, in the July 28, 1986 issue of *Forbes*, adds to the names of types of speculative grade issues. *Gyrojunk* bonds are those that once were supported by large and real assets but due to reorganization, divestitures and spinoffs, no longer have good assets supporting them. *Geriatric* issues are those of companies that once has some standing in industrial America and are now included in the Skid Row of industrial America. Others are *"borderline geriatrics . . . which are beyond middle age that have reconciled their aging to reality."* *Juvenile* junks are from younger issuers.

[2] W. Braddock Hickman, *Corporate Bond Quality and Investor Experience* (Princeton, NJ: Princeton University Press, 1958), p. 109. Hickman also quotes from *Measuring Business Cycles*, a 1946 publication by Arthur C. Burns and Wesley C. Mitchell:

> After a severe depression industrial activity rebounds sharply, but speculation does not. The following contraction in business is mild, which leads people to be less cautious. Consequently, in the next two or three cycles, while the cyclical advances become progressively smaller in industrial activity, they become progressively larger in speculative activity. Finally, the speculative boom collapses and a drastic liquidation follows, which ends this cycle of cycles and brings us back to the starting point.

[3] U.S. General Accounting Office, *High Yield Bonds—Issues Concerning Thrift Investments in High Yield Bonds* Washington, D.C.: Superintendent of Documents (1989), pp. 22-23.

[4] These include:

Edward I. Altman and Scott A. Nammacher, "The Default Rate Experience on High-Yield Corporate Debt." *Financial Analysts Journal* (July/August 1985), pp. 25-41.

Edward I. Altman, "Measuring Corporate Bond Mortality and Performance." *The Journal of Finance*, Vol. 44 No. 4 (September 1989), pp. 909-922.

Paul Asquith, David W. Mullins, Jr., and Eric D. Wolff, "Original Issue High Yield Bonds: Aging Analyses of Defaults, Exchanges and Calls." *The Journal of Finance*, Vol. 44 No. 4 (September 1989), pp. 923-952.

K. Scott Douglass and Douglas J. Lucas, *Historical Default Rates of Corporate Bond Issuers 1970-1988*, a special report of Moody's Investors Service, July 1989.

"First Boston Default Study." *High Yield Handbook* (The First Boston Corporation, January 1989), pp.44-48.

Gail I. Hessol and Thomas Kitto, "High-Yield Bond Default Rates." *Standard & Poor's CreditWeek* (August 7, 1989), pp. 21-23.

[5] For further discussion of junk bond mortality, see Laurie S. Goodman, "High Yield Default Rates: Is There Cause for Concern?" *Journal of Portfolio Management*, Winter, 1990.

[6] W. Braddock Hickman, "Corporate Bonds: Quality and Investment Performance," Occasional Paper 59. (New York, NY: National Bureau of Economic Research, 1957), pp. 16-17.

[7] David Zigas and Larry Light, "Don't Put Away the Smelling Salts Yet." *Business Week* (October 2, 1989), p. 93.

[8] Louis Lowenstein, "Taking Issue with the S.E.C.: Three New Reasons to Fear Junk Bonds." The *New York Times*, August 24, 1986.

9   U.S. General Accounting Office, *High Yield Bonds*, p. 3.

10 Hickman, "Corporate Bonds," p. 26.

11 "Bankruptcy Ruling Could Set Precedent For Deciding Secured Creditors' Claims." *Investor's Daily* (September 3, 1986), p. 2.

SECTION II

Chapter 8

BOND PRICING AND TRADITIONAL YIELD MEASURES

In Section I of this book, we described the different features of corporate bonds. In the six chapters in Section II we set forth the techniques for valuing corporate bonds. Here is a road map for our journey. In this chapter we explain how the price of a bond is determined and the conventional yield measures commonly used in the marketplace to assess the relative value of corporate bonds—yield to maturity and yield to call. The limitations of these yield measures are illustrated. In the next chapter, we describe a return measure that overcomes the limitations of the conventional yield measures—horizon return—and how it can be used in relative value analysis and assessing the potential performance of a corporate bond. In Chapter 10, the price volatility characteristics of bonds are explained. There we introduce the concepts of duration and convexity. Our focus in Chapter 9 is on option-free bonds. Chapters 11 and 13 set forth the state-of-the-art analytical techniques for valuing corporate bonds with embedded options. The option-adjusted spread approach is explained in Chapter 11. The option's approach is explained in Chapter 13, with background information on options provided in Chapter 12.

Pricing a Bond

The price of any financial instrument (common stock, bond, mortgage, real estate) is equal to the present (discounted) value of its *expected* cash flows. By discounting the cash flows, allowance is made for the timing of the cash flows.[1] Consequently, determining the price requires that an investor estimate the following:

- the expected cash flows, and
- the appropriate required yield.

The expected cash flows for some financial instruments are simple to determine; for others, the task may be quite complex. The required yield reflects the yield for financial instruments with *comparable* risk and features.

Assuming that a corporate issuer does not default, it is simple to compute the cash flows for a fixed-rate, option-free (that is, a noncallable, nonputable or nonconvertible) bond. The cash flows are (1) coupon interest payments to the maturity date and (2) the par (or maturity) value at maturity.

Two bonds will be used to illustrate how the price of a bond is calculated: a 7% coupon, 5-year bond and a 7% coupon, 20-year bond. Assuming that the next coupon payment for both bonds is six months from now, the second column of Tables 8–1 and 8–2 set forth the cash flow that the investor will realize every six months until the bond matures.

To calculate the price of each bond, the yield required by an investor must be determined. For purposes of our illustrations, we shall assume that the investor wants a 10% yield in order to invest in either of these bonds. The cash flows should be discounted at one-half the required yield, or 5% in our illustration. The third column of Tables 8–1 and 8–2 gives the present value of $1 for each period using an interest rate of 5%. The last column of the tables gives the present value of the cash flows, which is found by multiplying the cash flow in the second column by the present value of $1 at 5%. The sum of the present value of the cash flows is the price of the bond.

Table 8–1   Calculation of the Price of a 7%, 5-Year Bond Selling to Yield 10%

Period (1)	Cash flow per $100 par (2)	Present value of $1 at 5% (3) *	Present value of cash flow (4) = (2) × (3)
1	3.5	0.952380	3.33333
2	3.5	0.907029	3.17460
3	3.5	0.863837	3.02343
4	3.5	0.822702	2.87945
5	3.5	0.783526	2.74234
6	3.5	0.746215	2.61175
7	3.5	0.710681	2.48738
8	3.5	0.676839	2.36893
9	3.5	0.644608	2.25613
10	103.5	0.613913	63.54002

Price = Total present value =   88.41739

* Present value of $1 at 5% calculated as follows:

$$\frac{1}{(1.05)^{period}}$$

In practice, hand-held calculators and PC software are used to compute the price of a bond given the (1) coupon rate, (2) maturity date, and (3) required yield

The required yield is determined by investigating the yields offered on comparable bonds in the market. By comparable, we mean issues of the same credit quality, features, and maturity.[2] The required yield is typically expressed as an annual interest rate. Since the cash flows for corporate bonds are every six months, the market convention is to use one-half the annual interest rate as the periodic interest rate with which to discount the cash flows. This is the practice we followed in calculating the price in Tables 8–1 and 8–2.

**Table 8-2 Calculation of the Price of a 7%, 20-Year Bond
Selling to Yield 10%**

Period (1)	Cash flow per $100 par (2)	Present value of $1 at 5% (3) *	Present value of cash flow (4) = (2) × (3)
1	3.5	0.952380	3.33333
2	3.5	0.907029	3.17460
3	3.5	0.863837	3.02343
4	3.5	0.822702	2.87945
5	3.5	0.783526	2.74234
6	3.5	0.746215	2.61175
7	3.5	0.710681	2.48738
8	3.5	0.676839	2.36893
9	3.5	0.644608	2.25613
10	3.5	0.613913	2.14869
11	3.5	0.584679	2.04637
12	3.5	0.556837	1.94893
13	3.5	0.530321	1.85612
14	3.5	0.505067	1.76773
15	3.5	0.481017	1.68355
16	3.5	0.458111	1.60339
17	3.5	0.436296	1.52703
18	3.5	0.415520	1.45432
19	3.5	0.395733	1.38506
20	3.5	0.376889	1.31911
21	3.5	0.358942	1.25629
22	3.5	0.341849	1.19647
23	3.5	0.325571	1.13949
24	3.5	0.310067	1.08523
25	3.5	0.295302	1.03355
26	3.5	0.281240	0.98434
27	3.5	0.267848	0.93746
28	3.5	0.255093	0.89282
29	3.5	0.242946	0.85031
30	3.5	0.231377	0.80982

Table continues

Table 8–2 Calculation of the Price of a 7%, 20-Year Bond Selling to Yield 10% *(Continued)*

Period (1)	Cash flow per $100 par (2)	Present value of $1 at 5% (3) *	Present value of cash flow (4) = (2) × (3)
31	3.5	0.220359	0.77125
32	3.5	0.209866	0.73453
33	3.5	0.199872	0.69955
34	3.5	0.190354	0.66624
35	3.5	0.181290	0.63451
36	3.5	0.172657	0.60430
37	3.5	0.164435	0.57552
38	3.5	0.156605	0.54811
39	3.5	0.149147	0.52201
40	103.5	0.142045	14.70172

Price = Total present value = 74.26137

* Present value of $1 at 5% calculated as follows:

$$\frac{1}{(1.05)^{period}}$$

The price of a zero coupon bond is simply the present value of the maturity value. However, in the present value computation, the number of periods used for discounting is *double* the number of years to maturity of the bond, not the number of years.

Price/Yield Relationship for an Option-Free Bond

A fundamental property of a bond is that its price changes in the opposite direction of the change in the required yield. The reason is that the price of the bond is the present value of the cash flows. As the required yield increases, the present value of the cash flows decreases; hence, the price decreases. The opposite is true when the required yield decreases: the present value of the cash flows increases and, therefore, the price of the bond increases. This is il-

Table 8–3   Price/Yield Relationship for Six Bonds

Coupon/ Term	Required Yield						
	7%	8%	9%	10%	11%	12%	13%
7%/ 5	100.00	95.94	92.09	88.42	84.92	81.60	78.43
7%/20	100.00	90.10	81.60	74.26	67.91	62.38	57.56
10%/ 5	112.47	108.11	103.96	100.00	96.23	92.64	89.22
10%/20	132.03	119.79	109.20	100.00	91.98	84.95	78.78
13%/ 5	124.95	120.28	115.83	111.58	107.54	103.68	100.00
13%/20	164.07	149.48	136.80	125.74	116.05	107.52	100.00

lustrated in Table 8–3 for the two 7% coupon bonds whose price we calculated in Tables 8–1 and 8–2 and for four other bonds.

If we graphed the price/yield relationship for any option-free bond, we would find that it has the "bowed" shape shown in Figure 8–1. This shape is referred to as *convex*. The convexity of the price/yield relationship has important implications for the investment properties of a bond, as we will see in Chapter 10.

The Relationship Between Coupon Rate, Required Yield and Price

As yields in the marketplace change, the only variable that an investor can change to compensate for the new required yield in the market is the price of the bond. When the coupon rate is equal to the required yield, the price of the bond will be equal to its par value.

When yields in the marketplace rise above the coupon rate, the price of the bond adjusts so that any investor who wishes to purchase the bond can realize additional interest. To do so, the price of the bond must sell below its par value. The capital appreciation realized by holding the bond to maturity represents a form of interest payment to the investor to compensate for the lower coupon rate than the yield required in the market. A bond selling below its par

Figure 8–1   Price/Yield Relationship for an Option-Free Bond

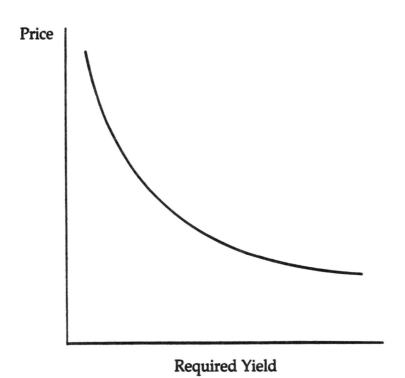

Required Yield

---

value is said to be selling at a *discount*. In our earlier calculation of bond price, we saw that when the required yield is greater than the coupon rate, the price of the bond is always less than the par value.

When the required yield in the market is below the coupon rate, the price of the bond must sell above its par value. This occurs because investors who would have the opportunity to purchase the bond at par would be getting a coupon rate in excess of what the market would require. As a result, investors would bid up the price of the bond because its yield is attractive. It will be bid up to a price at which it offers the required yield in the market. A bond whose price is above its par value is said to be selling at a *premium*.

The relationship between coupon rate, required yield and price is summarized below:

coupon rate < required yield   <———————>   price < par
coupon rate = required yield   <———————>   price = par
coupon rate > required yield   <———————>   price > par

These relationships can be verified for the six bonds whose price we show at various required yields in Table 8-3.

Relationship Between Bond Price and Time if Interest Rates are Unchanged

If the required yield is unchanged between the time a bond is purchased and the maturity date, what will happen to the price of the bond? For a bond selling at par value, the coupon rate is equal to the required yield. As the bond moves closer to maturity, the bond will continue to sell at par value. Thus, for a bond selling at par, its price will remain at par as the bond moves toward the maturity date.

The price of a bond will *not* remain constant for a bond selling at a premium or a discount. Table 8–4 shows the price movement of two 20-year bonds not selling at par value as they approach maturity. Notice that the discount bond will increase in price as it approaches maturity assuming the required yield does not change. For a premium bond, the opposite occurs. For both bonds, the price will equal par value at the maturity date.

Reasons for the Change in the Price of a Bond

The price of a bond will change due to one or more of the following reasons:

1. *A change in the level of interest rates in the economy.* For example, if interest rates in the economy increase (fall) because of Fed policy, the price of a bond will decrease (increase).

2. *As it moves toward maturity.* As we demonstrated, over time a discount bond rises in price over time if yields do not change; a premium bond's price declines over time if yields do not change.

Table 8–4 Price of Discount and Premium Bond as Bond Approaches Maturity

Bonds: 7% coupon, 20-year bond, selling at 74.26 to yield 10%
11.5% coupon, 20-year bond, selling at 112.87 to yield 10%

| | | Bond | |
After (years)	Years to Maturity	7% coupon (discount)	11.5% coupon (premium)
1	19	74.70	112.65
2	18	75.18	112.41
3	17	75.71	112.14
4	16	76.30	111.85
5	15	76.94	111.53
6	14	77.65	111.17
7	13	78.44	110.78
8	12	79.30	110.35
9	11	80.26	109.87
10	10	81.31	109.35
11	9	82.47	108.77
12	8	83.74	108.13
13	7	85.15	107.42
14	6	86.71	106.65
15	5	88.42	105.79
16	4	90.31	104.85
17	3	92.39	103.81
18	2	94.68	102.66
19	1	97.21	101.39
20	0	100.00	100.00

3. *A change in the required yield due to a change in the spread between corporates and Treasuries.* If the Treasury rate does not change, but the spread to Treasuries for all corporate bonds changes (narrows or widens), corporate bond prices will change.

4. *A change in the perceived credit quality of the issuer.* Assuming interest rates in the economy and yield spreads between cor-

porates and Treasuries do not change, the price of a corporate bond will increase (decrease) if its perceived credit quality has improved (deteriorated).

Accrued Interest and Invoice Price

When an investor purchases a bond between coupon payments, if the issuer is not in default, the investor must compensate the seller of the bond for the coupon interest earned from the time of the last coupon payment to the settlement date of the bond. This amount is called *accrued interest* and is computed as follows:

$$(\text{coupon rate}) \times \frac{\text{number of days from last coupon to settlement date}}{\text{number of days in coupon period}}$$

Market conventions determine the number of days in a coupon period and the number of days from the last coupon to settlement date. For corporate bonds, the day count convention is "30/360" which means a year is treated as having 360 days and each month as having 30 days. Therefore, the number of days in a coupon period is 180.

For example, suppose that a corporate bond in which the last coupon payment was made on March 1 is purchased with a settlement date of July 17. The number of days from settlement to the next coupon payment (September 1) is determined as follows:

Remainder of July	13	days
August	30	days
September 1	1	day
	44	days

Since there are 180 days in a coupon period, the number of days from the last coupon to the settlement date is 136 (180 minus 44). Accrued interest for this bond is then:

$$(\text{coupon rate}) \times \frac{136}{180}$$

There are financial calendars available that provide the day count. Most money managers use software programs that have this information programmed in.

The *invoice price* is the total proceeds that the buyer of the bond pays the seller. The invoice price is equal to the price agreed upon by the buyer and the seller plus accrued interest.

Conventional Yield Measures

An investor who purchases a corporate bond can expect to receive a dollar return from one or more of the following sources:

- the coupon interest payments made by the issuer,

- any capital gain (or capital loss—negative dollar return) when the bond matures, is called or is sold, and

- income from reinvestment of the coupon interest payments. This source of dollar return is referred to as *interest-on-interest*.

For corporate bonds, three yield measures are commonly cited by market participants—current yield, yield to maturity and yield to call. These yield measures are expressed as a percent return rather than a dollar return. However, the yield measure should consider each of the three potential sources of return cited above. Below we discuss the current yield and yield to maturity. Later in this chapter we cover the traditional analysis of callable bonds using the yield to call measure.

Current Yield

The current yield relates the *annual* coupon interest to the market price. The formula for the current yield is:

$$\text{current yield} = \frac{\text{annual dollar coupon interest}}{\text{price}}$$

For example, the current yield for a 7%, 20-year bond whose price is 74.26 is 9.43% as follows:

annual dollar coupon interest $= .07 \times \$100 = \$7$
price $= \$74.26$

current yield $= \dfrac{\$7}{\$74.26} = .0943$ or 9.43%

The current yield will be greater than the coupon rate when the bond sells at a discount; the reverse is true for a bond selling at a premium. For a bond selling at par, the current yield will be equal to the coupon rate.

The drawback of the current yield is that it considers only the coupon interest and no other source of return that will impact an investor's return. No consideration is given to the capital gain that the investor will realize when a bond is purchased at a discount and held to maturity; nor is there any recognition of the capital loss that the investor will realize if a bond purchased at a premium is held to maturity.

Yield to Maturity

The most popular measure of yield in the bond market is the yield to maturity. The yield to maturity is the interest rate that will make the present value of the cash flows from a bond equal to its invoice price (price plus accrued interest). Calculation of the yield to maturity of a bond is the reverse process of calculating the price of a bond. To find the price of a bond we determined the cash flows and the required yield, then we calculated the present value of the cash flows to obtain the price. To find the yield to maturity, we first determine the cash flows. Then we search by trial and error for the interest rate that will make the present value of the cash flows equal to the invoice price.[3]

To illustrate, consider a 7%, 20-year bond selling for 67.91. The cash flows for this bond are (1) 40 six-month payments of \$3.5 and (2) \$100 40 six-month periods from now. The present value using various discount (interest) rates is:

Interest rate	3.5%	4.0%	4.5%	5.0%	5.5%	6.0%	6.5%
Present value	100.00	90.10	81.60	74.26	67.91	62.38	57.56

When a 5.5% interest rate is used, the present value of the cash flows is equal to 67.91, which is the price of the bond. Hence, 5.5% is the semiannual yield to maturity.

The market convention adopted is to double the semiannual interest rate and call that interest rate the yield to maturity. Thus, the yield to maturity for the above bond is 11% (2 times 5.5%). The yield to maturity computed using this convention—doubling the semiannual yield—is called a *bond equivalent yield* or *coupon equivalent yield*.

The following relationship between the price of a bond, coupon rate, current yield and yield to maturity holds:

bond selling at	relationship
par	coupon rate = current yield = yield to maturity
discount	coupon rate < current yield < yield to maturity
premium	coupon rate > current yield > yield to maturity

The yield to maturity considers the coupon income and any capital gain or loss that the investor will realize by *holding the bond to maturity*. The yield to maturity also considers the timing of the cash flows. It does consider interest on interest; *however, it assumes that the coupon payments can be reinvested at an interest rate equal to the yield to maturity*. So, if the yield to maturity for a bond is 10%, for example, to earn that yield the coupon payments must be reinvested at an interest rate equal to 10%. The following illustration clearly demonstrates this.

Suppose an investor has $74.26 and places the funds in a certificate of deposit that pays 5% every six months for 20 years or 10% per year (on a bond equivalent basis). At the end of 20 years, the $74.26 investment will grow to $522.79. Instead, suppose an investor buys the following bond: a 7%, 20-year bond selling for $74.26. The yield to maturity for this bond is 10%. The investor would expect that at the end of 20 years, the total dollars from the investment will be $522.79.

Let's look at what the investor will receive. There will be 40 semiannual interest payments of $3.5 which will total $140. When the bond matures, the investor will receive $100. Thus, the total dollars that the investor will receive is $240 if he held the bond to maturity. But this is less than the $522.79 necessary to produce a yield of 10% on a bond equivalent basis by $282.79 ($522.79 minus $240). How is this deficiency supposed to be made up? If the investor reinvests the coupon payments at a semiannual interest rate of 5% (or 10% annual rate on a bond equivalent basis), then the interest earned on the coupon payments would be $282.79. Consequently, of the $448.53 total dollar return ($522.79 minus $74.26) necessary to produce a yield of 10%, about 63% ($282.79 divided by $448.53) must be generated by reinvesting the coupon payments.

Clearly, the investor will only realize the yield to maturity that is stated at the time of purchase if (1) the coupon payments can be reinvested at the yield to maturity, and (2) if the bond is held to maturity. With respect to the first assumption, the risk that an investor faces is that future reinvestment rates will be less than the yield to maturity at the time the bond is purchased. This risk is referred to as *reinvestment risk*. If the bond is not held to maturity, the price of the bond may have to be sold for less than its purchase price, resulting in a return that is less than the yield to maturity. The risk that a bond will have to be sold at a loss because interest rates rise is referred to as *interest-rate risk* or *price risk*.

Reinvestment risk: There are two characteristics of a corporate bond that determine the degree of reinvestment risk. First, for a given yield to maturity and a given coupon rate, the longer the maturity the more the bond's total dollar return is dependent on the interest-on-interest to realize the yield to maturity at the time of purchase. That is, the greater the reinvestment risk. The implication is that the yield to maturity measure for long-term coupon bonds tells little about the potential yield that an investor may realize if the bond is held to maturity. For long-term bonds, in high interest rate environments the interest-on-interest component may be as high as 70% of the bond's potential total dollar return.

The second characteristic that determines the degree of reinvestment risk is the coupon rate. For a given maturity and a given yield to maturity, the higher the coupon rate, the more dependent the bond's total dollar return will be on the reinvestment of the coupon payments in order to produce the yield to maturity at the time of purchase. This means that holding maturity and yield to maturity constant, premium bonds will be more dependent on interest on interest than bonds selling at par. In contrast, discount bonds will be less dependent on interest on interest than bonds selling at par. For zero coupon bonds, none of the bond's total dollar return is dependent on interest on interest. So, a zero coupon bond has no reinvestment risk if held to maturity.

Interest-rate risk: As we explained earlier in this chapter, a bond's price moves in the direction opposite the change in interest rates. As interest rates rise (fall), the price of a bond will fall (rise). For an investor who plans to hold a bond to maturity, the change in the bond's price prior to maturity is of no concern; however, for an investor who may have to sell the bond prior to the maturity date, an increase in interest rates subsequent to the time the bond was purchased will mean the realization of a capital loss. Not all bonds have the same degree of interest-rate risk. In Chapter 10, we shall explain the characteristics of a bond that determine its interest-rate risk.

Given the assumptions underlying yield to maturity, we now can drive home with an illustration the key point that yield to maturity has limited value in assessing the relative value of corporate bonds. Suppose that an investor who has a five year investment horizon is considering the following four noncallable corporate bonds:

Bond	Coupon Rate	Maturity (years)	Yield to Maturity
W	5%	3	9.0%
X	6%	20	8.6%
Y	11%	15	9.2%
Z	8%	5	8.0%

Assuming that all four corporate bonds are of the same credit quality, which one is the most attractive to this investor? An investor who selects Bond Y because it offers the highest yield to maturity is failing to recognize that the bond must be sold after five years, the price of the bond depending on the yield required in the market for 10 year, 11% coupon bonds at that time. Hence, there could be a capital gain or capital loss that will make the return

higher or lower than the yield to maturity promised now. Moreover, the higher coupon rate on Bond Y relative to the other three
bonds means that more of this bond's return will be dependent on
the reinvestment of coupon interest payments.

Bond W offers the second highest yield to maturity. On the surface, it seems to be particularly attractive because it eliminates the
problem faced by purchasing Bond Y of realizing a possible capital
loss when the bond must be sold prior to the maturity date. In addition, the reinvestment risk seems to be less than for the other
three bonds because the coupon rate is the lowest. However, the
investor would not be eliminating the reinvestment risk since after
three years he must reinvest the proceeds received at maturity for
two more years. The return that the investor will realize will depend on interest rates three years from now when the investor must
rollover the proceeds received from the maturing bond.

Which is the best bond? The yield to maturity doesn't seem to be
helping us identify the best bond. The answer depends on the expectations of the investor. Specifically, it depends on the interest
rate at which the coupon interest payments can be reinvested until
the end of the investor's investment horizon. Also, for bonds with a
maturity longer than the investment horizon, it depends on the
investor's expectations about interest rates at the end of the investment horizon. Consequently, any of these bonds can be the best
investment vehicle based on some reinvestment rate and some future interest rate at the end of the investment horizon. In the next
chapter, we shall present an alternative return measure for assessing corporate bonds.

Traditional Analysis of Callable Bonds

Throughout this chapter, our analysis on pricing and return measures has dealt with corporate bonds in which neither the issuer nor
the bondholder has the option to do anything. In this section, we'll
look at callable bonds. Our purpose here is fourfold. First, the disadvantages of the call feature from the investor's perspective are
explained. Second, the conventional methodology that has been
used to evaluate these bonds will be discussed. Third, we will describe the price/yield relationship for a callable corporate bond. Fi-

nally, we set the foundation for how bonds with embedded options, such as callable corporate bonds, should be viewed.

Disadvantages of Callable Bonds

The holder of a callable bond has given the issuer the right to call the issue prior to the expiration date. This results in two disadvantages to the bondholder. First, an issuer may call a bond when the yield on bonds in the market is lower than the issue's coupon rate. For example, if the coupon rate on a callable corporate bond is 13% and prevailing market yields are 7%, the issuer will find it economical to call the 13% issue and refund it with a 7% issue. From the investor's perspective, the proceeds received will have to be reinvested at a lower interest rate. Thus, callable bonds expose bondholders to reinvestment risk.

Second, as we shall explain later in this section, the price appreciation potential for a bond in a declining interest rate environment is limited when it is callable. The price of the callable bond will remain near its call price rather than rising to a higher price that would result for an otherwise comparable noncallable bond. This phenomenon for a callable bond is referred to as *price compression*.

Given these disadvantages of a callable corporate bond, why would any investor want to own one? If the investor receives sufficient compensation in the form of higher potential yield (lower price for the bond), an investor willing to accept call risk will be willing to hold a callable corporate bond.

Conventional Methodology

When a corporate bond is callable, the practice has been to calculate a yield to call as well as a yield to maturity. The former yield calculation assumes that the issuer will call the bond at the first call date. The procedure for calculating the yield to call is the same as for any yield calculation: determine the interest rate that will make the present value of the expected cash flows equal to the price. In the case of yield to call, the expected cash flows are the coupon payments to the first call date and the call price.

To illustrate the computation, consider an 18-year, 11% coupon bond with a maturity value of $100 selling for $116.90. Suppose that the first call date is 13 years from now and the call price is $105.50.

The cash flows for this bond if it is called in 13 years are (1) 26 coupon payments of $5.50 every six months and (2) $105.50 in 26 six-month periods from now.

The process for finding the yield to call is the same as for finding the yield to maturity. The present value for several periodic interest rates is shown below:

Annual interest rate	Semi-annual rate	Present value of 26 payments of $5.50	Present value of $105.50 26 periods from now	Present value of cash flows
8.0	4.00	87.91	38.05	125.96
8.5	4.25	85.56	35.75	121.31
9.0	4.50	83.31	33.59	116.90
9.5	4.75	81.14	31.57	112.71
10.0	5.50	79.06	29.67	108.73

Since a periodic interest rate of 4.5% makes the present value of the cash flows equal to the price, 4.5% is the yield to call. Therefore, the yield to call on a bond equivalent basis is 9%.

According to the conventional approach, conservative investors should calculate the yield to call and yield to maturity for a callable bond selling at a premium, selecting the lower of the two as a measure of potential return. It is the smaller of the two yield measures that investors should use to evaluate the relative value of bonds. Some investors calculate not just the yield to the first call date, but the yield to all possible call dates. Since most bonds can be called at any time after the first call date, the approach recommended has been to calculate the yield to every coupon anniversary date following the first call date. Then, all yield to calls calculated and the yield to maturity are compared. The lowest of these yields is called the *yield to worst*.[4] It is this yield that the conventional approach would have one believe should be used in relative value analysis.

Let's take a closer look at the yield to call as a measure of the potential return of a callable corporate bond. The yield to call does consider all three sources of potential return from owning a bond. However, as in the case of the yield to maturity, it assumes that all cash flows can be reinvested at the computed yield—in this case the yield to call—until the assumed call date. As we noted earlier in this chapter, this assumption may be inappropriate. Moreover, the yield to call assumes that (1) the investor will hold the bond to the assumed call date and (2) the issuer will call the bond on that date.

These assumptions underlying the yield to call are oftentimes unrealistic. They do not take into account how an investor will reinvest the proceeds if the issue is called. For example, consider two bonds, M and N. Suppose that the yield to maturity for bond M, a five-year noncallable bond, is 10% while for bond N the yield to call assuming the bond will be called in three years is 10.5%. Which bond is better for an investor with a five-year investment horizon? It's not possible to tell for the yields cited. If the investor intends to hold the bond for five years and the issuer calls the bond after three years, the total dollars that will be available at the end of five years will depend on the interest rate that can be earned from investing funds from the call date to the end of the investment horizon.

What return measure can take this into account? The horizon return framework explained in the next chapter does.

Price/Yield Relationship for a Callable Corporate Bond

We stated earlier in this chapter that the price/yield relationship for an option-free (i.e., noncallable) bond is convex. Figure 8–2 shows the price/yield relationship for both a noncallable bond and the same bond if it is callable. The convex curve a-a' is the price/yield relationship for the noncallable (option-free) bond. The unusual shaped curve denoted by a-b is the price/yield relationship for the callable bond.

The reason for the shape of the price/yield relationship for the callable bond is as follows. When the prevailing market yield for comparable bonds is higher than the coupon rate on the bond, it is unlikely that the corporate issuer will call the bond. For example, if the coupon rate on a bond is 8% and the prevailing yield on comparable bonds is 16%, it is highly improbable that the issuer will call an 8% bond so that it can issue a 16% bond. Since the bond is unlikely to be called, the callable bond will have the same price/yield relationship as a noncallable bond. However, even when the coupon rate is just below the market yield investors may not pay the same price for the bond had it been a noncallable bond because there is still the chance the market yield may drop further so that it is beneficial for the issuer to call the bond.

As yields in the market decline, the likelihood that yields will decline further so that the issuer will benefit from calling the bond increases. We may not know the exact yield level at which investors begin to view the issue likely to be called, but we do know that there is some level. In Figure 8–2, at yield levels below y*, the price/yield relationship for the callable bond departs from the price/yield relationship for the noncallable bond. If, for example, the market yield is such that a noncallable bond would be selling for 109 but since it is callable would be called at 104, investors would not pay 109. If they did and the bond is called, investors would receive 104 (the call price) for a bond they purchased for 109. Notice that for a range of yields below y*, there is price compression—that is, there is limited price appreciation as yields decline. The portion of the callable bond price/yield relationship below y* is said to exhibit negative convexity.

Breaking a Corporate Callable Bond into Its Component Parts

To develop an analytical framework for assessing relative value and evaluating the potential performance of callable bonds over some investment horizon, it is necessary to understand what the components of the bond owned are. A callable corporate bond is a bond in which the bondholder has sold the issuing corporation an option (more specifically, a call option) that allows the issuer to repurchase the contractual cash flows of the bond from the time the bond may be called until the maturity date.

Consider the following two bonds: (1) a callable bond with an 8% coupon, 20 years to maturity and callable in five years at 104 and (2) a 10-year 9% coupon bond callable immediately at par. For the first bond, the bondholder owns a 5-year noncallable bond and has sold a call option granting the issuer the right to call away from the bondholder 15 years of cash flows 5 years from now for a price of 104. The investor who owns the second bond has a 10-year noncallable bond and has sold a call option granting the issuer the right to immediately call the entire 10 year contractual cash flows or any cash flows remaining at the time the issue is called for 100.

Effectively, the owner of a corporate callable bond is entering into two separate transactions. First, he buys a noncallable corporate bond from the issuer for which he pays some price. Then, he sells the issuer a call option for which he receives the option price from the issuer. Therefore, we can summarize the position of a callable corporate bondholder as follows:

long a callable bond = long a noncallable bond + short a call option

In terms of price, the price of a callable corporate bond is therefore equal to the price of the two components parts. That is,

callable bond price = noncallable bond price – call option price

The call option price is subtracted from the price of the noncallable bond. The reason is that when the bondholder sells a call option, he receives the option price. Graphically this can be seen in Figure 8–2. The difference between the price of the noncallable bond and the callable bond at a given yield level is the price of the embedded call option.

Actually, the position is more complicated than we just described. The issuer may be entitled to call the bond at the first call date and anytime thereafter, or at the first call date and any subsequent coupon anniversary. Thus, the investor has effectively sold a strip (or package) of call options to the issuer. The call price may vary with the date the issue may be called. The underlying bond for the call option is the remaining coupon payments that would have been made by the issuer had the bond not been called. For exposition purposes, it is easier to understand the principles associated with the investment characteristics of callable corporate bonds by describing the investor's position as long a noncallable bond and short a call option.

While we have limited our discussion to callable bonds, the same logic applies to putable bonds. In the case of a putable bond, the bondholder has the right to sell the bond to the issuer at a designated price and time. A putable bond can be broken into two separate transactions. First, the investor buys a noncallable bond. Second, the investor buys an option from the issuer that allows the

Figure 8–2 Price/Yield Relationship for a Noncallable and Callable Bond

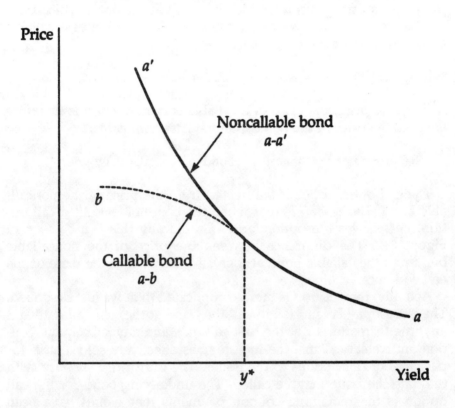

investor to sell the bond to the issuer. This type of option, as we explain in Chapter 12, is called a *put* option. Therefore, the position of a putable bondholder can be described as:

long a putable bond = long a noncallable bond + long a put option

The price of a putable bond is then

price of a putable bond = price of a noncallable bond + price of a put option

Because the valuation of bonds with embedded options requires an understanding of basic option theory, we include coverage of that topic in Chapter 12.

Yield Measure for Floating Rate Securities

The coupon rate for a floating rate security changes periodically based on some predetermined index (such as LIBOR or Treasuries). Since the value for the benchmark in the future is not known, it is not possible to determine the cash flows. This means that a yield to maturity cannot be calculated.

Effective Margin

A conventional measure used to estimate the potential return for a floating rate security is the security's *effective margin*. This measure estimates the average yield spread over the underlying index that the investor can expect to earn over the life of the security. The procedure for calculating the effective margin is as follows:

Step 1: Determine the cash flows assuming that the index rate does not change over the life of the security.

Step 2: Select a yield spread (margin).

Step 3: Discount the cash flows in step 1 by the current index rate plus the yield spread selected in step 2.

Step 4: Compare the present value of the cash flows as calculated in step 3 to the price. If the present value is equal to the security's price, the effective margin is the yield spread assumed in step 2. If the present value is not equal to the security's price, go back to step 2 and try a different yield spread.

For a security selling at par, the effective margin is simply the spread over the index.

To illustrate the calculation, suppose that a 6-year floating rate security selling for 99.3098 pays 6-month LIBOR plus 80 basis points. The coupon rate is reset every six months. Assume that LIBOR is currently 10%. Table 8–5 shows the calculation of the effective margin for this security. The second column shows current LIBOR. The third column sets forth the cash flows for the security.

The cash flow for the first 11 periods is equal to one-half LIBOR (5%) plus the semiannual spread of 40 basis points multiplied by 100. In the 12th six-month period, the cash flow is 5.4 plus the maturity value of 100. The top row of the last five columns shows the annual yield spread. The columns below the assumed yield spread show the present value of each cash flow. For example consider the assumed spread of 88 basis points. Adding one-half this assumed spread to the current LIBOR of 5% (10% annual), gives a discount rate of 5.44%. For the cash flow of $54 in period 6, the present value is:

$$\frac{\$5.4}{(1.0544)^6} = 3.9297.$$

The last row gives the total present value of the cash flows. For the five assumed yield spreads, the present value is equal to the price of the floating rate security (99.3098) when the assumed yield spread is 96 basis point. (Notice that the effective margin is 80 basis points, the same as the spread over the index (LIBOR), when the security is selling at par.)

There are two drawbacks to the effective margin as a measure of the potential return from investing in a floating rate security. First, this measure assumes that the index will not change over the life of the security. In Chapter 11, we present an approach that allows the investor to introduce interest rate volatility into the analysis of a floating rate security. Second, if the floating rate security has a cap or floor, this is not taken into consideration. Other approaches that we present in Chapters 11 and 13 can handle caps or floors.

Notes

1 Discounting is explained in any basic investment book.

2 In Chapter 10 we introduce a measure of interest-rate risk known as duration. Instead of talking in terms of a bond with the same maturity as being comparable, we will recast the analysis in terms of duration.

[3] In the illustrations presented in Section II of this book, we assume that the next coupon payment will be six months from now so that the invoice price is just the bond price.

[4] The yield to worst also takes into account maximum sinking fund redemptions (at 100) prior to the initial call date and the redemption of the remainder on the call date.

Table 8-5 Calculation of the Effective Margin for a Floating Rate Security

Floating rate security: Maturity = 6 years
Rate = LIBOR + 80 basis points
Reset every six months

| | | | *Present value of cash flow* | | | | |
| | | | *Assumed annual yield spread (in bp)* | | | | |
Period	Annual LIBOR (%)	Cash flow ($)*	80	84	88	96	100
1	10	5.4	5.1233	5.1224	5.1214	5.1195	5.1185
2	10	5.4	4.8609	4.8590	4.8572	4.8535	4.8516
3	10	5.4	4.6118	4.6092	4.6066	4.6013	4.5987
4	10	5.4	4.3755	4.3722	4.3689	4.3623	4.3590
5	10	5.4	4.1514	4.1474	4.1435	4.1356	4.1317
6	10	5.4	3.9387	3.9342	3.9297	3.9208	3.9163
7	10	5.4	3.7369	3.7319	3.7270	3.7171	3.7122
8	10	5.4	3.5454	3.5401	3.5347	3.5240	3.5186
9	10	5.4	3.3638	3.3580	3.3523	3.3409	3.3352
10	10	5.4	3.1914	3.1854	3.1794	3.1673	3.1613
11	10	5.4	3.0279	3.0216	3.0153	3.0028	2.9965
12	10	105.4	56.0729	55.9454	55.8182	55.5647	55.4385
	Present value		100.0000	99.8269	99.6541	99.3098	99.1381

* For periods 1-11:
   Cash flow = 100 (LIBOR + Assumed yield spread) (.5)

For period 12:
   Cash flow = 100 (LIBOR + Assumed yield spread) (.5) + 100

Chapter 9

ANALYSIS OF CORPORATE BONDS USING THE HORIZON RETURN FRAMEWORK

In the previous chapter, we explained and illustrated the conventional approaches used to analyze fixed-rate and floating-rate corporate bonds. We then highlighted the limitations of the conventional yield measures. If conventional measures such as the yield to maturity and yield to call offer little insight into the relative value of corporate bonds, what measure of return can be used? The proper measure is one that considers all three sources of potential dollar return over the investor's investment horizon. The return is then the interest rate that will make the invoice price grow to the projected total dollar return at the end of the investment horizon. The yield computed in this way is referred to as the *horizon return*. The horizon return is also referred to as the *total return and realized compound yield*. In this chapter we explain this measure and demonstrate how it can be applied to relative value analysis.

Horizon Return

The horizon return requires that the investor specify:

- an investment horizon
- a reinvestment rate

• a selling price for the bond at the end of the investment horizon (which depends on the assumed yield to maturity that the bond will sell for at the end of the investment horizon).

More formally, the steps for computing a horizon return over some investment horizon are as follows:

Step 1: Compute the total coupon payments plus the interest on interest based on the assumed reinvestment rate. The reinvestment rate is one-half the annual interest rate that the investor assumes can be earned on the reinvestment of coupon interest payments.[1]

Step 2: Determine the projected sale price at the end of the investment horizon. The projected sale price will depend on the projected yield on comparable bonds at the end of the investment horizon.

Step 3: Add the values computed in Steps 1 and 2. The sum is the total future dollars that will be received from the investment given the assumed reinvestment rate and projected required yield at the end of the investment horizon.

Step 4: To obtain the semiannual horizon return, use the following formula:

$$\left(\frac{\text{total future dollars}}{\text{purchase price of bond}}^{1/\text{length of horizon}} \right) - 1$$

Step 5: Since coupon interest is assumed to be paid semiannually, double the interest rate found in Step 4. The resulting interest rate is the horizon return expressed on a bond equivalent basis. Instead, the horizon return can be expressed on an effective annual interest rate basis by using the following formula:

$$(1 + \text{semiannual horizon return})^2 - 1$$

To illustrate the computation of the horizon return, suppose that an investor with a 3-year investment horizon is considering purchasing a 20-year, 8% coupon bond for $828.40. The yield to maturity for this bond is 10%. The investor expects that he can reinvest the coupon interest payments at an annual interest rate of 6% and that at the end of the investment horizon the 17-year bond will be selling to offer a yield to maturity of 7%. The horizon return for this bond is computed in Table 9–1.

Objections to the horizon return analysis cited by some portfolio managers are that it requires assumptions about reinvestment rates and future yields, as well as forcing a portfolio manager to think in terms of an investment horizon. Unfortunately, some portfolio managers find comfort in meaningless measures such as the yield to maturity because it is not necessary to incorporate any expectations. The horizon return framework enables the portfolio manager to analyze the performance of a bond based on different interest rate scenarios for reinvestment rates and future market yields. By investigating multiple scenarios, the portfolio manager can see how sensitive the bond's performance is to each scenario. There is no need to assume that the reinvestment rate will be constant for the entire investment horizon.

For portfolio managers who want to use the market's expectations of short-term reinvestment rates and the yield on the bond at the end of the investment horizon, implied forward rates can be calculated from the yield curve. Implied forward rates are explained in Chapter 10 and are calculated based on arbitrage arguments. A horizon return computed using implied forward rates is called an *arbitrage-free horizon return.*

Applications of Horizon Analysis

In the remainder of this chapter, we demonstrate how horizon analysis can be employed to assess the relative value of different corporate bonds and the relative value of corporate bonds compared to municipal bonds.

Comparing Coupon and Zero Coupon Corporates

For managers of tax-exempt portfolios who intend to hold a corporate bond until maturity, there is an analytical technique for assessing the relative value of a coupon and zero coupon corporate bond. The technique is best presented by means of an illustration.[2]

Suppose that a portfolio manager is considering the following two 12-year corporate bonds of the same quality rating: (1) a 12.6%

Table 9-1   Illustration of Horizon Return Calculation

Assumptions:

- Bond: 8%, 20-year bond selling for $828.40 (yield to maturity is 10%)
- Annual reinvestment rate: 6%
- Investment horizon: 3 years
- Yield for 17-year bonds at end of investment horizon: 7%

Calculations:

Step 1: Compute the total coupon payments plus the interest on interest assuming an annual reinvestment rate of 6%, or 3% every six months. The coupon payments are $40 every six months for 3 years or 6 periods (the planned investment horizon). The total coupon interest plus interest on interest is $258.74.*

Step 2: The projected sale price at the end of 3 years assuming that the required yield to maturity for 17-year bonds is 7% is found by determining the present value of 34 coupon payments of $40 plus the present value of the maturity value of $1,000, discounted at 3.5%. The price can be shown to be $1,098.51.

Step 3: Adding the amount in Steps 1 and 2 gives total future dollars of $1,357.25.

Step 4: Compute the following:

$$\left(\frac{\$1,357.25}{\$828.40}\right)^{1/6} - 1$$

$$= (1.63840)^{.16667} - 1$$

$$= 1.0858 - 1 = .0858 \text{ or } 8.58\%$$

Table continues

Table 9-1 Illustration of Horizon Return Calculation (Continued)

Step 5: Doubling 8.58% gives a horizon return of 17.16% on a bond equivalent basis. On an effective annual interest rate basis, the horizon return is

$(1.0858)^2 - 1$

$= 1.1790 - 1 = .1790 = 17.90\%$

---

* The formula is given in footnote 1 of the text. For this illustration, the semiannual coupon is $40, the semiannual reinvestment rate is 3%, and the length of the horizon is 6 (3 years). Therefore, the coupon interest plus interest on interest is:

$$\$40 \left[\frac{(1.03)^6 - 1}{.03} \right] = \$258.74$$

---

coupon bond selling at par and (2) a zero coupon bond selling at 24.98. Both bonds are intended to be held to the maturity date and therefore the investment horizon is 12 years. The yield to maturity for the zero coupon corporate bond is 11.9%. Since no reinvestment of coupon payments is required, the horizon return is 11.9%. The horizon return for the 12.6% coupon bond will depend on the rate at which the coupon payments can be reinvested. We can determine the reinvestment rate that will produce the same total future dollars from both investments. This rate is called the *break-even reinvestment rate.*

Suppose that instead of investing $100 in the 12.6% coupon bond, the portfolio manager decides to invest in the zero coupon bond. The semiannual yield to maturity is 5.95%; the $100 invested in the zero coupon bond will grow to $400 at the end of 24-periods (12 years), that is:

$\$100 \ (1.0595)^{24} \ = \ \$400$

If the portfolio manager places $100 in the 12.6% coupon bond, she will be indifferent between the zero coupon corporate bond and the 12.6% corporate bond if the latter produces total future dollars of $400. The total future dollars from holding an investment to maturity will be equal to the sum of (1) the coupon payments, (2) the maturity value, and (3) the interest on interest from reinvesting the coupon payments.

For the 12.6% coupon bond, the portfolio manager knows that for each $100 invested, $151.20 will be received from coupon payments (24 × $6.30) plus the maturity value of $100. Therefore, $251.20 ($151.20 + $100) will be received. For the 12.6% coupon bond to produce $400, interest on interest must equal $148.80 ($400 − $251.20). Alternatively, the coupon interest plus the interest on interest must equal $300. There is a formula that can be used to calculate the coupon plus interest on interest that will be realized from reinvesting the coupon payments at some reinvestment rate. The formula is:[3]

$$ C \left[\frac{(1+r)^n - 1}{r} \right] $$

where   C = semiannual coupon payment (in $ per $100 par)
          r = semiannual break-even reinvestment rate (in decimal)
          n = number of semiannual coupon payments (in decimal)

In our illustration, we know that the semiannual coupon payment is $6.30 and that the interest on interest should equal $300. Substituting these values into the above formula and a value of 24 for n, we have:

$$ 300 = 6.30 \left[\frac{(1+r)^{24} - 1}{r} \right] $$

By trial and error, we can find the value for r that will make the right side of the formula equal to 300. The value would be 5.53%. Therefore, if the portfolio manager believes she can realize at least an 11.06% (2 × 5.53%) reinvestment rate, the 12.6% corporate bond will provide more future dollars than the zero coupon corporate bond. If she expects to reinvest the coupon payments at a rate less than 11.06%, the zero coupon bond would be a better investment since it will provide a higher horizon return.

The break-even reinvestment rate can be generalized to compare two coupon bonds with the same maturity.

Comparing Municipal and Corporate Bonds

The conventional methodology for comparing the relative value of a tax-exempt municipal bond and a taxable corporate bond is to compute the *taxable-equivalent yield*. The taxable-equivalent yield is the yield that must be earned on a taxable bond in order to produce the same yield as a tax-exempt municipal bond. The formula is:

$$\text{taxable-equivalent yield} = \frac{\text{tax exempt yield}}{1 - \text{marginal tax rate}}$$

For example, suppose an investor in the 28% marginal tax bracket is considering a 10-year municipal bond with a yield to maturity of 7.2%. The taxable-equivalent yield is:

$$\frac{7.2\%}{1 - .28} = 10\%$$

If the yield offered on a comparable quality corporate bond with 10 years to maturity is more than 10%, those who use this approach would recommend that the corporate bond be purchased. If, instead, a yield of less than 10% is offered on a comparable corporate bond, the investor should invest in the municipal bond.

What's wrong with this approach? The tax-exempt yield of the municipal bond and the taxable-equivalent yield suffer from the same limitations that we discussed in the previous chapter with respect to yield to maturity. Consider the difference in reinvestment opportunities for a corporate and municipal bond. For the former, coupon payments will be taxed; therefore, the amount to be reinvested is not the entire coupon payment but an amount net of taxes. In contrast, since the coupon payments are free from taxes for a municipal bond, the entire coupon can be reinvested.

The horizon return framework can accommodate this situation by allowing us to explicitly incorporate reinvestment opportunities. There is another advantage to the horizon return framework compared to the conventional taxable-equivalent yield approach. Changes in tax rates (either because the investor expects his or her tax rate to change or the tax structure to change) can be incorporated into the horizon return framework.

Evaluating Potential Bond Swaps

Portfolio managers commonly swap an existing bond in a portfolio for another bond. Bond swaps can be categorized as follows: (1) pure yield pickup swaps, (2) substitution swaps, (3) rate anticipation swaps, and (4) intermarket spread swaps. Horizon return analysis can be used to assess the potential return from a swap.

Pure yield pickup swap: Switching from one bond to another that has a higher yield is called a pure yield pickup swap. The swap may be undertaken to achieve either higher current coupon income or higher yield to maturity,[4] or both. No expectation is made about changes in interest rates, yield spreads or credit quality.

Rate anticipation swap: A portfolio manager who has expectations about the future direction of interest rates will use bond swaps to position the portfolio to take advantage of the anticipated interest rate move. These are known as rate anticipation swaps. If rates are expected to fall, for example, bonds with greater price volatility will be swapped for existing bonds in the portfolio having lower price volatility (to take advantage of the larger change in price that will result if interest rate in fact do decline). The opposite will be done if rates are expected to rise.[5]

Substitution swap: In a substitution swap a portfolio manager swaps one bond for another bond that is thought to be identical in terms of coupon, maturity, price sensitivity to interest rate changes, and credit quality but offers a higher yield. This swap depends on a capital market imperfection. Such situations sometimes exist in the bond market due to temporary market imbalances. The risk that the portfolio manager faces is that the bond purchased may not be identical to the bond for which it is exchanged. For example, if credit quality is not the same, the bond purchased may be offering a higher yield because of higher credit risk rather than because of a market imbalance.

Horizon return analysis can be used to evaluate a substitution swap. Suppose a pension portfolio that is exempt from income taxes includes a single-A rated, 10%, 18-year corporate bond selling at par. We'll call this Bond A. Also suppose that the portfolio manager has the opportunity to swap into another bond, Bond B, that is also a single-A rated corporate bond but is selling at 100.41 to yield 10.2%. Bond B is a 10.25% coupon bond with 18.5 years to maturity. The portfolio manager believes that Bond B is cheap because it is offering a yield higher (10.2%) than Bond A (10%), a comparable-quality corporate bond. The portfolio manager has an investment horizon of six months and expects that Bond B will fall into line with other single-A rated bonds by the end of the investment horizon. Let's assume that the next coupon payment for both bonds is exactly six months from now, so that we need not consider reinvestment income.

Table 9-2 shows the horizon return for both bonds for three interest rate environments at the investment horizon (that is, six months from now): stable, falling 100 basis points, and rising 100 basis points. For each interest rate environment, four yield spreads are shown. For the first, the yield spread is unchanged at 20 basis points (10.2% − 10%). The second yield spread is zero (i.e., Bond B's yield spread has moved in the direction anticipated by the portfolio manager). The third yield spread assumes a narrowing of the yield spread to 10 basis points, which represents a partial adjustment rather than the full adjustment anticipated by the portfolio manager. Finally, the last yield spread assumes that the yield spread widens to 30 basis points rather than narrowing as expected.

Under all interest rate environments, when the yield spread narrows, Bond B will outperform Bond A. However, if the yield spread widens, Bond A will outperform Bond B. Even if the spread is unchanged, Bond B will outperform Bond A.

Since we analyzed this swap from the perspective of a pension fund, the tax implications of selling Bond A are not considered because a pension fund is exempt from income taxes. Managers of taxable entities would have to undertake a more comprehensive analysis that takes into account any tax implications such as a realized gain or loss from the sale of Bond A.

Intermarket spread swap: These swaps are undertaken when the portfolio manager believes that the current yield spread between two bonds in the market is out of line with its historical yield spread and that the yield spread will realign by the end of the investment horizon. Yields spreads between bonds exist for the following reasons:

Table 9-2 Analysis of a Substitution Swap

Held in Portfolio (Candidate for Sale): Bond A
   A-rated corporate, 10%, 18-year, selling at 100.00 to yield 10%
Candidate for Purchase: Bond B
   A-rated corporate, 10.25%, 18.5-year, selling at 100.41 to yield
   10.2%

Investment Horizon = 6 months

Expectations:
   The buy candidate currently is mispriced (underpriced).
   The spread between the bond held in the portfolio and the buy
   candidate will be zero at the horizon date.

	Bond A (Sell)			Bond B (Buy)		
Spread (in basis points)	Yield (%) 10.0	Price 100.00	Horizon Return (%)*	Yield (%) 10.2	Price 100.41	Horizon Return (%)*
Rates Stable:						
Spread = 20	10.0	100.00	5.00	10.20	100.41	5.10
Spread = 0	10.0	100.00	5.00	10.00	102.07	6.76
Spread = 10	10.0	100.00	5.00	10.10	101.23	5.92
Spread = 30	10.0	100.00	5.00	10.30	99.59	4.29
Falling Rates:						
Spread = 20	9.0	108.73	13.73	9.20	109.15	13.81
Spread = 0	9.0	108.73	13.73	9.00	111.04	15.69
Spread = 10	9.0	108.73	13.73	9.10	110.09	14.74
Spread = 30	9.0	108.73	13.73	9.30	108.23	12.89
Rising Rates:						
Spread = 20	11.0	92.30	−2.70	11.20	92.71	−2.56
Spread = 0	11.0	92.30	−2.70	11.00	94.17	−1.11
Spread = 10	11.0	92.30	−2.70	11.10	93.44	−1.84
Spread = 30	11.0	92.30	−2.70	11.30	91.99	−3.28

* Since there are no coupon payments to reinvest, the horizon return for both bonds can be computed as follows:

   (price 6 months from now at assumed yield − initial price + semiannual coupon) ÷ initial price

The semiannual coupon for Bond A is $5 and for Bond B $5.125.

1. There is a difference in the credit quality of bonds (for example, between Treasury bonds and double-A public utility bonds of the same maturity).

2. Difference in features of corporate bonds that make them more or less attractive to investors (for example, callable and noncallable bonds and putable and nonputable bonds).

To illustrate an intermarket spread swap and how to analyze its potential return using the horizon return framework, suppose a pension fund manager is holding Bond X, a single-A rated corporate bond with a 7.5% coupon rate and 10 years to maturity, selling at 93.35 to yield 8.5%. The pension fund manager observes that yields on 10-year double-A corporate bonds are offering a yield 20 basis points lower. Based on historical yield spreads, the pension fund manager feels that a 20 basis point yield spread between single-A and double-A corporates is too narrow and that a more appropriate yield spread for these two issues, based on recent historical patterns, is 30 basis points. Furthermore, he believes that the market will realign to a 30 basis point spread in six months.

Suppose that the pension fund manager has the opportunity to swap Bond X for Bond Y, a double-A rated corporate bond with a coupon rate of 7.5%, 10 years to maturity and selling for 94.64% to yield 8.3%. The yield spread between Bond X and Bond Y is 20 basis points. Table 9-3 shows the horizon return after six months for three interest rate environments: stable, falling 100 basis points and rising 100 basis points. Four yield spreads at the end of six months are shown for each interest rate environment. Bond Y will outperform Bond X if the yield spread between single-A rated and double-A rated corporate bonds widens; it will underperform Bond X if the yield spread remains unchanged or narrows.

Of course, as we noted in the illustration of the substitution swap, tax consequences must be considered for any taxable entity contemplating an intermarket spread swap. In addition, swaps must be weighted so that they take into consideration the fact that bonds with different features will perform differently when interest rates change. When a portfolio manager enters into an intermarket spread swap, he wants to improve performance if his expectations about the spread works out and not risk that the swap not work

Table 9-3 Analysis of an Intermarket Spread Swap

Held in Portfolio (Candidiate for Sale): Bond X
  A-rated corporate, 7.5%, 10-year, selling at 93.35 to yield 8.5%
Candidate for Purchase: Bond Y
  AA-rated corporate, 7.5%, 18.5-year, selling at 94.64 to yield
  8.3%

Investment Horizon = 6 months

Expectations:
  Spread between A and AA corporates will widen from 20
  basis points to 30 basis points.

	Bond X (Sell)			Bond Y (Buy)		
Spread (in basis points)	Yield (%) 8.5	Price 93.35	Horizon Return (%)	Yield (%) 8.3	Price 94.64	Horizon Return (%)
Rates Stable:						
Spread = 10	8.5	93.57	4.25	8.4	93.57	2.83
Spread = 20	8.5	93.57	4.25	8.3	94.81	4.14
Spread = 30	8.5	93.57	4.25	8.2	95.44	4.81
Spread = 40	8.5	93.57	4.25	8.1	96.08	5.48
Falling Rates:						
Spread = 10	7.5	100.00	11.14	7.4	100.67	10.33
Spread = 20	7.5	100.00	11.14	7.3	101.35	11.05
Spread = 30	7.5	100.00	11.14	7.2	102.04	11.78
Spread = 40	7.5	100.00	11.14	7.1	102.73	12.51
Rising Rates:						
Spread = 10	9.5	87.66	− 2.08	9.4	88.23	− 2.81
Spread = 20	9.5	87.66	− 2.08	9.3	88.81	− 2.20
Spread = 30	9.5	87.66	− 2.08	9.2	89.83	− 1.12
Spread = 40	9.5	87.66	− 2.08	9.1	89.97	− 0.97

out because changes in the level of interest rates affected the two
bonds differently.[6]

Notes

[1] The formula for computing coupon interest plus interest on interest is found by multiplying the semiannual dollar coupon payment by

$$\frac{(1 + \text{semiannual reinvestment rate})^{\text{length of horizon}} - 1}{\text{semiannual reinvestment rate}}$$

where the length of horizon is the number of six-month periods in the investment horizon.

[2] The reason we have qualified our example to a tax-exempt portfolio is because there is a tax disadvantage of taxable zero coupon bonds. A taxable investor must pay taxes on accrued interest on a zero even though no cash payment is made by the issuer.

[3] This is the same formula given in footnote 1 to calculate the coupon interest plus interest on interest.

[4] A swap of one imaginery number for a higher imaginery number.

[5] In the next chapter we will illustrate the characteristics of a bond that affect its price volatility with respect to interest rate changes.

[6] This can be done by dollar duration weighting the swap. Dollar duration is explained in the next chapter.

Chapter 10

BOND PRICE VOLATILITY FUNDAMENTALS

In the previous two chapters, our focus was on return measures. To evaluate the potential price performance of a corporate bond, we need to know about their price volatility characteristics when interest rates change. We know that the price of a corporate bond changes in a direction opposite to the change in interest rates. But some bonds rise or fall more than other bonds when interest rates change. In this chapter we will illustrate the price volatility characteristics of bonds. We first look at option-free bonds and then provide a framework for analyzing the price volatility of callable bonds.

Bond Price Volatility Properties

To see how the price of a bond changes as yield changes, we'll use the six bonds in Table 8–3 of Chapter 8 (see page 304). For each bond, Table 10–1 shows the dollar price change per $100 of par value and Table 10–2 shows the percentage price change for various yields assuming that the initial yield is 10%.

The following three properties of price volatility can be seen from these two tables:

- *Property 1:* For a given change in yield, price volatility is not the same for all bonds.

- *Property 2:* For small changes in yield, the absolute change in price is approximately the same regardless if yields increase or decrease.
- *Property 3:* When yields change by a large amount, a given change in basis points will produce a noticeably greater price increase if yield declines than it would produce a price decrease if yield increases.

An investment implication of this last property is that if an investor owns a bond, the capital gain that will be realized if yield decreases is greater than the capital loss that will be realized if yield increases by the same number of basis points.

As can be seen in Table 10–2, there are two characteristics of an option-free bond that determines its price volatility: coupon and term to maturity.

- *Characteristic 1:* For a given term to maturity and initial yield, the price volatility of a bond is greater the lower the coupon rate.
- *Characteristic 2:* For a given coupon rate and initial yield, the longer the term to maturity, the greater the price volatility.

An investment implication of the first characteristic is that bonds selling at a deep discount will have greater price volatility than bonds selling near or above par. Zero coupon bonds will have the greatest price volatility for a given maturity.

Measures of Price Volatility

Bond market participants need a way to measure a bond's price volatility or interest rate risk. Three measures that are commonly used are explained below.

Price Value of a Basis Point

The *price value of a basis point,* also referred to as the *dollar value of a basis point,* is the change in the price of the bond if the yield changes by 1 basis point. The price value of a basis point is expressed as the absolute value of the change in price.

Table 10-1 Dollar Price Change (Per $100 Par) for Six Bonds

Assumption: Initial yield is 10%

Increase in required yield:

		Change in basis points					
		1	*10*	*50*	*100*	*200*	*300*
				Yield			
Coupon	*Term*	10.01%	10.10%	10.50%	11.00%	12.00%	13.00%
7.00%	5	-0.04	-0.32	-1.41	-1.72	-3.32	-3.17
7.00%	20	-0.07	-0.68	-3.29	-6.35	-11.88	-16.70
10.00%	5	-0.04	-0.39	-1.91	-3.77	-7.36	-10.78
10.00%	20	-0.09	-0.85	-4.15	-8.02	-15.05	-21.22
13.00%	5	-0.04	-0.41	-2.05	-4.04	-7.90	-11.58
13.00%	20	-0.10	-1.03	-5.00	-9.69	-18.22	-25.74

Decrease in required yield:

		Change in basis points					
		-1	*-10*	*-50*	*-100*	*-200*	*-300*
				Yield			
Coupon	*Term*	9.99%	9.90%	9.50%	9.00%	8.00%	7.00%
7.00%	5	0.04	0.36	1.81	3.67	7.53	11.58
7.00%	20	0.07	0.69	3.53	7.34	15.84	25.74
10.00%	5	0.04	0.39	1.95	3.96	8.11	12.47
10.00%	20	0.09	0.86	4.44	9.20	19.79	32.03
13.00%	5	0.04	0.42	2.10	4.24	8.69	13.37
13.00%	20	0.10	1.04	5.35	11.06	23.74	38.33

It does not make a difference if we increase or decrease the required yield by 1 basis point to compute the price value of a basis point. (Recall the second property which states that the price change will be the same for small changes in yield.) For our six

Table 10–2 Percentage Price Change for Six Bonds

Assumption: Initial yield is 10%

Increase in required yield:

		Change in basis points					
		1	10	50	100	200	300
					Yield		
Coupon	Term	10.01%	10.10%	10.50%	11.00%	12.00%	13.00%
7.00%	5	-0.04	-0.40	-2.00	-3.95	-7.71	-11.29
7.00%	20	-0.09	-0.91	-4.43	-8.56	-15.99	-22.49
10.00%	5	-0.04	-0.39	-1.91	-3.77	-7.36	-10.78
10.00%	20	-0.09	-0.85	-4.15	-8.02	-15.05	-21.22
13.00%	5	-0.04	-0.37	-1.83	-3.63	-7.08	-10.38
13.00%	20	-0.08	-0.82	-3.98	-7.71	-14.49	-20.47

Decrease in required yield:

		Change in basis points					
		-1	-10	-50	-100	-200	-300
					Yield		
Coupon	Term	9.99%	9.90%	9.50%	9.00%	8.00%	7.00%
7.00%	5	0.04	0.41	2.05	4.15	8.51	13.10
7.00%	20	0.09	0.92	4.76	9.88	21.33	34.66
10.00%	5	0.04	0.39	1.95	3.96	8.11	12.47
10.00%	20	0.09	0.86	4.44	9.20	19.79	32.03
13.00%	5	0.04	0.37	1.88	3.80	7.79	11.98
13.00%	20	0.08	0.83	4.25	8.80	18.88	30.48

bonds, the price value of a basis point can be obtained from Table 10–1 which shows the dollar price change per $100 par for an increase or decrease of 1 basis point (yield of 9.99% or 10.01%).

Yield Value of an 8th

Another measure of the dollar price volatility of a bond is the change in the yield for a specified price change. This is found by first calculating the bond's yield if the bond's price is increased by, say, X dollars. Then the difference between the initial yield and the new yield is the yield value of an X dollar price change. The smaller the yield value of an X dollar price change, the greater is the *dollar* price volatility. This is because it would take more X dollar price movements to change the yield a specified number of basis points.

Corporate bonds are typically traded in 8ths of a percentage point. Consequently, investors in these markets compute the yield value of an 8th. The calculation of the yield value of an 8th for the two 10% coupon bonds selling to yield 10% is shown below:

Increasing the price by an 8th:

Bond	Initial price + 8th	Yield at new price	Initial yield	Yield value of an 8th
10%/5 year	100.125	9.968%	10.000%	.0032 = 3.2 bp
10%/20 year	100.125	9.985%	10.000%	.0013 = 1.3 bp

Modified Duration and Dollar Duration

A commonly employed measure of price volatility is modified duration. It is defined as a weighted average term-to-maturity.[1] The weights are the present value of each cash flow as a percent of the invoice price. The appendix to this chapter illustrates how it is computed.

Mathematically modified duration can be shown to be equal to the approximate percentage change in the price of a bond if yield changes by 100 basis points. For example, if the modified duration of a bond is 5, this means that a 100 basis point change in yield will change the bond's price by approximately 5%.

Dollar duration is the approximate dollar price change of a bond per $100 of par value if yield changes by 100 basis points. It is calculated as follows:

$$\text{dollar duration} = \frac{\text{modified duration} \times \text{price}}{100}$$

Table 10–3 shows the modified duration for our six bonds. Also shown in the table is the estimated percentage price change based on modified duration. Each value in the table is found using the following formula:

– (modified duration) × (yield change) × 100

Relationship Among Price Volatility Measures

For small changes in yield the various bond price volatility measures are related. For example, for a small change in yield, dollar duration is the same as the price value of a basis point. The yield value of an 8th is equal to the reciprocal of the price value of a basis point multiplied by a factor.

Beyond Duration: Convexity

Table 10–4 shows the difference between the actual percentage price change and the estimated percentage price change using modified duration. Notice that for small changes in yield, modified duration does a good job of estimating the actual percentage price change. However, for large changes in yield modified duration does not do as good a job. In fact, the larger the yield change, the poorer the approximation.

The approximation can be improved by using another parameter that influences the price volatility of a bond. This parameter is referred to as *convexity*. The procedure for calculating convexity is discussed in the appendix to this chapter. Table 10–5 shows the convexity of our six bonds and the percentage price change due to convexity. Each of the values in Table 10–5 are computed using the following formula:

.5 (convexity) × (yield change)^2 × 100

Modified duration and convexity can be used together to estimate the percentage price change. This is done by simply summing the estimated price changes in Tables 10–3 and 10–5. Table 10–6 shows the estimated price change using modified duration and convexity. The difference between the actual percentage price change

Table 10–3 Estimated Percentage Change in Price Based on Modified Duration

Increase in required yield:

Coupon	Term	Mod. Dur.	Change in basis points					
			1	10	50	100	200	300
			Yield					
			10.01%	10.10%	10.50%	11.00%	12.00%	13.00%
7.00%	5	4.05	-0.04	-0.41	-2.03	-4.05	-8.10	-12.15
7.00%	20	9.18	-0.09	-0.92	-4.59	-9.18	-18.36	-27.54
10.00%	5	3.86	-0.04	-0.39	-1.93	-3.86	-7.72	-11.58
10.00%	20	8.58	-0.09	-0.86	-4.29	-8.58	-17.16	-25.74
13.00%	5	3.71	-0.04	-0.37	-1.86	-3.71	-7.42	-11.13
13.00%	20	8.22	-0.08	-0.82	-4.11	-8.22	-16.44	-24.66

Decrease in required yield:

Coupon	Term	Mod. Dur.	Change in basis points					
			-1	-10	-50	-100	-200	-300
			Yield					
			9.99%	9.90%	9.50%	9.00%	8.00%	7.00%
7.00%	5	4.05	0.04	0.41	2.03	4.05	8.10	12.15
7.00%	20	9.18	0.09	0.92	4.59	9.18	18.36	27.54
10.00%	5	3.86	0.04	0.39	1.93	3.86	7.72	11.58
10.00%	20	8.58	0.09	0.86	4.29	8.58	17.16	25.74
13.00%	5	3.71	0.04	0.37	1.86	3.71	7.42	11.13
13.00%	20	8.22	0.08	0.82	4.11	8.22	16.44	24.66

Note: The percentage price change is calculated using the following formula:
- (modified duration) × (yield change) × 100

Illustrations using 7%, 20-year bond
modified duration = 9.18

If yield increases by 50 basis points (+0.0050):
- 9.18 × (+0.0050)× 100 = –4.59%

If yield decreases by 100 basis points (-0.0100):
- 9.18 × (–0.0100) × 100 = +9.18%

Table 10–4 Percentage Price Change not Explained by Modified Duration

Increase in required yield:

			Change in basis points					
			1	10	50	100	200	300
					Yield			
Coupon	Term	Mod. Dur.	10.01%	10.10%	10.50%	11.00%	12.00%	13.00%
7.00%	5	4.05	0.00	0.00	0.03	0.10	0.39	0.86
7.00%	20	9.18	0.00	0.01	0.16	0.62	2.37	5.05
10.00%	5	3.86	0.00	0.00	0.02	0.09	0.36	0.80
10.00%	20	8.58	0.00	0.01	0.14	0.56	2.11	4.52
13.00%	5	3.71	0.00	0.00	0.02	0.08	0.34	0.75
13.00%	20	8.22	0.00	0.00	0.13	0.51	1.95	4.19

Decrease in required yield:

			Change in basis points					
			-1	-10	-50	-100	-200	-300
					Yield			
Coupon	Term	Mod. Dur.	9.99%	9.90%	9.50%	9.00%	8.00%	7.00%
7.00%	5	4.05	0.00	0.00	0.02	0.10	0.41	0.95
7.00%	20	9.18	0.00	0.01	0.17	0.70	2.97	7.12
10.00%	5	3.86	0.00	0.00	0.02	0.10	0.39	0.89
10.00%	20	8.58	0.00	0.01	0.15	0.62	2.63	6.29
13.00%	5	3.71	0.00	0.00	0.02	0.09	0.37	0.85
13.00%	20	8.22	0.00	0.01	0.14	0.58	2.44	5.82

Note: The values in this table are found by subtracting the values in Table 10–3 from those in Table 10–1.

Table 10–5 Estimated Percentage Change in Price Using Convexity

| | | Con- | Yield change in basis points | | | | | |
Coupon	Term	vexity	1	10	50	100	200	300
7.00%	5	20.04	0.00	0.00	0.03	0.10	0.40	0.90
7.00%	20	132.08	0.00	0.01	0.17	0.66	2.64	5.94
10.00%	5	18.74	0.00	0.00	0.02	0.09	0.37	0.84
10.00%	20	117.48	0.00	0.01	0.15	0.59	2.35	5.29
13.00%	5	17.72	0.00	0.00	0.02	0.09	0.35	0.80
13.00%	20	108.86	0.00	0.01	0.14	0.54	2.18	4.90

Note: The values in this table are computed using the following formula:

$$.5 \times (\text{convexity}) \times (\text{yield change})^2 \times 100$$

Illustrations using 7%, 20-year bond
  Convexity = 66.04

If yield increases by 50 basis points (+0.0050):
  $.5 \times (132.08) \times (+0.0050)^2 \times 100 = .17\%$

If yield decreases by 100 basis points (–0.0100):
  $.5 \times (132.08) \times (–0.0100)^2 \times 100 = .66\%$

and the estimated percentage price change using modified duration and convexity is shown in Table 10–7. Notice that even for large changes in yield, the two parameters, modified duration and convexity, do a good job of approximating the actual percentage price change.

Formulas for Approximating Duration and Convexity

Later in this chapter and in the other chapters in this book, we will see that the standard formulas for duration and convexity are inappropriate for corporate bonds with embedded options. Since duration is a measure of the change in bond price for small changes in

Table 10–6   Percentage Price Change Using Modified Duration and Convexity

Increase in required yield:

		Change in basis points					
		1	10	50	100	200	300
				Yield			
Coupon	Term	10.01%	10.10%	10.50%	11.00%	12.00%	13.00%
7.00%	5	-0.04	-0.40	-2.00	-3.95	-7.70	-11.25
7.00%	20	-0.09	-0.91	-4.42	-8.52	-15.72	-21.60
10.00%	5	-0.04	-0.39	-1.91	-3.77	-7.35	-10.74
10.00%	20	-0.09	-0.85	-4.14	-7.99	-14.81	-20.45
13.00%	5	-0.04	-0.37	-1.83	-3.62	-7.07	-10.33
13.00%	20	-0.08	-0.82	-3.97	-7.68	-14.26	-19.76

Decrease in required yield:

		Change in basis points					
		-1	-10	-50	-100	-200	-300
				Yield			
Coupon	Term	9.99%	9.90%	9.50%	9.00%	8.00%	7.00%
7.00%	5	0.04	0.41	2.05	4.15	8.50	13.05
7.00%	20	0.09	0.92	4.76	9.84	21.00	34.48
10.00%	5	0.04	0.39	1.95	3.95	8.09	12.42
10.00%	20	0.09	0.86	4.44	9.17	19.51	31.03
13.00%	5	0.04	0.37	1.88	3.80	7.77	11.93
13.00%	20	0.08	0.83	4.25	8.76	18.62	29.56

Note: The values in this table are obtained by adding the corresponding values in Tables 10–3 and 10–5.

Table 10-7 Percentage Price Change not Explained by Using both Modified Duration and Convexity

Increase in required yield:

		Change in basis points					
		1	10	50	100	200	300
				Yield			
Coupon	Term	10.01%	10.10%	10.50%	11.00%	12.00%	13.00%
7.00%	5	0.00	0.00	0.00	0.00	-0.01	-0.04
7.00%	20	0.00	0.00	0.00	-0.04	-0.28	-0.89
10.00%	5	0.00	0.00	0.00	0.00	-0.01	-0.05
10.00%	20	0.00	0.00	0.00	-0.03	-0.24	-0.76
13.00%	5	0.00	0.00	0.00	0.00	-0.02	-0.05
13.00%	20	0.00	0.00	-0.01	-0.03	-0.22	-0.71

Decrease in required yield:

		Change in basis points					
		-1	-10	-50	-100	-200	-300
				Yield			
Coupon	Term	9.99%	9.90%	9.50%	9.00%	8.00%	7.00%
7.00%	5	0.00	0.00	0.00	0.00	0.01	0.05
7.00%	20	0.00	0.00	0.00	0.04	0.33	1.18
10.00%	5	0.00	0.00	0.00	0.00	0.02	0.05
10.00%	20	0.00	0.00	0.00	0.03	0.28	1.01
13.00%	5	0.00	0.00	0.00	0.00	0.02	0.05
13.00%	20	0.00	0.00	0.01	0.04	0.27	0.92

Note: The values in this table are calculated by subtracting the values in Table 10–6 from those in Table 10–2.

interest rates, the following formula, known as *effective duration*, can be used to approximate duration:

effective duration =

$$\frac{\text{Price if yield decreases by } x \text{ basis points} - \text{Price if yield increases by } x \text{ basis points}}{\text{Initial price} (2x)}$$

For example, consider the 7% coupon, 20-year bond selling at 74.26 to yield 10%. Suppose we evaluate the price changes for a 20 basis point change up and down. Then:

Initial price = 74.26
For $x = .002$
Price if yield decreases by 20 basis points = 75.64
Price if yield increases by 20 basis points = 72.92
then,

$$\text{effective duration} = \frac{75.64 - 72.92}{(74.26) \, 2 \, (.0020)} = 9.16$$

From Table 10–3, we see that the modified duration for this bond is 9.18. The effective duration is 9.16, a good approximation.

To approximate convexity, the following formula, called *effective convexity*, can be used:

effective convexity =

$$\frac{\text{Price if yield decreases by } x \text{ basis points} + \text{Price if yield increases by } x \text{ basis points} - 2 \, (\text{Initial Price})}{2 \, (\text{Initial price}) \, (x) \, (x)}$$

Once again, consider the 7% coupon, 20-year bond selling at 74.26 to yield 10%. Then:

$$\text{effective convexity} = \frac{75.64 + 72.92 - 2 \, (74.26)}{2 \, (74.26) \, (.002) \, (.002)} = 67.33$$

From Table 10–5 we see that convexity is equal to 66.04. Effective convexity of 67.33 approximates convexity well.

Use of Modified Duration and Convexity in Assessing Interest Rate Risk and Relative Value

Modified duration and convexity are parameters used by market participants to assess the interest rate risk of a bond and relative value of bonds. Unfortunately, many market participants often rely on modified (or dollar) duration as the sole measure of the interest rate risk associated with a bond. As a result, some market participants will infer that if two bonds have the same dollar duration but different yields (as measured by yield to maturity), the one with the higher yield is more attractive. In this section, we'll demonstrate why such a practice is improper.

Properties of Convexity

The convexity properties of *all* option-free bonds are summarized below.

- *Property 1:* As the yield increases (decreases) the dollar duration of a bond decreases (increases).

This is illustrated in Table 10–8.

- *Property 2:* For a given yield and maturity, the lower the coupon rate, the greater the convexity of a bond.

This can be seen from the computed convexity for the six bonds in Table 10–5.

- *Property 3:* For a given yield and modified duration, the lower the coupon the smaller the convexity.

This property is demonstrated in Table 10–9. Notice that all three bonds are selling to yield 10% and have a modified duration of approximately 8.6 years. The convexity of the three bonds decreases as the coupon rate decreases.

The first property of convexity has interesting implications for bond investors. As yield declines, an investor who owns a bond would want its price to increase as much as possible—hence, an investor wants dollar duration to increase. The opposite is true if yield increases: An investor wants the dollar duration to decline

Table 10-8　Dollar Duration for Two Bonds at Different Yields

	10% coupon/5 years			10% coupon/20 years		
Yield	Price	Modified duration	Dollar duration	Price	Modified duration	Dollar duration
6%	117.06	4.02	4.706	146.23	10.46	15.296
7%	112.47	3.98	4.476	132.03	9.97	13.163
8%	108.11	3.94	4.260	119.79	9.49	11.368
9%	103.96	3.90	4.054	109.20	9.03	9.861
10%	100.00	3.86	3.860	100.00	8.58	8.580
11%	96.23	3.82	3.676	91.98	8.15	7.496
12%	92.64	3.78	3.502	84.95	7.74	6.575
13%	89.22	3.75	3.346	78.78	7.35	5.790
14%	85.95	3.71	3.189	73.34	6.98	5.119

Note: Dollar duration is calculated as follows:

$$\frac{\text{modified duration} \times \text{price}}{100}$$

Table 10-9　Convexity of Bonds Selling at Same Yield and with Same Modified Duration but Different Coupon Rates

Bond		Yield to maturity	Modified duration	Convexity
Coupon	Maturity			
7%	16.5 years	10%	8.56	121.10
10%	20.0	10%	8.58	117.48
13%	22.5	10%	8.61	109.62

when yield increases. For this reason, investors commonly refer to the shape of the price/yield relationship for an option-free bond as having "positive" convexity—"positive" indicating that it is a good attribute of a bond. Later in this chapter, we will find that callable corporate bonds exhibit "negative" convexity, which means dollar duration may not change in the desired direction as yield declines.

Without going into details, convexity is measuring the rate of change of dollar duration as yield changes. Table 10–10 shows the percentage change in dollar duration for the two bonds in that table assuming the initial yield is 10%. The greater the rate of change of dollar duration, the greater the convexity of a bond. Since the dollar duration of all option-free bonds always changes in the right direction, greater convexity is a desirable property. Consequently, two bonds may have the same dollar duration but different convexities. They will not perform the same.

It is often thought that for two bonds with the same dollar duration, the one with the higher convexity will outperform the other. This is not true because the market will price convexity. The bond with the higher convexity will sell at a higher price and therefore offer a lower yield. Consequently, to obtain greater convexity, the investor must pay for it. The performance of a bond over some investment horizon, as measured by horizon return, will depend on actual market volatility. The greater actual market volatility, the greater the benefit from improving convexity. Thus, the yield to maturity giveup that an investor would be willing to pay to obtain higher convexity depends on the investor's expectations of future interest rate volatility.

Limitations of Duration and Convexity Measures

We presented the basics concerning duration and convexity as a measure of the price volatility of interest rates. There are three assumptions that underlie their use. First, it is assumed that the yield curve is flat. (The yield curve is discussed in the next chapter.) This means that all interest rates—short, intermediate and long—are equal. Second, it is assumed that when the yield curve shifts, the shift is parallel. That is, all interest rates rise and fall by the same rate. Thus, the flattening, steepening or twisting of the yield curve is not consistent with the use of duration and convexity. Third, it is assumed that the cash flows of the bond do not change when inter-est rates change. When a bond is callable, this assumption may be violated because as interest rates change, the likelihood that the is-suer will call the bond changes. Therefore, the expected cash flows change when interest rates change. Finally, while duration for a Treasury security reflects changes in interest rates for Treasuries, changes in the price of a corporate bond reflects changes in both the Treasury rate and the spread to Treasuries.

The first assumption is not critical. The second, however, is criti-cal. When the yield curve does not shift in a parallel fashion, dura-tion and convexity may be a misleading measure of price volatility when interest rates change. Third, for callable bonds, there are only special circumstances where duration and convexity will be appro-priate. We'll discuss this in the next section.

Finally, an approach that takes into consideration the change in spread on a corporate bond's price volatility has been recently sug-gested.[2] This measure is referred to as *spread duration*. It involves the estimation of a "sector spread beta," which is an empirical rela-tionship of how the spread in a corporate bond sector tends to change as the spread in the corporate bond market as a whole changes. For a portfolio of corporate bonds, the spread duration is equal to the weighted average of the durations of the corporate sec-tors represented in the portfolio. The weight of each sector is the product of the sector spread beta and the market value percentage of the sector in the portfolio.

Price Volatility of Callable Bonds

At the end of Chapter 8, we explained how the price of a callable bond can be viewed as follows:

price of a callable bond = price of a noncallable bond − call option price

This means that the price volatility of a callable bond will depend on (1) the price volatility of the noncallable bond when interest rates change and (2) the price volatility of the call option when in-terest rates change. For example, if interest rates decline, the price

Table 10–10   Percentage Change in Dollar Duration as Yield Changes

Assumption: Initial yield = 10%

	Percentage change in dollar duration	
Yield change from	*10% / 5 year*	*10% / 20 year*
7% to 6%	5.14%	16.20%
8% to 7%	5.11	15.79
9% to 8%	5.08	15.53
10% to 9%	5.03	14.93
Initial yield = 10%		
10% to 11%	-4.77	-12.63
11% to 12%	-4.73	-12.29
12% to 13%	-4.45	-11.94
13% to 14%	-4.69	-11.59

of a noncallable bond will rise. The amount it will rise by depends on the duration of the noncallable bond. But, when interest rates decline, the value of the call option the bondholder sold to the issuer increases in value. Since the call option price is subtracted from the noncallable bond price, this reduces the price appreciation of the callable bond. This is why the callable bond exhibits the negative convexity or price compression we discussed in Chapter 8.

From our discussion of callable bonds in Chapter 8, we see that its price will depend on the price of the call option. In this section, we saw that the price volatility of a callable bond will depend on the price volatility of the call option. Therefore, to evaluate the price and price volatility of a callable bond, it is necessary to understand the fundamentals of option theory. This is the subject Chapter 12.

Appendix

Duration

First formulated by Frederick Macaulay in 1938[3], duration is a weighted average term-to-maturity of the security's cash flows. The weights in this weighted average are the present values of each cash flow as a percent of the present value of all the bond's cash flows (i.e., the weights are the present value of each cash flow as a percent of the bond's full price).

Mathematically, Macaulay duration *on a coupon date* for a semiannual pay bond is computed as follows:

Macaulay duration =

$$\frac{1 \times PVCF_1 + 2 \times PVCF_2 + 3 \times PVCF_3 + \ldots + n \times PVCF_n}{2 \times PVTCF}$$

where

  n = number of periods until maturity (specifically, number of years to maturity times 2)

  t = the period when the cash flow is expected to be received ($t = 1, \ldots n$)

  $PVCF_t$ = the present value of the cash flow in period t discounted at the yield to maturity

  $PVTCF$ = the total present value of the cash flow of the bond where the present value is determined using the yield to maturity. This is simply the price of the bond.

For an option-free bond on a coupon date and with semiannual payments, the cash flow for periods 1 through n - 1 is one-half the annual coupon interest. The cash flow in period n is the semiannual coupon interest plus the maturity value. The formula can be easily extended to fractional periods when a bond is not on its coupon date.

Table A10-1   Calculation of Macaulay Duration for the 10%, 5-Year Coupon Bond Selling at Par

Period t	Cash Flow	PV of $1 @ 5%	PVCF$_t$	t × PVCF$_t$
1	$ 5	0.952380	4.761904	4.7619
2	5	0.907029	4.535147	9.0703
3	5	0.863837	4.319187	12.9576
4	5	0.822702	4.113512	16.4540
5	5	0.783526	3.917630	19.5882
6	5	0.746215	3.731076	22.3865
7	5	0.710681	3.553406	24.8738
8	5	0.676839	3.384196	27.0736
9	5	0.644608	3.223044	29.0074
10	105	0.613913	64.460890	644.6089
			Total	810.7822

Macaulay duration =

$$\frac{1 \times \text{PVCF}_1 + 2 \times \text{PVCF}_2 + 3 \times \text{PVCF}_3 + \ldots + n \times \text{PVCF}_n}{2 \times \text{PVTCF}}$$

$$\frac{810.7822}{2 \times 100} = 4.05$$

For a bond selling on its coupon date, the total present value of the cash flows is simply the quoted price (or flat price) of the bond. For a bond not selling on a coupon date, the total present value of the cash flows is the bond's quoted price plus accrued interest.

Table A10-1 shows the details involved in calculating the Macaulay duration for the 10%, 5-year bond selling at 100 to yield 10%.

The relationship between Macaulay duration and bond price volatility is:[4]

percentage change in price =

$$- \frac{1}{(1 + \frac{yield}{2})} \times \text{Macaulay duration} \times (\text{yield change}) \times 100$$

The relationship is exact for infinitesimal changes in yields, but is only approximate for larger changes.

The first two expressions on the right hand side of this equation are combined into one term and called *modified duration*; that is,

$$\text{modified duration} = \frac{\text{Macaulay duration}}{(1 + \frac{yield}{2})}$$

The relationship can then be expressed as follows:

percentage price change =

– (modified duration) × (change in yield) × 100

This is the equation we used in the chapter to calculate the estimated percentage price change due to duration in Table 10-3.

Convexity

The convexity of an option-free fixed income security *on a coupon date* for a semiannual pay bond can be estimated using the following formula:

convexity =

$$\frac{1 \times 2 \times PVCF_1 + 2 \times 3 \times PVCF_2 + 3 \times 4 \times PVCF_3 + \ldots + n \times (n+1) \times PVCF_n}{4 \times (1 + yield/2)^2 \times PVTCF}$$

where the terms are the same as defined earlier for Macaulay duration.

Table A10–2 Computation of Convexity for the 10%, 5-Year Bond Selling at Par

Period t	Cash Flow	PV of $1 @ 5%	PVCFt	t × t × PVCFt
1	$ 5	0.952380	4.761904	9.5238
2	5	0.907029	4.535147	27.2109
3	5	0.863837	4.319187	51.8303
4	5	0.822702	4.113512	82.2702
5	5	0.783526	3.917630	117.5289
6	5	0.746215	3.731076	156.7052
7	5	0.710681	3.553406	198.9907
8	5	0.676839	3.384196	243.6621
9	5	0.644608	3.223044	290.0740
10	105	0.613913	64.460890	7,090.6980
			Total	8,268.4941

convexity =

$$\frac{1\times2\times PVCF_1 + 2\times3\times PVCF_2 + 3\times4\times PVCF_3 + \ldots + n\times(n+1)\times PVCF_n}{4\times(1+yield/2)^2\times PVTCF}$$

$$\frac{8,268.4941}{4\times(1.05)^2\times100} = 18.74$$

In Table A10-2 we show the detailed calculations for the convexity of the 10%, 5-year bond selling at 100 to yield 10%.

Duration provides a first approximation to the percentage price change. Convexity provides a second approximation, based on the following relationship:[5]

approximate percentage price change due to convexity =

.5 × (convexity) × (yield change)^2 × 100

It should be noted that the formula gives only an approximation of that part of the price change that is due solely to the curvature of the price/yield relationship. This is the relationship used to calculate the values in Table 10–5.

Notes

[1] Actually, as explained in the appendix to this chapter, this is the definition for Macaulay duration. Modified duration is equal to Macaulay duration divided by one plus one-half the yield to maturity.

[2] See Martin L. Leibowitz, William S. Krasker and Ardavan Nozari, "Spread-Duration: A New Tool for Bond Portfolio Management," Chapter 14 in Frank J. Fabozzi (ed.), *Fixed Income Portfolio Strategies* (Chicago, IL: Probus Publishing Company, 1989).

[3] Frederick Macaulay, *Some Theoretical Problems Suggested by the Movement of Interest Rates, Bond Yields, and Stock Prices in the U.S. Since 1856* (National Bureau of Economic Research, New York, 1938).

[4] Mathematically, the relationship is obtained by taking the first derivative of the price function and then dividing by the price. See Appendix A of Frank J. Fabozzi, *Fixed Income Mathematics* (Chicago, IL: Probus Publishing Company, 1988).

[5] Mathematically this is derived from the second term of the Taylor series for the price function. See Appendix A in Fabozzi, *Fixed Income Mathematics*.

Chapter 11

OPTION-ADJUSTED SPREAD APPROACH TO THE VALUATION OF CORPORATE BONDS

In this chapter, we shall explain how to value a corporate bond by taking into account (1) the term structure of interest rates, (2) the options embedded in the corporate bond, and (3) the expected volatility of interest rates. The approach we present is called the option-adjusted spread approach. Since this approach relies on the term structure of interest rates, we begin this chapter with a discussion of that topic.

The Term Structure of Interest Rates

In Chapter 8, we explained that the price of a bond is the present value of its expected cash flow. In our illustrations, we used the same interest rate to discount every cash flow from the bond. This means that the investor is willing to accept the same yield on a cash flow six months from today as he is willing to accept on a cash flow to be received 20 years from today. This is an unrealistic assumption. The proper method for valuing a package of cash flows such as those from a corporate bond is to discount each cash flow at an interest rate that is based on when the cash flow will be received. Essentially, the interest rate that is appropriate to discount a cash flow for some time period t is equal to: (1) the interest rate on a zero coupon Treasury security maturity at time t plus (2) a risk premium associated with the corporate bond.

The interest rate on a zero coupon Treasury security is constructed from the yield curve which is the graphical depiction of the relationship between the yield on Treasury securities for different maturities. Figure 11–1 shows four hypothetical yield curves.

While a yield curve is typically constructed based on observed yields for on-the-run Treasuries, the term structure of interest rates is the relationship between maturity and the yield on zero coupon Treasury securities. Any noncallable security can be properly viewed as a package of zero coupon instruments. That is, each zero coupon instrument in the package has a maturity equal to its coupon payment date and, in the case of the principal, the maturity date. The value of the security should equal the value of all the component zero coupon instruments. If this does not hold, it is possible to generate arbitrage profits.[1] To determine the value of each zero coupon instrument, it is necessary to know the yield on the zero coupon Treasury corresponding to that maturity. This yield is called the *spot rate* and the graphical depiction of the relationship between the spot rates and maturity is called the *spot rate curve* or the *term structure of interest rates*.

It would seem logical that the observed yield on stripped or zero coupon Treasury securities can be used to construct an actual spot rate curve. However, there are problems with this approach. First, the liquidity of the zero coupon market is not as great as that of the coupon Treasury market. Second, there are maturity sectors of the zero coupon Treasury market that attract specific investors who may be willing to give up yield in exchange for an attractive feature associated with that particular maturity sector, thereby distorting the spot yield curve. For example, unlike domestic taxable entities, the tax code of some foreign countries grants investors preferential tax treatment on zero coupon Treasuries. As a result, there is often considerable participation by certain foreign investors in long maturity zero coupon Treasury bonds, driving down yields in that maturity sector.

Instead of using the yield on zero coupon Treasury securities, spot rates are estimated using sophisticated statistical techniques. A

Figure 11-1   Four Hypothetical Yield Curves

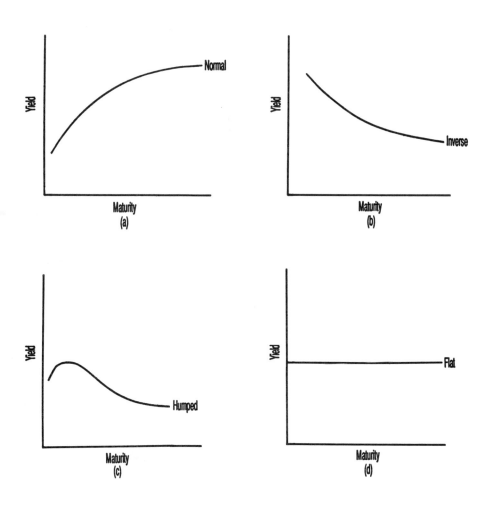

review of these techniques is beyond the scope of this book. Instead, in our analysis, we will take the spot rates as given.

Implied Forward Rates

A product of the spot rate curve (term structure of interest rates) is the implied forward rates. It is easiest to explain this concept by means of an illustration.

Suppose that an investor has a one year investment horizon and is faced with the following two alternatives:

Alternative 1: buy a one-year Treasury bill

Alternative 2: buy a six-month Treasury bill and when it matures in six months buy another six-month Treasury bill

The investor will be indifferent between the two alternatives if they produce the same yield over the one-year investment horizon. The investor knows the spot rate on the six-month Treasury bill and the one-year Treasury bill. However, he does not know what yield will be available on a six-month Treasury bill purchased six months from now. The yield on a six-month Treasury bill six months from now is called the *forward rate*. Given the spot rate for the six-month Treasury bill and the one-year bill, the forward rate on a six-month Treasury bill that will make the investor indifferent to the two alternatives can be determined as described below.

By investing in the one-year Treasury bill, the investor will receive $100 at the end of one year. The price (cost) of the one-year Treasury bill would be:

$$\frac{100}{(1 + y_2)^2}$$

where y_2 is one-half the bond equivalent yield of the theoretical one-year spot rate.

Suppose that the investor purchased a six-month Treasury bill for $D. At the end of six months, the value of this investment would be:

$$D (1 + y_1)$$

where y_1 is one-half the bond equivalent yield of the theoretical six-month spot rate.

Let f_2 be one-half the forward rate on a six-month Treasury bill available six months from now. Then the future dollars available at the end of one year resulting from the $D investment will be:

$$D (1 + y_1) (1 + f_2)$$

Suppose that today we wanted to know how many $D the investor must invest in order to have $100 one year from now. This can be found as follows:

$$D (1 + y_1) (1 + f_2) = 100$$

Solving we get,

$$D = \frac{100}{(1 + y_1) (1 + f_2)}$$

The investor will be indifferent between the two alternatives confronting him if he makes the same dollar investment and receives $100 at the end of one year from both alternatives. That is, the investor will be indifferent if:

$$\frac{100}{(1 + y_2)^2} = \frac{100}{(1 + y_1) (1 + f_2)}$$

Solving for f_2, we get:

$$f_2 = \frac{(1 + y_2)^2}{(1 + y_1)} - 1$$

Doubling f_2 gives the bond equivalent yield for the six-month forward rate.

To illustrate this, suppose that the following spot rates are determined:

six-month bill spot rate = .080, therefore y_1 = .0400
one-year bill spot rate   = .083, therefore y_2 = .0415

Substituting into the equation, we have:

$$f_2 = \frac{(1.0415)^2}{1.0400} - 1$$
$$= .043$$

The forward rate on a six-month Treasury security, quoted on a bond equivalent basis is 8.60% (.043 × 2).

Since we used the theoretical spot rates to compute the forward rate, the resulting forward rate is called the *implied forward rate*. Although we demonstrated only how to get the six-month implied forward rate six months from now, it is a simple exercise to compute the six-month implied forward rate for any number of periods from now.

In fact, the implied forward rate for any length of time can be calculated from the yield curve. For example, the 10-year forward rate four years from now can be calculated. If one believes that the implied forward rates are the market's consensus of future interest rates, then the implied forward rates can be used in the horizon return framework, explained in Chapter 9. Recall that in the horizon return framework, it is necessary to determine short-term reinvestment rates and the expected yield on the bond at the end of the investment horizon. But these are nothing more than forward rates. When a horizon return is calculated based on implied forward rates, it is called an *arbitrage-free horizon return*.

Whether one believes that the implied forward rates reflect the market's consensus of future interest rates depends on whether one believes in one of the theories of the term structure of interest rates described next.

Overview of Theories of the Term Structure of Interest Rates

In Figure 11–1 we presented four hypothetical yield curves. Panel A shows an upward sloping yield curve; that is, yields rise as maturity increases. This shape is commonly referred to as a "normal" or "positive" yield curve. Panel B shows a downward sloping or "inverted" yield curve in which yields decline as maturity increases. Panel C shows a "humped" yield curve. Finally, Panel D shows a "flat" yield curve. Historically, all four yield curves have been observed at different points in the business cycle.

Two theories have evolved to explain the observed shapes of the yield curve: the expectations theory and the market segmentation theory.[2]

According to the expectations theory, the shape of the yield curve is determined by market participants' (borrowers' and lenders') expectations of future interest rates. That is, the shape is determined by expected forward interest rates. There are two forms of the expectations theory: the pure expectations theory and the liquidity premium theory.

Proponents of the pure expectations theory, also called the unbiased expectations theory, argue that the shape of the yield curve is determined *only* by expected forward interest rates. When interest rates are expected to rise, the yield curve will be normal or positive; when they are expected to fall, the yield curve will be inverted or negative. If the pure expectations theory holds, the implied forward rates that we discussed earlier will be the market's unbiased estimate of the yields expected in the future.

The biased expectations theory asserts that the shape of the yield curve is determined by *both* expectations of future interest rates and a premium demanded (in terms of higher yield demanded) for either extending maturity or moving out of a maturity sector that provides a better asset/liability match. Consequently, the forward rates embody both interest rate expectations and a yield premium. According to this theory, the implied forward rates will not be an unbiased estimate of the market's expectations of future interest rates because it embodies a yield premium.

The market segmentation theory postulates that the major reason for the shape of the yield curve is that due to asset/liability management constraints (either regulatory or self-imposed), creditors (borrowers) restrict their lending (financing) to specific maturity sectors. Thus, the shape of the yield curve is determined by supply and demand for securities within the specific maturity sector. The market segmentation theory basically asserts that creditors and borrowers will not freely substitute securities from one maturity sector to another when lending or financing based on interest rate expectations. The expectations theory, in contrast, assumes that market participants (creditors and borrowers) will move from one maturity sector to another based on their interest rate expectations.

In the applications of the term structure to the valuation of corporate bonds (and options modeling discussed in the next chapter), the assumption is that the unbiased expectations theory best describes the term structure of interest rates. Therefore, the implied forward rates derived from the spot rates are the market's unbiased estimate of expected future interest rates.

Estimating the Option-Adjusted Spread for a Corporate Bond

The traditional analysis of the yield premium for a corporate bond involves calculating the difference between the yield to maturity (or yield to call) of a corporate bond and the yield to maturity of a comparable maturity coupon Treasury. The latter is obtained from the yield curve. For example, consider the following two 10% coupon, 20-year bonds:

Issue	Price	Yield to Maturity
Treasury	101.5305	9.82%
Corporate	92.3338	10.95%

The yield spread for these two bonds is 113 basis points. Therefore, the yield premium is said to be 113 basis points. However, the drawbacks of this procedure are (1) the yield to maturity for neither bond is calculated properly because it fails to take into consideration the term structure of interest rates; and (2) in the case of a callable and/or putable bond, expected interest rate volatility will alter its expected cash flow. For now, let's focus only on the first problem: failure to incorporate the term structure of interest rates.

Static Option-Adjusted Spread

In traditional yield spread analysis, an investor compares the yield to maturity of a corporate bond with the yield to maturity of a similar maturity on-the-run Treasury security. This means that the yield to maturity of a 20-year zero coupon corporate bond and a 10%, 20-year corporate coupon bond would both be compared to a 20-year Treasury security. Such a comparison makes little sense since the cash flow characteristics of the two corporate bonds will not be the same as that of the benchmark Treasury.

The proper procedure to compare corporate bonds of the same maturity but with different coupon rates is to compare the corporate bond with a portfolio of Treasury securities that have the same cash flow. For example, consider the 10%, 20-year corporate bond selling for 92.3338. The cash flow per $100 par value for this corporate bond (assuming that the issue is not called or put) is 39 semi-annual payments of $5 and a payment in 20 years (40 six-month periods) of $105. A portfolio that will replicate this cash flow, would include 40 zero coupon Treasury with maturities coinciding with the amount and timing of the cash flows of the corporate bond.

The corporate bond's value is equal to the value of all of the cash flows. The corporate bond's value assuming the cash flows are riskless will equal the present value of the replicating portfolio of Treasury securities. In turn, these cash flows are valued at the spot rates. Table 11–1 shows how to calculate the price of the Treasury issue assuming the spot rate curve shown in the table. The price would be 101.5305. The corporate bond's price is 92.3338, a lower value than the package of zero coupon Treasury securities because investor's are demanding a premium for the risk associated with holding a corporate bond rather than a riskless package of securities.

The spread to Treasuries is determined as follows. It is the spread that will make the present value of the cash flows from the corporate bond when discounted at the spot rate plus the spread equal to the corporate bond's price. A trial-and-error procedure is required to determine the spread. This spread is called the *option-adjusted spread*.

To illustrate how this is done, let's use the corporate bond in our previous illustration. Select some spread, say 80 basis points. To each spot rate in Table 11–1, 80 basis points is added. So, for example, the 3-year (period 6) spot rate is 8.1% (.073 + .008). The spot rate plus the 80 basis points is then used to calculate the present

Table 11-1 Price of a 10%, 20-Year Corporate Based Bond on Spot Rates

Period	Assumed spot rate	Cash flow	Present value of $1	PV of cash flow
1	0.070	5	0.9662	4.8309
2	0.071	5	0.9329	4.6630
3	0.071	5	0.9006	4.5032
4	0.072	5	0.8681	4.3404
5	0.072	5	0.8379	4.1896
6	0.073	5	0.8065	4.0323
7	0.075	5	0.7728	3.8641
8	0.077	5	0.7392	3.6959
9	0.079	5	0.7056	3.5282
10	0.081	5	0.6723	3.3616
11	0.082	5	0.6427	3.2137
12	0.085	5	0.6069	3.0343
13	0.086	5	0.5785	2.8925
14	0.088	5	0.5473	2.7363
15	0.090	5	0.5167	2.5836
16	0.092	5	0.4870	2.4348
17	0.093	5	0.4618	2.3089
18	0.095	5	0.4337	2.1687
19	0.096	5	0.4103	2.0517
20	0.096	5	0.3915	1.9577
21	0.096	5	0.3736	1.8680
22	0.096	5	0.3565	1.7825
23	0.097	5	0.3365	1.6823
24	0.097	5	0.3209	1.6045
25	0.099	5	0.2988	1.4942
26	0.099	5	0.2847	1.4237
27	0.100	5	0.2678	1.3392
28	0.100	5	0.2551	1.2755
29	0.100	5	0.2429	1.2147
30	0.100	5	0.2314	1.1569
31	0.102	5	0.2140	1.0698
32	0.102	5	0.2036	1.0178

(Table continues)

Table 11-1 Price of a 10%, 20-Year Corporate Based Bond on Spot Rates (Continued)

Period	Assumed spot rate	Cash flow	Present value of $1	PV of cash flow
33	0.103	5	0.1907	0.9534
34	0.103	5	0.1813	0.9067
35	0.103	5	0.1725	0.8623
36	0.103	5	0.1640	0.8200
37	0.105	5	0.1506	0.7529
38	0.107	5	0.1380	0.6900
39	0.107	5	0.1310	0.6550
40	0.109	105	0.1197	12.5697

Total present value = 101.5305

value of 95.2431 (see Table 11–2). Since the present value is not equal to the corporate bond's price (92.3338), the spread we seek is not 80 basis points. Table 11–3 shows the present value when a 120 basis point spread is tried. The present value is equal to the corporate bond price. Therefore 120 basis points is the option-adjusted spread.

This procedure assumes that the cash flows will not change because interest rates do not change and, as a result, the expected cash flow of a bond will not change since it will not be called or put. An option-adjusted spread calculated based on this assumption is referred to as a *static option-adjusted spread*. Next we look at how to incorporate expected interest rate volatility into the analysis.

Option-Adjusted Spread

We stated earlier that there were two drawbacks to the traditional analysis. Previously, we showed how to overcome the first problem: failure to incorporate the term structure of interest rates. This lead to the static option-adjusted spread. Now we'll look at the second drawback: failure to take into account future interest rate volatility that would affect the expected cash flow for a callable or putable bond.

Table 11-2 Present Value of a 10%, 20-Year Corporate Bond Based on Spot Rates Plus 80 Basis Points

Period	Assumed spot rate	Spread + 80 bp	Cash flow	PV of $1	Present value
1	0.070	0.078	5	0.9625	4.8123
2	0.071	0.079	5	0.9254	4.6272
3	0.071	0.079	5	0.8903	4.4514
4	0.072	0.080	5	0.8548	4.2740
5	0.072	0.080	5	0.8219	4.1096
6	0.073	0.081	5	0.7880	3.9402
7	0.075	0.083	5	0.7523	3.7614
8	0.077	0.085	5	0.7168	3.5839
9	0.079	0.087	5	0.6817	3.4083
10	0.081	0.089	5	0.6470	3.2351
11	0.082	0.090	5	0.6162	3.0810
12	0.085	0.093	5	0.5796	2.8980
13	0.086	0.094	5	0.5504	2.7521
14	0.088	0.096	5	0.5187	2.5937
15	0.090	0.098	5	0.4879	2.4397
16	0.092	0.100	5	0.4581	2.2906
17	0.093	0.101	5	0.4328	2.1639
18	0.095	0.103	5	0.4050	2.0249
19	0.096	0.104	5	0.3817	1.9084
20	0.096	0.104	5	0.3628	1.8141
21	0.096	0.104	5	0.3449	1.7244
22	0.096	0.104	5	0.3278	1.6392
23	0.097	0.105	5	0.3082	1.5412
24	0.097	0.105	5	0.2929	1.4643
25	0.099	0.107	5	0.2717	1.3586
26	0.099	0.107	5	0.2579	1.2897
27	0.100	0.108	5	0.2417	1.2086
28	0.100	0.108	5	0.2293	1.1467
29	0.100	0.108	5	0.2176	1.0879
30	0.100	0.108	5	0.2064	1.0322
31	0.102	0.110	5	0.1902	0.9509
32	0.102	0.110	5	0.1803	0.9013

(Table continues)

**Table 11-2   Present Value of a 10%, 20-Year Corporate Bond
Based on Spot Rates Plus 80 Basis Points
(Continued)**

Period	Assumed spot rate	Spread + 80 bp	Cash flow	Present value of $1	PV of cash flow
33	0.103	0.111	5	0.1682	0.8411
34	0.103	0.111	5	0.1594	0.7969
35	0.103	0.111	5	0.1510	0.7550
36	0.103	0.111	5	0.1431	0.7153
37	0.105	0.113	5	0.1309	0.6543
38	0.107	0.115	5	0.1195	0.5975
39	0.107	0.115	5	0.1130	0.5650
40	0.109	0.117	105	0.1029	10.8033

Total present value = 95.2431

To understand the second drawback, consider a 10%, 20-year corporate bond that is immediately callable and current interest rates are 10%. The probability that the issuer will call the bond increases as interest rates decline. If interest rates do fall and the bond is called, the cash flows will change. A small drop in rates will not be sufficient to justify calling the bond by the issuer. The rate must drop enough so that it will be economic for the issuer to call the bond. For example, a decline of interest rates from 10% to 9.50% six months from now may not make it attractive to call the issue given the cost of refunding. In addition to the interest rate, that cost will be determined by (1) the remaining maturity on the bond, (2) the call price, and (3) fees for registering and underwriting the new issue.

Not only is the direction of interest rates important but so is the path of interest rates. For example, consider the four possible interest rate paths shown in Figure 11-2 (see pages 376–77) in which the interest rate begins at 11% and ends at 10.7% at the end of 20 years assuming that interest rates can rise or fall by 7% every six months.

Table 11–3 Present Value of a 10%, 20-Year Corporate Bond Based on Spot Rates Plus 120 Basis Points

Period	Assumed spot rate	Spread + 120 bp	Cash flow	PV of $1	Present value
1	0.070	0.082	5	0.9606	4.8031
2	0.071	0.083	5	0.9219	4.6095
3	0.071	0.083	5	0.8852	4.4258
4	0.072	0.084	5	0.8483	4.2413
5	0.072	0.084	5	0.8141	4.0703
6	0.073	0.085	5	0.7790	3.8951
7	0.075	0.087	5	0.7423	3.7113
8	0.077	0.089	5	0.7059	3.5294
9	0.079	0.091	5	0.6700	3.3501
10	0.081	0.093	5	0.6348	3.1738
11	0.082	0.094	5	0.6034	3.0169
12	0.085	0.097	5	0.5665	2.8324
13	0.086	0.098	5	0.5369	2.6847
14	0.088	0.100	5	0.5051	2.5253
15	0.090	0.102	5	0.4742	2.3710
16	0.092	0.104	5	0.4444	2.2219
17	0.093	0.105	5	0.4190	2.0950
18	0.095	0.107	5	0.3914	1.9568
19	0.096	0.108	5	0.3682	1.8408
20	0.096	0.108	5	0.3493	1.7465
21	0.096	0.108	5	0.3314	1.6570
22	0.096	0.108	5	0.3144	1.5721
23	0.097	0.109	5	0.2951	1.4754
24	0.097	0.109	5	0.2798	1.3991
25	0.099	0.111	5	0.2591	1.2957
26	0.099	0.111	5	0.2455	1.2276
27	0.100	0.112	5	0.2297	1.1483
28	0.100	0.112	5	0.2175	1.0874
29	0.100	0.112	5	0.2059	1.0297
30	0.100	0.112	5	0.1950	0.9751
31	0.102	0.114	5	0.1793	0.8967
32	0.102	0.114	5	0.1697	0.8483

(Table continues)

Table 11-3 Present Value of a 10%, 20-Year Corporate Bond Based on Spot Rates Plus 120 Basis Points (Continued)

Period	Assumed spot rate	Spread + 120 bp	Cash flow	PV of $1	Present value
33	0.103	0.115	5	0.1580	0.7902
34	0.103	0.115	5	0.1494	0.7472
35	0.103	0.115	5	0.1413	0.7066
36	0.103	0.115	5	0.1336	0.6682
37	0.105	0.117	5	0.1220	0.6101
38	0.107	0.119	5	0.1112	0.5561
39	0.107	0.119	5	0.1050	0.5248
40	0.109	0.121	105	0.0954	10.0176

Total present value = 92.3338

Suppose that the following rule is established for calling of the bond: if interest rates are 7% or less with at least five years remaining to maturity, then the bond will be called. For path 1 in Figure 11–2, the bond would not be called given this rule. Therefore, the cash flow for the bond at each six-month period is not different from that of a noncallable bond. For the other three paths in Figure 11–2, however, the bond would be called. Therefore, the cash flow at the projected call date is the call price plus the coupon interest.

For each path a cash flow can be determined based on (1) the rule for a bond to be called and (2) the call provisions. Suppose that for our hypothetical callable bond, the bond may not be called for 5 years (10 periods) and the call schedule is as follows: if called at the end of 5 years but before 9 years, the call price is 104; if called after 9 years, the call price is 103. Given this information and the rule for calling, Figure 11–3 shows the cash flow for the four paths in Figure 11–2. For example, for path 4 the bond would be called in period 13 (i.e., in 6.5 years), when the rate first reaches 7%. The cash flow in period 13 is the call price of 104 plus semiannual coupon interest of 5, or 109.

Figure 11-2 Four Possible Interest Rate Paths Assuming Interest Rates Can Rise or Fall by 7% Every Six Months

Period	Path 1	Path 2	Path 3	Path 4
1	11.0	11.0	11.0	11.0
2	11.8	10.2	10.2	10.2
3	12.6	9.5	9.5	9.5
4	11.7	8.8	8.8	8.8
5	12.5	8.2	8.2	8.2
6	13.4	7.7	8.8	8.8
7	12.5	7.1	8.2	8.2
8	11.6	6.6	8.8	8.8
9	10.8	6.2	9.4	9.4
10	11.5	5.7	10.0	8.7
11	12.3	5.3	10.7	8.1
12	13.2	5.7	11.5	7.5
13	14.1	6.1	10.7	7.0
14	13.1	6.5	9.9	6.5
15	14.1	7.0	9.2	6.1
16	13.1	6.5	8.6	5.6
17	12.2	6.0	8.0	5.2
18	13.0	5.6	7.4	4.9
19	13.9	5.2	6.9	4.5
20	14.9	4.9	6.4	4.2
21	13.9	4.5	6.0	3.9
22	12.9	4.8	6.4	4.2
23	12.0	5.2	6.8	4.5
24	11.2	5.5	7.3	4.8
25	10.4	5.1	6.8	5.1
26	9.6	5.5	7.3	5.5
27	10.3	5.1	6.8	5.9
28	11.0	4.8	7.3	6.3
29	11.8	5.1	7.8	6.7
30	12.6	5.5	8.3	7.2
31	11.8	5.8	8.9	7.7
32	12.6	6.2	9.5	8.3
33	11.7	6.7	10.2	8.8

(Figure continues)

Figure 11-2 Four Possible Interest Rate Paths Assuming Interest Rates Can Rise or Fall by 7% Every Six Months (Continued)

Period	Path 1	Path 2	Path 3	Path 4
34	10.9	7.1	9.5	9.5
35	10.1	7.6	10.1	10.1
36	9.4	8.2	10.8	10.8
37	8.8	8.8	10.1	10.1
38	9.4	9.4	10.8	10.8
39	10.0	10.0	10.0	10.0
40	10.7	10.7	10.7	10.7

There are obviously an enormous number of interest rate paths. For each path there is a corresponding cash flow. Let's imagine for the moment that we can analyze each path. For each path, the present value of the cash flows of the bond can be calculated. The discount rate used to calculate the cash flows will be based on the spot rate for the period plus a spread. Therefore, for each path a present value can be calculated. An average of all the present values can be computed. If the average present value is equal to the market price of the corporate bond, then the spread used to calculate the present value along each path is the option-adjusted spread. If it is not, the present value along each path is calculated again using a different spread. Once again, if the average present value is equal to the market price of the corporate bond, this new spread is the option-adjusted spread. If not, the process continues until a spread is found that satisfies this condition.

Notice how the expected interest rate volatility comes into play. When constructing the interest rate paths, the amount by which the interest rate can rise or fall each period must be assumed. In our illustration, we assumed that the interest rate can rise or fall each period by 7%. Suppose, instead, that expected interest rate volatilityis 13%. Figure 11-4 shows the interest rate paths in Figure 11-2 based on 13% volatility every six months. The corresponding

Figure 11-3 Cash Flow Corresponding to Four Possible Interest Rate Paths Assuming Interest Rates Can Rise or Fall by 7% Every Six Months

Period	Path 1	Path 2	Path 3	Path 4
1	$ 5	$ 5	$ 5	$ 5
2	5	5	5	5
3	5	5	5	5
4	5	5	5	5
5	5	5	5	5
6	5	5	5	5
7	5	5	5	5
8	5	5	5	5
9	5	5	5	5
10	5	109	5	5
11	5	0	5	5
12	5	0	5	5
13	5	0	5	109
14	5	0	5	0
15	5	0	5	0
16	5	0	5	0
17	5	0	5	0
18	5	0	5	0
19	5	0	108	0
20	5	0	0	0
21	5	0	0	0
22	5	0	0	0
23	5	0	0	0
24	5	0	0	0
25	5	0	0	0
26	5	0	0	0
27	5	0	0	0
28	5	0	0	0
29	5	0	0	0
30	5	0	0	0
31	5	0	0	0
32	5	0	0	0

(Figure continues)

Figure 11–3 Cash Flow Corresponding to Four Possible Interest Rate Paths Assuming Interest Rates Can Rise or Fall by 7% Every Six Months (Continued)

Period	Path 1	Path 2	Path 3	Path 4
33	5	0	0	0
34	5	0	0	0
35	5	0	0	0
36	5	0	0	0
37	5	0	0	0
38	5	0	0	0
39	5	0	0	0
40	105	0	0	0

cash flow for each path is shown in Figure 11–5. The greater volatility assumed results in a different cash flow pattern for paths 3 and 4. Note also that in path 1 while the interest rate declines below 7% in period 37, the rule for calling specifies that if the bond does not have at least 5 years remaining to maturity, it will not be called.

Thus far, we have skirted the question of the complexity of evaluating all paths. In practice, techniques such as Monte Carlo simulation can be employed to estimate the option-adjusted spread.[3] To do this, it is necessary to specify how the term structure will shift each period. This is accomplished by specifying a probability distribution for the short-term Treasury rate. A change in the short-term Treasury rate will determine how the entire term structure will shift. The assumed probability distribution must be consistent with the existing term structure of interest rates. These nuances, however, are beyond the scope of this chapter.

A summary of the procedure to calculate the option-adjusted spread is given below and in Figure 11–6.

1. From the Treasury yield curve estimate the term structure of interest rates (spot rates) and the implied forward rates.

2. Select a probability distribution for short-term Treasury spot rates. The probability distribution should be selected such

Figure 11–4 Four Possible Interest Rate Paths Assuming Interest Rates Can Rise or Fall by 13% Every Six Months

Period	Path 1	Path 2	Path 3	Path 4
1	11.0	11.0	11.0	11.0
2	12.4	9.6	9.6	9.6
3	14.0	8.3	8.3	8.3
4	12.2	7.2	7.2	7.2
5	13.8	6.3	6.3	6.3
6	15.6	5.5	7.1	7.1
7	13.6	4.8	6.2	6.2
8	11.8	4.1	7.0	7.0
9	10.3	3.6	7.9	7.9
10	11.6	3.1	8.9	6.9
11	13.1	2.7	10.1	6.0
12	14.8	3.1	11.4	5.2
13	16.8	3.5	9.9	4.5
14	14.6	3.9	8.6	3.9
15	16.5	4.5	7.5	3.4
16	14.3	3.9	6.5	3.0
17	12.5	3.4	5.7	2.6
18	14.1	2.9	4.9	2.3
19	15.9	2.6	4.3	2.0
20	18.0	2.2	3.7	1.7
21	15.6	1.9	3.3	1.5
22	13.6	2.2	3.7	1.7
23	11.8	2.5	4.2	1.9
24	10.3	2.8	4.7	2.1
25	9.0	2.4	4.1	2.4
26	7.8	2.7	4.6	2.7
27	8.8	2.4	4.0	3.1
28	10.0	2.1	4.5	3.5
29	11.3	2.3	5.1	4.0
30	12.7	2.6	5.8	4.5
31	11.1	3.0	6.6	5.0
32	12.5	3.4	7.4	5.7
33	10.9	3.8	8.4	6.4

(Figure continues)

**Figure 11-4 Four Possible Interest Rate Paths Assuming Interest
            Rates Can Rise or Fall by 13% Every Six Months
            (Continued)**

Period	Path 1	Path 2	Path 3	Path 4
34	9.5	4.3	7.3	7.3
35	8.2	4.9	8.2	8.2
36	7.2	5.5	9.3	9.3
37	6.2	6.2	8.1	8.1
38	7.0	7.0	9.1	9.1
39	8.0	8.0	8.0	8.0
40	9.0	9.0	9.0	9.0

that it is consistent with (a) the current term structure of interest rates and (b) the historical behavior of interest rates.
This will prevent the possiblility of arbitrage along the yield
curve.

3. Use the probability distribution and Monte Carlo simulation
   to randomly select a large number of interest rate paths (say,
   1,000).

4. For bonds with embedded options (such as callable or putable bonds), develop rules for determining the exercise of an
   option.

5. For each path found in (3), determine the cash flows given
   (a) information about the corporate bond (e.g., call provisions) and (b) the rules established in (4).

6. For an assumed spread and the term structure, calculate a
   present value for each path.

7. Calculate the average present value from all the paths.

8. Compare the average present value to the market price of
   the corporate bond. If they are equal, the assumed spread
   used in (6) is the option-adjusted spread. If they are not, try
   another spread and repeat (7) and (8).

Figure 11-5 Four Possible Interest Rate Paths Assuming Interest Rates Can Rise or Fall by 13% Every Six Months

Period	Path 1	Path 2	Path 3	Path 4
1	$ 5	$ 5	$ 5	$ 5
2	5	5	5	5
3	5	5	5	5
4	5	5	5	5
5	5	5	5	5
6	5	5	5	5
7	5	5	5	5
8	5	5	5	5
9	5	5	5	5
10	5	109	5	109
11	5	0	5	0
12	5	0	5	0
13	5	0	5	0
14	5	0	5	0
15	5	0	5	0
16	5	0	109	0
17	5	0	0	0
18	5	0	0	0
19	5	0	0	0
20	5	0	0	0
21	5	0	0	0
22	5	0	0	0
23	5	0	0	0
24	5	0	0	0
25	5	0	0	0
26	5	0	0	0
27	5	0	0	0
28	5	0	0	0
29	5	0	0	0
30	5	0	0	0
31	5	0	0	0
32	5	0	0	0

(Table continues)

Figure 11–5 Four Possible Interest Rate Paths Assuming Interest Rates Can Rise or Fall by 13% Every Six Months (Continued)

Period	Path 1	Path 2	Path 3	Path 4
33	5	0	0	0
34	5	0	0	0
35	5	0	0	0
36	5	0	0	0
37	5	0	0	0
38	5	0	0	0
39	5	0	0	0
40	105	0	0	0

Illustration

While it is too complicated to work through the calculation of an option-adjusted spread here, let's look at the result of one analysis. Table 11–4 summarizes the results of an option-adjusted spread analysis by Hayre and Lauterbach for three callable corporate bond issues.[4] The analysis is based on closing prices as of September 20, 1988.

The traditional analysis would suggest that the ITT bond is particularly attractive because it trading at 168 basis points over the Treasury yield curve. In fact, in terms of just spread off Treasuries, it would seem that this issue is the most attractive of the three issues. However, the option-adjusted spread analysis suggests just the opposite. Regardless of the assumed volatility of interest rates, the ITT issue is the least attractive on an option-adjusted spread basis.

Notice also the impact of the volatility assumption on the option-adjusted spread. The higher the assumed volatility of interest rates,the lower the option-adjusted spread. In the case of the ITT issue, if assumed volatility is 20% per annum, then the option-adjusted spread is negative—quite a different story than traditional yield spread analysis would tell us.

Figure 11–6

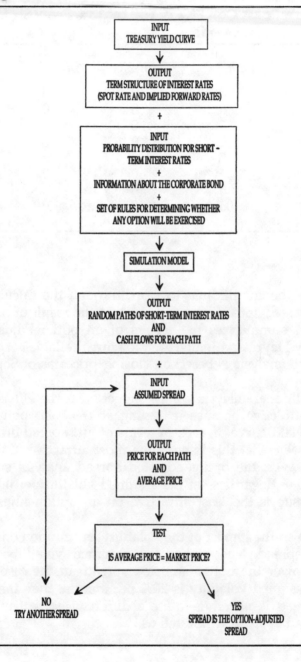

Valuing the Embedded Option

In Chapter 8, we stated that the price of a callable bond is equal to the price of a noncallable bond minus the value of the embedded call option. A byproduct of the option-adjusted spread analysis is the implied value of the embedded call option.

The procedure for obtaining this value after an option-adjusted spread is estimated is as follows. First, use the option-adjusted spread to determine what a noncallable corporate bond would sell for. This price, which is called the implied noncallable bond price, is determined by adding the option-adjusted spread to the spot rates and calculating the present value of the cash flows to maturity. Next, subtract the callable bond's market price from the implied noncallable bond price. The difference is the value of the embedded call option.

For the ITT issue, the value of the embedded call option, as calculated by Hayre and Lauterbach, was as follows:

	Volatility assumed		
	10%	15%	20%
Option-adjusted spread (bp)	57	30	–4
Implied noncallable price	105.06	105.94	107.07
Market price	101.58	101.58	101.58
Value of embedded call option	3.48	4.36	5.49

Notice that the value of the embedded call option is a byproduct of the option-adjusted spread analysis and not valued explicitly. In Chapter 13, an approach will be discussed that values the option explicitly.

Applications to Other Bond Structures with Embedded Options

While our focus has been on callable corporate bonds, the option-adjusted spread analysis can be extended to any corporate bond structure such as putable bonds and floating rate notes. It can easily accomodate more than one embedded option simultaneously. For example, if a corporate bond is both callable and putable, the cash flow along a path will take into account that the bond may be called before it is put if interest rates fall sufficiently (based on the rule established for calling) or be put before it is called if interest rates rise. In the case of floating rate notes, the presence of any interest rate cap or floor can be easily accommodated.

Junk bond structures typically have multiple embedded options. Consider, for example, the payment-in—kind (PIK) bond. If rates decline sufficiently, the bond may be called; however, if interest rates rise, the issuer has the option of putting to the bondholder another bond with the same coupon as the issue. The option-adjusted spread approach can handle PIK bonds.

In the case of bonds with sinking fund provisions, the probability that an issue will be called away for sinking fund purposes can be incorporated into the analysis.

Effective Duration and Convexity

In the previous chapter, we described the price performance characteristics of noncallable and callable bonds. Measures of price volatility to interest rate changes such as modified duration and convexity can be computed for bonds where the cash flow is independent of changes in future interest rates. In addition to modified duration and convexity, we also presented a general formula for the price sensitivity of a bond, effective duration and convexity. These measures are calculated by determining how much the price of a bond will change if interest rates change by a small amount in both directions.

Within the option-adjusted spread framework, effective duration and convexity can be computed by increasing and decreasing short-term Treasury rates by a small amount. When changing interest rates, the option-adjusted spread is kept constant. This will produce two average prices (present values): one when short-term interest rates are increased and one when short-term interest rates are decreased. The average prices are then substituted into the formula for effective duration and convexity given in the previous chapter.

For the three issues in Table 11–4, the effective duration and convexity are shown in Table 11–5. Also shown is the effective duration and convexity for the bonds if they were not callable, which are essentially the modified durations. Look at the ITT bond which was callable in less than one year from the date that the analysis was performed. Notice that for the ITT bond, effective duration for the callable bond is much lower than for the bond if it had been a noncallable bond. The convexity for this bond is negative. The lower effective duration and the negative convexity are due to the fact that the bond has a coupon rate that is higher than the prevailing market yield (10.8% coupon versus 10.2% using the yield to maturity as the prevailing market yield—see Table 11–4). In contrast, the effective duration for the callable GMAC bond is almost identical to its noncallable duration despite the fact that the bond is immediately callable. The reason is that the coupon rate on the issue is 8% while the prevailing yield (as measured by the bond's yield to maturity) is 9.86%. Therefore, this bond is trading as if it is a noncallable bond.

Price Performance

In Chapter 8, we showed that the price/yield relationship for an option-free bond is convex. At the end of that chapter, we explained that the price/yield relationship for a noncallable bond will exhibit negative convexity as yields drop. While we stated what the price/yield relationship would look like, we did not show how it could be calculated.

The option-adjusted spread analysis can be used to construct the price/yield relationship for changes in interest rates. In this case, the interest rate that changes is the short-term Treasury rate. This is done by changing the short-term Treasury rate, keeping the same option-adjusted spread, and calculating the average price (present value) along all the paths. This procedure will trace out the price/yield relationship.

When this was done for the ITT bond, the price/yield relationship shown in Figure 11–7 resulted, which also shows the relationship for the bond if it was noncallable. Compare this figure with Figure 8–2 in Chapter 8 (page 320). The shapes are identical. For the ITT bond, once the short-term Treasury rate falls below about 12%, the bond will exhibit negative convexity. That is what the calculated values for effective duration and convexity for the ITT bond tell us in Table 11–5.

Table 11-4 Option Adjusted Spread for Three Callable Corporate Bonds

Issuer	S&P Rating	Maturity	Next Call Date	Next Call Price	Curr. Price	Coupon (%)	YTM	Trsy. Yield Spread	OAS at Volatility of		
									10%	15%	20%
ITT Fin.	A	07/01/92	07/01/89	100.00	101.58	10.800	10.27	168	57	30	-4
Marriot	A-	02/01/96	02/01/93	100.00	99.59	9.625	9.70	85	65	50	37
GMAC	AA-	07/15/07	Callable now	104.00	84.19	8.000	9.86	82	71	54	41

Note: Based on closing prices and Treasury rates on September 20, 1988.
Source: Lakhbir Hayre and Kenneth Lauterbach, "Stochastic Valuation of Debt Securities," in Frank J. Fabozzi (ed.), *Managing Institutional Assets* (New York, NY: Harper & Row, 1990).

Table 11-5 Effective Duration and Convexity for Three Callable Corporate Bonds

Issuer	Maturity	Next Call Date	Current Price	Effective Duration		Effective Convexity	
				Callable	Noncallable	Callable	Noncallable
ITT Fin.	07/01/92	07/01/89	101.58	1.1	3.0	-0.3258	0.1872
Marriot	02/01/96	02/01/93	99.59	4.6	5.1	0.2135	0.5683
GMAC	07/15/07	Callable now	84.19	8.1	8.4	0.5328	1.6818

Note: Volatility assumption is 15% per annum.
Source: Lakhbir Hayre and Kenneth Lauterbach, "Stochastic Valuation of Debt Securities," in Frank J. Fabozzi (ed.), *Managing Institutional Assets* (New York, NY: Harper & Row, 1990).

Figure 11-7 Projected Price Paths for the ITT Bond

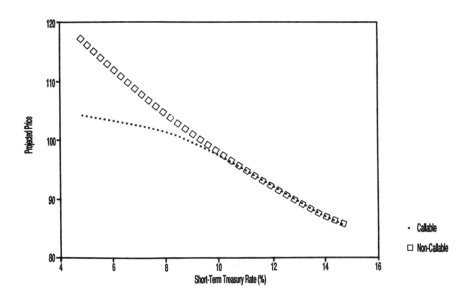

Source: Lakhbir Hayre and Kenneth Lauterbach, "Stochastic Valuation of Debt Securities," in Frank J. Fabozzi (ed.), *Managing Institutional Assets* (New York, NY: Harper Row, 1990).

The Limitations of Option-Adjusted Spread Analysis

While the option-adjusted spread analysis is clearly superior to traditional analysis, it does have its limitations. The option-adjusted spread analysis helps us identify securities that promise to pay a spread after adjusting for the embedded option if (1) the bond is held to the effective maturity date and (2) the cash flows from the bond can be reinvested in investment vehicles with a yield equal to the yield on the noncallable corporate bond plus the option-adjusted spread. Moreover, the key ingredients in the analysis are (1) a spot rate curve, (2) expected interest rate volatility, and (3) a rule for determining when an embedded option will be exercised. If these ingredients are incorrect, the results of the analysis will be misleading.

Notes

[1] This is, in fact, what government dealer firms do when they create stripped (or zero coupon) Treasury securities. For an illustration, see Frank J. Fabozzi and T. Dessa Fabozzi, *Bond Markets, Analysis and Strategies* (Englewood Cliffs, NJ: Prentice Hall, 1988), Chapter 6.

[2] For a detailed discussion of these theories see, Richard W. McEnally, "The Term Structure of Interest Rates," Chapter 53 in Frank J. Fabozzi and Irving M. Pollack (eds.), *The Handbook of Fixed Income Securities* (Homewood, IL: Dow Jones-Irwin, 1987).

[3] There are other techniques such as binomial lattices and solving differential equations. These approaches are beyond the scope of this chapter. The interested reader who would like to delve into these mathematical techniques are referred to the following articles: Thomas Ho and Sang-Bin Lee, "Term Structure Movements and Pricing Interest-Rate Contingent Claims," *Journal of Finance* (June 1986), and Kenneth B. Dunn and John J. McConnell, "Valuation of GNMA Mortgage-Backed Securities," *Journal of Finance* (December 1981), for a discussion of binomial lattices and solving differential equations, respectively. For a description of the simulation procedure, see Lakhbir Hayre and Kenneth Lauterbach, "Stochastic Valuation of Debt Securities," in Frank J. Fabozzi (ed.), *Managing Institutional Assets* (New York, NY: Harper & Row, 1990).

[4] See Hayre and Lauterbach, "Stochastic Valuation of Debt Securities."

Chapter 12

BASICS OF OPTIONS

I n the next chapter we will present an options approach that can be used to value corporate bonds with embedded options. In this chapter we will provide the basics of options. The focus is on the characteristics of options, not option strategies.

Options Defined

An option is an agreement in which the writer of the option grants the buyer of the option the right, but not the obligation, to purchase from or sell to the writer a designated instrument at a specified price within a specified period of time. The writer, also referred to as the seller, grants this right to the buyer in exchange for a certain sum of money called the *option price* or *option premium*. The price at which the instrument may be bought or sold is called the *exercise* or *strike price*. The date after which an option is void is called the *expiration date* or *maturity date*.

When an option grants the buyer the right to purchase the designated instrument from the writer, it is called a *call option*. When the option buyer has the right to sell the designated instrument to the writer (seller), the option is called a *put option*. The buyer of an option is said to be *long the option*; the writer (seller) is said to be *short the option*.

An option is said to be an *American option* if the buyer may exercise the option at any time up to and including the expiration date.

Figure 12-1 Summary of Terms of an Option and Basic Option Positions

---

Terms of an option:
- Underlying instrument
- Right to buy or sell the underlying instrument
  - right to buy: call option
  - right to sell: put option
- Exercise or strike price
- Expiration or maturity date
- When the option may be exercised
  - at any time up to and including expiration date: American option
  - only at the expiration date: European option
- Option buyer pays option writer (seller)
  - amount paid is called option price or option premium

Basic option positions:
- long call position = buy a call option
- short call position = sell a call option
- long put position = buy a put option
- short put position = sell a put option

An option is said to be a *European option* if the buyer may only exercise the option on the expiration date. There is no particular reason why the geographical adjectives are used to describe the conditions for exercising the option.

Figure 12-1 summarizes the terms of an option and basic option positions.

Profit/Loss Profile for Basic Option Positions

The maximum amount that an option buyer can lose is the option price. The maximum profit that the option writer (seller) can realize is the option price. The option buyer has substantial upside return potential while the option writer has substantial downside risk. This is illustrated below.

Figure 12–2 summarizes the profit/loss profile for the four basic option positions at the expiration date of the option. The horizontal axis represents the price of the underlying instrument at the expiration date and the vertical axis represents the profit or loss. The terms of both the call and put options used in the illustrations are as follows:

underlying instrument = 10% coupon bond currently with 15 years
and 2 months to maturity
par value = $100
strike price = $100
time to expiration of option = 2 months

We also assume that the current price of the underlying bond is $100 (i.e., the bond is selling at par) which means that the yield to maturity on this bond is currently 10%. The profit/loss profile for the four basic option positions will depend on the price of the underlying bond at the expiration date. The price, in turn, will depend on the yield on 15 year bonds with a 10% coupon, since in 2 months the underlying bond will have only 15 years to maturity.

Long Call Position (Buying a Call Option)

We shall assume that price of the call option is $5. Therefore, the buyer pays the seller $5 to purchase the call option. If the price of the bond at the expiration date is less than or equal to $100 (which means that the market yield is greater than 10%), then the investor would not exercise the option. The option buyer will lose the entire option price of $5. Notice, however, that this is the maximum loss that the option buyer will realize regardless of how low the price of the bond declines.

If the price of the bond is greater than $100 (that is, a market yield at expiration that is less than 10%), the option buyer will exercise the option. By exercising, the option buyer purchases the bond for $100 (the strike price) and can sell it in the market for a higher price. The option buyer will realize a loss at expiration if the price

Figure 12–2 Profit/Loss for Basic Option Positions

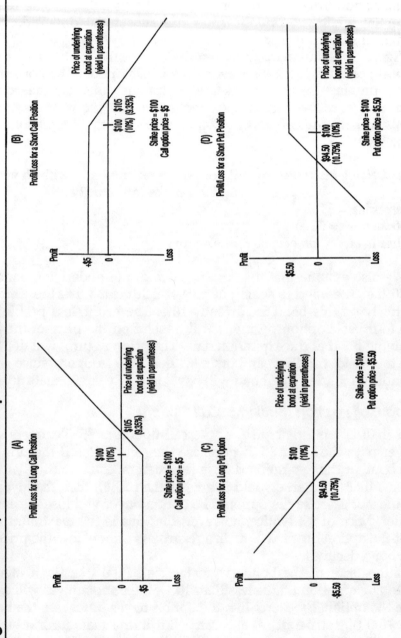

of the bond is greater than $100 but less than $105 (which corre-
sponds to a market yield at expiration of 10% and approximately
9.35%, respectively). The option buyer will break even if the price
of the bond at expiration is $105. It is the break-even price because
it cost the option buyer $5 to acquire the call option and $100 to
exercise the option to purchase the bond. A profit will be realized if
the price of the bond at expiration is greater than $105 (that is, the
market yield declines below 9.35%).

Figure 12–2a shows the profit/loss profile. While the break-even
point and the loss will depend on the option price, the shape
shown in the figure will hold for all buyers of call options. The
shape indicates that the maximum loss is the option price and that
there is substantial upside potential.

Short Call Position (Writing a Call Option)

Once again, assume the call price is $5. The profit/loss profile of
the short call position is the mirror image of the profit/loss profile
of the long call strategy. That is, the profit (loss) of the short call
position for any given price of the bond at the expiration date is the
same as the loss (profit) of the long call position. Consequently, the
maximum profit that the short call position can produce is the option price; the maximum loss is only limited by how high the price
of the bond can increase (i.e., how low the market yield can fall) by
the expiration date, less the option price. This can be seen in Figure
12–2b.

Long Put Position (Buying a Put Option)

Assume that the price of the put option is $5.50, so that the option
buyer pays the option writer this amount to purchase the put option. If the price of the bond is equal to $100 or greater than $100
because the market yield has fallen below 10%, the buyer of the put
option will not exercise it, resulting in a loss of $5.50 (the option
price). The investor will exercise the option when the price of the
bond at expiration is less than $100 (market yield at expiration
above 10%). If the market yield is higher than approximately
10.75%, the price of the bond will be less than $94.50, resulting in a
profit from the position. For market yields between 10% and about
10.75%, the investor will realize a loss; however, the loss is less than

$5.50. The break-even market yield is approximately 10.75% since this will result in a bond price of $94.50.

Figure 12–2c shows the profit/loss for this position. As with the long call option position, the loss is limited to the option price. However, the profit potential is substantial: the theoretical maximum profit being generated if the bond price falls to zero.

Short Put Position (Selling or Writing a Put Option)

The profit/loss profile for a short put option is the mirror image of the long put option. The maximum profit from this strategy is the option price. As can be seen in Figure 12–2d, the maximum loss is only limited by how low the price of the bond can fall by the expiration date less the option price received for writing the option.

Option Price

In the next chapter we will discuss an approach that can be used to value a bond with issuer or bondholder options by determining the fair price of the option embedded in the bond. Here option pricing will be explained.

Basic Components of the Option Price

The cost to the buyer of an option is primarily a reflection of the option's *intrinsic* value and any additional amount over its intrinsic value. The premium over intrinsic value is often referred to as *time value* or *time premium*.

Intrinsic value: The intrinsic value of an option is the economic value of the option if it is exercised immediately. Since the buyer of an option need not exercise the option, and, in fact, will not do so if there is no economic value that will result from exercising, the intrinsic value cannot be less than zero.

The intrinsic value of a call option on a bond is the difference between the current bond price and the strike price. For example, if the *strike price* for a call option is $100 and the *current bond price* is $107, the intrinsic value is $7. That is, if the option buyer exercised the option and simultaneously sold the bond, the option buyer would realize $107 from the sale of the bond, which would be covered by acquiring the bond from the option writer for $100, thereby netting $7.

When a call option has intrinsic value, it is said to be "in the money." Our call option with a strike price of $100 is in the money when the price of the underlying bond is greater than $100. When the strike price of a call option exceeds the current bond price, the call option is said to be "out of the money" and has no intrinsic value. A call option for which the strike price is equal to the current bond price is said to be "at the money."

These relationships in terms of strike price and current bond price, or alternatively in terms of prevailing market rate and coupon rate, are summarized below for a call option:

- if current bond price > strike price (or if prevailing market rate < coupon rate), then
  1. The intrinsic value is the difference between the current bond price and strike price
  2. The option is said to be "in the money"

- if current bond price = strike price (or the prevailing market rate = coupon rate), then
  1. The intrinsic value is zero
  2. The option is said to be "at the money"

- if current bond price < strike price (or the prevailing market rate > coupon rate) then
  1. The intrinsic value is zero
  2. The option is said to be "out of the money"

For a put option, the intrinsic value is equal to the amount by which the current bond price is below the strike price. For example, if the strike price of a put option is $100 and the current bond price is $88, the intrinsic value is $12. That is, if the buyer of the put option exercises it and simultaneously sells the bond, he will net $12. The bond will be sold to the writer for $100 and purchased in the market for $88.

When the put option has intrinsic value, the option is said to be in the money. For our put option with a strike price of $100, the option will be in the money when the bond price is less than $100.

A put option is out of the money when the current bond price exceeds the strike price. A put option is at the money when the strike price is equal to the current bond price.

These relationships are summarized below for a put option:

- if current bond price < strike price (or the prevailing market rate > coupon rate), then
  1. The intrinsic value is the difference between the strike price and current bond price
  2. The option is said to be "in the money"
- if current bond price = strike price (or prevailing market rate = coupon rate), then
  1. The intrinsic value is zero
  2. The option is said to be "at the money"
- if current bond price > strike price (or the prevailing market rate < coupon rate), then
  1. The intrinsic value is zero
  2. The option is said to be "out of the money"

Time value: The time value of an option is the amount by which the option price exceeds the intrinsic value. That is,

  time value of an option = option price − intrinsic value

For example, if the price of a call option with a strike price of $100 is $18 when the current bond price is $107, then for this option:

  intrinsic value = $107 − $100 = $7
  time value of option = $18 − $7 = $11

If the current bond price is $88 instead of $107, then the time value of this option is $18 since the option has no intrinsic value. For an at-the-money or out-of-the-money option, the time value of the option is equal to the option price since the intrinsic value is zero.

At the expiration date, the time value of the option will be zero. The option price at the expiration date will be equal to its intrinsic value.

Why would an option buyer be willing to pay a premium over the intrinsic value? The reason is that the option buyer believes that at some time prior to expiration, changes in the market yield will increase the value of the rights conveyed by the option.

Determinants of the Option Price

While we can easily determine the value of an option at the expiration date and the intrinsic value of an option at any time prior to the expiration date, the fair value or price of the option at any time prior to the expiration date must be estimated. Here we will discuss the factors that will influence the fair or "theoretical" value of an option.[1]

The following six factors will influence the option price:

1. current price of the underlying instrument,

2. strike price,

3. time to expiration,

4. risk-free interest rate over the life of the option,

5. coupon rate, and

6. expected interest rate volatility over the life of the option.

The impact of each of these factors will depend on whether (1) the option is a call or a put and (2) the option is an American option (an option that may be exercised up to and including the expiration date) or a European option (an option that may be exercised only at the expiration date).

1. Current price of the underlying instrument: For a call option, as the current price of the underlying bond increases (decreases), the option price increases (decreases). For a put option, as the current price of the bond decreases (increases), the option price increases (decreases).

2. Strike price: All other factors constant, the higher the strike price, the lower the price of a call option. For a put option, the opposite is true: the higher the strike price, the higher the price of a put option.

3. Time to expiration: For American options, all other factors constant, the longer the time to expiration the higher the option price. No general statement can be made for European options.

4. Risk-free interest rate over the life of the option: Holding all other factors constant, the price of a call option on a bond will increase as the short-term risk-free interest rate rises. For a put option, the opposite is true: an increase in the short-term risk-free interest rate will decrease the price of a put option.

5. Coupon rate: Coupons tend to decrease the price of a call option because the coupons make it more attractive to hold the bond than the option. Thus, call options on coupon bearing bonds will tend to be priced lower than other similar call options on noncoupon bearing bonds. For put options, coupons tend to increase their price.

6. Expected interest rate volatility over the life of the option: As the expected interest rate volatility over the life of the option increases, the price of an option increases. The reason is that the greater the expected volatility, as measured by the standard deviation or variance of interest rates, the greater the probability that the price of the underlying bond will move in the direction that will benefit the option buyer.

Option Pricing Models [2]

Several models have been developed to estimate the theoretical or fair price of an option. These models are based on an arbitrage or riskless hedge valuation model. Our purpose here is not to describe option pricing models, but, instead, to bring to the reader's attention the more commonly available models that are commercially available from software vendors. Most of the dealer firms have developed their own option pricing models.

The Black-Scholes Option Pricing Model and Binomial Model

The most popular option pricing model for call options on common stock is the Black-Scholes option pricing model.[3] The key insight of the Black-Scholes option pricing model is that a synthetic option can be created by taking an appropriate position in the underlying common stock and borrowing or lending funds at the risk-free interest rate.

There are several assumptions underlying the Black-Scholes option pricing model that are necessary to create the synthetic option and therefore price the option. These assumptions and their limitations when applied to options on bonds are summarized below:

1. The volatility of the price of the bond is constant over the life of the option. We know from Chapter 10 that the price volatility of a bond declines as a bond moves toward its maturity date.

2. The risk-free interest rate over the life of the option is constant. Obviously, this assumption is untenable for options on bonds since it is the change in the interest rate that will effect the price of the underlying bond and therefore the price of the option.

3. The probability distribution assumed for the price of the underlying security when applied to options on bonds may mean that negative interest rates are possible. This is, of course, an unrealistic assumption.

4. The original Black-Scholes model assumed that the option is a European call option on a nondividend paying stock. If applied to price a call option on a bond, this means that the bond is a zero coupon bond. Subsequent modifications to the Black-Scholes model permitted the pricing of American call options on dividend paying stocks. The Black-Scholes model for pricing options on bonds can also be modified to accommodate coupon payments.

Another option pricing model that overcomes some, but not all, of the limitations of the Black-Scholes model is the binomial option pricing model.[4] As in the case of the Black-Scholes model, the binomial model assumes a particular probability distribution for the *price* of the underlying bond.

Binomial Models Based on Yields

Rather than assume a probability distribution for the price of the underlying bond, the binomial option pricing model has been applied to bonds by assuming a probability distribution model for the yield rather than the bond price. While this model is clearly superior to the Black-Scholes model and the binomial model based on prices, it does have a limitation. All option pricing models to be theoretically valid must satisfy what is known as the *put-call parity relationship*. This is the relationship between the price of a put option, the price of a call option, the price of the underlying security, the strike price and the risk-free interest rate. The problem with the binomial model based on yields is that it does not satisfy the put-call parity relationship. The reason why it violates this relationship is that this model fails to take into consideration the yield curve, thereby allowing arbitrage opportunities.

Yield Curve or Arbitrage-Free Models

The most elaborate models which take into consideration the yield curve and as a result do not permit arbitrage opportunities are called *yield curve option pricing models* or *arbitrage-free option pricing models*. These models can incorporate different volatility assumptions along the yield curve. While these models are theoretically superior to the other models we described, they require extensive computer time to solve.[5] Nevertheless, such models are the most appropriate ones to use to value options embedded in corporate bonds.

Price Sensitivity of the Option Price

When one of the six factors that affects the price of an option changes, the option price will change. Since the price of a bond with an embedded option will be affected by how the price of the embedded option changes, we will look at the sensitivity of the option price to three of the factors—the price of the underlying bond, time to expiration and expected interest rate volatility. We focus our attention on call options.[6]

The Call Option Price and the Price of the Underlying Bond

Figure 12–3 shows the theoretical price of a call option based on the price of the underlying bond. The horizonal axis is the price of the underlying bond at any point in time. The vertical axis is the option price. The shape of the theoretical price of a call option given the price of the underlying bond would be the same regardless of the actual option pricing model used. In particular, the relationship between the price of the underlying bond and the theoretical call price is convex. Thus, option prices also exhibit convexity.

The line from the origin to the strike price on the horizontal axis in Figure 12–3 is the intrinsic value of the call option when the price of the underlying bond is less than the strike price since the intrinsic value is zero. The 45 degree line extending from the horizontal axis is the intrinsic value of the call option once the price of the underlying bond exceeds the strike price. The reason is that the intrinsic value of the call option will increase by the same dollar amount as the increase in the price of the underlying bond. For example, if the exercise price is $100 and the price of the underlying bond increases from $100 to $101, the intrinsic value will increase by $1. If the price of the bond increases from $101 to $110, the intrinsic value of the option will increase from $1 to $9. Thus, the slope of the line representing the intrinsic value after the strike price is reached is 1.

Since the theoretical call option price is shown by the convex line, the difference between the theoretical call option price and the intrinsic value at any given price for the underlying bond is the time value of the option.

Figure 12–4 shows the theoretical call option price but with a tangent line drawn at the price of p^*. The tangent line in Figure 12–4 can be used to estimate what the new option price will be (and therefore what the change in the option price will be) if the price of the underlying bond changes. Because of the convexity of the relationship between the option price and the price of the underlying bond, the tangent line does a good job of approximating what the new option price will be for a small change in the price of the underlying bond. For large changes, however, the tangent line does

Figure 12–3 Theoretical Call Price and Price of Underlying Bond

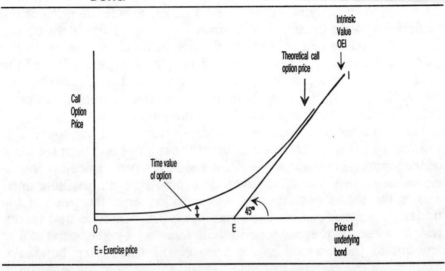

Figure 12–4 Estimating the Theoretical Option Price with a Tangent Line

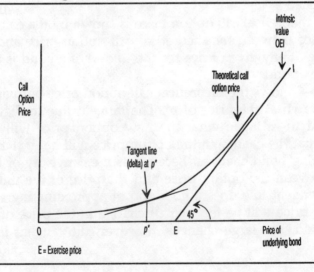

not do as good a job in approximating what the new option price will be.

The slope of the tangent line shows how the theoretical call option price will change for small changes in the price of the underlying bond. The slope of the tangent line is commonly referred to as the *delta* or *hedge ratio* of the option. Specifically,

$$\text{delta} = \frac{\text{change in price of call option}}{\text{change in price of underlying bond}}$$

For example, a delta of .5 means that a $1 change in the price of the underlying bond will change the price of the call option by $.50.

Figure 12–5 shows the theoretical call option price with three tangent lines drawn. The steeper the slope of the tangent line, the greater the delta. When an option is deep out of the money (that is, the price of the underlying bond is substantially below the strike price), the slope of the tangent line is relatively flat (see line 1 in Figure 12–5). This means a delta close to zero. To understand why, consider a call option with a strike price of 100 and 2 months to expiration. If the price of the underlying bond is $20, its price would not increase by much if the price of the underlying bond increased by $1 from $20 to $21.

For a call option that is deep in the money, the delta will be close to 1. That is, the call option price will increase almost dollar for dollar with an increase in the price of the underlying bond. In terms of Figure 12–5, the slope of the tangent line approaches the slope of the intrinsic value line after the strike price. As we stated earlier, the slope of that line is 1. Thus, the delta for a call option varies from zero (for deep out of the money call options) to one (for deep in the money call options). The delta for an at the money call option is approximately 0.5.

In the previous chapter, we measured the convexity of an option-free bond. We also can measure the convexity of a call option. Recall from the previous chapter that the convexity of a bond is measuring the change in the dollar duration. For call options, convexity measures the change in delta. The measure of convexity for options is commonly referred to as *gamma* and is measured as follows:

Figure 12–5 Delta of a Call Option at Three Prices for the Underlying Bond

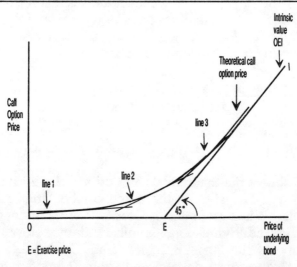

$$gamma = \frac{\text{change in delta}}{\text{change in price of underlying bond}}$$

The Call Option Price and Time to Expiration

All other factors constant, the longer the time to expiration, the greater the option price. Since each day the option moves closer to the expiration date, the time to expiration decreases. The *theta* of an option measures the change in the option price as the time to expiration decreases. That is,

$$theta = \frac{\text{change in price of option}}{\text{decrease in time to expiration}}$$

Assuming that the price of the underlying bond does not change so that the intrinsic value of the option does not change, theta measures how quickly the time value of the option changes as the option moves towards expiration.

The Call Option Price and Expected Interest Rate Volatility

All other factors constant, a change in the expected interest rate volatility will change the option price. The *vega* of an option measures the dollar price change in the price of the option for a 1% change in expected interest rate volatility. That is,

$$\text{vega} = \frac{\text{change in option price}}{1\% \text{ change in expected interest rate volatility}}$$

Notes

[1] For a more detailed discussion of the impact of these factors on the price of an option, see: Mark Pitts and Frank J. Fabozzi, *Interest Rate Futures and Options* (Chicago, IL: Probus Publishing Company, 1990), Chapter 7.

[2] For a more extensive discussion of this topic, see: Chapter 7 in Pitts and Fabozzi, *Interest Rate Futures and Options* and Lawrence J. Dyer and David P. Jacob, "Guide to Fixed Income Option Pricing Models," Chapter 3 in Frank J. Fabozzi (ed.), *The Handbook of Fixed Income Options* (Chicago, IL: Probus Publishing Company, 1989).

[3] Fischer Black and Myron Scholes, "The Pricing of Corporate Liabilities." *Journal of Political Economy* (May-June 1973), pp. 637-659.

[4] The following are credited with the development of the binomial option pricing model: John Cox, Stephen Ross and Mark Rubinstein, "Option Pricing: A Simplified Approach," *Journal of Financial Economics* (September 1979), pp. 229-262; Richard Rendleman and Britt Barter, "Two-State Option Pricing," *Journal of Finance* (December 1979), pp. 1093-1110; and William Sharpe, *Investments* (Englewood Cliffs, NJ: Prentice-Hall, 1981), Chapter 16.

[5] For a discussion of yield curve or arbitrage-free option pricing models see: Pitts and Fabozzi, *Interest Rate Futures and Options*;

Dyer and Jacob, "Guide to Fixed Income Option Pricing Models," and; Ravi E. Dattatreya and Frank J. Fabozzi, "A Simplified Model for the Valuation of Debt Options," Chapter 4 in *The Handbook of Fixed Income Options*.

[6] For a more detailed discussion see: James F. Meisner and John A. Richards, "Option Premium Dynamics: With Applications to Fixed Income Portfolio Analysis," in Frank J. Fabozzi and T. Dessa Garlicki (eds.), *Advances in Bond Analysis and Portfolio Strategies* (Chicago, IL: Probus Publishing Company, 1987) and Pitts and Fabozzi, *Interest Rate Futures and Options*, Chapter 7.

Chapter 13

AN OPTIONS APPROACH TO THE VALUATION OF CORPORATE BONDS

As explained in Chapter 8, the traditional procedure for assessing the relative value of callable bonds is to first compute the
yield to call for a bond and then compare that measure (assuming it
is less than the yield to maturity) to the yield on various callable
bonds. However, as we explained in the same chapter, this procedure will not permit an investor to assess the relative performance
of callable bonds over a predetermined investment horizon. In
Chapter 11, we presented a framework for assessing relative value
based on option-adjusted spread analysis. Using that framework,
the value of the embedded option is not calculated directly. Instead,
it is computed after an option-adjusted spread is determined. In
this chapter, we present a framework that values the option directly. We refer to this approach as the *options approach*. At the end
of this chapter, we combine the horizon return framework explained in Chapter 9 with the options approach.

Breaking a Callable Bond into its Component Parts

Recall from Chapter 8 that the price of a callable corporate bond is
equal to the price of its two components parts. That is,

   callable bond price = noncallable bond price – call option price

The call option price is subtracted from the price of the noncallable bond because the bondholder has sold a call option to the issuer. The call option price can be estimated using one of the option pricing models described in the previous chapter. Because the analysis proceeds based on the estimated option price, the approach is referred to as the options approach.

To illustrate the options approach, consider the General Motors Acceptance Corporation 12% coupon bond of June 2005 that is callable in June 1990 at 102. A bondholder who owned this bond on June 1, 1988, effectively owned a noncallable bond with 17 years to maturity and sold a call option granting the issuer (GMAC) the right to call away from the bondholder 15 years of cash flows beginning June 1, 1990. The exercise price for this call option is 102.

The price of the noncallable bond and the theoretical price of the embedded call option at each yield level are shown in Table 13–1. The theoretical price of the call option is based on a binomial option pricing model.[1] Recall from our discussion of the determinants of an option's price in the previous chapter that an assumption about expected future interest rate volatility is required as an input into the option pricing model. The volatility assumption to compute the theoretical call option price in Table 13–1 is 12% per year.

The difference between the price of the noncallable bond and the theoretical price of the call option is the price of the callable bond. A graph of the price/yield relationship in Table 13–1 is shown in Figure 13–1. The shape is consistent with the price/yield relationship for callable bonds we described in Chapters 8 and 11.

We know that the price of a call option increases when the expected interest rate volatility increases. Table 13–2 shows the theoretical price of the call option when interest rate volatility is assumed to be 20% per year. The theoretical price of the call option is greater in Table 13–2 than in Table 13–1 because of the higher interest rate volatility assumed. Since the theoretical price of the call option is higher, the price of the callable bond is lower in Table 13–2 than in Table 13–1.

This also can be seen in Figure 13-2 which shows the price/yield relationship assuming: (1) the issue is not callable, (2) the issue is callable and interest rate volatility is assumed to be 12% per year,

Table 13–1 Price/Yield Relationship and Theoretical Option Price for GMAC 12% of June 2005 Callable at 102 in June 1990 (Settlement 6/1/88, 12% Interest Rate Volatility Assumption)

Assumptions to compute theoretical call option price:
Binomial option pricing model
Interest rate volatility: 12%
Short-term interest rate: 6%

Yield	Noncallable bond price	Theoretical option price	Theoretical callable bond price
20.51	60	0.000	60.000
20.18	61	0.000	61.000
19.86	62	0.000	62.000
19.55	63	0.000	63.000
19.24	64	0.000	64.000
18.95	65	0.000	65.000
18.66	66	0.000	66.000
18.39	67	0.000	67.000
18.11	68	0.000	68.000
17.85	69	0.001	68.999
17.59	70	0.001	69.999
17.34	71	0.001	70.999
17.10	72	0.002	71.998
16.86	73	0.002	72.998
16.63	74	0.003	73.997
16.40	75	0.005	74.995
16.18	76	0.006	75.994
15.96	77	0.008	76.992
15.75	78	0.012	77.988
15.54	79	0.016	78.984
15.33	80	0.020	79.980
15.13	81	0.027	80.973
14.94	82	0.036	81.964
14.75	83	0.046	82.954
14.56	84	0.057	83.943
14.38	85	0.075	84.925

Table 13-1 Price/Yield Relationship and Theoretical Option Price for GMAC 12% of June 2005 Callable at 102 in June 1990 (Settlement 6/1/88, 12% Interest Rate Volatility Assumption) (Continued)

Yield	Noncallable bond price	Theoretical option price	Theoretical callable bond price
14.20	86	0.095	85.905
14.02	87	0.116	86.884
13.85	88	0.146	87.854
13.68	89	0.183	88.817
13.51	90	0.223	89.777
13.35	91	0.265	90.735
13.19	92	0.330	91.670
13.03	93	0.398	92.602
12.87	94	0.469	93.531
12.72	95	0.557	94.443
12.57	96	0.667	95.333
12.42	97	0.783	96.217
12.28	98	0.904	97.096
12.00	100	1.235	98.765
11.73	102	1.606	100.394
11.46	104	2.112	101.888
11.33	105	2.380	102.620
11.20	106	2.661	103.339
11.07	107	3.012	103.988
10.95	108	3.373	104.627
10.83	109	3.742	105.258
10.71	110	4.134	105.866
10.59	111	4.596	106.404
10.47	112	5.067	106.933
10.35	113	5.548	107.452
10.24	114	6.056	107.944
10.13	115	6.631	108.369
10.02	116	7.215	108.785
9.91	117	7.808	109.192
9.80	118	8.429	109.571
9.69	119	9.111	109.889
9.59	120	9.801	110.199
9.48	121	10.499	110.501

Table 13–1 Price/Yield Relationship and Theoretical Option Price for GMAC 12% of June 2005 Callable at 102 in June 1990 (Settlement 6/1/88, 12% Interest Rate Volatility Assumption) (Continued)

Yield	Noncallable bond price	Theoretical option price	Theoretical callable bond price
9.38	122	11.220	110.780
9.28	123	11.996	111.004
9.18	124	12.778	111.222
9.08	125	13.567	111.433
8.98	126	14.372	111.628
8.89	127	15.224	111.776
8.79	128	16.080	111.920
8.60	130	17.813	112.187
8.42	132	19.632	112.368
8.24	134	21.466	112.534
8.07	136	23.362	112.638
7.90	138	25.267	112.733
7.73	140	27.210	112.790
7.24	146	33.106	112.894
6.79	152	39.075	112.925
6.36	158	45.066	112.934
5.96	164	51.064	112.936
5.57	170	57.064	112.936

and (3) the issue is callable and interest rate volatility is assumed to be 20% per year. Notice that the price/yield relationship for the callable bond assuming 20% interest rate volatility begins to depart from the price/yield relationship for the bond if it is not callable at a higher yield than the price/yield relationship for the callable bond assuming 12% interest rate volatility. When the market yield is deep in the money, the price/yield relationship for the callable bond is the same regardless of the interest rate volatility assumption.

Table 13–2 **Price/Yield Relationship and Theoretical Option Price for GMAC 12% of June 2005 Callable at 102 in June 1990 (Settlement 6/1/88, 20% Interest Rate Volatility Assumption)**

Assumptions to compute theoretical call option price:
Binomial option pricing model
Interest rate volatility: 20%
Short-term interest rate: 6%

Yield	Noncallable bond price	Theoretical option price	Theoretical callable bond price
20.51	60	0.019	59.981
20.18	61	0.024	60.976
19.86	62	0.029	61.971
19.55	63	0.035	62.965
19.24	64	0.044	63.956
18.95	65	0.055	64.945
18.66	66	0.066	65.934
18.39	67	0.078	66.922
18.11	68	0.092	67.908
17.85	69	0.112	68.888
17.59	70	0.134	69.866
17.34	71	0.158	70.842
17.10	72	0.182	71.818
16.86	73	0.208	72.792
16.63	74	0.248	73.752
16.40	75	0.290	74.710
16.18	76	0.334	75.666
15.96	77	0.379	76.621
15.75	78	0.427	77.573
15.54	79	0.491	78.509
15.33	80	0.564	79.436
15.13	81	0.640	80.360
14.94	82	0.718	81.282
14.75	83	0.800	82.200
14.56	84	0.887	83.113
14.38	85	1.006	83.994
14.20	86	1.128	84.872
14.02	87	1.254	85.746

Table 13-2 Price/Yield Relationship and Theoretical Option Price for GMAC 12% of June 2005 Callable at 102 in June 1990 (Settlement 6/1/88, 20% Interest Rate Volatility Assumption) (Continued)

Yield	Noncallable bond price	Theoretical option price	Theoretical callable bond price
13.85	88	1.384	86.616
13.68	89	1.518	87.482
13.51	90	1.665	88.335
13.35	91	1.851	89.149
13.19	92	2.041	89.959
13.03	93	2.235	90.765
12.87	94	2.434	91.566
12.72	95	2.637	92.363
12.57	96	2.855	93.145
12.42	97	3.125	93.875
12.28	98	3.399	94.601
12.00	100	3.964	96.036
11.73	102	4.550	97.450
11.46	104	5.285	98.715
11.33	105	5.664	99.336
11.20	106	6.049	99.951
11.07	107	6.439	100.561
10.95	108	6.835	101.165
10.83	109	7.272	101.728
10.71	110	7.752	102.248
10.59	111	8.238	102.762
10.47	112	8.730	103.270
10.35	113	9.228	103.772
10.24	114	9.731	104.269
10.13	115	10.240	104.760
10.02	116	10.821	105.179
9.91	117	11.414	105.586
9.80	118	12.013	105.987
9.69	119	12.618	106.382
9.59	120	13.227	106.773
9.48	121	13.842	107.158

Table 13-2   Price/Yield Relationship and Theoretical Option
             Price for GMAC 12% of June 2005 Callable at 102
             in June 1990 (Settlement 6/1/88, 20% Interest Rate
             Volatility Assumption) (Continued)

Yield	Noncallable bond price	Theoretical option price	Theoretical callable bond price
9.38	122	14.479	107.521
9.28	123	15.172	107.828
9.18	124	15.871	108.129
9.08	125	16.575	108.425
8.98	126	17.283	108.717
8.89	127	17.996	109.004
8.79	128	18.713	109.287
8.60	130	20.250	109.750
8.42	132	21.832	110.168
8.24	134	23.431	110.569
8.07	136	25.076	110.924
7.90	138	26.797	111.203
7.73	140	28.529	111.471
7.24	146	33.925	112.075
6.79	152	39.541	112.459
6.36	158	45.311	112.689
5.96	164	51.183	112.817
5.57	170	57.117	112.883

Option-Adjusted Yield

Given the above relationship for a callable bond, an investor wants to know if the noncallable bond is correctly priced in the sense that he is being rewarded adequately for the credit risk associated with owning the bond. Although in our previous illustrations we have started with the price of the noncallable bond and computed the theoretical price of the callable bond by subtracting the theoretical price of the call option, the price that the noncallable bond will sell at in the market is not directly observable. It can be estimated by rewriting the relationship as:

Figure 13–1   Price/Yield Relationship for GMAC 12%, June 2005, Callable at 102 in June 1990 (Settlement 6/1/88)

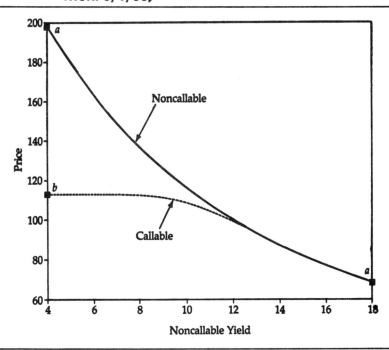

noncallable bond price = callable bond price + call option price

Can we estimate the price of the noncallable bond? We can, if we can determine the price of the callable bond and the call option price. Given the estimated call option price based on some option pricing model and the observed market price of the callable bond, adding the two prices gives the implied price of the noncallable bond.

Given the implied price of the noncallable bond, it is then simple to compute the yield on this bond if it is not called but held to maturity. Recall from Chapter 8 that yield is the interest rate that will make the present value of the cash flows for the bond if held to maturity equal to the price. The yield computed is referred to as the *option-adjusted yield*.[2]

**Figure 13–2 Price/Yield Relationship for GMAC
Callable Bond for June 1, 1988 Settlement, Based
on Two Interest Rate Volatility Assumptions**

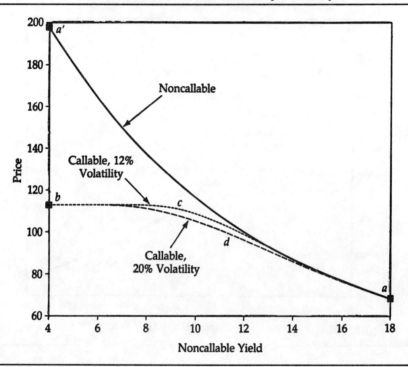

To illustrate the option-adjusted yield, suppose an investor is considering an 8% coupon callable corporate bond selling at 102 with 20 years to maturity and callable at 104. Suppose also that using an option pricing model, the call option price is estimated to be 4.21. Then the option-adjusted yield is computed by first calculating the implied price for the noncallable bond as follows:

  observed callable bond price = 102
  theoretical call option price = 4.21
  noncallable bond price = 102 + 4.21 = 106.21

The option-adjusted yield is computed by finding the interest rate that will make the present value of 40 coupon payments of $4 every six months plus $100 at the end of 40 six-month periods equal to $104.21. The calculated six-month interest rate which satisfies this is 3.7%. Doubling this interest rate gives the option-adjusted yield of 7.4% on a bond equivalent yield basis.

For an actual application, consider once again the GMAC callable bond. Suppose that for June 1, 1988 settlement, the *observed* price for the bond is 106.933. Also suppose that based on an option pricing model and a volatility assumption of 12% per year, the theoretical option price for the call option is 5.067. The implied noncallable bond price is found as follows:

   observed callable bond price = 106.933
   theoretical call option price = 5.067
   noncallable bond price = 106.933 + 5.067 = 112

The option-adjusted yield is found by determining the interest rate that will make the present value of the cash flow if this bond is not called and held to maturity equal to the implied price of the noncallable bond (112) plus the accrued interest. There is no accrued interest on this bond since we assumed the settlement date is on a coupon date (June 1). The semiannual interest rate that will make the present value of the cash flows equal to 112 is 5.237%. Doubling this interest rate gives the option-adjusted yield computed on a bond equivalent basis. The option-adjusted yield is therefore 10.474%.

The option-adjusted yield is the implied yield on the noncallable bond. A noncallable bond is priced fairly if the option-adjusted yield for a callable bond is the proper yield for a noncallable bond with the same features and of the same issuer. A bond is rich or overvalued if the option-adjusted yield is less, and cheap or undervalued if the option-adjusted yield is more.

An option-adjusted yield spread can be calculated by computing the difference between the yield to maturity on an otherwise "comparable" Treasury security and the option-adjusted yield on the hypothetical noncallable corporate bond. Herein lies a problem with the options approach as commonly employed in practice: What is a comparable Treasury security? A Treasury with the same maturity? The same duration? The same average life? There are problems with each of these measures.

In our discussion of the option-adjusted spread approach in Chapter 11, a comparable Treasury did not have to be identified. Instead, a corporate bond was compared to a package of zero coupon Treasury securities. There is no reason why this approach cannot be used within the options approach rather than calculating an option-adjusted yield spread as discussed above. Using this approach, a spread to the spot rates would be sought that would make the present value of the cash flow if the bond is not called equal to the implied noncallable bond price.

Option-Adjusted Duration and Convexity

In Chapter 10 we discussed modified duration and convexity for an option-free bond. For a callable bond, it is inappropriate to use modified duration and convexity because the expected cash flows change as the interest rate changes. We also presented a formula for effective duration and convexity which provide an approximation to modified duration and convexity, respectively. In the options approach, effective duration and convexity also can be estimated. An alternative approach is to use information about the price volatility characteristics of the embedded call option to estimate duration. We explain this approach below.

Option-Adjusted Duration

The duration of a callable bond after adjusting for the call option, commonly referred to as the *option-adjusted (modified) duration*, can be shown to be equal to [3]

option-adjusted duration =

$$\frac{Price_{NCB}}{Price_{CB}} \times Dur_{NCB} \times (1 - delta)$$

where

$Price_{NCB}$ = price of noncallable bond

$Price_{CB}$ = price of callable bond

Dur_{NCB} = modified duration of the noncallable bond

delta = delta of the call option

As can be seen, the option-adjusted duration depends on the following three elements:

(1) the ratio of the price of the noncallable bond to the price the callable bond. Recall that the difference between the price of a noncallable bond and a callable bond is equal to the price of the call option. The greater (smaller) the price of the call option, the higher (lower) the ratio. Thus we see that the option-adjusted duration will depend on the price of the call option.

(2) the duration of the corresponding noncallable (option-free) bond.

(3) the delta of the call option. As we explained in the previous chapter, the delta measures the change in the price of the call option when the price of the underlying bond changes.

Let's apply the option-adjusted duration formula to the following two extreme cases—a deep discount callable bond and a premium callable bond with a coupon rate substantially above the prevailing market yield. First consider the deep discount bond.

For a deep discount bond, the coupon rate is substantially below the current market yield. For example, a 20-year bond with a coupon rate of 5% will trade at a deep discount when the current market yield on comparable bonds is 15%. Since it would not be economic for the corporate issuer to call the 5% coupon bond and replace it with a 15% coupon bond, the call option is deep out of the money. The option price would be small for this bond and therefore the ratio of the noncallable bond price to the callable bond price would be close to one. From the previous chapter, recall our discussion of the delta of a call option. When the option is deep out of the money, the delta is close to zero. Therefore,

$$\frac{Price_{NCB}}{Price_{CB}} = 1$$

$$delta = 0$$

Substituting into the formula for the option-adjusted duration, we have:

option-adjusted duration $= 1 \times Dur_{NCB} \times (1 - 0)$

$$= Dur_{NCB}$$

Thus, the option-adjusted duration of a deep discount callable bond will be the same as its duration assuming it is noncallable.

Now let's consider the duration of a premium callable bond with a coupon rate substantially greater than the current market yield. As an example, consider a 20-year bond with a coupon rate of 16% when the current market yield is 6% (the bond would sell at a premium). The call option would be deep in the money since it would be highly beneficial for the corporate issuer to call the issue and issue new bonds with a coupon rate of 6%. Once again, recall that the delta of a deep in the money call option is 1. Substituting 1 for delta into the formula for the option-adjusted duration, we have:

$$\text{option–adjusted duration} = \frac{Price_{NCB}}{Price_{CB}} \times Dur_{NCB} \times (1-1)$$

$$= 0$$

Thus, the option-adjusted duration for a premium callable bond in which the coupon rate is substantially greater than the current market yield would be zero.

Any where in between a deep discount bond and a premium bond with a high coupon rate relative to the prevailing market yield, the option-adjusted duration of a callable bond will be less than the duration of a noncallable bond.

Let's see how this would be applied to the GMAC callable bonds. Suppose that the observed price is 106.933 and the theoretical call option price is 5.067. The implied price of the noncallable bond is 112 and the option-adjusted yield is 10.474%. The modified duration of the noncallable bond selling for 112 and with a yield of 10.474% would be 7.67. Based on the same option pricing model that generated the theoretical call option price of 5.067, the delta for the call option would be 0.486. The option-adjusted duration for the GMAC callable bond based on the above information would be:

P_{NCB} = implied price of noncallable bond = 112

P_{CB} = observed price of callable bond   = 106.933

Dur_{NCB} = duration of noncallable bond = 7.67

delta   = delta of call option = 0.486

$$\text{option–adjusted duration} = \frac{112}{106.933} \times 7.67 \times (1-0.486)$$

$$= 4.13$$

Option-Adjusted Convexity

The option-adjusted convexity using an options approach can be found as follows:

option-adjusted convexity =

$$\frac{Price_{NCB}}{Price_{CB}} \; [Con_{NCB} \times (1-delta) - Price_{NCB} \times (gamma) \times (Dur_{NCB})^2]$$

where

Con_{NCB} = convexity of the noncallable bond

gamma = gamma of the call option

The option-adjusted duration depends on the price of the call option (i.e., the ratio of the price of the noncallable bond to the price of the callable bond), the duration of the noncallable bond and the delta. The option-adjusted convexity depends on the same three factors plus the convexity of the noncallable bond and the gamma of the call option. As explained in the previous chapter, the gamma of the call option measures the convexity of the call option.

Since the gamma of a call option is positive and the delta is between 0 and 1, option-adjusted convexity will be less than the convexity of the noncallable bond. Unlike the convexity for an option-free bond which is always positive, the option-adjusted convexity may be negative. This occurs when the term in the square bracket is negative. That is, when

$$\text{Con}_{\text{NCB}} \times (1 - \text{delta}) < \text{Price}_{\text{NCB}} \times (\text{gamma}) \times (\text{Dur}_{\text{NCB}})^2$$

When will this condition result? When the yield falls such that the call option moves deep in the money, the delta will approach 1. The term on the left hand side will approach 0 and the term on the right hand side will be positive, resulting in a negative value for the term in the square brackets in the option-adjusted convexity formula.

Continuing with the GMAC callable bond, assume the same information earlier. The convexity of the noncallable bond is 91.82. The gamma for the call option (based on the option pricing model used to calculate the theoretical call option price) is 0.02878. The option-adjusted convexity is then:

P_{NCB} = implied price of noncallable bond = 112

P_{CB} = observed price of callable bond = 106.933

Dur_{NCB} = duration of noncallable bond = 7.67

Con_{NCB} = convexity of noncallable bond = 91.82

delta = delta of call option = 0.486

option-adjusted convexity =

$$\frac{122}{106.933} \; [91.82 \times (1 - 0.486) - 112 \times 0.02878 \times (7.67)^2]$$

$$= -149$$

The option-adjusted convexity is negative in this example because the option-adjusted yield is 10.474%, which is less than the coupon rate of 12%. The call option is therefore in the money.

Tables 13–3 and 13–4 show the price/yield relationship for the GMAC callable bond, the duration for the noncallable bond, the duration for the callable bond, the convexity of the noncallable bond, the delta of the call option, the gamma of the call option and the convexity of the callable bond. Tables 13–3 and 13–4 assume that interest rate volatility will be 12% and 20%, respectively. Notice in both tables that the duration of the callable bond approaches the duration of the noncallable bond as the yield rises above the coupon rate of 12%. As yields decline below 12%, the difference between the duration of the callable bond and the noncallable bond increases.

Using the Options Approach to Evaluate Corporate Bonds with Other Embedded Interest Rate Options

While our illustrations have been limited to callable bonds, the options approach can be extended to value putable bonds. Extending the approach to include more than one embedded option is difficult because options are not additive. For example, consider a corporate bond that is both putable and callable. Using the options approach, the price of the bond can be specified as:

callable and putable bond price =
  noncallable bond price – call option price + put option price

The theoretical value for both the call option and put option can be estimated using an option pricing model and the estimated values substituted into the above relationship. However, exercise of the call option will make the put option worthless and likewise exercise of the put option will make the call option worthless. The option that might be exercised first depends on the path of interest rates. The advantage of the option-adjusted spread approach explained in Chapter 11 is that it takes the possible paths of interest rates into account rather than trying to value the options directly.

The options approach has also been used to value floating rate securities with a cap and/or floor. A one-period cap and floor are nothing more than a put option and call option, respectively. Since the floor and cap apply to each reset period, a cap and a floor are equivalent to a package of puts and calls. The holder of a floating rate security has effectively sold a package of puts and purchased a package of calls. The options approach would suggest that a floating rate note can be valued as follows:

Table 13-3 Option Adjusted Duration and Convexity for GMAC 12% of June 2005 Callable at 102 in June 1990 (Settlement 6/1/88, 12% Interest Rate Volatility Assumption)

Assumptions to compute theoretical call option price:
Binomial option pricing model
Interest rate volatility: 12%
Short-term interest rate: 6%

Yield	Noncallable bond Price	Dur.	Con.	Call option Price	Delta	Gamma	Callable bond Price	Dur.	Con.
20.51	60	4.96	45.4	0.000	0.00	.000001	60.000	4.9	45.4
20.18	61	5.03	46.5	0.000	0.00	.000003	61.000	5.0	46.5
19.86	62	5.10	47.6	0.000	0.00	.000004	62.000	5.1	47.6
19.55	63	5.17	48.7	0.000	0.00	.000007	63.000	5.1	48.7
19.24	64	5.24	49.7	0.000	0.00	.000011	64.000	5.2	49.7
18.95	65	5.30	50.8	0.000	0.00	.000016	65.000	5.3	50.8
18.66	66	5.37	51.8	0.000	0.00	.000026	66.000	5.3	51.8
18.39	67	5.43	52.9	0.000	0.00	.000037	67.000	5.4	52.8
18.11	68	5.49	53.9	0.000	0.00	.000051	68.000	5.4	53.8
17.85	69	5.56	54.9	0.001	0.00	.000077	68.999	5.5	54.8
17.59	70	5.62	55.9	0.001	0.00	.000105	69.999	5.6	55.7
17.34	71	5.68	57.0	0.001	0.00	.000139	70.999	5.6	56.6
17.10	72	5.74	58.0	0.002	0.00	.000198	71.998	5.7	57.5

16.86	73	5.80	59.0	0.002	0.00	.000262	72.998	5.8	58.3
16.63	74	5.86	59.9	0.003	0.00	.000331	73.997	5.8	59.0
16.40	75	5.92	60.9	0.005	0.00	.000455	74.995	5.9	59.6
16.18	76	5.98	61.9	0.006	0.00	.000587	75.994	5.9	60.2
15.96	77	6.04	62.8	0.008	0.00	.000725	76.992	6.0	60.7
15.75	78	6.09	63.8	0.012	0.00	.000942	77.988	6.0	60.9
15.54	79	6.15	64.7	0.016	0.00	.001187	78.984	6.1	60.9
15.33	80	6.20	65.7	0.020	0.00	.001441	79.980	6.1	60.9
15.13	81	6.26	66.6	0.027	0.00	.001775	80.973	6.2	60.5
14.94	82	6.31	67.5	0.036	0.01	.002191	81.964	6.2	59.7
14.75	83	6.36	68.4	0.046	0.01	.002620	82.954	6.2	58.9
14.56	84	6.42	69.4	0.057	0.01	.003079	83.943	6.3	57.7
14.38	85	6.47	70.3	0.075	0.01	.003725	84.925	6.3	55.8
14.20	86	6.52	71.1	0.095	0.02	.004383	85.905	6.3	53.6
14.02	87	6.57	72.0	0.116	0.02	.005054	86.884	6.4	51.2
13.85	88	6.62	72.9	0.146	0.03	.005875	87.854	6.4	48.0
13.68	89	6.67	73.8	0.183	0.03	.006795	88.817	6.4	44.1
13.51	90	6.72	74.6	0.223	0.04	.007724	89.777	6.4	39.9
13.35	91	6.77	75.5	0.265	0.05	.008673	90.735	6.4	35.4
13.19	92	6.82	76.3	0.330	0.06	.009839	91.670	6.4	29.5
13.03	93	6.86	77.2	0.398	0.07	.011006	92.602	6.3	23.3
12.87	94	6.91	78.0	0.469	0.08	.012174	93.531	6.3	16.8

Table 13–3 Option Adjusted Duration and Convexity for GMAC 12% of June 2005 Callable at 102 in June 1990 (Settlement 6/1/88, 12% Interest Rate Volatility Assumption) (Continued)

Yield	Noncallable bond Price	Dur.	Con.	Call option Price	Delta	Gamma	Callable bond Price	Dur.	Con.
12.72	95	6.96	78.8	0.557	0.09	.013406	94.443	6.3	9.5
12.57	96	7.00	79.6	0.667	0.11	.014725	95.333	6.2	1.4
12.42	97	7.05	80.4	0.783	0.12	.016032	96.217	6.2	−7.0
12.28	98	7.09	81.2	0.904	0.14	.017327	97.096	6.1	−15.8
12.00	100	7.18	82.8	1.235	0.18	.019921	98.765	5.9	−35.2
11.73	102	7.27	84.4	1.606	0.22	.022422	100.394	5.8	−55.9
11.46	104	7.35	85.9	2.112	0.26	.024551	101.888	5.4	−76.7
11.33	105	7.39	86.7	2.380	0.29	.025551	102.620	5.3	−87.4
11.20	106	7.43	87.4	2.661	0.31	.026493	103.339	5.2	−98.1
11.07	107	7.47	88.2	3.012	0.34	.027128	103.988	5.0	−107.5
10.95	108	7.51	88.9	3.373	0.37	.027716	104.627	4.8	−117.0
10.83	109	7.55	89.6	3.742	0.40	.028259	105.258	4.6	−126.4
10.71	110	7.59	90.3	4.134	0.42	.028689	105.866	4.5	−135.5
10.59	111	7.63	91.1	4.596	0.45	.028756	106.404	4.3	−142.5
10.47	112	7.67	91.8	5.067	0.48	.028778	106.933	4.1	−149.3
10.35	113	7.71	92.5	5.548	0.51	.028757	107.452	3.9	−155.9
10.24	114	7.75	93.2	6.056	0.54	.028601	107.944	3.7	−161.7
10.13	115	7.78	93.9	6.631	0.57	.028099	108.369	3.5	−165.1
10.02	116	7.82	94.6	7.215	0.59	.027564	108.785	3.3	−168.2
9.91	117	7.86	95.2	7.808	0.62	.026997	109.192	3.1	−170.9

118	9.80	7.89	95.9	8.429	0.65	.026317	109.571	2.9	−172.7
119	9.69	7.93	96.6	9.111	0.67	.025370	109.889	2.7	−172.0
120	9.59	7.96	97.2	9.801	0.70	.024405	110.199	2.5	−171.0
121	9.48	8.00	97.9	10.499	0.72	.023425	110.501	2.3	−169.6
122	9.38	8.03	98.6	11.220	0.75	.022384	110.780	2.2	−167.3
123	9.28	8.07	99.2	11.996	0.77	.021192	111.004	2.0	−163.1
124	9.18	8.10	99.9	12.778	0.79	.020000	111.222	1.8	−158.6
125	9.08	8.14	100.5	13.567	0.81	.018809	111.433	1.7	−153.6
126	8.98	8.17	101.1	14.372	0.83	.017610	111.628	1.5	−148.1
127	8.89	8.20	101.8	15.224	0.84	.016387	111.776	1.4	−141.7
128	8.79	8.24	102.4	16.080	0.86	.015178	111.920	1.2	−134.9
130	8.60	8.30	103.6	17.813	0.89	.012809	112.187	1.0	−120.3
132	8.42	8.36	104.8	19.632	0.91	.010663	112.368	0.8	−105.4
134	8.24	8.43	106.0	21.466	0.93	.008606	112.534	0.6	−89.6
136	8.07	8.49	107.2	23.362	0.95	.006928	112.638	0.4	−75.7
138	7.90	8.55	108.4	25.267	0.96	.005337	112.733	0.3	−61.3
140	7.73	8.61	109.5	27.210	0.97	.004155	112.790	0.2	−50.0
146	7.24	8.78	112.8	33.106	0.99	.001608	112.894	0.0	−22.1
152	6.79	8.94	116.0	39.075	0.99	.000538	112.925	0.0	−8.4
158	6.36	9.10	119.1	45.066	0.99	.000135	112.934	0.0	−2.3
164	5.96	9.25	122.0	51.064	1.00	.000029	112.936	0.0	−0.5
170	5.57	9.39	124.8	57.064	1.00	.000004	112.936	0.0	−0.0

price of a floating rate note =
  price of a pure floater + value of a package of put options
  – value of a package of call options

The price of a pure floater is the price of a floating rate security without any cap or floor. Models are available to estimate the value of a package of puts and calls. Once again, the problem with using the above formula is that the options are not additive and depend on the path of interest rates. As we explained in Chapter 11, this complication can be handled within the option-adjusted spread framework.

In defense of the options approach, its advocates cite the ease of implementation compared to the option-adjusted spread approach. For a good number of participants, the increased accuracy is simply not worth the increased resources needed to implement the more complex procedures required by the option-adjusted spread approach. The options approach will provide a good estimate of the option-adjusted yield for a corporate bond with only one embedded option, such as a bond that is only callable, or a bond with more than one option when all but one of the options is deep out of the money.

Horizon Return Analysis and Performance Profiles of Callable Bonds

The option-adjusted yield obtained from the options approach suffers from the same drawbacks that we discussed for the other yield measures in Chapter 8 and the option-adjusted spread measure discussed in Chapter 11. Moreover, even if a callable bond is identified as cheap using the options approach or the option-adjusted spread approach, that bond may not be appropriate for a portfolio manager whose performance evaluation is based on the return over some horizon, as is the performance of most money managers.

Using the horizon return analysis approach that we discussed in Chapter 9, the performance of a callable bond can be compared to that of a noncallable bond under different market scenarios. However, the two bonds must have equivalent duration to be comparable. In the case of a callable bond, the duration that would be ap-

Table 13–4 Option Adjusted Duration and Convexity for GMAC 12% of June 2005 Callable at 102 in June 1990 (Settlement 6/1/88, 20% Interest Rate Volatility Assumption)

Assumptions to compute theoretical call option price:
Binomial option pricing model
Interest rate volatility: 20%
Short-term interest rate: 6%

Yield	Noncallable bond Price	Dur.	Con.	Call option Price	Delta	Gamma	Callable bond Price	Dur.	Con.
20.51	60	4.96	45.4	0.019	0.00	.000845	59.981	4.9	44.0
20.18	61	5.03	46.5	0.024	0.00	.000987	60.976	5.0	44.8
19.86	62	5.10	47.6	0.029	0.00	.001130	61.971	5.0	45.5
19.55	63	5.17	48.7	0.035	0.00	.001274	62.965	5.1	46.2
19.24	64	5.24	49.7	0.044	0.00	.001493	63.956	5.1	46.7
18.95	65	5.30	50.8	0.055	0.01	.001716	64.945	5.2	47.1
18.66	66	5.37	51.8	0.066	0.01	.001939	65.934	5.3	47.5
18.39	67	5.43	52.9	0.078	0.01	.002161	66.922	5.3	47.9
18.11	68	5.49	53.9	0.092	0.01	.002397	67.908	5.4	48.2
17.85	69	5.56	54.9	0.112	0.01	.002718	68.888	5.4	48.1
17.59	70	5.62	55.9	0.134	0.02	.003036	69.866	5.5	48.1
17.34	71	5.68	57.0	0.158	0.02	.003352	70.842	5.5	47.9
17.10	72	5.74	58.0	0.182	0.02	.003665	71.818	5.5	47.7
16.86	73	5.80	59.0	0.208	0.03	.003982	72.792	5.6	47.4
16.63	74	5.86	59.9	0.248	0.03	.004400	73.752	5.6	46.7

Table 13–4 Option Adjusted Duration and Convexity for GMAC 12% of June 2005 Callable at 102 in June 1990 (Settlement 6/1/88, 20% Interest Rate Volatility Assumption) (Continued)

Yield	Noncallable bond			Call option			Callable bond		
	Price	Dur.	Con.	Price	Delta	Gamma	Price	Dur.	Con.
16.40	75	5.92	60.9	0.290	0.04	.004812	74.710	5.7	45.9
16.18	76	5.98	61.9	0.334	0.04	.005218	75.666	5.7	45.0
15.96	77	6.04	62.8	0.379	0.05	.005621	76.621	5.7	44.0
15.75	78	6.09	63.8	0.427	0.05	.006018	77.573	5.7	43.0
15.54	79	6.15	64.7	0.491	0.06	.006480	78.509	5.7	41.5
15.33	80	6.20	65.7	0.564	0.07	.006963	79.436	5.8	39.8
15.13	81	6.26	66.6	0.640	0.07	.007438	80.360	5.8	38.1
14.94	82	6.31	67.5	0.718	0.08	.007906	81.282	5.8	36.2
14.75	83	6.36	68.4	0.800	0.09	.008367	82.200	5.8	34.2
14.56	84	6.42	69.4	0.887	0.10	.008828	83.113	5.8	32.1
14.38	85	6.47	70.3	1.006	0.11	.009336	83.994	5.8	29.6
14.20	86	6.52	71.1	1.128	0.12	.009835	84.872	5.8	26.9
14.02	87	6.57	72.0	1.254	0.13	.010323	85.746	5.7	24.1
13.85	88	6.62	72.9	1.384	0.14	.010803	86.616	5.7	21.2
13.68	89	6.67	73.8	1.518	0.15	.011274	87.482	5.7	18.2
13.51	90	6.72	74.6	1.665	0.16	.011739	88.335	5.7	15.0
13.35	91	6.77	75.5	1.851	0.17	.012198	89.149	5.7	11.6
13.19	92	6.82	76.3	2.041	0.18	.012646	89.959	5.6	8.0
13.03	93	6.86	77.2	2.235	0.20	.013084	90.765	5.6	4.4
12.87	94	6.91	78.0	2.434	0.21	.013511	91.566	5.5	0.6

12.72	95	6.96	78.8	2.637	0.22	.013929	92.363	5.5	−3.2
12.57	96	7.00	79.6	2.855	0.24	.014328	93.145	5.4	−7.2
12.42	97	7.05	80.4	3.125	0.25	.014669	93.875	5.4	−11.1
12.28	98	7.09	81.2	3.399	0.27	.015000	94.601	5.3	−15.2
12.00	100	7.18	82.8	3.964	0.30	.015630	96.036	5.2	−23.7
11.72	102	7.27	84.4	4.550	0.33	.016222	97.450	5.1	−32.5
11.46	104	7.35	85.9	5.285	0.36	.016563	98.715	4.9	−40.6
11.33	105	7.39	86.7	5.664	0.38	.016714	99.336	4.8	−44.8
11.20	106	7.43	87.4	6.049	0.39	.016857	99.951	4.7	−49.0
11.07	107	7.47	88.2	6.439	0.41	.016991	100.561	4.6	−53.2
10.95	108	7.51	88.9	6.835	0.43	.017117	101.165	4.5	−57.5
10.83	109	7.55	89.6	7.272	0.44	.017167	101.728	4.4	−61.5
10.71	110	7.59	90.3	7.752	0.46	.017135	102.248	4.3	−65.1
10.59	111	7.63	91.1	8.238	0.48	.017097	102.762	4.2	−68.6
10.47	112	7.67	91.8	8.730	0.50	.017051	103.270	4.1	−72.2
10.35	113	7.71	92.5	9.228	0.51	.017000	103.772	4.0	−75.7
10.24	114	7.75	93.2	9.731	0.53	.016942	104.269	3.9	−79.3
10.13	115	7.78	93.9	10.240	0.55	.016879	104.760	3.8	−82.9
10.02	116	7.82	94.6	10.821	0.56	.016680	105.179	3.7	−85.5
9.91	117	7.86	95.2	11.414	0.58	.016465	105.586	3.6	−87.9
9.80	118	7.89	95.9	12.013	0.60	.016246	105.987	3.5	−90.3
9.69	119	7.93	96.6	12.618	0.61	.016023	106.382	3.4	−92.7

Table 13–4 Option Adjusted Duration and Convexity for GMAC 12% of June 2005 Callable at 102 in June 1990 (Settlement 6/1/88, 20% Interest Rate Volatility Assumption) (Continued)

Yield	Noncallable bond Price	Dur.	Con.	Call option Price	Delta	Gamma	Callable bond Price	Dur.	Con.
9.59	120	7.96	97.2	13.227	0.63	.015797	106.773	3.2	−95.0
9.48	121	8.00	97.9	13.842	0.64	.015568	107.158	3.1	−97.3
9.38	122	8.03	98.6	14.479	0.66	.015308	107.521	3.0	−99.3
9.28	123	8.07	99.2	15.172	0.67	.014961	107.828	2.9	−100.4
9.18	124	8.10	99.9	15.871	0.69	.014613	108.129	2.8	−101.4
9.08	125	8.14	100.5	16.575	0.70	.014265	108.425	2.7	−102.3
8.98	126	8.17	101.1	17.283	0.72	.013915	108.717	2.6	−103.1
8.89	127	8.20	101.8	17.996	0.73	.013564	109.004	2.5	−103.8
8.79	128	8.24	102.4	18.713	0.75	.013212	109.287	2.4	−104.4
8.60	130	8.30	103.6	20.250	0.77	.012414	109.750	2.2	−104.1
8.42	132	8.36	104.8	21.832	0.79	.011589	110.168	2.0	−103.0
8.24	134	8.43	106.0	23.431	0.82	.010769	110.569	1.8	−101.3
8.07	136	8.49	107.2	25.076	0.84	.009946	110.924	1.6	−98.9
7.90	138	8.55	108.4	26.797	0.86	.009118	111.203	1.4	−95.4
7.73	140	8.61	109.5	28.529	0.87	.008301	111.471	1.3	−91.5
7.24	146	8.78	112.8	33.925	0.92	.006038	112.075	0.8	−77.0
6.79	152	8.94	116.0	39.541	0.95	.004126	112.459	0.5	−60.3
6.36	158	9.10	119.1	45.311	0.97	.002635	112.689	0.3	−43.8
5.96	164	9.25	122.0	51.183	0.98	.001563	112.817	0.1	−29.3
5.57	170	9.39	124.8	57.117	0.99	.000854	112.883	0.1	−17.9

propriate is either the effective duration or option-adjusted duration.

To illustrate how to evaluate the performance of a callable bond relative to a noncallable bond of the same duration, consider a 12% coupon, 30-year bond callable after 5 years at 109.60.[4] Suppose also that (1) the current interest rate is 12% (thus, the bond is selling at par), (2) the option-adjusted duration is estimated to be 7.4 years, (3) the callable bond is fairly priced, and (4) the portfolio manager considering this bond is concerned with its performance over a six-month investment horizon.

Figure 13–3 shows the performance profile of this callable bond relative to a noncallable bond of the same duration (7.4 years). This example assumes the callable bond is fairly priced. The horizontal axis measures the change from the current rate (12%) at the end of the six-month horizon. The difference in the horizon return between the callable bond and the noncallable bond is shown on the vertical axis. This performance profile demonstrates that if interest rates do not change by more than 100 basis points above or below the current rate of 12%, the callable bond will outperform the noncallable bond with equal duration. However, the callable bond will underperform the equivalent duration noncallable bond if interest rates change by more than 100 basis points in either direction. Thus, the attractiveness of this bond will depend on the portfolio manager's expectations about how much interest rates will change at the end of six months. If interest rates are expected to be stable, the callable bond will be more attractive relative to the noncallable bond.

In the previous example, it was assumed that the callable bond was fairly priced. Now, let's look at the performance profile if the callable bond is priced 50 basis points too rich; that is, the option-adjusted yield is 50 basis points less than a noncallable bond of the same issuer. Assuming that this mispricing is corrected in six months, the performance profile is shown in Figure 13–4. Notice that regardless of what happens to interest rates at the end of six months, this bond will underperform the equivalent duration noncallable bond.

If, on the other hand, the callable bond is cheap by 50 basis points and corrects in six months, the callable bond will provide incremental returns even if interest rates rise or fall by 300 basis points, as shown in Figure 13-5. Remember that the performance profiles shown in Figures 13-4 and 13-5 assume that the mispricing will be corrected at the end of the six month period. If the bond continues to get cheaper, the callable bond will underperform relative to the noncallable bond. In one study, Latainer and Jacob tested the option's framework by investigating the six-month performance of callable long telephone bond issues that were identified as being 25 basis points cheap or rich based on the estimated option-adjusted yield. Their empirical results indicate that, on average, bonds identified as cheap provided incremental returns of 127 basis points relative to bonds that were identified as rich. In addition, 70% of the callable bonds identified as cheap in their study would have provided a higher horizon return.

Using the Options Approach to Value Convertible Bonds

In Chapter 7 we discussed convertible bonds. However, in our discussion of convertible bonds, we did not address the following questions:

1. What is a fair value for the conversion premium per share?

2. How do we handle convertible bonds with call and/or put options?

3. How does a change in interest rates affect the stock price?

The options approach to valuation can help us answer these questions.

Consider first a noncallable/nonputable convertible bond. The investor who purchases this bond would be entering into the following two separate transactions:

1. buying a noncallable/nonputable straight bond and

2. buying a call option (or warrant) on the stock where the number of shares that can be purchased with the call option is equal to the conversion ratio.

Figure 13-3   Six-Month Performance of a 30-Year, 12% Coupon Bond Callable After 5 Years at 109.6 Relative to an Equivalent-Duration Noncallable Bond

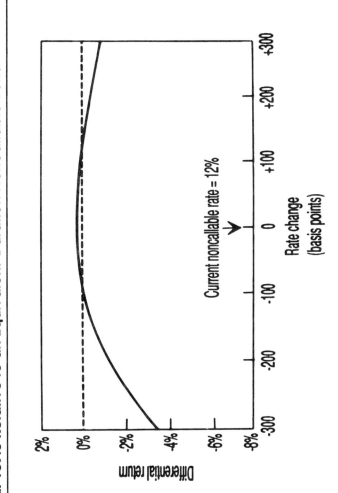

Source: Gary Latainer and David Jacob, "Modern Techniques for Analyzing Value and Performance of Callable Bonds," in Frank J. Fabozzi and T. Dessa Garlicki (eds.), *Advances in Bond Analysis and Portfolio Strategies* (Chicago, IL: Probus Publishing Company, 1987), p. 278.

Figure 13–4 Six-Month Performance of a 30-Year, 12% Coupon Bond Callable After 5 Years at 109.6, Priced 50 Basis Points Rich, Relative to an Equivalent Noncallable Bond

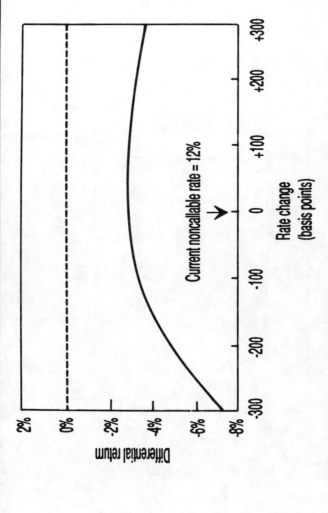

Source: Gary Latainer and David Jacob, "Modern Techniques for Analyzing Value and Performance of Callable Bonds," in Frank J. Fabozzi and T. Dessa Garlicki (eds.), *Advances in Bond Analysis and Portfolio Strategies* (Chicago, IL: Probus Publishing Company, 1987), p. 281.

Figure 13–5   **Six-Month Performance of a 30-Year, 12% Coupon Bond Callable After 5 Years at 109.6, Priced 50 Basis Points Cheap, Relative to an Equivalent Duration Non-callable Bond**

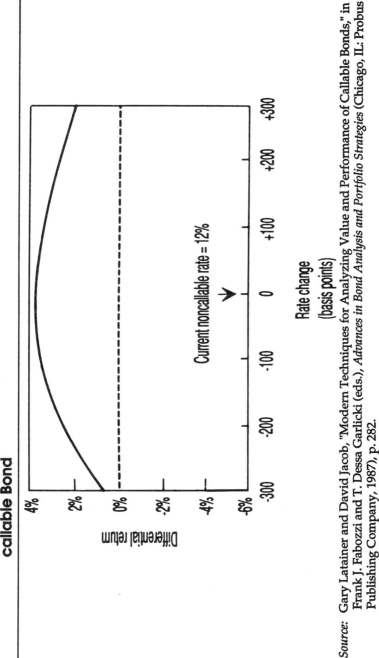

Source: Gary Latainer and David Jacob, "Modern Techniques for Analyzing Value and Performance of Callable Bonds," in Frank J. Fabozzi and T. Dessa Garlicki (eds.), *Advances in Bond Analysis and Portfolio Strategies* (Chicago, IL: Probus Publishing Company, 1987), p. 282.

The question is: What is the fair value for the call option? The fair value depends on the factors that we discussed in Chapter 12 which effect the price of a call option. One key factor is the expected price volatility of the stock: the greater the expected price volatility, the higher the value of the call option. The theoretical value of a call option can be valued using the Black-Scholes option pricing model or the binomial option pricing model. Therefore, as a first approximation to the value of a convertible bond, the following formula can be used:

Convertible bond value =
  Straight value + Price of the call option on the stock

The price of the call option is added to the straight value because the investor has purchased a call option on the stock.

Now let's add in a common feature of a convertible bond: the issuer's right to call the bond. The issuer can force conversion by calling the bond. For example, suppose that the call price is $1,030 per $1,000 par and the conversion value is $1,700. If the issuer calls the bonds, the optimal strategy for the investor is to convert the bond and receive shares worth $1,700.[5] The investor, however, loses any premium over the conversion value that is reflected in the market price. Therefore, the analysis of convertible bonds must take into account the value of the issuer's right to call the bond. In turn, this depends on (1) future interest rate volatility and (2) economic factors that determine whether it is optimal for the issuer to call the bond.

The Black-Scholes option pricing model cannot handle this situation. Instead, the binomial option pricing model can be used to simultaneously value the bondholder's call option on the stock and the issuer's right to call the bonds. The bondholder's put option can also be accommodated. To link interest rates and stock prices together (the third question we raised above), statistical analysis of historical movements of these two variables must be estimated and incorporated into the model.

While the options approach offers a great deal of promise and models have been proposed as far back as 1977, we have not seen wide spread use of this approach.[6]

Notes

[1] The theoretical option price for this illustration was provided by Andrew Ho of Kidder Peabody.

[2] When the analysis is applied to callable corporate bonds that have no other embedded options, the term *call-adjusted yield* is commonly used.

[3] See Appendix A in Frank J. Fabozzi, *Fixed Income Mathematics* (Chicago, IL: Probus Publishing Company, 1988) for the derivation of this formula.

[4] This example is adapted from Gary D. Latainer and David P. Jacob, "Modern Techniques for Analyzing Value and Performance of Callable Bonds," in Frank J. Fabozzi and T. Dessa Garlicki (eds.), *Advances in Bond Analysis & Portfolio Strategies* (Chicago, IL: Probus Publishing Company, 1987).

[5] Actually, the conversion value would be less than $1,700 because the per share value after conversion would decline.

[6] See, for example: Michael Brennan and Eduardo Schwartz, "Convertible Bonds: Valuation and Optimal Strategies for Call and Conversion," *Journal of Finance* (December 1977), pp. 1699-1715; Jonathan Ingersoll, "A Contingent-Claims Valuation of Convertible Securities," *Journal of Financial Economics* (May 1977), pp. 289-322; Michael Brennan and Eduardo Schwartz, "Analyzing Convertible Bonds," *Journal of Financial and Quantitative Analysis* (November 1980), pp. 907-929; and George Constantinides, "Warrant Exercise and Bond Conversion in Competitive Markets," *Journal of Financial Economics* (September 1984), pp. 371-398.

Index

A

Accrued interest, 140-141
Acquisition activity, 205
Adelphia Communications, 53
Adjustable-debt, 159-160
Affirmative covenants, 58
Alaskan Housing Finance Corporation, 183
Allegheny Corporation, 228
Altman, Edward I., 268, 269, 270, 297n
American Airlines, Inc., 243
American Bar Foundation, 43n
American Express Company, 145, 228-229
American option, 391, 399
American Telephone and Telegraph Company, 178
AMR Corporation, 243
Anheuser-Busch Companies, Inc., 177, 178, 179
Ann Taylor, Inc., 257, 281
Annuity note, 197
ANR Pipeline Company, 195
Arbitrage-free horizon return, 327, 366
Arbitrage-free option pricing models, 402
Archer-Daniels-Midland Company, 186-188
Arizona Public Service, 202

Asquith, Paul, 269
Atchison, Topeka & Santa Fe, 86
Atlas Corporation, 242
"At the money" option, 397
Availability, of bonds, 243

B

"Baby bonds", 48
Balloon payment, 189
Baltimore Gas & Electric Company, 72, 166, 194, 209
Baltimore and Ohio Railroad Company, 60, 86
Bankruptcy Reform Act of 1978
    and airlines, 90-91, 104n
    and original issue bonds, 155
    and railroads, 88-89, 103n
    and speculative-grade bonds, 287-291
Banks
    average maturity of corporate new issues, 131
    and corporate bond investments, 10
Barnett, S.C., 111-112
Barron's, 266
Baruch, Bernard M., 220n
BCI Holding Corporation, 257
Beatrice Companies, 257

BellSouth Capital Funding Corpora-
tion, 97
Bell Telephone System, 114
Beneficial Corporation, 118, 138, 145
Binomial lattices, 390n
Binomial option pricing model, 401-
402
Black and Decker Manufacturing
Company, 209
Black-Scholes option pricing model,
400-401, 440
Blanket indenture, 46, 55
Blind pools, 286
Bond. See Corporate bond
Bond indentures. See Indentures
Bond price volatility, 339-360
measures of, 340-350
modified duration, 343-344, 351-354
properties, 339-340
Bond pricing, 299-309, 339-360
Bond ratings, 23-41
Bond swaps, evaluating potential,
332-335
Bond value, factors determining, 33-
34. See also Interest payments
Book-entry, 47-48
Braniff International Corporation, 291
Break-even reinvestment rate, 329
Break-even time, 235
Bridge financing, 257
Bristol-Myers Company, 186
Bullet bonds, 182
Burlington Northern Railroad Com-
pany, 77-78, 86, 209

C

Callable bonds, 314-315, 317-321, 354-
355, 409, 420-423, 430-439. See also
Debt retirement
Call option, 249-250, 391, 403, 404, 406,
425
Call protection, 180
Canal Electric Company, 72
Canadian Pacific Limited, 110, 112-113

Canadian sinking fund, 196
Carolina Power & Light Company,
178, 200
Cash calls. See Outright redemptions
Cash flow tests, 59
Cato Corporation, 118
Central Maine Power Company, 201
Charter Company, 145
Chase Manhattan Bank, 95-96, 167
Chemical Banking Corporation, 164-
165
Chesapeake and Ohio Railway Com-
pany, 60, 78, 86
Chicago & North Western Railway
Company, 89
Chrysler Corporation, 257
Cincinnati Gas & Electric Company,
72, 181
C.I.T. Financial Corporation, 123
CIT Group Holdings, Inc., 116-117
Citibank, N.A., 51, 60
Citicorp, 60, 96, 110, 159, 167
Citizens Utilities Company, 69-70
Coastal Corporation, 206
Collars, 166
Collateralized mortgage obligations,
8, 9, 10
Columbus Southern Power Company,
98
Commercial paper, 108
Common stock, and convertible
bonds, 223, 224
Commonwealth Edison, 98
Computer software, 183, 301, 309, 400
Conditional sales agreements, 84
Conflict of interest, and trustee, 50-51
Connecticut Light and Power Com-
pany, 71-72
Consolidated Rail Corporation, 87
Continental Cablevision, 53
Continental Telephone Company of
California, 193
Conversion parity price, 232, 234
Conversion premium, 234
Conversion price, 232
Conversion ratio, 232

Conversion value, 234
Convertible bonds, 223-253, 436, 440
  characteristics, 232-237
  convertible strategies, traditional, 244-250
  definition, 223-224
  liquid yield option notes, 239-241
  price risk, 238-239
  provisions, 227-232
  usable securities, 241-244
Convertible hedge, 245, 247-248
Convertible strategies, 244-250
Convex, 304
Convexity, and prices, 344, 347-350, 358-360, 403
Corporate bond
  accrued interest and invoice price, 308
  definition, 3-4, 6
  horizon return framework, 325-337
  interest payments, 135-171
  invoice price, 309
  maturity of, 107-133
  municipals compared, 331
  new issues, volume of, 13-18
  ownership of, 11-12
  outstanding, by issuer type, 8, 9
  price volatility fundamentals, 339-360
  price/yield relationship, 303-308
  pricing, 299-309
  puts, 116-120
  ratings, 23-41
  size of market, 7-9
  speculative-grade, 255-295
  trading, 18-23
  valuation of, 361-390, 409-441
  yield measures, 299, 303-307, 309-314
Corporate debt
  estimated total, 7-8
  and income tax, 4, 4ln
  non-financial, 7
  ownership, 9-13
Corporate financial reports, 46, 52
Counterfeiting, 7
Coupon rate, 304-306, 312, 400

Covered call options, 249-250
CP National Corporation, 118
Credit enhancements, and unsecured debt, 96-99
Credit review, examined, 24-25, 28
CSX Corporation, 60
Currencies, 142-145
Currently callable issue, 180
Curtis Publishing Company, 150-151

D

Dana Corporation, 227
Dart Drug Stores, Inc., 285
Dart & Kraft, Inc., 54
Daylin, Inc., 291
DCS Capital Partnership, 81
Debenture, 6, 110-111, 157
Debt covenants, changes in, 62-63
Debtholder's lists and reports, 51-54
Debt issues, 45, 10ln. See also Indentures
Debt ratings, 24-28
Debt restrictions, 58
Debt retirement, 173-222
  call and refunding provisions, 177-185
  defeasance, 211-216
  eminent domain, redemption through, 204
  maintenance and replacement funds, 197-201
  net worth redemptions, 205-220
  outright redemptions, 185-188
  premature redemption, 176-177
  purchase fund, 196-197
  sale of assets, 201-205
  sinking fund, 188-196
  tenders, 208-211
Debt vs. equity, determination, 4-5
Debt with variable coupons, 158-160
Decapitalization, 28
Deep discount callable bond, 421-422
Defaults
  rates, 1970-1988, 273

remedies, 49, 55
on speculative-grade bonds, 287-291
Defeasance, 211-216
Delta of an option, 405, 406, 421
Depository Trust Company, 47-48
Detroit, Toledo and Ironton Railway
    Company, 89-90
Dewing, Arthur Stone, 109, 132n, 224,
    252n
Differential equations, 390n
Discount, and bond prices, 305, 311
Dividend restrictions, 59-60
Dividends, as income from trust, 84-
    85
Dodd, David L., 247
Donaldson, Lufkin & Jenrette, 266
Dow Chemical Company, 81
Drew, Daniel, 224, 252n
Drexel Burnham Lambert, 274
Dual coupon issues, 145-146
Duff & Phelps Inc., 24, 26-27
Duke Power Company, 203
Duration, 356-357

E

Eastman Kodak Company, 46, 182
Economic defeasance, 211, 212
Effective convexity, 350
Effective margin, 321, 322
Electric utility companies
    average maturity of corporate new
        issues, 131
    indenture changes, 57
    secured debt, 63, 69-76
Ellis, Charles D., 32, 44n
Ellsworth Convertible Growth and In-
    come Fund, Inc., 248
Elmira and Williamsport Railroad
    Company, 113
Embedded call option, 385
Equipment bonds, 84
Equipment trust certificates, 83
Equipment trust financing, 83-90

Equitable Life Leasing Corporation,
    123, 183
Equity vs. debt, determination, 4-5
Erie Railway, 224
Eurodollars, 142
European option, 392, 399
Event risk, 25
Exercise price, 391
Expectations theory, of yield curve,
    367
Expiration date, 391
Exxon Corporation, 214
Exxon Shipping Company, 170n

F

"Faux-currencies", 142, 169n
Federal Aviation Act of 1958, 92
Federated Department Stores, Inc., 59
Finance companies
    average maturity of corporate new
        issues, 131
Financial Accounting Standards
    Board, 211, 214
Financial Security Assurance, 98
First Boston Corporation, 264, 266
First Mortgage Bonds, 72
First Mortgage and Collateral Trust
    Bonds, 72
First Refunding Mortgage Bonds, 72
Fisk, James Jr., 224
Fitch Investors Service, Inc., 24, 26-27,
    32, 35, 36-37, 255
Floaters, market for, 166-168
Floating rate notes, 159, 385, 386
Floating rate securities, 163, 324, 425
Florida East Coast Railway Company,
    90
Florida Power & Light, 199-200, 203
Ford Motor Credit Company, 47, 54,
    137, 170n
Foreign debt, 7-9
Foreign investors, 362
Forstmann & Company, Inc., 79-80

4% Perpetual Consolidated Debenture
  Stock, 110
Fox Television Stations, Inc., 5, 41-43n
Fruehauf Finance Company, 46

G

Gamble Skogmo, Incorporated, 149
Gamma, measure of convexity, 405
Gannett Company, 145
Gas companies
  average maturity of corporate new
    issues, 131
  and secured debt, 76-77
General Electric Credit Corporation,
  79-80
General Motors Acceptance Corpora-
  tion, 94-95, 137, 152, 154, 165, 170n,
  213, 410-416
General and Refunding Mortgage
  Bonds, 73
Georgia Power Company, 98, 202-203
Gimmicks, 3, 41n
Global registered note, 47
Gould, Jay, 224
Government bonds, 6
Graham, Benjamin, 247
Graham-Newman Corporation, 248
Grant, James, 175
Grant, W.T. Company, 289, 292
Green Bay & Western Railroad, 110
Griffin, Merv, 267, 268
Growth companies, 256
GTE Corporation, 76
Gulf Oil (Great Britain) Limited, 81
Gulf States Utilities Company, 257

H

Hamilton, Alexander, 190
Harcourt Brace Jovanovich, Inc., 157-
  158
Harnischfeger Corporation, 196
Harris Corporation, 46

Harvard Study, 269
Hayre, Lakbhir, 383, 385
Hedge, and convertible bonds, 244-
  248
Hedge ratio of the option, 405
Hercules Incorporated, 142
Heritage Communications, 53
Hertz Corporation, 145
Hickman, W. Braddock, 123-124, 133n,
  175, 260, 270, 287, 294n
High Income Trust Securities, 274
Holiday Inns, Inc., 97-98
Horizon return analysis, 430-436
Horizon return framework, 325-337,
  366
Hospitals, and mortgage debt, 79
Household corporate bond invest-
  ments, 10
Household Finance Corporation, 145
Houston Lighting & Power Company,
  200
Houston Natural Gas, 56-57
Hovnanian Enterprises, Inc., 147
Hudson & Manhattan Railroad Com-
  pany, 150
Hudson's Bay Oil and Gas Company,
  Ltd., 80
Humana, Inc., 79

I

ICN Pharmaceuticals, Inc., 119-120
Illinois Bell Telephone Company, 76
Illinois Central Gulf Railroad Com-
  pany, 47, 86
Imperial Savings Association, 277
Implied forward rates, 364-366
Income bonds, 147-151
Income tax, and securities, 4
Indentures, 5, 45-105
  blanket, 46, 55
  consolidation, 54-55
  conveyance of assets, 54-55
  covenants, 55-63
  and debt ratings, 25, 27-28, 44n

definitions and provisions, 47
denominations, 48
form of securities, 47-48
lease of assets, 54
merger, 54-55
supplemental, 55-57
trustee, 46, 50-51
Indiana & Michigan Electric Company, 69
Industrial companies, 7-8, 13-16, 78-79, 131
Inland Steel Company, 78
Insider trading scandals, 266
In-substance defeasance, 211
Insull, Samuel, 63, 102n
Insurance companies
  and credit enhancement, 98-99
  and junk bond market, 275, 276
Integrated Resources Inc., 141, 262-264
Interest coverage tests, in covenants, 59
Interest on interest, 309
Interest payments, and bond value, 135-171
  accrued interest, 140-141
  currencies, 142-145
  dual coupon issues, 145-146
  floating rate notes, 166-168
  income bonds, 147-151
  original issue discount bonds, 151-153
  participating bonds, 146-147
  payment and record date, 139
  payment in kind bonds, 156-158
  timing of, 136-138
  variable coupons, 158-160
  variations, 141-142
  zero coupon bonds, 153-156
  zero coupon deferred interest, 156-158
Interest rates
  risk, 312, 313-314
  term structure of, 362
  volatility, 371, 400, 407
Intermarket spread swap, 333, 335-336
Intermediate-term debt, 108, 120
International companies

average maturity of new issues, 131
International Harvester Company.
    See Navistar
    International Transportation Company
International treaty organizations, 7
Internorth, Inc., 203
Intrinsic value of option, 396-398
Investment companies, and bonds, 13
Investment-grade corporate bonds,
    maturity, 129-130
Investment restrictions, 236
Investment value, 236

J

Jacob, David, 436
J.C. Penney Company, 152, 154
Jim Walter Corporation, 58
John Deere Credit Company, 137
Jones & Laughlin Steel Corporation, 78
Junk bonds, 386. See also Speculative-
    grade bonds

K

Kimberly-Clark Corporation, 191
KN Energy, Inc., 51, 62-63, 64-68
Koger Company, 146
Kroger Company, 257

L

Latainer, Gary, 436
Lauterbach, Kenneth, 383, 385
Lease arrangements, 84
Leaseback of property, restrictions, 60-61
Lease Obligation Bonds, 81-82
Legal defeasance 211, 212
Letter of credit, 97-98
Leveraged buyouts, 205, 257, 285

LIBOR, 159, 321, 322
Liquid yield option notes, 239-241
Listed bond trading, 18-21, 23, 43n
Loan agreement. *See* Indenture
LOBS, 81-82
London Interbank Offered Rate
    (LIBOR), 159 321, 322
Long call position, 393-395
Long coupon, 136
Long Island Lighting Company, 51,
    72, 73, 257
Long put position, 395
Long-term debt, 108-120, 127
Long the option, 391
Louisville and Nashville Railroad
    Company, 80, 86, 87
LTV Corporation, 261-262, 266, 269,
    280, 281-282
LYONS, 239-241

M

McCarthy, Crisanti & Maffei, Inc., 24,
    26-27, 52-53
Macaulay, Frederick, 356-358
Mackay, Charles, 220n
McLean Industries, 261, 262
Magma Copper Company, 170
Maintenance and replacement funds,
    197-201
Mandatory specific sinking fund, 190
Manufacturers Hanover, 167
Market segmentation theory, yield
    curve, 367-368
Martin Marietta Corporation, 151-152
Maturity date, 391
Maturity, of securities, 107-133
May Department Stores Company, 51,
    58-59, 61, 107, 190, 210
Medium-term debentures (notes), 6,
    43n, 108, 120-123
Merger activity, 205
Merrill Lynch & Company, 239
Merrill Lynch Taxable Bond Index, 124
Mesa Capital Corporation, 282

Metromedia Broadcasting Corpora-
    tion, 5
Minstar Inc., 206
"Mirror bonds", 80
Missouri-Kansas-Texas Railroad Com-
    pany, 195-196
Missouri Pacific Railroad Company,
    86, 149-150
Model indenture, 46
Model mortgage bond indenture, 46-
    47
Monroe, Ann, 43n
Monte Carlo simulation, 379, 381
Moody's Bond Record, 224
Moody's Investors Service, 16, 24-30,
    35, 37-39, 255
Morgan Guaranty Trust Company,
    214
Mortgage bond indenture, 46-47
Mortgages, 8
Mountain States Telephone & Tele-
    graph Company, 209
Mullins, David, 269
Municipal bonds, compared to corpo-
    rate, 331
Mutual funds, 10, 13, 273, 286

N

Nabisco, RJR Inc., 120
National Steel Corporation, 78
Navistar International Transportation
    Company, 257, 278
Negative covenants, 58-62
Negative pledge clause, and unse-
    cured debt, 99-101, 105n
NeoRx Corporation, 230
Net worth, 205-208
New bond issues, volume, 13-18
New York CSA, 84
New York Plan, 84
New York Stock Exchange, and bond
    trading, 20-23
New York Telephone Company
    mortgage debt, 76

trading suspension, 21
"Nine bond rule", 20
Noncallable bond, 417
Nonconvertible debt, 13
Nonmandatory specific sinking fund, 192
Non-utility companies, and secured debt, 77-83
Norfolk & Western Railway, 86, 87
Northern Central Railway, 113
Northern Pacific Railway, 209
Northern Securities Company, 146
Northern States Power Company, 210-211
Novation, 211, 212

O

Ohio Edison, 194
Ontario & Quebec Railway Company, 112
Open-ended indenture, 46
Open-ended mortgage, 63
Option-adjusted convexity, 423-425
Option-adjusted (modified) duration, 420-421
Option-adjusted spread approach, 361-390
  duration and convexity, 386-387
  estimating for a corporate bond, 368-386
  limitations of, 389
  price performance, 387
  term structure of interest rates, 361, 362-368
Option-adjusted yield, 417-419
Option premium. See Option price
Option price, 391, 402, 403
Option pricing models
  binomial, 401, 402, 407n, 440
  Black-Scholes, 400-401, 407n, 440
  price sensitivity, 402-407
  yield curve, 402, 407-408n
Options approach to valuation of corporate bonds, 409-441

bonds with embedded interest rate options, 425-430
component parts of callable bond, 409-416
convertible bonds, valuation of, 436-440
horizon return analysis, 430
option-adjusted convexity, 423-425
option-adjusted duration, 420-423
option-adjusted yield, 416-420
Options, characteristics of, 391-408
  defined, 391
  price, 396-400
  profit/loss profile for basic positions, 392-396
Oregon Short Line Railroad Company, 146
Original issue discount bonds, 151-153
"Out of the money" option, 397
Outright redemptions, 185-188
Over-the-counter market, 18-19, 23
Owens-Corning Fiberglas Corporation, 190

P

Pacific Gas & Electric, 194
Pacific Power & Light, 204
Pan American World Airways, Inc., 244
Par amount of offerings, term to maturity, 128
Participating bonds, 146-147
Payment-in-kind, 48, 156-158, 281, 386
"Peg date", 59
Pembroke Capital Company Inc., 81
Penn Central Transportation Company, 33, 88, 113
Pennsylvania Railroad Company, 113
Pension funds, 9-10, 275-276
Peoples Express Airlines, Inc., 56, 93-94, 104n
PepsiCo, Inc., 96, 154
Perpetual issues, 110

Perpetual warrant, 242
Petro-Lewis Corporation, 281
Philadelphia Plan equipment trust
    certificate, 84
Piedmont Aviation, 92-93, 104n
"Poison puts", 119-120
Preferred stock, 42n
Premium pricing, 305
Premium callable bond, 421-422
Premium payback period, 235
Premium recovery period, 235
Presidio Oil Company, 170n
Price compression, 315
Price risk, and bonds, 238-239, 312
Price/yield relationship, 410-417
Primerica Corporation, 162
Private Export Funding Corporation,
    82
Public offerings, 1973-1988, 13-17
Public Service Company of New
    Hampshire, 72, 73-76, 288
Public Utility Holding Company Act,
    198, 218n
Pullman Leasing Company, 89
Purchase fund, 196
Pure yield pickup swap, 332
Putable bonds, 319-320, 385
Put option, 320, 391, 425

R

Railroads, and secured debt, 77, 83-90,
    103n
Rate anticipation swap, 332
Ratings
    changes, summary, 29-30
    debt ratings, 24-28, 35-36, 52-53
    definitions, 24-28, 35-36
    designations, 16
    importance of, 31-34
    limitations on use of, 28, 29
    on speculative-grade bonds, 255
    split, 34
    symbols, 26-27
Realized compound yield, 325

Reconstruction Finance Corporation,
    90
Redemption prices, 177-178
Refunding, 180, 181, 184-185
Registered form, 47
Reinvestment rate, break-even, 329
Reinvestment risk, 312-313
Release and substitution of property
    clauses, 202
Reports, by trustee, 51-52
Republic Steel, 78, 261, 262
Resorts International Inc., 267-268
Restricted subsidiaries, 59
Restrictive covenants. See Negative
    covenants
Restructurings, 257
RLC Corporation, 81
Rogers, James, 168-169n
Ryder System, Inc., 81

S

Safe Harbor Water Power Corpora-
    tion, 72
Sale/leaseback transaction, 61
Savings Association Insurance Fund,
    277
Savings and loans, and junk bonds,
    276
Schuylkill Navigation Company, 84
SCI Television, Inc., 53
Seaboard Airline Railroad, 90
Seagram Company, Ltd., 96
Secured debt, 63, 69-94
    non-utility mortgage bonds, 77-79
    other, 79-83
    utility mortgage bonds, 63, 69-77
Secured equipment financing
    airlines, 83, 90-94
    railroads, 83-90, 103n
Secured Facility Bonds, 82
Secured Lease Obligation Bonds, 81-82
Securities
    corporate bond investments, 10, 13
    debt vs. equity, determination, 4-5

maturity of, 107-133
Securities Industry Association, 21
SFBs, 81-82
"Shadow bonds", 80
Shearson/Lehman Corporate Bond
    Index, 264
Shell Canada Limited, 81
Shenandoah Life Insurance Company
    v. Valero Energy Corporation, 102
Short call position, 395
Short coupon, 136
Short the option, 391
Short put option, 396
Short sale, of stocks, 245
Sierra Pacific Power Company, 69, 71,
    72
Signal Capital Corporation, 89
Simons v. Cogan, 102
Sinking funds, 188, 196, 386
SLOBs, 81-82
Sohio Pipe Line Company, 96
South Carolina Electric and Gas Com-
    pany, 204
South Carolina Generating Company,
    204
Southern Bell Telephone, 21
Southern California Edison, 194, 203
Southern Company, 194
Southern Pacific Transport, 86
Southern Railway, 86
Southland Corporation, 286-287
Southwestern Bell Telephone, 21
Speculative-grade bonds, 255-295
    buyers of, 272-277
    defaulted and bankrupt issues, 287-
        291
    high-yield bond performance and
        default rates, 261-272
    market, 258-261
    reducing risk, 277-287
Spot rate, 362, 364, 368
Spot rate curve, 362, 36
Spread duration, 354
Standard Oil Company, 96
Standard & Poor's Corporation, 24-27,
    32-35, 39-41, 255, 264

Static option-adjusted spread, 368-371
Step-down floaters, 164
Stepped-down interest rate, 145
Stepped-up coupon issues, 145
Stock repurchase restrictions, 59-60
Strike price, 391, 399
Substitution swap, 332-333
Sunshine Mining Company, 282
Swan Brewery Company Limited, 208
Swedish Export Credit Corporation,
    109-110
Synthetic convertibles, 241, 242
System Energy Resources, Inc., 71, 203

T

Tangible net worth, 207
Taxable-equivalent yield, 331
Telecommunications industry, and
    long-term debt, 126
Telephone companies
    average maturity of corporate new
        issues, 131
    and secured debt, 76
Tenders, 208-211
Term structure of interest rates, 361-
    368
Texaco, Inc., 268, 270
Texaco Limited, 81
Texas Air Corporation, 56, 93, 115-116
Texas Gas Transmission Company, 60
Texas International Company, 258
Texas & Pacific Railway, 86
Texas Utilities Electric Company, 72,
    98
"Theoretical" value of option, 399,
    403-404, 407n
Theta of an option, 406
Thrift institutions
    and corporate bonds, 10
    average maturity of corporate new
        issues, 131
    and secured debt, 82-83
Time premium, 396
Time value of option, 396, 398-399

Toronto, Grey & Bruce Railway Company, 112
Total return, 325
Transamerica Commercial Finance Company, 162
Transamerica Financial Corporation, 61-62, 152
Transcontinental Gas Pipe Line Corporation, 195
Transportation companies
   average maturity of corporate new issues, 131
Trans World Airlines, 92
Trustee, of debt issues, 46, 50-51
Trust Indenture Act of 1939, 46
Turner Broadcasting, 115

U

Underwritten offerings, 13, 122
Union Carbide Corporation, 81
Union Pacific Railroad, 86, 87, 146
United Illuminating Company, 63
United States Steel Corporation, 123
Unlisted issues, 18, 21, 23
Unrestricted subsidiaries, 59
Unsecured debt, 94-101
   credit enhancements, 96-99
Usable securities, 241-244
U.S. Treasury issues, 6
U.S. West Capital Funding, Inc., 96
USX Corporation, 215
Utilities, 7-8, 13-16, 126. See also under individual names

V

Vanderbilt, Cornelius, 224
Variable-rate debt, 159-160
Vega of an option, 407
Vehicle leasing, 81

W

Wabash Railway Company, 90
Warrant, 241
Washington Water Power Company, 204
Water companies
   average maturity of corporate new issues, 131
Weberman, Ben, 20, 133n, 294n
Wells Fargo & Company, 159
Western Air Lines, Inc., 244
Western Union, 261, 262, 282
Wickes Companies, Inc., 137, 145, 183, 292-293
Wisconsin Michigan Power, 204
Wisconsin Natural Gas Company, 204
Wolff, Eric, 269
Working capital maintenance, 59
W. T. Grant Company, 289, 292

Y

Yield curve, 33, 367-368, 402
Yield to maturity, and bond market, 310-314
Yield to worst, 316, 323n
Youngstown Sheet and Tube Company, 78

Z

Zapata Corporation, 261, 262
Zero coupon bonds, 153, 158, 170n, 239, 281, 303, 313, 327, 329-330
Zero coupon Treasury security, 362, 368, 390n